HOSPITALITY FINANCIAL MANAGEMENT

Robert E. Chatfield

College of Business
University of Nevada, Las Vegas

Michael C. Dalbor

William F. Harrah College of Hotel Administration
University of Nevada, Las Vegas

PEARSON

Prentice
Hall

Upper Saddle River, New Jersey 07458

Library of Congress Cataloging-in-Publication Data

Dalbor, Michael C.,
    Hospitality financial management / Michael C. Dalbor, Robert E. Chatfield.
      p. cm.
    Includes index.
    ISBN 0-13-048287-0
    1. Hospitality industry—Finance.   I. Chatfield, Robert E.   II. Title.

    TX911.3.F5D35 2004
    647.94′068′1—dc22

                                                                      2004008181

Executive Editor: Vernon R. Anthony
Associate Editor: Marion Gottlieb
Editorial Assistant: Beth Dyke
Assistant Editor: Ann Brunner
Senior Marketing Coordinator: Elizabeth Farrell
Marketing Manager: Ryan DeGrote
Marketing Assistant: Les Roberts
Executive Assistant: Nancy Kesterson
Director of Production and Manufacturing: Bruce Johnson
Managing Editor—Production: Mary Carnis
Manufacturing Buyer: Cathleen Petersen
Production Liaison: Denise Brown
Full-Service Production and Composition: Penny Walker/The GTS Companies/York, PA Campus
Design Director: Cheryl Asherman
Design Coordinator: Mary E. Siener
Cover Design: Allen Gold
Cover Image: Epoxy/Getty Images—Photodisc
Cover Printer: Coral Graphics
Printer/Binder: Courier Westford

Pearson Prentice Hall™ is a trademark of Pearson Education, Inc.
Pearson® is a registered trademark of Pearson plc
Prentice Hall® is a registered trademark of Pearson Education, Inc.

Pearson Education LTD.
Pearson Education Singapore, Pte. Ltd
Pearson Education, Canada, Ltd
Pearson Education–Japan

Pearson Education Australia PTY, Limited
Pearson Education North Asia Ltd
Pearson Educación de Mexico, S.A. de C.V.
Pearson Education Malaysia, Pte. Ltd

10 9 8 7
ISBN 0-13-048287-0

In memory of my father, William O. Chatfield and to my mother, Ellie M. Chatfield, both have taught me many valuable life long lessons.

Robert E. Chatfield

This book is dedicated to my father and mother,
John B. Dalbor and Dorothy G. Dalbor
La manzana cae cerca del arbol

Michael C. Dalbor

Brief Contents

For information about all Prentice Hall Hospitality Management and Culinary Arts titles visit www.prenhall.com/pineapple

Access this book's companion website at www.prenhall.com/chatfield

Contents

For information about all Prentice Hall Hospitality Management and Culinary Arts titles visit www.prenhall.com/pineapple

Access this book's companion website at www.prenhall.com/chatfield

Brief Biographies

Robert E. Chatfield is professor of finance and director of MBA programs at the College of Business, University of Nevada, Las Vegas. Previously, he was an associate professor of finance at Texas Tech University and an assistant professor of finance at the University of New Mexico.

Professor Chatfield has been teaching financial management for over 25 years and has taught financial management to hospitality students at UNLV for the past 15 years. He has worked as a financial consultant to the gaming industry in Las Vegas. He has also received teaching excellence awards both at Texas Tech University and Purdue University.

Professor Chatfield has been a productive researcher, publishing in a number of leading finance journals, including *Financial Management*, *Journal of Financial and Quantitative Analysis*, the *Financial Review*, *International Journal of Forecasting*, *Journal of Money, Credit and Banking*, *Quarterly Journal of Business and Economics*, and *Journal of Economics and Business*.

Professor Chatfield enjoys athletics and especially likes to participate in tennis, white-water rafting, and is a novice ballroom dancer.

Michael C. Dalbor is an assistant professor in the William F. Harrah College of Hotel Administration at the University of Nevada, Las Vegas. He holds a B.S. in Food Service and Housing Administration from the Pennsylvania State University and an M.B.A. in finance from Loyola College in Maryland. He also holds a Ph.D. in Hotel, Restaurant, and Institutional Finance from the Pennsylvania State University.

He has published articles in the *Journal of Hospitality Tourism Research*, the *Cornell Hotel and Restaurant Administration Quarterly*, the *Appraisal Journal*, the *International Journal of Hospitality Management*, and the *Journal of Hospitality Financial Management*. He is active in the Association of Hospitality Financial Management Education and the Council on Hotel, Restaurant, and Institutional Education. He has worked in various management positions in the hospitality industry, including food and beverage management and as a purchasing agent. He has also conducted numerous market analyses and feasibility studies as a hotel consultant and has been a commercial real estate appraiser specializing in hotel valuation.

Preface

Hospitality Financial Management is intended as a first finance course for hospitality and tourism students. It may also be useful to hospitality industry professionals who want to know more about the financial management function in the hospitality industry.

This book focuses primarily on long-term finance decisions, especially the hospitality firm's capital budgeting decision. Given the fixed asset intensiveness of the industry, capital budgeting is an important process for hospitality and tourism students to understand. Additionally, a significant amount of background information is required to fully understand this process.

The text has a number of features to facilitate learning and understanding. Each chapter begins with a list of objectives and an introduction to the chapter content. Chapters conclude with discussion questions and problems that demonstrate key concepts. Problems that may be solved by using Excel spreadsheets are indicated with **EXCEL** in the margin, with spreadsheets accessible online at www.prenhall.com/chatfield. Key terms and concepts are identified and defined in the glossary.

Chapter 1 provides an introduction to hospitality financial management. Various types of business organization are discussed along with an introduction to agency problems and the concept of value creation. Chapter 2 provides an introduction to financial markets and financial instruments. Foreign exchange and commodity markets are also discussed.

Chapter 3 reviews the major financial statements and discusses some of the key ratios used in the hospitality industry. It also discusses the limitations of ratio analysis. Chapter 4 introduces the student to the concept of risk and return. The important features of the chapter include the market portfolio and the capital asset pricing model.

Chapter 5 covers the time value of money. This includes discounting and compounding and demonstrates a wide variety of applications. The appendix to this chapter demonstrates how to solve time value of money problems using two different financial calculators. Chapter 6 discusses bonds and preferred stock. This chapter explains the basic approach to both bond and preferred stock valuation. It also includes examples of bonds and preferred stocks issued by hospitality firms.

Chapter 7 covers common stock. It features common stock terminology as well as an introduction to basic common stock valuation. Chapter 8 focuses on the cost of capital. This chapter elaborates on how the weighted cost of capital is derived.

Chapter 9 is an introduction to capital budgeting. This chapter covers the calculation of net investment and the subsequent cash flows. Chapter 10 builds on the concepts of Chapter 9 by examining the different methods used to determine whether a capital budgeting project will create value. Such methods as net present value, internal rate of return, and payback are thoroughly explained. The appendix to this chapter provides an example of a capital budgeting project.

Chapter 11 introduces the student to hotel valuation. The chapter begins with hotel market studies and also discusses the hotel appraisal process. The income capitalization approach is emphasized. Chapter 12 provides an introduction to capital structure. It shows the impact of capital structure on firm value and reviews some major capital structure theories. The text concludes with a glossary to help students become familiar with key terms.

A variety of online tools and resources, for both instructors and students, enhance the text's content. An Instructor's Manual and Test Bank are provided through the www.prenhall.com catalog website – password protected. A Student Companion Website, accessed at www.prenhall.com/chatfield, contains power point slides reinforcing the key points in each chapter and Excel spreadsheet templates for solutions of chapter problems where applicable. Excel supplemental products are available at a discounted price when packaged with this textbook (ISBN: 013-151681-7). Please consult with your local Pearson Prentice Hall sales representative for details.

ACKNOWLEDGMENTS

The authors wish to acknowledge helpful comments and suggestions made by the following professors: Andrew Feinstein, Percy Poon, and Mike Sullivan. Special thanks to the reviewers of this text: Francis A. Kwansa, University of Delaware; Woody Kim, Oklahoma State University; Melih Madanoglu, Virginia Tech; Richard S. Savich, California State Polytechnic University; and Larry Yu, The George Washington University.

We would like to thank Marion Gottlieb who was our constant contact at Prentice Hall. We appreciate her prodding, reminders, and encouragement that were instrumental in providing the motivation we needed to finish this project. Karen Slaght's editing is much appreciated. Also Penny Walker was professional and a delight to work with in guiding us through the production process. These are the three professionals we dealt with directly in finishing this project. We are sure there are many others who we are also indebted to and we wish to thank them as well.

Thanks also to Melih Madanoglu of Virginia Tech University for offering input regarding solutions to problems using Excel spreadsheets.

Robert E. Chatfield extends a special thanks to his wife, Hyun Kyung Chatfield. Her many hours spent reading the manuscript, answering questions, testing the book in the classroom and recommending many student-friendly improvements are greatly appreciated.

Michael C. Dalbor would like to thank his wife Cindy for her love and support. Her patience and understanding during this process facilitated the project immensely.

Introduction | 1

Chapter Objectives

- To be introduced to the scope of hospitality financial management
- To explain the relationships between finance and other functional areas of business management
- To review the different forms of business organization
- To understand the three main decisions in financial management
- To understand the goal of wealth maximization
- To understand the different types of agency relationships
- To understand the ways managers act to increase value
- To understand how projects are undertaken to create value
- To be briefly introduced to the remainder of the text

1.1 INTRODUCTION

The world of hospitality financial management is an important and exciting place to be. The financial decisions made by hospitality managers have important implications for not only the managers and owners of the company, but the overall industry as well. Some of the more exciting developments related to hospitality finance include the following.

- The decision in 1992 to split Marriott Corporation into two separate companies—Marriott International and Host Marriott
- The initial public common stock offering of Boston Chicken in 1993. Investors who purchased the stock at the beginning of trading earned over 100 percent on their investment by the end of the first day
- The spin-off of a new restaurant company, Darden Corporation, from General Mills in 1995. Darden Corporation now includes the Olive Garden, Red Lobster, Bahama Breeze, and Smokey Bones restaurant chains
- The spin-off of a new casino/hotel company, Park Place Entertainment, from Hilton Hotels in 1998. Park Place Entertainment includes Grand Casinos and Caesar's Palace

There are many other examples of financial decisions that have had an impact on the hospitality industry. It is important to understand the thought processes behind these and other types of financial decisions. For example, how does McDonald's decide where to open a new restaurant? How does Hyatt Corporation decide the best way to finance its next hotel project? How does Hilton know whether or not to pay its investors dividends? These are just a few of the types of questions that the study of financial management can help answer.

The purpose of this textbook is to introduce the hospitality student to the field of financial management. After completing your course in conjunction with this textbook, the authors hope that you will be better informed about how important financial decisions are made within hospitality firms. An understanding of how financial decisions are made is important because financial management has continued to be recognized as an important component of the hospitality curriculum by many hospitality company recruiters. Additionally, the concepts discussed herein can often apply directly to your own personal financial circumstances.

Some hospitality students may fail to grasp the significance of financial management because it may be of little interest to them initially. However, as we will discuss throughout the text, there are really no business decisions that will not have an impact on the financial position of the hospitality organization. It matters not whether you are in food and beverage operations, sales and marketing, or human resources, you will be responsible for making decisions that will impact the wealth of the owners (and possibly yourself). This text will describe how we can determine if a decision or project creates value. Value creation is an integral part of financial management.

But what, specifically, is financial management? Financial management is the process of making decisions about assets, the financing of those assets, and the distribution of any potential cash flows generated by the assets. Financial management therefore involves these three major decisions, all of which impact the different departments of a hospitality organization.

1.2 THE RELATIONSHIP OF FINANCIAL MANAGEMENT TO OTHER FUNCTIONAL AREAS OF MANAGEMENT

Hospitality students often take a sequence of quantitative courses, usually beginning with financial accounting. Many of them subsequently take managerial accounting, followed by a financial management course. It is important to understand that although all of these courses are quantitative, accounting and finance are separate academic fields—more like cousins, as opposed to being twin brothers or sisters.

One major difference is that there are many different types of accounting. Financial accounting, for example, is the recording and classifying of financial information for use by others. Other types of accounting include managerial, tax, auditing, and cost accounting. On the other hand, financial management uses accounting information (an income statement, for example) to help make value-maximizing decisions. Accordingly, students are often required to take both accounting and finance courses because they can be used to help evaluate the financial condition of a firm and also to decide which future projects to undertake.

(Another important difference between accounting and finance is that financial and managerial accounting often focuses on earnings—accrual-based earnings.) You may recall from your accounting course(s) that accrual-based financial statements (such as the income statement) show revenues when they are earned and expenses when they are incurred. This may or may not be the same time period in which cash is received or paid. Another example is depreciation—an expense that reduces taxable income but is not an actual cash outlay. (Financial managers and investors are generally more concerned with cash flow because hospitality firms pay employees and suppliers with cash, lenders are repaid with cash, and owners are often paid cash dividends.) Therefore, the value of a project or a firm is much more dependent on cash flows rather than accounting-type earnings.)

Financial management is also closely related to the field of economics. Many hospitality students are required to take at least one course in economics. Macroeconomics is important to financial management because of key factors such as interest rates and foreign exchange rates. Microeconomics is related to finance because financial managers must understand how individual investors behave the way they do. Marginal analysis (such as the concept of declining marginal utility) is an important concept in microeconomics. Additionally, marginal analysis is often used in financial management to determine if a project's incremental benefits exceed its incremental costs.

Another important area of management is marketing. Marketing is related to financial management in at least two ways. First, marketing projects often involve capital expenditures that require a complete analysis before implementation. Second, changes in the marketing plan can affect the cash flows of a project and must therefore be considered when the evaluation of a potential project is conducted.

Other management functions are related to finance, including strategic management, operations management, human resources management, management information systems, and even property maintenance and security. Nevertheless, for a manager to be effective in the firm, he or she should have a fundamental understanding of financial management principles.

1.3 ORGANIZATION OF THE FIRM

In this section of the text, we will briefly review the different types of business organization and discuss the important differences between them.

The most common type of business in the United States is the sole proprietorship in which individuals are in business for themselves. Although this form of business is easy and inexpensive to establish, the owner assumes unlimited liability for the liabilities of the business. Another problem for this type of organization is the relative difficulty in raising capital. On the other hand, the business itself is not taxed; any profits are simply part of the individual owner's personal income.

A partnership is developed when two or more people form a business. Like the sole proprietorship, it is easy and inexpensive to organize. Similarly, it can be difficult to raise capital, and the partners have unlimited liability and share the responsibility for the liabilities of the business. A special type of partnership is the limited partnership, which features a general partner who has unlimited liability for the business. On the other hand, the limited partners are only responsible for their investment in the business. However, the general partners have more control over the decisions affecting the business and usually receive extra compensation for these management duties.

The focus of this textbook will be on the corporate form of business organization, although much of the discussion and analysis can be applied to other forms of business. A corporation must first have a charter and be incorporated within a specific state. Once a charter has been established, the owners (stockholders) of the corporation elect a board of directors to make decisions regarding corporate policy. The board of directors does not typically handle day-to-day operations but instead makes policy decisions such as the hiring of executives and the corporation's auditors.

A corporation has some advantages over other types of business organizations, including unlimited life and a lack of dependency on any one individual. Another advantage is the limited liability for its owners. In other words, investors can lose the value of their investment, but they are not responsible for the liabilities of the business. Finally, it is generally easier for a corporation to raise either debt or equity capital than it is for a sole proprietor or partnership. A chart summarizing the features of the six major types of business organizations is shown in Exhibit 1-1.

On the other hand, corporations are more difficult to organize and are generally subject to more stringent regulation by federal and state governments. Additionally, corporations suffer from double taxation. The corporate entities

Type	Advantages	Disadvantages
Sole proprietorship	Ease of formation Greater control Single taxation	Unlimited liability Relative difficulty in raising capital
Partnership	Ease of formation Greater control Single taxation	Unlimited liability Relative difficulty in raising capital
Limited liability partnership	Ease of formation Limited liability Single taxation	Relative difficulty in raising capital
Corporation	Unlimited life Limited liability Relative ease in raising capital	Relatively difficult to form Increased regulation Double taxation of dividends
Limited liability company	Ease of formation Limited liability Single taxation	Finite life Restrictions on transferability
Subchapter S corporation	Limited liability Single taxation	Increased regulation Restrictions on formation

Exhibit 1-1   Comparison of business organizations.

themselves are taxed, and any dividends paid to shareholders are also taxed as the shareholder's personal income.

Another potential issue facing a corporation is the control over the direction of the company. A person or group of persons can effectively take control of the company with 51 percent of the outstanding shares of common stock. Another issue is the relationship between the owners and the management of the corporation. Problems can develop when management takes actions to benefit themselves at the expense of the owners. Problems between owners and lenders can also arise in the corporation. These will be discussed later in this chapter.

In addition to the pure form of the corporation, there are other hybrid forms of business organization. One is the limited liability company, or LLC. This type of organization uses the limited liability features of a corporation while being taxed in a manner similar to that of a partnership, thus avoiding double taxation. However, the LLC must specify a date of dissolution, and one cannot join the company without approval from the other members. A variety of firms such as those in the legal and accounting professions are organized as a limited liability partnership, or LLP. In these organizations, the personal liability of the partners is limited.

A similar type of organization is the subchapter S corporation, allowing for an organization to avoid separate federal taxation. However, to receive this classification, firms must meet certain requirements, including a maximum of 75 owners, each of whom must be a resident or citizen of the United States.

In order to raise equity capital through public markets (stock exchanges), the corporation must meet certain requirements of the **Securities and Exchange Commission (SEC).** Once these are met, the corporation can issue either common stock or preferred stock. Common stock is the most prevalent type of stock issued. Common stockholders are considered to have a residual claim on the cash flows of the firm; in other words, all other parties receive payment before common stockholders. They bear the most risk of any supplier of capital to a corporation.

On the other hand, preferred stockholders are paid before the common shareholders. They have a dividend that is based on the par value of the stock. However, preferred stockholders generally do not have the right to vote as the common stockholders do. Additionally, preferred stock is not issued nearly as often as common stock is. For example, closing stock prices are listed each weekday in the *Wall Street Journal*. Common stock prices take up approximately seven pages of the paper, whereas preferred stock listings take up less than one-half of one page.

Preferred stock, with its fixed dividend, is similar to a bond. Bonds are a form of debt capital issued by a corporation. Corporations issue bonds to investors, who receive interest payments and a repayment of their loan at the end of a specific term. Corporate bonds, just like common and preferred stock, can be traded on exchanges. A comparison of preferred stock and bonds is shown in Exhibit 1-2.

These financial instruments will be discussed in greater detail in Chapter 2.

Armed with a basic understanding of the organization of the firm, we can proceed in an attempt to develop a basic understanding of financial management in the hospitality industry.

Security	Features
Preferred stock	Shown in equity section of balance sheet
	Shareholder paid a fixed dividend
	Shareholder paid after bondholders, before common stockholders
	Shareholder cannot vote for board of directors
	Dividends not tax deductible for issuing corporation
	Often convertible to common stock
	Sometimes callable by the issuing corporation
Bonds	Shown as a corporate liability
	Bondholder receives a fixed interest payment
	Bondholder paid before shareholders
	Bondholders have very limited influence on corporation
	Interest payments are tax deductible for issuing corporation

Exhibit 1-2   Comparison of preferred stocks and bonds.

1.4 A BASIC UNDERSTANDING OF FINANCIAL MANAGEMENT

As previously discussed, financial management involves the three major decisions of the firm: the **investment decision,** the **financing decision,** and the **dividend decision.** We will discuss these decisions briefly using Exhibit 1-3.

Assets		Liabilities	
Cash	$ 50,000	Accounts payable	$ 150,000
Accounts receivable	$ 40,000	Notes payable	$ 50,000
Inventory	$ 110,000		
Total current assets	$ 200,000	Total current liabilities	$ 200,000
		Long-term debt	$ 300,000
Fixed assets	$ 800,000		
		Total liabilities	$ 500,000
		Owner's equity	
		Preferred stock	$ 50,000
		Common stock	$ 150,000
		Retained earnings	$ 300,000
		Total equity	$ 500,000
Total assets	$1,000,000	Total liabilities and owner's equity	$1,000,000

Exhibit 1-3
SHC
Balance Sheet,
December 31, 200X.

Beginning with a simplified balance sheet, we can begin to examine the three major financial decisions of the firm. The balance sheet, of course, is based on the fundamental accounting equation that states that assets must equal liabilities plus owner's equity. You may recall from your accounting courses that current assets include accounts such as cash, accounts receivable, and inventory. Fixed assets are items such as land, building, and equipment. We have shown only two major categories to simplify the presentation.

Assets are things of value that are controlled by the firm. In this example, the Sample Hotel has only 20 percent of its total assets in current assets. This is not unusual for a hotel company that owns real estate because the assets with the highest costs are land, building, and equipment. These are the assets that typically produce the greatest amount of revenue for the firm. The selection of which assets to hold is called the investment decision. The investment decision for firms is parallel to that of an individual on a microeconomic level. Because resources are limited, which assets will be the best for us to own? A significant portion of this textbook involves how to determine if an asset is worth the investment.

Moving to the right side of the balance sheet, we can see that we have liabilities (both current and long term from lenders) and owner's equity. Current liabilities are debts owed to others (such as accounts payable and notes payable), whereas long-term liabilities are debts that will take longer than a year to pay (such as bonds). Owner's equity includes preferred stock, common stock, and retained earnings. Both lenders and owners have claims on the assets. The lenders have a priority claim. How should we pay for the assets that we decide to acquire? Should we borrow money, issue stock, or use retained earnings (or some combination of all three)? This decision is called the financing decision. In our example, the corporation has decided to finance the $1,000,000 worth of assets using equal amounts of debt and equity. The proportion of debt used versus equity will vary across segments of the hospitality industry and even across firms within one segment of the same industry. Researchers are still investigating how firm managers decide the amount of debt or equity to have on their balance sheets.

Finally, we know that people invest in firms to make money. If they purchase common stock, not only are they hoping that the price of their stock will increase, but they also are hoping to receive dividends. Firms have a choice regarding dividend payments. They may choose to pay dividends to their shareholders or else they can *retain these earnings* and use them to finance new assets. Many firms will do a combination—pay out some earnings as dividends and retain the rest for future growth. This decision is the dividend decision. All three financial decisions should be made to create or maximize the value of the owners' investment.

1.5 WEALTH MAXIMIZATION 💲

The goal of financial management is to maximize the wealth of the owners. When a firm has common stock that is publicly traded, it is maximizing the stock price. Wealth maximization means raising the stock price to its highest possible level.

Although sometimes emphasized in certain contexts, revenue maximization is not the financial goal of a hospitality organization. Profits are a function of revenues and expenses. Therefore, if revenues increase but expenses increase at the same rate or at a greater rate, then profits will not increase or could even decline. We can say that maximizing revenues is a necessary but insufficient condition to increase cash flows and, thus, the stock price. This is another reason why hospitality managers must be effective in managing both revenues and expenses.

Given the goal of financial management, it is important to know how stock prices are determined. In very general terms, the price of a share of stock is the sum of all cash flows received from the ownership in the stock. Although we cannot yet specifically determine the price of a share of stock, we can introduce the three major factors affecting the value of these dividends:

1. The size of the dividends. All else being equal, larger dividends will yield a higher stock price.
2. The timing of the dividends. All else being equal, the sooner the dividends are received, the higher the stock price.
3. The risk associated with the dividends. People generally prefer less risk to more risk. Accordingly, the lower the risk associated with the dividends, the higher the stock price.

Three factors

Now that we have some understanding of the determinants of the wealth of the owners, we can address the goal of wealth maximization. Why should this be the financial goal of the firm? If we think of the income statement in reverse, it can help explain the logic of this goal.

In terms of the priority claim on the firm's cash flow, the owners have the lowest priority and are paid last. This can be seen by visualizing the flow of a vertical income statement from top to bottom. Revenues are generated and are usually shown first. In general, direct operating expenses such as labor, benefits, supplies, and cost of goods sold are shown next. Subsequent to these expenses are the undistributed expenses such as marketing, maintenance, and energy. Last but not least are fixed expenses, such as real estate taxes, insurance, and interest paid to lenders. Income taxes are paid to governmental authorities with the owners accruing the posttax earnings.

The owners are paid after taxes because the government is paid beforehand through taxes. Before the government is paid, lenders are paid with principal and interest. Before the lenders are the other current liabilities, such as suppliers and employees. Thus, we have covered most of the typical expenses of a hospitality operation: costs of employees, suppliers, various administrative costs (marketing, for example), costs of borrowing, and taxes to the government. Accordingly, if we have made the owners happy (who get paid last), then we probably have satisfied the requirements of the other parties, who get paid before the owners. It will be important to remember throughout this textbook the importance of satisfying the needs of the suppliers of financial capital.

Additionally, it is important for students to understand that the goal of wealth maximization is not achieved at the expense of other departments in a hospitality organization. Hospitality financial management should be considered in conjunction with other functional areas. Basically, a good financial decision is a good business decision and vice versa. For example, good relations with employees should help increase productivity, employee retention, and future dividends. Likewise, we cannot expect to maximize the wealth of the owners without an effective marketing program. The goal of wealth maximization, like other goals in the hospitality operation, can be viewed as a long-term goal. Arguably, all of the managerial decisions made within the hospitality firm have implications for the owners.

1.5.1 Different Individuals, Differing Objectives

Hotel investments often involve numerous parties: a developer/owner, a management company, and usually a franchise company (such as Choice Hotels or Holiday Inn). A common way for hotel companies to operate is through the use of hotel management companies. Courtyard by Marriott is largely developed through the use of management contracts. Marriott Corporation constructs the property and sells it to a group of owners on completion. Once the sale is completed, Marriott Corporation manages the property for a fee. The advantage to Marriott Corporation is they do not have to own the real estate and can maintain the image of Courtyard through effective and consistent management. On the other hand, the owners pay management fees knowing their property is being managed by a large, experienced hospitality company.

Accordingly, when a management company signs an agreement to work for the owners, an **agency relationship** is established. The term *agency* originated from the practice of corporations delegating decision making to their hired agents (management), who theoretically act in the best interest of principals (outside financiers). Basically, **agency problems** are caused by the conflicting interests among a corporation's various stakeholders. Stakeholders include management, owners, creditors, employees, suppliers, and government.

The design of the contract between the two parties is crucial to the success of the enterprise. Given that each individual in the relationship is attempting to maximize his or her own welfare, this can lead to different ideas about what is the best course of action. Because most corporations have numerous stakeholders, the corporation is actually a complex web of relationships between them. Some of the typical agency problems arising from these agency relationships are as follows.

Frequently agency problems occur between managers and owners. For example, one type of problem is shirking, which can occur if a manager only receives a high, fixed salary that is guaranteed. With no positive incentive to increase profits, the manager may choose to simply work as few hours as possible (without incurring the risk of termination). One way to solve this problem is to offer the manager stock in the company or a portion of the profits. The basic strategy here is to align the incentives for the manager with those of the owners.

Another classic agency problem between managers and owners relates to excessive consumption of perquisites, such as the use of corporate jets, fancy offices, and other executive privileges. The incentive compensation method for solving this problem has already been mentioned. Other methods include threat of termination and/or takeover of the company. Finally, another way to solve this problem is through the use of increased monitoring of management actions. To better control this type of problem, the board of directors of the company can hire competent auditors, who can discover and reveal any excessive spending by management that decreases the value of the firm.

Other agency relationships exist in the hospitality industry. One of these is the owner–lender relationship. The ability to raise debt capital is important to the hospitality industry. However, the primary task of managers is to maximize the wealth of the shareholders, not necessarily increase the price of the company bonds. Accordingly, there can also be agency problems between bondholders (lenders) and shareholders. There are circumstances in which managers can invest in risky ventures that, if the project pays off, the benefits will largely accrue to the shareholders. On the other hand, if the project fails, the loss will be greater to the bondholders. The splitting of Marriott Corporation into two separate companies in October 1992 is an example. On the day of the announcement, the value of Marriott bonds decreased by approximately 30 percent, while the value of Marriott common stock increased approximately 12 percent. Although controversial at the time, the action taken by Marriott was intended to increase the wealth of the shareholders. Since then, Marriott International has operated very successfully as a hotel management company. Host Marriott began operating as a real estate investment trust (REIT) in 1999 and leases hotels and resorts to subsidiaries. Overall, one could certainly argue that the decision to split into separate companies led to a successful outcome.

1.5.2 Taking Actions to Increase Value

The goal of wealth maximization may seem distant and far away to a hospitality operations manager. But once again thinking of the income statement, we can easily think of actions taken by managers that will help increase value.

One example would be controlling expenses. Labor expense is usually the largest expense for most hotels and the second largest for most restaurants. If managers can increase employee efficiency and decrease labor costs, cash flow will increase. Controlling food and beverage costs also increases cash flow (this is usually the largest expense category for food and beverage operations).

From a sales perspective, increasing revenues (assuming costs remain the same) will also help increase cash flow. Discounting room rates or prices can, in the proper context, perform this function. Another way to increase value is opening an existing restaurant at different hours. This was the idea that McDonald's had about opening for breakfast many years ago. Using their existing locations that served only lunch and dinner, McDonald's developed a new menu and only had to incur some incremental labor costs to develop and later dominate the fast-food breakfast market.

It is important for students to understand that in reality, most of the everyday tasks completed by managers are done for the financial well-being of the firm. Specifically, most hospitality managers increase shareholder value by decreasing expenses, increasing revenue, or some combination of the two. In a general sense, managers take actions to address the three factors affecting the stock price discussed earlier.

1.5.3 Undertaking Projects to Create Value

Successful companies often use good ideas to create value for their shareholders. These ideas can turn into significant opportunities that not only change the financial position of the company but also the industry in which the company operates. There are many hospitality examples, but we discuss only a few here.

Kemmons Wilson, the founder of Holiday Inns, built his Holiday Inn hotel chain on good ideas. He got many of his ideas after traveling with his family to Washington, DC. Along the way, he found roadside accommodations to be of only minimal and inconsistent quality. He was upset by many motels charging extra fees for children staying in the same room with their parents and not offering any food and beverage service.

Recognizing the needs of traveling families like his own, he developed a chain of hotels that offered his guests swimming pools, food and beverage service, and the opportunity for children under the age of 12 to stay with their parents for no extra charge. Although common today, these simple ideas were revolutionary when first implemented.

Other innovations by Wilson had a larger impact on the hotel business as we know it today. Holiday Inn had the first nationwide reservation system, known as Holidex. Furthermore, Holiday Inns was the first to partner with a gas company and accept their credit cards for payment at Holiday Inn hotels (Holiday Inns at one time accepted the Gulf credit card).

Another lodging giant, Marriott Corporation, pioneered the guest rewards program in the hotel industry and was the first to offer in-room video checkout. Additionally, many good ideas are not thought of by the company but instead by their loyal customers and recognized by the company. For example, Marriott conducted extensive consumer research before they designed the Courtyard by Marriott prototype. By listening to their customers, Marriott designed rooms tailored for the business traveler by offering two telephones, dataports, in-room coffee, exercise facilities, and other amenities frequently requested by this market segment. Accordingly, good ideas helped Marriott create value for their shareholders and spur their tremendous growth.

So far we have given examples of good ideas that created value for shareholders. However, we have looked at these ideas in hindsight. How do we know in advance if we have a good idea or not? In other words, how do we know our potential project will create value? The project could be a new hotel, a new wing of rooms, a new gaming boat, or any number of different projects undertaken nearly every day in the hospitality industry. Can we be certain about the outcome?

Unfortunately, we do not live in a world with perfect information, nor can we predict the future with certainty. Nevertheless, managers must make decisions about which assets to invest in. We call this situation decision making under uncertainty. Uncertainty can also be defined as **risk.** Risk should not really be thought of as "taking a chance" but instead as the potential for outcomes to be different from our expectations. The greater the outcome is from our expectations, the greater the risk (for better or for worse).

Therefore, knowing that nearly every undertaking has some risk associated with it, we can incorporate this into our calculations regarding **value creation.** Later in this textbook, we will discuss the different types of risk and how they are measured. But for now, let us take a preliminary look at the "big picture" of value creation. Consider the new hotel project shown in Exhibit 1-4.

Looking at the proposed hotel project, we see the project generates incremental benefits of $5,000,000. The term *incremental* refers to the additional benefits or costs attributable to this project alone. By subtracting the costs from the benefits, we obtain the net incremental benefits of $1,000,000.

Should we invest in the new project? In the absence of other information, it appears that we should. Why? If we invest in the new hotel, the shareholders will be wealthier. How much wealthier will they become? The project summary indicates that the owners will become $1,000,000 wealthier. Thus, the new hotel

Projected incremental benefits	$5,000,000
Projected incremental costs	($4,000,000)
Projected net incremental benefits	$1,000,000

Exhibit 1-4 New hotel project summary.

project *creates value*. On the other hand, suppose the costs were *greater* than the benefits. We would then have a value-destroying project, and it would be rejected.

Thus far, we have discussed the investment decision. If the aforementioned project were undertaken, the financing decision would also have to be involved. Finally, after the project began to generate economic benefits, the managers would be involved in the dividend decision. Thus, all three financial decisions made by managers either affect or are affected by the process of value creation.

1.6 A GENERAL OUTLINE OF THE TEXTBOOK

This book deals mainly with the process of value creation in detail. Each chapter contains chapter objectives provided as an informal benchmark against which students can measure their progress. In addition to the text itself, each of the following chapters contains a chapter summary and a list of key terms used in the chapter. A glossary defining the key terms is provided at the end of the book. Finally, the chapters contain a number of questions and problems.

Chapter 2 provides the student with an introduction to the financial world at large, specifically in the form of capital markets and financial instruments. Included in this chapter is a discussion of stock and bond exchanges, hospitality lenders, and the importance of hedging risk by using forward and futures markets. Chapter 3 reviews the major financial statements and the uniform system of accounts. The chapter also examines the relationship between the financial statements and various ratios used by financial managers.

Chapter 4 introduces students to the concept of risk and the different types of risk. Moreover, it develops in detail the relationship between risk and return. Chapter 5 begins the heart of the textbook, the time value of money. This concept is key to determining whether or not a project creates value for the owners. Chapters 6 and 7 discuss the procedures for the valuation of bonds, preferred stock, and common stock. This helps the student become familiar with the financing decision. Chapter 8 discusses the important concept of cost of capital.

Chapter 9 begins a two-chapter introduction to the important concept of capital budgeting. Important concepts are introduced in Chapter 9, and Chapter 10 provides an applied example of deciding whether or not to invest in a new hospitality project. These chapters relate to the first of the major financial decisions, the investment decision.

Chapter 11 builds on the capital budgeting concepts from Chapters 9 and 10 to discuss in detail the valuation of hospitality investments such as hotels. Finally, Chapter 12 discusses the concept of capital structure management. Although this involves the financing decision, it shows how firms must not only find value-creating projects but must also try to minimize the cost of capital for those who supply funds for the project.

In summary, the first ten chapters cover the time value of money, risk and return, the cost of capital, and investment in long-term assets (an example of which we discussed in the previous section). The last two chapters involve more specific topics in hospitality finance: valuation/appraisal and capital structure. Prepared with basic knowledge of the time value of money and risk and return, these later chapters provide more detail regarding the important decisions that financial managers make.

1.7 SUMMARY

This chapter defined financial management and discussed how finance and accounting are different. Furthermore, the three major financial decisions were introduced as well as a discussion of the goal of hospitality financial management and the ways managers increase and create value. The student was briefly introduced to a value-creating project. Finally, a brief outline of the other chapters in the text was presented.

KEY TERMS

Agency problem
Agency relationship
Dividend decision
Financing decision
Investment decision
Risk
Securities and Exchange Commission (SEC)
Value creation

DISCUSSION QUESTIONS

1. What is financial management?
2. How is financial management different from accounting?
3. What are the advantages of a corporation? The disadvantages?
4. What are the three fundamental decisions of financial management?
5. What three factors affect the present worth of future dividends?
6. What is the difference between wealth maximization and value creation?
7. How do hospitality managers increase (maximize) value for their shareholders? Give some examples from your own experience.
8. Define an agency relationship. Who are the most typical parties involved in agency relationships in financial management?
9. Why do agency problems exist in financial management?
10. How do we know if a proposed project creates value for the shareholders?
11. How can a good decision in one functional area of hospitality management affect the financial position of the owners? Give some examples.
12. Describe some of the recent developments in hospitality financial management that have been in the news but have not been discussed in this chapter.

Financial Markets and Financial Instruments | 2

Chapter Objectives

- To understand why individuals invest
- To understand the different stock markets and how trading takes place
- To be able to calculate a holding period return
- To learn about the bond market
- To understand the money market and various money market instruments
- To understand the potential financial impact of fluctuations in foreign exchange rates
- To learn about risk hedging techniques such as forward and futures contracts
- To learn about some common indicators of stock market performance

---

WALT DISNEY COMPANY

The Walt Disney Company, one of the hospitality industry's oldest companies, began in 1923 with a cartoon character called Mickey Mouse. The common stock of the company is part of the Dow Jones Industrial Average.

The company is involved in theme parks such as Disneyland in California, Disney World in Florida, Euro Disney in France, and Disneyland in Tokyo. Additionally, the company owns Touchstone Motion Pictures along with the ABC television network and ESPN.

In 1992 Disney announced the issuance of $300 million in bonds that would mature in 100 years. Disney was the first company since 1954 to offer bonds with a 100-year maturity. The Disney bonds were callable beginning July 15, 2023, at a price that declined to 100 percent of face value after July 15, 2043.

The issue was met with some skepticism, as investors thought Disney was only trying to lock in a lower interest rate. Additionally, if interest rates were to fall, the value of the bonds would rise, but of course, Disney can eventually buy them back, perhaps at a lower price. This makes the bond issue less appealing to potential investors.

2.1 INTRODUCTION

Financial markets are places in which the suppliers of financial instruments (firms) meet the buyers of these instruments (investors) through financial intermediaries (such as brokers). A tremendous variety of financial instruments is available for investors to choose from. This chapter discusses the different types of existing financial markets and their importance. Additionally, it discusses the functioning of these markets, the parties involved, and the financial instruments that are part of financial markets. Moreover, it introduces the student to a variety of topics such as foreign exchange, forward and futures contracts, and stocks and bonds.

2.2 WHY PEOPLE INVEST

To some students, investing is something that *other people* do. Perhaps they think this because they do not have much disposable income to invest. However, they may not realize that their pursuit of a college education is really an investment. Although different from stocks or bonds, it is an investment nonetheless. Many students defer full-time employment in hopes of working full time later at a higher salary. The motivation of "giving something up" today to earn something in the future is similar to that of Wall Street investors.

Investors are hoping to make money, of course, but they are also doing something else. They are deferring present consumption in hopes of increased future consumption. This would be much more difficult to do without relatively efficient capital markets and a tremendous variety of financial instruments from which to choose. However, this is only one side of the story. From the hospitality firm's perspective, firms need capital to fund their operations in the form of equity (common or preferred stock) and debt (bonds or other loans). Let us examine equity capital first.

2.2.1 Description of Stock

We briefly introduced the features of common and preferred stock in Chapter 1 in our discussion of corporations. As you may recall, shares of stock owned by investors are a source of equity financing for companies that issue them. There are two types of equity issued. Preferred stockholders receive a specified dividend that is expressed as a percentage of the price. On the other hand, common stockholders cannot receive dividends until preferred stockholders are paid. Moreover, although there is no guarantee of common stockholders receiving a dividend, prospective investors often examine the history of a company to assess the likelihood of future dividend payments. Despite these disadvantages, common stockholders are allowed to vote on important issues at the annual shareholders meeting, whereas preferred stockholders are not. The most important decision shareholders make involves voting for the board of directors, which in turn makes decisions about the management team, the auditing firm, and many other issues.

When investors purchase stock, they hope to increase their future purchasing power in two ways: by receiving a stream of dividend payments and by eventually selling their stock at a higher price than what they paid, which is called a capital gain. Shareholders must pay income taxes on any dividends paid by the corporation in the year they are distributed. On the other hand, taxes on capital gains can be deferred until the share of stock is actually sold. Additionally, capital gains are currently taxed at a lower rate than ordinary dividends.

Investors are concerned with the return on their equity investments. One of these types of returns is called a **holding period of return,** which is calculated as follows:

$$\frac{(\text{Price at sale} - \text{Purchase price}) + \text{Dividends received}}{\text{Purchase price}} \times 100$$

$$= \text{Holding period return \%}$$

For example, assume you purchased a share of stock one year ago for $10. During the year you received $1 in dividends, and today you sell the stock for $12. What is your holding period return? Using the preceding formula:

$$\frac{(\$12 - \$10) + \$1}{\$10} \times 100 = 30\%$$

This return, of course, is calculated before taxes. If dividend income is taxed at 27 percent and capital gains are taxed at 20 percent, you will receive $.73 in after-tax dividends and $1.60 in after-tax capital gains. Therefore, your overall after-tax return is lowered to 23.3 percent ($2.33/$10).

An important part of the holding period return calculation is the price of the stock. What affects the price of stocks? Although supply and demand definitely plays a key role, the price is largely dependent on the current and future prospective cash flows of the company. As you may recall from Chapter 1, there are three factors affecting the **present value** of these cash flows: timing, magnitude, and risk. Each of these factors will be discussed in greater detail later in this book.

2.2.2 Description of Bonds

Bonds represent a method of debt financing for a company and are basically a promise to repay investors over a period of time. Unlike common stock, bond-holders do not have a true ownership claim on the assets of the firm. Nevertheless, they receive a return on their investment in the form of semiannual interest payments and the return of the face value of the bond (called the **principal**) at the end of the term. Much like dividends, this represents a series of cash payments that can be valued. Thus, bonds can be traded like stocks (although they are usually not traded in the same volume).

Bond prices are indexed relative to 100. Therefore, if a $1,000 bond is selling at 100, the price is $1,000. However, if its price increases to 102, the price is $1,020. If the price decreases to 98, it is selling for $980. Although the price of the bond often changes, the amount of interest it pays does not. For example, a $1,000 bond paying 13 percent interest will yield $130 in interest each year for an investor, regardless of what happens to the price. Bond prices are also based on the present value of the cash flows of the bond. The same three factors that determine the present value of dividends for common stocks also affect principal and interest payments of bonds. Exhibit 2-1 shows how bond prices are typically presented in the financial press.

The exhibit contains a fictitious bond issued by Hilton Corporation. Reading from left to right, the name of the company is first, followed by two sets of numbers. The first set is the annual interest rate on the bond—in this case, 7¼ percent.

Bond	Current yield	Volume	Close	Net chg
Hilton 7¼ 04	7.2	40	101	+½

Exhibit 2-1 Bond pricing.

The second set of numbers is the last two numbers of the year the bond matures. The next column shows the current yield, which is simply the amount of annual interest earned divided by the current price. Note that this yield is *not* the return an investor will receive if she holds the bond until maturity. The yield to maturity calculation will be shown in Chapter 6 on Stock and Bond Valuation. The next column is the volume of bonds traded that day, expressed in thousands of dollars. Accordingly, $40,000 of the Hilton bonds were traded in this example. The next column shows the closing price, with the principal value of the bond indexed to 100. Finally, the net change column measures the change in closing price from the last day of trading.

There are a number of differences between stocks and bonds. One of the most important relates to federal taxes. Under the current tax system in the United States, debt financing has an inherent advantage over equity financing. This is because interest payments on bonds are tax-deductible expenses for the issuing firms, and the interest expense is included on the income statement. On the other hand, dividend payments to stockholders are not considered operating expenses and do not appear on the income statement. This is one of the reasons why firms often choose to finance their assets (in part) with debt instead of equity. It is important to note that most hospitality firms use some combination of debt and equity to finance their assets.

The remainder of this chapter focuses on capital markets and some of the most common financial instruments.

2.3 CAPITAL MARKETS

Capital markets are those markets in which debt and equity issues are traded. Many people think primarily of the stock market when they hear the term *capital markets*. However, there are many other types of capital markets, including the bond market and mortgage market. There is also more than one stock market. We begin with an examination of the various stock markets.

2.3.1 New York Stock Exchange

The New York Stock Exchange (NYSE) is the oldest stock market in the United States. It was founded in 1792 and became designated as a national securities exchange by the Securities and Exchange Commission (SEC) in 1934. The NYSE is a physical location in which buyers and sellers conduct secondary trading of financial instruments, including bonds. The difference between primary and secondary trading will be discussed later.

In general, the NYSE lists most of the largest corporations in the United States. As of this writing, there are 2,800 different companies offering securities on the NYSE. These companies must meet certain standards to be listed on the

NYSE. Additionally, the NYSE is not only for American companies—there are over 470 non-U.S. companies listed.

The NYSE offers membership to securities dealers and brokerage firms in the form of "seats" on the trading floor. Only member firms are allowed to deal in securities offered on the exchange. Each of the 1,336 seats carries a price and can be bought and sold between competing firms. However, although the NYSE is a major exchange, it is not the only place for firms to list their securities.

2.3.2 NASDAQ

NASDAQ is an acronym that stands for National Association of Security Dealers and Automated Quotations. The growth of the economy and the interest by investors in smaller companies has contributed to the growth of NASDAQ, as evidenced by the increase in stock ownership by American households. In 1971, only 27 percent of American households owned stock, but by 1999, the number had grown to approximately 45 percent. NASDAQ serves an important function by allowing companies that are too small to be listed on the NYSE access to financial capital. However, NASDAQ is also home to many large companies such as Microsoft and Intel.

NASDAQ is known as an over-the-counter (OTC) market because it is not a physical location like the NYSE. It was created in 1971 as the first electronic stock market via a network of securities dealers. Although the NYSE lists the largest companies, NASDAQ is the fastest-growing securities market and in 1994 surpassed the NYSE in the number of shares traded. NASDAQ is actually comprised of two separate markets: a National market, which contains stocks of 4,400 companies, and the Small Cap market, which contains stocks of 1,800 companies. The key element in the system is composed of dealers who act as **"market makers"** and compete with each other for business. A market maker is someone who helps stabilize prices by helping to guarantee trades between buyers and sellers. If buyers or sellers cannot be found, market makers utilize securities from their own personal inventory to help ensure the liquidity of stock issues.

2.3.3 Other Stock Exchanges

There are also smaller regional stock exchanges in the United States, which include the Pacific Stock Exchange as well as exchanges in Boston, Chicago, Cincinnati, and Philadelphia. In addition, the United States is not the only country with stock markets. Many other countries also have stock markets on which both domestic and foreign companies are listed. Some of the largest include the Tokyo Stock Exchange and the London Stock Exchange. Given the increasing use of technology and globalization of information, many investors track the performance of other stock exchanges around the world. The financial crisis in East Asia in 1998 that affected the U.S. and other stock markets demonstrates the increasing links between the various exchanges and economies.

2.3.4 Bond Market

The bond market is not really separate from the stock market. Many bonds, like stocks, are traded on the NYSE. However, the majority of corporate and U.S. Treasury bonds are traded on OTC markets. As previously discussed, bonds are different financial instruments than stocks. Although bonds represent a contractual agreement between lender and borrower, most bonds (with the exception of government bonds) are not guaranteed. Accordingly, the safety of bonds is scrutinized carefully by investors. Investment services firms such as Moody's and Standard & Poor's rate the "safety" of bonds in terms of the probability of company payments of interest and principal to investors. Companies that do not make interest payments on their bond issues on time are said to be in **default.**

In terms of bond ratings, the lower the letter in the alphabet, the greater quality of bond. For example, a B bond is riskier than an A bond. Additionally, the more of the same letters in the rating, the greater quality of bond. Standard & Poor's rates bonds using all capital letters. For example, AAA bonds are higher quality than AA bonds. Moody's rates bonds with a capital letter followed by lowercase letters. In other words, Aaa bonds are rated higher than Aa bonds. Companies with C-rated bonds are highly speculative and the lowest rate.

As previously mentioned, most bonds represent a series of interest payments and the repayment of principal. In addition to being affected by the size and timing of payments, the price of a bond is also affected by the current assessment of the risk of those payments. The higher the risk of the payments, the lower the present value or price. Think of it this way: If you are holding a bond from McDonald's Corporation paying you 8 percent interest and a comparable bond is issued and pays 10 percent, your bond would not be as desirable (because of the lower interest payments), and the price of your bond should decline (all else being equal). The price declines because the interest and principal payments are discounted at a higher rate. This **discounting** will be discussed in later chapters.

Some bonds are callable, which means that the issuer has the right to repurchase the bonds at a certain price within a certain period of time. This feature is used by the issuing company to protect themselves in case interest rates drop. The call price has to be high enough to entice investors to want to purchase the bonds despite this feature. Other aspects of bonds will be discussed in Chapter 6.

2.3.5 Mortgage Market

The mortgage market refers to the pooling of home mortgages by government-sponsored agencies such as the Federal National Mortgage Association (Fannie Mae) and the Government National Mortgage Association (Ginnie Mae). These government agencies purchase mortgages from lenders and resell them to investors in the form of securities. The investors receive income from those making the mortgage payments. These securities are primarily sold to institutional investors such as insurance companies and pension funds and can be traded like bonds. These instruments are referred to as **mortgage-backed securities** or pass-throughs. Because these instruments are not actually issued by the federal government itself, their return is not guaranteed. However, they are generally considered to be very low risk and earn lower returns than commercial paper.

2.4 MONEY MARKET

The money market represents the market for debt instruments that are short term, meaning they will mature in one year or less. The most common money market instruments are certificates of deposit (CDs), commercial paper, and treasury bills.

CDs are debt securities issued through commercial banks. They are available not only to institutional investors in large denominations but also to small investors in denominations of only $100. The maturities and interest rates will vary. Commercial paper is a short-term debt instrument with maturities ranging up to 270 days. It is typically issued by well-known, quality companies to investors who are looking for safety yet want a return on their investment. Commercial paper is rated much like corporate bonds.

Treasury bills are used by the Federal Reserve to help fund the operations of the U.S. government. The most common maturities are three, six, and twelve months, with the smallest denomination being $10,000. Treasury bills are auctioned weekly or monthly by the Federal Reserve, although investors can also buy them directly from brokers and certain banks. Treasury bills are actually **zero coupon securities,** meaning that investors buy the bonds at a discount, and the bonds gain value as they near maturity; no interest payments are made. The federal government also issues treasury notes, which have longer maturities than bills. On October 31, 2001, the federal government announced that it would no longer issue the 30-year Treasury bond.

All of the Treasury issues are backed by the credit of the U.S. government; therefore, their return is essentially guaranteed. Additionally, the instruments can be sold rather easily if needed. The rate of return on these instruments has an important implication in finance. Investors consider the return on these securities to be the **risk-free rate of return.** The return on treasury bills, for example, is often quite low for short maturities. However, the risk associated with them is virtually nonexistent. This direct relationship between risk and return will be discussed later in the book.

2.5 RAISING FINANCIAL CAPITAL AND SECURITY TRADING

We discussed earlier that firms finance assets with debt and equity issues. A new common stock issue by a firm is called an initial public offering (IPO). The firm first establishes a relationship with an investment banker, who effectively acts as an intermediary between the firm and potential investors. The investment banker provides consulting services to the firm regarding the price of the new issue and completes the necessary legal work required by the SEC. Investment bankers often work with bankers in other firms to help sell the new issue to the public. The investment banker will purchase the issue from the firm and then reissue the stock to the public through brokers. The initial sale of the stock is called the **primary market.**

Investment banking firms make a significant amount of fees when they help with an IPO. A recent scandal involving investment banking showed some firms were falsely touting certain stocks and enticing clients to buy them for the firm to get more investment banking business. In the spring of 2003 a number of investment firms settled a major case with the state of New York and were forced to pay large fines.

On the other hand, most trading of stocks occurs on the **secondary market,** which represents investors trading among themselves through brokers. Although the firm is usually concerned about the share price (because managers and employees may also own stock), no new funds are raised for the company in this process. Let us examine this process in more detail.

Let's say you would like to purchase 100 shares of Hilton Hotel (which is listed on the NYSE with the ticker symbol HLT). You place a call to your broker, who contacts your broker's representative at the stock exchange. Each company listed on the stock exchange is assigned a specialist. Similar to a market maker for OTC stocks, a specialist is someone responsible for maintaining a balance in supply and demand for the stock and preventing large swings in prices. Your broker's representative then contacts the specialist with your order to buy at your specified price. The specialist either matches your order to buy with someone who wants to sell or sells you stock from their own inventory. Once the trade is finished, a confirmation is sent back to your broker. Although you now own one share of stock, you will not be sent the stock certificate. Stock certificates are generally kept by the brokers for their customers.

The pricing of stocks is based on a "bid" and an "ask" price. The bid price is what a prospective buyer is willing to pay for a share. The ask price is the amount for which a broker will sell it to you. The difference between the two is called the bid-ask spread and represents a small profit for the broker. Stock prices were once expressed in dollars and eighths of a dollar. However, in late 2000 stock prices changed to dollars and cents.

The buying and selling process of stocks moves quite quickly. According to the NYSE, it takes an average of 22 seconds from the time an order is placed until a confirmation of that transaction is received at a broker's office. The speed of the process indicates the heavy reliance on computers by the stock exchanges. Although normally well functioning, a software problem in June 2001 at the NYSE led to a trading halt of approximately 90 minutes. Trading was eventually restored, but the problem is indicative of the financial markets' significant reliance on advanced technology and the potential problems that sometimes occur.

2.6 FINANCIAL MARKETS AND HEDGING RISK

Is there ever a time when investments are made to avoid losing money as opposed to making money? Consider the purchase of homeowners insurance. Although mortgage companies require such insurance, homeowners pay a monthly premium to insure their home and valuables. Hopefully, nothing will happen to the house, and the value of the asset is maintained. Conversely, if the house burns down, they file a claim, the house is rebuilt, and the valuables are replaced. Thus, the homeowners are effectively hedging risk. Either way, they will have a home and personal property. Financial instruments are available to help hospitality managers hedge risk as well.

2.6.1 Forward and Futures Contracts

Some assets are purchased immediately, or "on the spot," such as a share of stock. Other examples could include the purchase of commodities such as wheat or pork bellies. If we make the purchase today, we would pay the spot price, or cash price. However, in some cases we may want to order assets for delivery (and payment) sometime in the future. One of the problems with this is that prices can change over time, which creates uncertainty for both the buyer and the seller of the asset. A good example is a farmer taking bushels of wheat to market. The price of wheat may change dramatically between the time of harvest and the time he or she gets to the market to make a sale. This circumstance created the need for financial instruments known as forward and futures contracts.

A **forward contract** is an agreement about a sale of an asset that will be delivered in the future. The price agreed on for future delivery is called the forward price. An important feature of a forward contract is that cash payment is not required until delivery is made. The details of the transaction, such as the amount of the asset to be delivered and the price of the asset, are negotiated between the two parties. However, one of the problems with forward contracts is that both parties are locked into the agreement and must trust the other to perform. Moreover, because of the specific nature of forward contracts, they are very difficult to sell to a third party. Accordingly, the uncertainties and other difficulties associated with the forward contract led to the development of another type of financial instrument.

A **futures contract** is similar to a forward contract in that the contract involves a future delivery of an asset at a price (called the forward price). However, the features of a futures contract are largely standardized as opposed to being negotiated between the two parties. The contract is actually between a trader and a clearinghouse that guarantees contract performance and the solvency of the two parties. Contract sizes and delivery dates are standardized, making them much easier to sell to a third party. These contracts are traded on either the Chicago Board of Trade or the Chicago Mercantile Exchange. The value of the contract changes each day because the value of the underlying asset changes. The process of settling the value of the contract between the parties is called "marking to market."

If one party wants to exit from the contract, they can either sell their contract or else take an opposite position (in other words, instead of buying bushels of wheat on a certain date, you sell bushels of wheat on a certain date). This effectively offsets the position in the contract. Taking a second and opposite position is quite common. It is estimated that only 5 percent of futures contracts are actually fulfilled. In addition to commodities, forward and futures contracts can be used with foreign currencies and commodities to help hospitality managers hedge risk.

2.6.2 Foreign Exchange Markets

As trade barriers between countries are removed, more U.S. companies are doing business overseas. This means that revenues, and consequently profits, are generated in a variety of foreign currencies, making knowledge of exchange rate movements important. When foreign currencies are compared to a domestic currency, this can be done using either direct or indirect quotes. For companies based in the United States, a direct quote would indicate the cost of one unit of foreign currency in U.S. dollars. For example, on March 18, 2003, the spot exchange rate as a direct quote for the euro was $1.0633. In other words, one euro would cost you approximately $1.06. An indirect quote is simply the inverse of the direct quote. Using the previous example, the indirect quote would indicate that $1.00 was equal to .9405 euros on that date. In other words, it would cost an individual in Europe .9405 euros to obtain one U.S. dollar.

Foreign exchange rates are important to hospitality companies. McDonald's, for example, generated approximately 65 percent of their revenues from locations outside the United States in 2002. Nevertheless, the SEC requires that profits from overseas must be "repatriated" and converted to U.S. dollars before they are reported to investors. Because exchange rates between currencies frequently change, this means that reported profits could also change. Let us look at an example.

Let's say that you manage a hospitality company in France and have earned profits of 100,000 euros. When you started the year, the exchange rate was 1 euro per $1. However, by the end of the year, the exchange rate is 2 euros per $1. Have your profits increased or decreased? Let us look at the calculations.

$$\text{January 1: 100,000 euros} \times \frac{\$1}{1 \; euro} = \$100,000$$

After rate change:

$$\text{December 31: 100,000 euros} \times \frac{\$1}{2 \; euro} = \$50,000$$

As can be seen from these calculations, you have experienced a foreign exchange loss. Remember, we are interested in the value of the profits in terms of dollars. The number of euros has not changed—but their value in terms of U.S. dollars has. Think of it this way: At the beginning of the year, it took 1 euro to purchase $1 worth of goods. At the end of the year, however, it took 2 euros to buy the same amount of U.S. goods. You are then worse off holding euros than you were before the change in the exchange rate. A good exercise would be to calculate the effect on dollar profits if the exchange rate changed from 1 euro per $1 to .50 euro per $1.

The previous example shows how devaluation of currency can affect profits. Although there are a number of factors affecting exchange rates, one of the primary ones is the difference between the expected rate of inflation for the two countries. We will not discuss further how exchange rates change but instead will focus on how hospitality managers can hedge this foreign exchange rate risk.

If you calculated the exchange rate change to .50 euro per $1, you can see that you are now a hero (or heroine) because you have doubled your profits in terms of dollars. However, the first example revealed the possibility of cutting your profits in half. Therefore, one can understand the uncertainty (and risk) involved if you choose to do nothing.

On the other hand, a hospitality manager could hedge the risk by using a forward or futures contract to sell euros for U.S. dollars at an agreed rate of exchange. This way, the exchange rate would be locked in and the uncertainty would be eliminated. Who would be interested in selling dollars to our firm? A likely candidate would be a European company operating in the United States that needed to sell U.S. dollars and buy euros.

The use of the euro as currency was not agreed to until 1991, and it was finally coined and distributed in 2002. The introduction of the currency was expected to help unify the European area and increase the flow of goods and services across countries. The single currency was formally issued in the countries of Austria, Belgium, Finland, France, Germany, Greece, Ireland, Italy, Luxembourg, Netherlands, Portugal, and Spain.

2.6.3 Commodity Markets

Not only must hospitality managers worry about repatriating profits, but they must also be concerned about costs. Consider a restaurant operation that sells large quantities of orange juice. If there is poor weather and the orange crop is damaged, prices will probably increase. This can put a hospitality manager in a bind because it is unlikely that prices can be raised substantially in the short term without adversely affecting revenues. What options are available to the hospitality manager?

The first option would be to do nothing and hope for the best. Depending on the crop damage, the price increase may be modest. Additionally, a hospitality manager could try substituting a less-expensive juice for orange juice on the menu. Another option would be to buy a forward or futures contract. Although no cash payment is required up front, futures contracts deal in large quantities. For example, orange juice contracts are traded in 15,000-pound units. Only a major restaurant company could handle such a large delivery of orange juice on the date the contract is executed. How could a smaller company deal with a contract of this size?

Let's say you have a futures contract to purchase orange juice for $1.00 per gallon. If the spot price of orange juice increases to $1.25 per gallon, your contract has increased in value. You could then sell your contract at a profit and use the profits to pay for the price increase from a local orange juice purveyor in the quantity desired. Thus, even small restaurateurs can utilize the futures market to help them hedge price risk.

2.7 KEY FINANCIAL INTERMEDIARIES: LENDERS TO THE HOSPITALITY INDUSTRY

In the beginning of the chapter we mentioned the idea of financial intermediaries that help make capital markets function. Although brokers definitely play a key role in the overall financial marketplace, lenders are of critical importance to the hospitality industry. Although most hospitality firms use common stock to finance assets, many only finance a percentage of assets this way. The remaining financing must come from debt instruments. Bonds, which are a type of debt, were previously discussed. However, hospitality firms often use loans instead. This section will discuss the different types of lenders to the hospitality industry.

2.7.1 Commercial Banks

Commercial banks, who have traditionally been the largest lender to the hospitality industry, take in capital from depositors to whom they provide a return on their money in the form of interest. To be able to pay this interest, banks will lend the money to businesses and individuals. The interest rate on the loan is the rate of return of the bank. Because banks are willing to bear this risk, the banks earn the difference between the interest rate charged on loans and the interest rate paid to depositors. This is called the spread. The larger the spread, the more money for the bank. In addition to the interest spread, commercial banks also generate revenue by charging fees for making loans. Given the importance of interest expense to lenders and borrowers alike, it is important to understand how it is calculated. Interest expense is calculated as follows:

$$\text{Interest} = \text{Principal} \times \text{Rate} \times \text{Time}$$

Commercial banks offer many types of loans. One type is a fully amortized loan. This means that each payment contains a portion that is interest and a portion that is principal. As stated in the bond discussion, principal is the amount of money that was originally borrowed. Most home mortgage loans are fully amortized, and the interest portion is tax deductible. On the other hand, some commercial loans are interest only, with the principal being repaid only at the end of the loan term—called a balloon payment.

Banks have also become more involved in investments for individuals. Treasury instruments, certificates of deposit, individual retirement accounts, and other instruments are also offered by banks. For many years banks had been prevented from underwriting securities, although this is now allowed for certain issues. However, banks are still not allowed to sell insurance.

2.7.2 Real Estate Investment Trusts (REITs)

These companies manage real estate portfolios for shareholders. The stock of the REIT is traded on one of the stock markets. Equity REITs are those that actually own real estate and pass income from the real estate on to the owners. Mortgage REITs lend money to the industry and provide interest income to the owners. REITs are exempt from corporate income taxes if they distribute at least 95 percent of their earnings to shareholders. They have become a popular method of financing hotels over the past decade, but their popularity can be affected by changes in tax laws. One of the better-known REITs in the hospitality industry is Host Marriott Corporation. After its creation along with Marriott International in 1992, Host Marriott became a REIT in January 1999.

2.7.3 Insurance Companies and Pension Funds

These two large institutional investors serve different purposes but have similar investment strategies; both receive monthly cash flows (premiums for life insurance firms). Life insurance companies are expected to invest these premiums to meet the needs of the insured when it is time to collect, whereas pension funds receive money from company payroll accounts and meet the needs of individuals after they retire.

Insurance companies are regulated by the individual states, whereas many pension funds are regulated by the Pension Benefit Guaranty Corporation. The investments made by these institutions are scrutinized carefully to ensure that they remain solvent. Certain real estate investments are considered quite speculative and, therefore, may be considered too risky for institutional lenders. The poor performance of many hotel markets in the early 1990s forced these lenders to reconsider their lending practices to the hotel industry. Therefore, although insurance companies and pension funds will still lend funds to hospitality firms, the frequency and magnitude have declined in recent years.

2.8 STOCK MARKET PERFORMANCE

When someone talks about the performance of the stock market, it is not always clear what they are referring to. Instead of tracking the performance of the entire listing of stocks traded on the different exchanges, investors will examine certain stock market indicators or indices. We will discuss two of the more popular indicators in the following sections.

Company	Symbol	Company	Symbol
Alcoa	AA	Honeywell	HON
American Express	AXP	International Business Machines	IBM
AT&T	T	Intel	INTC
Boeing	BA	International Paper	IP
Caterpillar	CAT	Johnson & Johnson	JNJ
Citigroup	C	J.P. Morgan	JPM
Coca-Cola	KO	McDonald's	MCD
Disney	DIS	Merck	MRK
DuPont	DD	Microsoft	MSFT
Eastman Kodak	EK	Minnesota Mining and Mfg	MMM
Exxon Mobil	XOM	Philip Morris	MO
General Electric	GE	Procter and Gamble	PG
General Motors	GM	SBC Communications	SBC
Hewlett-Packard	HWP	United Technologies	UTX
Home Depot	HD	Wal-Mart	WMT

Source: Dow Jones Web site.

Exhibit 2-2   Dow Jones Industrial Average Components as of May 2003.

2.8.1 Dow Jones Industrial Average

Dow Jones and Company is a corporation that has been tracking the performance of the stock market for many years. They established a way of tracking the general performance of the stock market by creating a price-weighted index of the common stock of 30 large companies that are considered industry leaders. The index is often referred to simply as "the Dow." A list of the current 30 companies is provided in Exhibit 2-2.

This index is the oldest stock market index in use and is widely reported in the financial press. The index is a weighted average of the stock prices, based on the value of each stock. It should be noted that although the Dow industrial stocks are probably reported the most, Dow Jones also tracks an index of 20 transportation companies and 15 utility companies. The three indices are combined into the Dow Jones Composite Average.

2.8.2 Standard & Poor's 500

Standard & Poor's (S&P) is a financial services corporation that rates stocks, bonds, and commercial paper. Additionally, the company tracks the performance of the stock market and creates an index of 500 stocks, primarily those listed on the New York Stock Exchange. The index, commonly known as the S&P 500, is often reported in conjunction with the performance of the Dow. It is calculated using a weighted average based on the value of the 500 individual stocks. A comparison of the annual returns of the two stock market indices since 1950 is shown in Exhibit 2-3.

2.8.3 Market Performance in Terms of Return

As shown in Exhibit 2-3, the two indices have overall average returns that are fairly close together. The average, or mean return, of the S&P 500 is 9.63 percent, whereas the mean return for the Dow is 9.01 percent. The mean will change, of

Year	S&P 500 % gain (loss)	Dow % gain (loss)	Year	S&P 500 % gain (loss)	Dow % gain (loss)	Year	S&P 500 % gain (loss)	Dow % gain (loss)
1950	22.51	17.64	1968	7.66	4.28	1986	14.62	23.49
1951	14.44	14.36	1969	(11.36)	(15.19)	1987	2.03	1.34
1952	11.64	8.43	1970	0.10	4.81	1988	12.39	8.83
1953	(6.52)	(3.77)	1971	10.79	6.12	1989	27.25	27.79
1954	44.21	43.97	1972	15.63	14.58	1990	(6.56)	(4.86)
1955	23.76	20.77	1973	(17.37)	(16.81)	1991	26.31	20.23
1956	3.34	2.27	1974	(29.72)	(27.58)	1992	4.48	4.93
1957	(13.44)	(12.77)	1975	31.38	37.68	1993	7.06	13.47
1958	36.90	33.97	1976	19.15	17.87	1994	(1.55)	2.15
1959	8.03	16.40	1977	(11.50)	(17.10)	1995	34.13	33.36
1960	(3.00)	(9.35)	1978	1.06	(2.38)	1996	20.26	25.04
1961	24.28	20.62	1979	12.31	4.47	1997	31.00	23.94
1962	(11.81)	(10.81)	1980	25.77	15.37	1998	26.67	15.95
1963	18.89	17.01	1981	(9.73)	(9.36)	1999	19.53	24.80
1964	12.97	14.56	1982	14.76	19.37	2000	(10.14)	(6.18)
1965	9.06	10.89	1983	17.26	19.99	2001	(13.04)	(7.10)
1966	(13.09)	(18.94)	1984	1.40	(3.72)			
1967	20.09	15.20	1985	26.36	28.63			

Sources: Yahoo! Finance Web site (1950–1999) and *Wall Street Journal* (2000–2001).

Exhibit 2-3 Annual Performance of S&P 500 and DJIA.

course, depending on the time period examined. The market has recently had two consecutive years of negative returns, something that has not occurred since 1973–1974. The market has not had three consecutive years of negative returns since the 1939–1941 period.

Another important aspect of returns is their **standard deviation.** As the student is aware, a return on the stock market is not guaranteed. An interesting feature of stock market performance is the variation of returns. Although the mean return for the S&P 500 for the past 52 years is 9.63 percent, the returns have ranged from nearly negative 30 percent to over 44 percent.

One of the reasons the stock market is considered risky is the inability to obtain a mean return on a consistent basis. How can we assess the risk of the stock market? There are ways of quantifying the differences between the actual returns in any given year and the overall average. One quantifiable measure of this uncertainty is called **variance.** Another way is the square root of the variance, called the standard deviation. The standard deviations for the two market indicators are nearly identical with the standard deviation of returns for the S&P 500 being 16.2 percent, as compared to 16.1 percent for the Dow. Standard deviation calculations will be shown in greater detail in Chapter 4.

By examining the rate of return patterns of the two indices, we can see that they generally follow each other fairly consistently. A measure of how returns move together over time is called the **correlation coefficient,** which is a number that ranges from −1.0 to +1.0. Returns that move together perfectly have a correlation coefficient of +1.0, whereas those that move in exact opposite directions have a correlation coefficient of −1.0. In reality, most assets have returns that move somewhere between 0 and +1.0. Correlation coefficients are important when calculating the risk of groups of assets called portfolios, which are discussed later in the book.

2.9 SUMMARY

This chapter described the motivations for investors and how financial markets are used to help firms and investors alike. The student was introduced to the capital markets including stock, bond, and mortgage markets. The importance of fluctuations in foreign exchange rates and the specifics of stock trading were also presented. Financial instruments that are used to hedge risk such as forward and future contracts were discussed. The most important financial intermediaries to the hospitality industry—lenders—were reviewed and compared. Finally, the chapter discussed some common stock market indicators and compared their performance.

KEY TERMS

Correlation coefficient
Default
Discounting
Forward contract
Futures contract
Holding period of return
Market maker
Mortgage-backed securities
Present value
Primary market
Principal
Risk-free rate of return
Secondary market
Standard deviation
Variance
Zero coupon securities

DISCUSSION QUESTIONS

1. Why do people invest?
2. What are the key differences between common stock and preferred stock?
3. How is a holding period return calculated?
4. What is a bond? How does it differ from common stock?
5. Describe the two largest stock markets.
6. In general, what will happen to the value of a bond when interest rates rise? Why?
7. Describe the process companies use to raise equity capital.
8. What is the difference between a futures contract and a forward contract?
9. Assume that you are a restaurant manager facing a potential price increase for orange juice. What options are available to you to deal with this problem?

10. Describe the major lenders to the hospitality industry.

11. Describe two of the most common stock market indicators.

12. How can we measure the total risk of an investment?

PROBLEMS

Problems designated with **Excel** *can be solved using* **Excel** *spreadsheets accessible at* http://www.prenhall.com/chatfield.

1. Assume that you own a share of stock that has achieved the following historical returns.

Year	Return percentage
1	10%
2	(4%)
3	25%
4	13%
5	.5%

Calculate the average return for the share of stock over the past five years.

2. Assume that you own a portfolio of five separate stocks. Each yields a different return and represents a different proportion of your portfolio. The stocks and their returns are as follows.

Stock	Percentage of portfolio	Return percentage
1	15%	10%
2	25%	8%
3	40%	6%
4	10%	12%
5	10%	5%

What is the weighted average return for your portfolio?

3. Joe Smith purchased a share of stock for $58. During the year he received $2.40 in dividends. At the end of the year he sold the stock for $64. Calculate the holding period return for his investment (excluding taxes).

4. Sally Jones purchased a share of stock for $42. During the year she received $1.80 in dividends. At the end of the year she sold her stock for $40.50. Calculate the holding period return for her investment (excluding taxes).

5. You would like to purchase five 8.5 percent $10,000 bonds that are currently selling for 102.

   a. How much will it cost you to purchase these bonds?

   b. How much interest will you earn in one year from these five bonds?

6. Assume that a $10,000 bond paying 12 percent interest is currently selling at 104.

   a. What is the current selling price of the bond in dollars?

   b. What is the current yield of this bond?

7. A $100,000 bond is currently selling at 98, and the current yield on the bond is 6.2 percent. What is the interest rate on the bond?

8. Hans Stern is a manager of a McDonald's in Germany, and he is interested in the indirect quote for U.S. dollars and euros. The direct quote of the euro per U.S. dollar is 1.75euro/$1. What is the indirect quote?

9. Assume that you are a manager of an American hospitality firm in France. You are forecasting a net income of 200,000 euros. Also assume that the exchange rate has changed from $1/1euro to $.50/1euro. When you repatriate your profits to dollars, has your net income increased or decreased from the change in the exchange rate?

EXCEL   10. Examine the return data from the S&P 500 index and the Dow Jones Industrial Average. Using a spreadsheet program such as Excel, calculate the correlation coefficient of their returns between 1992 and 2001.

11. You purchase a German sports car for 117,000 euros. At the time of your purchase, the exchange rate was 1.72euro/$1. Now the exchange rate has changed to 1.67euro/$1. Does your sportscar cost more or less in U.S. dollars now than when you purchased it? By how much?

12. Jennifer Annisette purchased two acres of land for $50,000 and received 50 percent financing of the purchase price from the bank (the loan is interest free). A home developer is interested in developing houses on Jennifer's land and is offering her $30,000 per acre for her land. What is Jennifer's net holding period return on her investment?

Review of Financial Statements and Selected Ratios

3

Chapter Objectives

- To review the income statement
- To review the Uniform System of Accounts format
- To review the balance sheet
- To understand the relationship between the income statement and the balance sheet
- To review the statement of retained earnings
- To review the statement of cash flows
- To review ratios of particular importance to the hospitality industry and understand the limitations of ratio analysis

PROPER RATIOS

Most introductory accounting courses teach basic ratios. Some of them try to teach students what an "acceptable" current ratio is. The current ratio is one of the first ratios students learn, and it is generally considered to be one of the easiest to remember. Additionally, it is one of the more important ratios from the lender's perspective.

However, it is important to remember that industries are not homogenous. As an example, one accounting text mentions that a "normal" ratio for most companies in most industries is between 1.6 and 1.9. Moreover, a current ratio of 2.0 is considered "good." Can we assume, then, that the higher the current ratio, the better? Some current ratios of different companies follows.

Company	2002 Current ratio
International Paper	1.7
Microsoft	3.8
3M Corporation	1.4
Marriott Corporation	.79
McDonald's	.71

(continued)

Let us look at the current ratio of two large and successful hospitality companies. Both of them have current ratios well below the "acceptable" range. How can this be?

We have to remember that we cannot simply assume ratio "rules" are the same for each company. Industries are not all alike, and companies within the same industry can differ significantly. It may be such that the shareholders of the hospitality companies shown do not want management tying up their investment in current assets. They want management to invest in long-term assets because they are more effective in producing cash flows to maximize the wealth of the owners.

3.1 INTRODUCTION

This chapter provides a review of the major financial statements that students should have worked with in earlier courses, such as financial and/or managerial accounting. One financial statement indicates the performance of an operation over a period of time—the **income statement.** Another indicates the financial position of the operation at a particular point in time—the **balance sheet.** The **statement of retained earnings** shows the changes of the owner's position during an operating cycle. And finally, the **statement of cash flows** explains the changes in the cash account for an operating cycle. Each of these are reviewed in this chapter.

Once the statements are completed, new information can be generated by utilizing ratio analysis. Although many ratios can be calculated, Chapter 3 focuses on the most commonly used by managers, owners, and lenders. Additionally, this chapter discusses the limitations of ratio analysis.

3.2 REVIEW OF THE INCOME STATEMENT

The income statement provides details on the revenues and expenses of a hospitality operation for a period of time. Students need to be very familiar with the construction of the income statement because it is frequently used as the major tool to assess management's capabilities. Furthermore, income statements can be compiled for individual departments, divisions, and properties and reported to outsiders.

Most "line items" shown on the income statement represent expenses. Typically, the largest expense category for hotels is labor cost, whereas the largest for food service operations is cost of goods sold (with labor cost usually second largest). Accordingly, the importance of the income statement and its frequent use led to a special construction for the hospitality industry.

3.2.1 Uniform System of Accounts for Hotels

The **Uniform System of Accounts** for hotels is a standardized income statement that provides the hospitality industry with numerous advantages. For one, it allows new properties to understand immediately the proper format of their income statements. Second, it allows easier comparison between properties. Additionally, it can be used for properties of all different sizes. Finally, it is a system that has been time tested since its design in 1925. Although the Uniform System has been updated since that time, the changes in recent years have been relatively minor.

The Uniform System of Accounts for hotels is unique to the hotel industry. Instead of focusing on one particular area of expense (such as labor cost or cost of goods sold) like retail or manufacturing concerns, it allows management to focus on different functional areas of a full-service hotel. Thus, labor expense can be appropriately attributed to an individual department to help determine that department's profitability, as opposed to examining a single good or service. This chapter discusses primarily the income statements for multidepartment hotel properties.

3.2.2 Hotel Income Statement

Before examining a detailed income statement for an individual hotel property, let us examine a consolidated income statement from Hilton Hotels shown in Exhibit 3-1.

As shown in Exhibit 3-1, the income statement is somewhat short and rather general, grouping revenues together into large categories based on corporate ownership. However, this is a "corporate" income statement that is a summary of operations typically shown to investors who are usually not concerned with the statistics of an individual property. The statistics provided on the statement are for an entire system of properties and would be of little value to a department manager at the property level or other internal users. Accordingly, department managers would be more interested in results at the property level. The level of detail in the statement will vary, depending on the needs of the user. An income statement for a sample hotel property is shown in Exhibit 3-2.

The focus of the income statement for use at the property level is on the operated departments—primarily rooms, food and beverage, and telephone. However, there may be other important departments such as casino operations or a golf course that are treated in a similar manner. The operated department income of each department represents the profit that each department contributes to the rest of the property. It is also important to note that each department will have a supporting schedule that provides more details on both revenue and expenses for each department. The total operated department income for the property is also called its contribution margin.

The remainder of the income statement comprises undistributed operating expenses—expenses that are not directly attributable to any one department. These include expenses such as administrative and general, marketing, maintenance, and utilities. The final section of the statement includes fixed expenses such as real estate taxes, property insurance, interest, depreciation, amortization, rent, and management fees. The last item is income taxes, and it is based on a percentage of the income before income taxes.

3.2.3 Restaurant Income Statement

Just as the hotel industry has a uniform income statement, so too does the restaurant industry. However, the corporate income statements for restaurant companies

(in millions, except per share amounts)	*2000*	Year ended December 31, *2001*	*2002*
Revenue			
Owned hotels	$2,429	2,122	2,100
Leased hotels	398	168	111
Management and franchise fees	350	342	329
Other fees and income	274	418	355
	3,451	3,050	2,895
Other revenue from managed and franchised properties	945	943	952
	4,396	3,993	3,847
Expenses			
Owned hotels	1,571	1,468	1,462
Leased hotels	365	152	101
Depreciation and amortization	382	391	348
Impairment loss and related costs	—	—	21
Other operating expenses	241	336	294
Corporate expense, net	62	71	66
	2,621	2,418	2,292
Other expenses from managed and franchised properties	945	943	952
	3,566	3,361	3,244
Operating Income	830	632	603
Interest and dividend income	86	64	43
Interest expense	(453)	(385)	(328)
Interest expense, net, from unconsolidated affiliates	(16)	(17)	(19)
Net gain (loss) on asset dispositions	32	(44)	(14)
Income Before Income Taxes and Minority Interest	479	250	285
Provision for income taxes	(200)	(77)	(81)
Minority interest, net	(7)	(7)	(6)
Net Income	$ 272	166	198
Basic Earnings Per Share	$ .74	.45	.53
Diluted Earnings Per Share	$ .73	.45	.53

See notes to consolidated financial statements

Source: Hilton Hotels Web site, http://media.corporate-ir.net/media_files/NYS/HLT/reports/ar2002.pdf.

Exhibit 3-1 Consolidated statements of income.

	Net revenue	Cost of sales	Payroll expense	Other expense	Operated dept income (loss)
Operated Department					
Rooms	$5,000,000		$1,000,000	$200,000	$3,800,000
Food and beverage	2,500,000	$1,000,000	1,000,000	200,000	1,300,000
Telephone	500,000	150,000	50,000	20,000	430,000
Rentals and other income	20,000				20,000
Total operated departments	8,020,000	1,150,000	2,050,000	420,000	4,400,000
Undistributed operating expenses					
Administrative and general			500,000	600,000	1,100,000
Marketing			200,000	100,000	300,000
Franchise fees				250,000	250,000
Energy				300,000	300,000
Property maintenance			150,000	250,000	400,000
Total undistributed expenses			850,000	1,500,000	2,350,000
Income before fixed charges	8,020,000	1,150,000	2,900,000	1,920,000	2,050,000
Real estate taxes				160,000	160,000
Property insurance				80,000	80,000
Interest				450,000	450,000
Management fees				305,000	305,000
Depreciation & amortization				100,000	100,000
Income before income taxes					955,000
Income taxes					287,000
Net income					$ 698,000

Exhibit 3-2   Sample hotel income statement for the year ended December 31, 2002.

are also generalized and abbreviated. The income statement for Outback Steakhouse is shown in Exhibit 3-3.

Similar to hotel income statements, more detailed income statements can be produced for internal users. A sample income statement is shown in Exhibit 3-4.

The major difference between this statement and the hotel income statement is the lack of segmentation of payroll costs across departments. Additionally, other income, which could include items such as vending and pay phone commissions, is either shown as a minor revenue (after food and beverage) or else as a reduction of uncontrollable expenses. Furthermore, all items are expressed as a percentage of total revenue, with the exception of food and beverage cost of sales, which are shown as a percentage of food and beverage revenue, respectively.

	YEARS ENDED DECEMBER 31,		
	2002	2001	2000
REVENUES			
Restaurant sales	$2,342,826	$2,107,290	$1,888,322
Other revenues	19,280	19,843	17,684
TOTAL REVENUES	2,362,106	2,127,133	1,906,006
COSTS AND EXPENSES			
Cost of sales	858,737	807,980	715,224
Labor and other related	572,229	507,824	450,879
Other restaurant operating	476,697	418,871	358,347
Depreciation and amortization	75,691	69,002	58,109
General and administrative	89,868	80,365	75,550
Provision for impaired assets and restaurant closings	5,281	4,558	-
Contribution for "Dine Out for America"	-	7,000	-
Income from operations of unconsolidated affiliates	(6,180)	(4,517)	(2,457)
	2,072,323	1,891,083	1,655,652
INCOME FROM OPERATIONS	289,783	236,050	250,354
OTHER INCOME (EXPENSE), NET	(3,322)	(2,287)	(1,918)
INTEREST INCOME (EXPENSE), NET	1,212	2,438	4,450
INCOME BEFORE ELIMINATION OF MINORITY PARTNERS' INTEREST AND PROVISION FOR INCOME TAXES	287,673	236,201	252,886
ELIMINATION OF MINORITY PARTNERS' INTEREST	39,546	30,373	33,884
INCOME BEFORE PROVISION FOR INCOME TAXES	248,127	205,828	219,002
PROVISION FOR INCOME TAXES	87,341	72,451	77,872
INCOME BEFORE CUMULATIVE EFFECT OF A CHANGE IN ACCOUNTING PRINCIPLE	160,786	133,377	141,130
CUMULATIVE EFFECT OF A CHANGE IN ACCOUNTING PRINCIPLE (NET OF TAXES)	(4,422)	-	-
NET INCOME	$ 156,364	$ 133,377	$ 141,130
BASIC EARNINGS PER COMMON SHARE			
Income before cumulative effect of a change in accounting principle	$ 2.10	$ 1.74	$ 1.82
Cumulative effect of a change in accounting principle (net of taxes)	(0.06)	-	-
Net income	$ 2.04	$ 1.74	$ 1.82
BASIC WEIGHTED AVERAGE NUMBER OF COMMON SHARES OUTSTANDING	76,734	76,632	77,470
DILUTED EARNINGS PER COMMON SHARE			
Income before cumulative effect of a change in accounting principle	$ 2.03	$ 1.70	$ 1.78
Cumulative effect of a change in accounting principle	(0.06)	-	-
Net income	$ 1.97	$ 1.70	$ 1.78
DILUTED WEIGHTED AVERAGE NUMBER OF COMMON SHARES OUTSTANDING	79,312	78,349	79,232

The information in the summary consolidated statements of income shown above is a replication of the information in the consolidated statements of income in Outback Steakhouse, Inc.'s 2002 Financial Report. For complete consolidated financial statements, including notes, and management's discussion and analysis of financial condition and results of operations, please refer to the Company's annual report on Form 10-K for the year ended December 31, 2002, filed by the Company with the Securities and Exchange Commission or the accompanying 2002 Financial Report.

Source: Outback Steakhouse Web site at http://media.corporate-ir.net/media_files/NYS/osi/reports/outback2002.pdf.

Exhibit 3-3 Outback Steakhouse, Inc. and Affiliates Consolidated Statements of Income in thousands, except per share amounts.

	Amounts	Percentage (%)
Sales		
Food	$1,500,000	75.0
Beverage	500,000	25.0
Total revenue	2,000,000	100.0
Cost of sales		
Food	600,000	40.0
Beverage	100,000	20.0
Total cost of sales	700,000	35.0
Gross profit	1,300,000	65.0
Other income	20,000	1.0
Total income	1,320,000	66.0
Controllable expenses		
Salaries and wages	600,000	30.0
Employee benefits	100,000	5.0
Direct operating expenses	60,000	3.0
Marketing	40,000	2.0
Energy	50,000	2.5
Maintenance	30,000	1.5
Total controllable expenses	880,000	44.0
Income before occupation costs	440,000	22.0
Interest	25,000	1.25
Depreciation	35,000	1.75
Income before income taxes	380,000	19.0
Income taxes	150,000	7.5
Net income	$ 230,000	11.5

Exhibit 3-4   Sample restaurant income statement.

3.3 REVIEW OF THE BALANCE SHEET

The balance sheet is used to represent the financial position of the firm for a specific point in time. There are really no significant differences in the balance sheets used by management as compared to those seen by external users. Moreover, there is no Uniform System for the balance sheet because all balance sheets follow a specific format.

The balance sheet is comprised of three major sections: assets, liabilities, and owner's equity. Assets are items that are owned by the firm; liabilities are claims on the assets by creditors or lenders to the firm. Owner's equity represents the claims to the assets by the owners. All of the assets are essentially claimed by someone—in other words, the total assets must equal total liabilities and owner's equity. This is known as the fundamental accounting equation. Balance sheets for Park Place Entertainment are shown in Exhibit 3-5.

The assets of a firm are listed in order of liquidity, with the most liquid assets being listed first. Cash and cash equivalents include items such as cash on hand,

	December 31,	
	2002	**2001**
Assets		
Cash and equivalents	$ 351	$ 328
Accounts receivable, net	185	222
Inventories, prepaids, and other	138	141
Income taxes receivable	3	9
Deferred income taxes	100	111
Total current assets	777	811
Investments	143	201
Property and equipment, net	7,649	7,731
Goodwill	834	1,811
Other assets	271	254
Total assets	$9,674	$10,808
Liabilities and Stockholders' equity		
Accounts payable	$ 53	$ 46
Current maturities of long-term debt	325	7
Accrued expenses	637	583
Total current liabilities	1,015	636
Long-term debt, net of current maturities	4,585	5,301
Deferred income taxes, net	1,023	1,021
Other liabilities	94	83
Total liabilities	6,717	7,041
Commitments and contingencies		
Stockholders' equity		
Common stock, $0.01 par value, 400.0 million shares authorized, 323.7 million and 322.4 million shares issued at December 31, 2002 and 2001, respectively	3	3
Additional paid-in capital	3,801	3,788
Retained earnings (accumulated deficit)	(569)	255
Accumulated other comprehensive loss	(16)	(35)
Common stock in treasury, at cost at December 31, 2002 and 2001, 23.1 million shares and 21.1 million shares, respectively	(262)	(244)
Total stockholders' equity	2,957	3,767
Total liabilities and stockholders' equity	$9,674	$10,808

Source: Park Place Entertainment Web site at
http://investor.parkplace.com/downloads/Park2002AR.pdf.

Exhibit 3-5 Park Place Entertainment Corporation and Subsidiaries consolidated balance sheets (dollars in millions, except par value).

checking accounts, certificates of deposit, and commercial paper. Accounts receivable is presented net of allowance for doubtful accounts. Inventories are also considered a current asset and are recorded at the lower of cost or market value.

Deferred income taxes result from differences in reporting to investors against reporting to the Internal Revenue Service. In other words, the differences between income taxes payable and income tax expense results in deferred income taxes. Furthermore, the federal government allows firms with an operating loss to use either a **tax carryback** against previous years or a **tax carryforward** for future years. This would represent an asset to the firm. A subtotal for current assets is always presented to analyze the position of the firm. This will be discussed in greater detail in the ratio analysis section of the chapter.

Investments are items such as stocks and bonds of other companies that the firm intends to hold for more than a year. Property and equipment are shown at cost less accumulated depreciation. Note that for Park Place, the greatest concentration of assets is in property and equipment. This is quite typical for hotel and casino firms. Other long-term assets include items such as Goodwill and other intangibles. Goodwill is an intangible asset that is obtained when the price paid for an asset exceeds the value of the assets. Other assets could represent patents and franchise fees.

The liabilities of the firm are also divided between "current" (due within one year) and long term. Current maturities of long-term debt is the portion of the long-term debt that is due within one year of the balance sheet date. For example, if a firm borrows $5,000,000, and $500,000 is due within six months, the firm will present $500,000 as a current maturity of long-term debt and $4,500,000 as a long-term liability.

Owner's equity shows common stock, additional paid-in-capital and retained earnings. Retained earnings is the account that is reduced when dividends are declared. It does not represent cash, however. It simply represents the accumulation of net income earned by the firm in previous periods less any dividends declared. A firm must have positive retained earnings to declare a dividend. Also included in this section is treasury stock, representing the repurchase of the firm's stock and shown as a reduction in owner's equity.

As discussed in the previous chapter, many companies do business around the world. Accordingly, all asset and liabilities must be presented in an average of exchange rates during the year. Any gains or losses from translations are reported in the owner's equity section as "Other comprehensive income (loss)." For many hospitality firms, this line item can be significant.

3.4 RELATIONSHIP BETWEEN THE INCOME STATEMENT AND THE BALANCE SHEET

It is important for hospitality students to be taught the differences between the income statement and the balance sheet because the two statements are reported separately and serve very different functions. However, the two statements are presented together, and it is also important to understand how the statements relate to one another. The relationships are explained in Exhibit 3-6.

As shown in Exhibit 3-6, assets are utilized to generate revenue (and also cash flow). The majority of assets are fixed—land, building, and equipment are necessary to produce a wide variety of revenues. There is one key exception to the usage of assets to produce revenue: depreciation is related to building and

Balance sheet accounts	Income statement line items
Assets	**Revenues**
Examples:	Examples:
Inventory	Rooms
Land	Food
Building	Beverage
Equipment	Casino
Liabilities	**Expenses**
Examples:	Examples:
Accounts payable	Cost of goods sold
Wages payable	Labor expense
Income taxes payable	Income tax expense
Owner's equity	**Net income**
Example:	
Retained earnings	

Balance sheet	
Report assets, liabilities, and owner's equity on December 31, 2001	
	Income statement
	Report revenue and expenses for the month of January 2002
Balance sheet	
Report assets, liabilities, and owner's equity on January 31, 2002	

Exhibit 3-6 Relationship between the income statement and the balance sheet.

equipment and is shown on the income statement. Nevertheless, depreciation expense is a "paper expense" that is used to lower taxable income and thereby generate tax savings.

Liabilities are associated with expenses on the income statement. Accounts payable is related to food and beverage cost, whereas wages payable is affiliated with labor expense. The last major balance sheet category is owner's equity. The major link with the income statement is the retained earnings account. Net income increases retained earnings, and a net loss reduces retained earnings (along with dividends declared). Dividends, however, are not an operations expense and do not appear on the income statement.

The bottom portion of the figure displays the relationship between the two statements over time. The purpose of the balance sheet is to reveal the financial position of the firm for a specific point in time, often the end of the month or a quarter. The income statement is then compiled to demonstrate the

Retained earnings, beginning of year	$40,000
Net income	$50,000
Dividends declared	$10,000
Retained earnings, end of year	$80,000

Exhibit 3-7   Sample statement of retained earnings for the year ended 2002.

performance of the firm for a period of time, often a month, three months, or a year. After the performance of the firm is shown on the income statement, another balance sheet is completed that incorporates the earnings or losses of the period.

3.5 STATEMENT OF RETAINED EARNINGS

The statement of retained earnings is now often included in a consolidated statement of stockholder's equity. However, given the importance of retained earnings and its link to the income statement, we focus on the calculation of the ending balance in retained earnings. A sample statement of retained earnings is shown in Exhibit 3-7.

The calculation of the ending balance of retained earnings is straightforward. Net income is added to the beginning balance, and any dividend declarations are subtracted to obtain the final balance. Occasionally, unusual adjustments must be made to retained earnings. Adjustments would include errors made in a prior period or a change in an accounting principle.

Retained earnings is only a small portion of the stockholder equity account that is usually presented by corporations. Items that can affect stockholder's equity in a given period include issuance or repurchase of stock, unrealized gains or losses on investments, and foreign exchange contracts. However, any further in-depth analysis of these items is beyond the scope of this text.

3.6 STATEMENT OF CASH FLOWS

The statement of cash flows is important because cash is considered the lifeblood of the business. Suppliers are paid in cash, lenders are paid in cash, and dividends are paid in cash. Additionally, as you may recall from your accounting courses, earnings from the income statement are accrual based and do not represent cash flows into the business.

Recent accounting scandals involving Enron, Tyco International, and other companies have revolved largely around the ability of the average investor to assess the current and future cash flows of the company. Many investors have argued that cash flows are more readily observable than are accrual-based earnings (either dividends are paid or they are not). Therefore, the statement of cash flows receives greater scrutiny than ever before.

A hospitality firm may derive cash inflows (or outflows) from three basic sources: operating, investing activities, or financing activities. Operating activities are those for which the firm is primarily in business (selling rooms or food, for example). A successful and vibrant firm should be able to generate most of its cash flows from operating activities. The other two activities are those related to investing (primarily securities and equipment) and financing (loans and dividend payments).

One of the difficulties for most students in compiling the statement of cash flows is the conversion of accrual-based figures to cash flows. For example, although depreciation is an expense shown on the income statement, it is a noncash expense that is shown to reduce taxable income. Therefore, because we never spent the cash to begin with, we must add it back to net income. Other items that require adjustments are accrual items. Increases in current assets (inventory, for example) represent decreases to cash flows and must be subtracted. Liabilities act in an opposite fashion with cash. An increase in accounts payable, for example, means that we bought inventory on credit (as opposed to cash). Therefore, this cash "saved" means an increase to cash. Exhibit 3-8 shows a statement of cash flows for the year 200x for the Sample Hotel.

As stated previously, most investors are concerned with the statement of cash flows from operating activities. A very rough estimate of this number is found by taking net income from the income statement and adding back depreciation. Although this is not exact, many of the accrual items will tend to balance out, leaving depreciation and perhaps amortization as the largest noncash expenses that need to be added back to derive a rough estimate of cash flow. Cash flows become more important later in valuation because value is primarily related to cash flows, not accrual-based earnings.

Students should also note the importance of cash flow relative to accrual-based earnings and the survivability of the business. It is possible for firms to

Net cash flow from operating activities:	
Net income	$698,000
Depreciation and amortization	100,000
Increase in accounts receivable	(10,000)
Increase in accounts payable	8,000
Net cash flow from operating activities	$796,000
Net cash flow from investing activities:	
Purchase of investments	($500,000)
Purchase of equipment	(200,000)
Net cash flow from investing activities	($700,000)
Net cash flow from financing activities:	
Proceeds from bank loan	$150,000
Payment of dividends	(80,000)
Net cash flow from financing activities:	$ 70,000
Total net cash flow:	$166,000
Cash balance 1/1/2xx2	$ 34,000
Cash balance 12/31/2xx2	$200,000

Exhibit 3-8 Sample hotel statement of cash flow for the year ended 200X.

have a negative net income and a positive cash flow. The opposite can also occur: a positive net income and a negative cash flow. However, the latter situation can cause business failure if it occurs over a long period of time.

3.7 VALIDITY OF FINANCIAL STATEMENTS

In early 2002, Wall Street investors became concerned about the accuracy of financial statements of some major corporations. The major (although not the only) focus was on Enron Corporation. Enron was at one time the seventh-largest corporation in the United States and was hoping to eventually become the largest. In early 2001, the company's common stock was selling for approximately $80 per share; however, the accounting of some of the company's transactions fell under intense scrutiny by October. On December 3, the company filed for bankruptcy, and the stock price in early 2002 was less than $1.00 per share. Employees were outraged because many of them were encouraged to purchase large amounts of Enron stock and keep them in their 401(k) plans. What went wrong for Enron?

Although many of the transactions were complex, some of them involved the establishment of various partnerships that were separate from but related to Enron. Enron would obtain loans for the partnerships while not disclosing the loans on Enron's balance sheet along with declaring "earnings" on their Enron's income statements that were not really there. The investigation is currently ongoing as of this writing, and more detailed information is forthcoming. Nevertheless, the practice that produced bogus financial statements is falling under increased scrutiny.

The effects of the Enron case were immediate and widespread. The public began to ask questions about the accounting practices that were essentially approved by Enron's auditor, Arthur Andersen. Partners and employees of Arthur Andersen were called before the U.S. Congress to testify about their knowledge of these transactions. In addition, the way auditors were engaged by companies came into question along with the issue of federal regulation of the accounting profession and tougher accounting standards. Finally, investors became concerned that there were more companies like Enron that used questionable accounting practices when compiling their financial statements.

One of the fundamental principles of an efficient market is the lack of information asymmetry and the accessibility of accurate and timely information. Without them, investors lose confidence in capital markets, and the impact on the economy can be devastating. If breaches of ethical standards are discovered in the investigation, the wrongdoers will be prosecuted, and the accounting profession can be improved to detect such actions. Hopefully, such a circumstance is a rarity and not an established practice.

Nevertheless, a significant amount of responsibility lies with the investors as well. In financial management, one of our tasks is to conduct some analysis to help make better-informed decisions. It is not the task of the financial manager to compile the financial statements; he or she usually assumes that the information supplied to make a decision is reasonably accurate and correct. We will also make this assumption as we analyze financial information. However, it is important for the student to understand that when financial managers utilize analytical tools such as ratio analysis, the results often raise more questions than answers and usually require further investigation. This is true even with the relatively simple financial statement examples we display in this chapter. It is one of the functions of this text to make the student a more critical reviewer of financial statements, even when they are compiled correctly.

3.8 RATIO ANALYSIS

One of the major tools used by financial managers and financial analysts is ratio analysis. Ratios are important because they are used by various individuals to help evaluate the financial position or performance of a firm. However, ratios can be misleading if not used properly because a ratio is simply one number placed over another.

Therefore, ratios become more meaningful when they are used appropriately as the beginning of a detailed investigation into a particular portion of a hospitality operation. One appropriate use is to compare ratios to industry standards when measuring performance. Ratios for different industries are compiled by sources such as Robert Morris Associates as well as a variety of sources on the World Wide Web. Industry comparisons are primarily used by lenders and investors to assess performance.

However, when utilizing industry comparisons, one must be careful in consideration of the benchmark used. For example, although it could be done, it would not be logical to compare a hotel or restaurant operation to the overall hospitality industry. This is because the hospitality industry is not homogeneous and contains many different segments such as hotels, motels, restaurants, cruise ships, amusement parks, and many others. Moreover, it is also important to understand that even within a particular industry segment there are many subsegments. For example, if you want to compare the ratios of McDonald's to the overall restaurant industry, this comparison could be misleading because McDonald's is a fast-food chain, and the "industry average" that is calculated could be heavily weighted by other types of restaurants.

This brings us to the final caveat regarding comparisons to industry averages. Despite the plethora of sources of financial information on the World Wide Web, it does not necessarily mean the information is appropriate for the purpose of your analysis. There are a number of potential pitfalls in utilizing industry averages.

For example, how many firms are included in the average? The size and type of firms can have a significant impact on the overall average. Certain firms may be included in an industry average one year but not the next because of takeovers and bankruptcies. Additionally, large firms can dominate a sample of an industry and distort the overall picture.

Moreover, not all firms use the same accounting methods (such as depreciation and inventory valuation methods). Furthermore, firms compile their statements over different periods of time—some use the calendar year and others use the fiscal year. These are all important considerations when making comparisons.

Hospitality operations managers frequently compare common hotel operation ratios, such as average daily rate, occupancy rate, and REVPar, to a prior period or goal. However, the caveats similar to those used in comparing ratios to industry averages also need to be considered here. For example, the events of September 11, 2001, adversely affected the occupancy of many hotels that month.

Therefore, comparisons with previous September months may not be meaning-ful. Additionally, changes such as renovations and revised advertising strategies can make comparisons difficult even for the same property.

3.8.1 Classes of Ratios

A large number of ratios can be utilized for purposes of financial analysis, and we do not intend to list them all. Instead, using surveys of interested parties such as controllers, loan officers, and investors, we will discuss the most popular ratios. Furthermore, these ratios are used for different purposes. Accordingly, we divide them into six different classes: liquidity, turnover, solvency, profitability, activity, and investor. The calculation of these different ratios will be used in conjunction with the financial statements of the Jamestown Hotel, which are presented in Exhibits 3-9 through 3-11.

	Revenue	Cost of sales	Payroll expense	Other expense	Operated dept income (loss)
Operated Departments					
Rooms	$3,000,000		$ 600,000	$200,000	$2,200,000
Food	1,300,000	$500,000	200,000	50,000	550,000
Beverage	400,000	100,000	75,000	25,000	200,000
Telephone	100,000	50,000	25,000	5,000	20,000
Rentals and other income	5,000				5,000
Total operated departments	4,805,000	650,000	900,000	280,000	2,975,000
Undistributed operating expenses					
Administrative and general			150,000	200,000	350,000
Marketing			100,000	100,000	200,000
Franchise fees				100,000	100,000
Energy				140,000	140,000
Property maintenance			100,000	75,000	175,000
Total undistributed expenses			350,000	615,000	965,000
Income before fixed charges	$4,805,000	$650,000	$1,250,000	895,000	2,010,000
Real estate taxes				55,000	55,000
Property insurance				30,000	30,000
Interest				250,000	250,000
Management fees				165,000	165,000
Depreciation and amortization				50,000	50,000
Income before income taxes					1,460,000
Income taxes					368,000
Net income					$1,092,000

Exhibit 3-9 Jamestown Hotel Income Statement for the year ended December 31, 2002.

Assets	
Current assets	
Cash and cash equivalents	$1,500,000
Marketable securities	700,000
Accounts receivable, net	200,000
Inventory	150,000
Prepaid expenses	50,000
Total current assets	2,600,000
Fixed assets	
Land	2,000,000
Building	5,000,000
Equipment	1,500,000
Less: Accumulated depreciation	2,000,000
Net fixed assets	6,500,000
Other assets	
Long-term investments	50,000
Franchise fees	75,000
Total assets	$9,225,000
Liabilities	
Current liabilities	
Accounts payable	$1,500,000
Income taxes payable	1,000,000
Total current liabilities	2,500,000
Long-term debt	3,000,000
Stockholders' equity	
Common stock, $1.00 par value; 500,000 authorized, 150,000 issued	150,000
Paid in capital	600,000
Retained earnings	2,975,000
Total stockholders' equity	3,725,000
Total liabilities and owner's equity	$9,225,000

Exhibit 3-10   Jamestown Hotel Balance Sheet, December 31, 2002.

Dividends paid to common shareholders	$250,000
Common shares outstanding	150,000
Market price per share	$ 92.00
Earnings per share	$ 7.28
Dividends per share	$ 1.67

Exhibit 3-11   Other key information for Jamestown Hotel during 2002.

3.8.1.1 Liquidity Ratios and Working Capital.   **Liquidity ratios** are used by various parties to help measure a firm's ability to pay its short-term debts. These ratios are used by lenders to determine if there are enough current assets that can be converted to cash to pay off short-term debts. The first important liquidity ratio is the current ratio. For the Jamestown Hotel, the current ratio calculation is as follows.

$$\frac{\text{Current assets}}{\text{Current liabilities}} = \text{Current ratio}$$

$$\frac{\$2,600,000}{\$2,500,000} = 1.04$$

The current ratio for the Jamestown Hotel is very close to 1.0, having only $100,000 more current assets than current liabilities. Some accounting textbooks will generalize about the "appropriate" current ratio for a business to have; however, this is very difficult because current ratios for manufacturing or retail firms may not be appropriate for hospitality firms. Many reasons could explain the low value of this ratio for the Jamestown Hotel. For one, many hospitality firms have very few receivables. Second, and more important, hospitality firms (particularly hotels) are fixed-asset intensive; the owners want management to invest in assets that will produce cash flows. In the hotel business, this means investments in land, buildings, and equipment. Accordingly, it is not unusual for hotel firms to have lower current ratios than in other industries, and a relatively low current ratio does not necessarily indicate problems within the operation.

Another important liquidity ratio is called the quick, or acid-test, ratio. It is very similar to the current ratio except that "less liquid" assets such as inventories and prepaid expenses are excluded from the numerator because these current assets are often difficult to convert into cash. The market value of inventory may not be known, and there may be only a limited market available for this asset. Additionally, it may be difficult to obtain refunds for prepaid expenses.

Another important assumption about the quick ratio is the likelihood of obtaining receivables. Remember that accounts receivable are often expressed as a net figure after subtracting an estimate of those that will not be repaid. Because this number includes an estimate made by management, the actual amount of cash received may differ significantly from that shown on the company's most recent balance sheet. Nevertheless, the quick ratio calculation for the Jamestown Hotel is as follows.

$$\frac{\text{Current assets} - \text{Inventories} - \text{Prepaid expenses}}{\text{Current liabilities}} = \text{Quick ratio}$$

$$\frac{\$2,600,000 - \$150,000 - \$50,000}{\$2,500,000} = .96$$

The quick ratio for the Jamestown Hotel is .96 and is lower than the current ratio. This will always be the case, assuming that the company has inventory and prepaid expenses. It serves largely the same purpose as the current ratio, except that it is considered to be a more stringent liquidity measure.

An item that is related to the current and quick ratios is working capital, which is not a shareholder's equity account nor is it a separate account shown on the balance sheet. It must be calculated based on information provided on the balance sheet. The formula for working capital is shown as:

Working capital = Current assets minus current liabilities

Working capital represents the difference between current assets and current liabilities. Most new businesses need to obtain working capital to become established. This means that they must have an excess of items such as cash and inventory above and beyond what they owe. In the case of the Jamestown Hotel, there is $100,000 in working capital. Again, it is not unusual for established hospitality firms to be in this situation.

3.8.1.2 Turnover Ratios.   Turnover ratios help measure management's effectiveness when employing the resources at their disposal. The major turnover ratios examined here are inventory turnover, asset turnover, and fixed asset turnover.

The inventory turnover ratio involves the use of an average inventory figure, which is done because the amount of inventory often changes from month to month. Accordingly, the average taken involves calculating the average of the inventory values shown on the beginning and end-of-year balance sheets. We can improve the accuracy of this ratio by taking more periods into account if we have the information. For illustration purposes, let us assume that the food inventory at the Jamestown Hotel was $100,000 at the beginning of the year and $120,000 at the end of the year. Therefore, the average inventory for the year is ($100,000 + $120,000)/2 = $110,000. The rest of the calculation is as follows.

$$\frac{\text{Cost of sales}}{\text{Average inventory}} = \text{Inventory turnover}$$

$$\frac{\$500,000}{\$110,000} = 4.55 \text{ times}$$

The inventory turnover ratio should then be compared to previous periods or industry averages for comparable hotels. A too-low inventory turnover ratio may be indicative of unpopular menu items or an investment policy that purchases too much inventory. Hospitality operations must manage inventory carefully because of the expense of receiving and storing it. On the other hand, a very high inventory turnover ratio may be facing stockouts of certain items desired by customers. Accordingly, management must strike a careful balance within a reasonable range for this ratio.

Another key turnover ratio is the asset turnover ratio, which presents the amount of sales that are generated by the assets. In the United States, it indicates how many dollars of sales are generated for every dollar of assets. Similar to the inventory turnover ratio, averages can be calculated for the total asset value. However, a single figure is often used because assets often do not change as rapidly as inventory. For the Jamestown Hotel, the calculation is

$$\frac{\text{Sales}}{\text{Total assets}} = \text{Asset turnover}$$

$$\frac{\$4,805,000}{\$9,225,000} = .52 \text{ times}$$

The asset turnover ratio indicates that management is generating approximately $.52 for every $1 of assets. All interested parties usually prefer to see a relatively high asset turnover ratio. We would like to obtain the most revenue-generating ability from our asset base. However, given the fact that most hotel operations are fixed-asset intensive, we may be more interested in knowing the productivity of our fixed assets alone as opposed to using the total asset figure. Accordingly, we can examine the fixed-asset turnover ratio for the Jamestown Hotel as well.

$$\frac{\text{Sales}}{\text{Fixed assets}} = \text{Fixed asset turnover}$$

$$\frac{\$4,805,000}{\$6,500,000} = .74 \text{ times}$$

As can be seen from the calculation, each \$1 of fixed assets is generating \$.74 of revenue. This ratio is an improvement over the asset turnover ratio because the denominator in the ratio is smaller. However, caution must be used when assessing this ratio.

We have mentioned the fixed-asset intensiveness of the hotel business. This also means there is usually a significant amount of accumulated depreciation on the balance sheet. Over time, and without significant investment in new fixed assets, the net value of the fixed asset will decline, which improves this ratio. In other words, management may appear to be more effective by delaying investment in new fixed assets. However, in the long run, this strategy would fail because eventually the hotel would deteriorate, adversely affecting occupancy and room rates as well.

3.8.1.3 Solvency Ratios.

The purpose of **solvency ratios** is to indicate the degree of financial leverage used by the company. The concept of financial leverage is illustrated when a firm borrows money to finance its assets (as opposed to using equity). Ratios in this category are examined by lenders to obtain a clear picture of the risk they may be taking if they lend money to the firm. Lenders will want to be assured that they will be repaid in the event of bankruptcy.

Additionally, owners are concerned with the degree of financial leverage, but for a different reason. Owners often want the firm to borrow money to help increase the rate of return they can obtain from the investment of their capital. If the firm can earn a return that is higher than the cost of the borrowed funds, then financial leverage makes sense. However, if the reverse is true, then the firm is better off not borrowing the funds.

The use of debt is quite common in the hospitality industry, particularly for hotels. In addition to increasing returns, another advantage of debt under the American system of taxation is that interest expense is tax deductible, whereas dividend payments are not. Nevertheless, firms must be careful with debt because as more debt is used, risk and the chance for bankruptcy increase. A more detailed discussion of capital structure policy is provided in Chapter 12. The solvency ratios examined here are debt to assets, debt to equity, times interest earned, and fixed-charge coverage.

The debt-to-assets ratio compares the total amount of debt (both short-term and long-term) to the amount of assets held by the firm. The calculation of the debt-to-assets ratio for the Jamestown Hotel is as follows.

$$\frac{\text{Total debt}}{\text{Total assets}} = \text{Debt-to-assets ratio}$$

$$\frac{\$5,500,000}{\$9,225,000} = .60 \text{ or } 60\%$$

The ratio indicates that approximately 60 percent of Jamestown Hotel's assets are financed by lenders. The percentage of assets financed with debt will vary across the hospitality industry. Managers may borrow less to maintain some "unused debt capacity" in case of a good investment opportunity in the future. On the other hand, managers may use debt because of the type of assets they have. Managers often attempt to match the term of the loan with the life of the asset.

Given the long-term nature of the majority of hotel assets, long-term debt is often used to finance them. Recognizing the importance of long-term debt, other ratios can be calculated that use long-term debt instead of total debt. However, the interpretation of the ratio is largely the same as the debt-to-assets ratio.

Lenders are not only concerned with the comparison of debt to assets but also with comparing debt to the equity of the firm. If a firm is successful in generating and retaining earnings, then the proportion of debt decreases (all else being the same), thereby reducing the risk to existing lenders. The debt-to-equity ratio for the Jamestown Hotel is

$$\frac{\text{Total debt}}{\text{Total equity}} = \text{Debt-to-equity ratio}$$

$$\frac{\$5,500,000}{\$3,725,000} = 1.48 \text{ or } 148\%$$

The ratio indicates that the lenders have a lower margin of safety with the Jamestown Hotel, perhaps more than in other industries such as retail or manufacturing. However, this is not unusual for the hotel industry because a significant amount of the debt (particularly the long-term debt) is guaranteed by real estate. If the circumstances call for a bankruptcy filing, then the lenders will be in a position to foreclose on the loan and take the hotel as collateral. Although the lender may not be interested in being a hotel owner, the fixed assets are tangible, and there is often a reasonably liquid market for them. Moreover, this situation is probably better for the lender than perhaps a pharmaceutical firm that owns intangible assets such as patents.

Regardless of the amount or type of debt used by a firm, all parties, including management, lenders, and owners, are concerned with the firm's ability to make periodic interest payments. This ratio is called the interest coverage ratio or the times interest earned ratio. The ratio uses earnings before interest and taxes (EBIT). The calculation for the Jamestown Hotel is as follows.

$$\frac{\text{Earnings before interest and taxes}}{\text{Interest expense}} = \text{Times interest earned}$$

$$\frac{\$1,710,000}{\$250,000} = 6.84 \text{ times}$$

In this example, the Jamestown Hotel generates earnings from operations that are 6.84 times greater than its interest payments. The interest coverage may be lower in the hotel industry than others because of the extensive use of financial leverage to finance operations. Students should also be reminded that the particular earnings figure used in this ratio is rarely expressed as such on the income statement. An easy way to calculate EBIT is to start with net income and simply add back income taxes and interest expense.

3.8.1.4 Profitability Ratios. In this chapter *profits* are considered to be the same as net income from the income statement. Profits margins are used to assess management's ability to produce a return for the owners. Owners and investors generally react favorably to firms that can produce an increasing stream of earnings. Net income is most often compared to total revenue, total assets (investment), and shareholder equity. The first ratio, the net profit margin, is calculated as follows.

$$\frac{\text{Net income}}{\text{Total revenue}} = \text{Net profit margin}$$

$$\frac{\$1,092,000}{\$4,805,000} = .227 \text{ or } 22.7\%$$

The profit margin indicates that for every \$1 of revenue, approximately 22.7 cents is being returned to the owners in the form of earnings. This margin will vary widely in the hospitality industry and depends on the type of business as well as the time of year being examined. Additionally, although the profit margin percentage itself may sometimes appear to be somewhat low, this percentage may translate into a large amount of dollars in absolute terms.

Another important profitability ratio is the return on investment (ROI), also called the return on assets. It compares the profits of the firm to the investment in assets made by the firm. Investors are concerned with using this ratio to assess management's effectiveness in using the assets to generate earnings for the owners. The calculation for the Jamestown Hotel is as follows.

$$\frac{\text{Net income}}{\text{Total assets}} = \text{Return on investment (Assets)}$$

$$\frac{\$1,092,000}{\$9,225,000} = .118 \text{ or } 11.8\%$$

The ratio indicates that management is generating approximately 12 cents of profits for every \$1 of assets. If assets are going to change significantly during the year, then it may be appropriate to use an average asset figure for the calculation. Another factor that will affect this ratio is the amount of depreciated fixed assets. A large amount of depreciated assets will lower the denominator and make the ratio appear larger. A significant new investment in assets could push the ratio much lower.

Another profitability ratio makes use of the two ratios previously discussed. Called the DuPont ratio, it breaks down the return on investment into two components: profit margin and asset turnover. This return on investment calculation shows the important interaction between the profit margin and the ability of assets to generate sales. For the Jamestown Hotel, the calculation is as follows.

$$\frac{\text{Net income}}{\text{Total revenue}} \times \frac{\text{Total revenue}}{\text{Total assets}} = \text{Return on investment (Assets)}$$

$$\frac{\$1,092,000}{\$4,805,000} \times \frac{\$4,805,000}{\$9,225,000} = .2273 \times .5209 = .118 \text{ or } 11.8\%$$

The calculation reveals that most of the ROI is derived from the higher asset turnover. For companies seeking a higher ROI, the ratio reveals a trade-off.

Companies with low profit margins must attempt to produce a higher asset turnover ratio, or vice versa. Very successful companies are those that have high percentages for both components.

The final profitability ratio to be analyzed is the return on stockholder equity ratio. This ratio is calculated as follows for the Jamestown Hotel.

$$\frac{\text{Net income}}{\text{Stockholder's equity}} = \text{Return on equity}$$

$$\frac{\$1,092,000}{\$3,725,000} = .293 \text{ or } 29.3\%$$

This is a key ratio that is examined by investors when considering an investment; it is affected by the amount of financial leverage used to finance the operations. As more financial leverage is used, expected return for the shareholders will increase, along with the risk associated with the investment. Similar to the return on investment ratio, the denominator in this ratio can be an average for the year.

3.8.1.5 Activity Ratios.   This section will discuss the major operating ratios utilized by management in the hospitality industry. These ratios are typically not available to outside investors but are usually calculated at the property level (although sometimes overall occupancy and average room rate ratios are reported by hotel companies). The ratios discussed here are occupancy percentage, average daily rate (ADR), revenue per available room (REVPAR), average check, food cost percentage, and beverage cost percentage.

The occupancy percentage is probably the single most calculated ratio in the hotel industry. It is important because the occupancy "drives" most of the other operating departments in a full-service hotel. A variety of occupancy percentages can be calculated, such as paid occupancy and complimentary occupancy. Nevertheless, each is calculated by dividing the occupied room nights by the available room nights. Assuming that the Jamestown Hotel has 150 rooms and that in 2002 the hotel generated 37,500 room nights, the calculation is as follows.

$$\frac{\text{Occupied room nights}}{\text{Available room nights}} = \text{Occupancy percentage}$$

$$\frac{37,500}{(150 \times 365)} = .685 \text{ or } 68.5\%$$

The occupancy calculation goes along with assumptions that there are 365 nights in a year (with the exception of leap years) and that rooms are not sold twice in the same night. This latter assumption means that 100 percent is the highest achievable occupancy. Some operations will not include complimentary rooms in this calculation because it lowers the average rate. However, complimentary rooms must be serviced, and complimentary guests can generate revenue in other areas of a full-service hotel. Furthermore, the correct number of occupied room nights is a useful number because a significant amount of budgeting is done on a per occupied room basis.

Another major ratio is the average daily rate (ADR), also called the average room rate. Considering that most hotels offer a variety of room rates to customers and that this ratio only represents an overall average for the property, many hotel managers will compile an average rate for each market segment that they serve. The Jamestown Hotel ADR is

$$\frac{\text{Rooms revenue}}{\text{Occupied room nights}} = \text{Average daily rate}$$

$$\frac{\$3,000,000}{37,500} = \$80.00$$

One must be careful when comparing the average room rates of various properties. The comparison of the average room rate of a luxury hotel property with a limited-service property is not very meaningful. Accordingly, a more appropriate comparison would be to budget a figure for the property or the average room rate for an earlier period.

Although we have shown how to calculate occupancy and average room rates separately, comparison of these figures alone can be misleading. For example, a limited-service hotel may have a high occupancy percentage but a very low average room rate. On the other hand, a luxury hotel may face an opposite situation.

Accordingly, there is a need to use a ratio that incorporates both occupancy and average room rate together. This is the purpose of REVPAR, which can provide a more comprehensive picture of property performance. The calculation can be completed in one of two ways.

$$\frac{\text{Rooms revenue}}{\text{Available room nights}} = \text{REVPAR}$$

or

$$\text{Occupancy percentage} \times \text{Average room rate} = \text{REVPAR}$$

$$\frac{\$3,000,000}{54,750} = \$54.79$$

Most hotel managers now prefer to examine REVPAR as a measure of performance because there is usually a trade-off between occupancy and average room rate. Managers will attempt to maximize REVPAR because it focuses on rooms revenue as a whole, not just the separate components.

Average check is utilized in food and beverage operations to assess the average amount of revenue generated per customer. Many restaurants have incentive programs for their servers to help increase the average check by serving wine or dessert. Gross profit margins on food items are normally much lower than rooms, so many operations see increasing the average check as a major goal. Assuming 55,000 food customers at the Jamestown Hotel in 2002, the average food check would be calculated in the following manner.

$$\frac{\text{Food revenue}}{\text{Number of customers}} = \text{Average food check}$$

$$\frac{\$1,300,000}{55,000} = \$23.64$$

This average check could then be subsequently used in budgeting once we had calculated the number of customers visiting the food service operations. The number of customers could be derived from the number of occupied room nights and an estimated capture percentage of local guests. If we are interested in the average beverage check, we would substitute beverage revenue and the number of bar customers in the same ratio.

Food and beverage cost of sale ratios are also important indicators of the potential profitability of food and beverage operations. The basic ratios are cost of sales divided by revenue. This would apply to the Jamestown Hotel in the following manner.

$$\frac{\text{Food cost of sales}}{\text{Food revenue}} = \text{Food cost percentage}$$

$$\frac{\$500,000}{\$1,300,000} = .3856 \text{ or } 38.5\%$$

$$\frac{\text{Beverage cost of sales}}{\text{Beverage revenue}} = \text{Beverage cost percentage}$$

$$\frac{\$100,000}{\$400,000} = .25 \text{ or } 25.0\%$$

An important consideration is the calculation of the cost of food sold. As you may recall from your accounting classes, this requires subtracting items such as employee and complimentary meals from the cost of food used and distributing those expenses to the appropriate departments.

3.8.1.6 Investor Ratios. This class of ratios is primarily, but not exclusively, of interest to hospitality investors. These ratios are related to common stock and involve earnings and the stock price. The ratios previously discussed in this chapter will have an effect on the ratios in this section, including the price-to-earnings (P/E) ratio, dividend payout ratio, and dividend yield.

The key information needed to calculate the preceding ratios are listed in a supplementary schedule shown in Exhibit 3-11. The P/E ratio for the Jamestown Hotel is calculated in the following manner.

$$\frac{\text{Market price of common shares}}{\text{Earnings per share}} = \text{Price-to-earnings ratio}$$

$$\frac{\$92.00}{\$7.28} = 12.64 \text{ times}$$

In the case of the Jamestown Hotel, the market price is more than 12 times its earnings. Although there is no theoretical evidence that a P/E ratio is either "too low" or "too high," investors examine this ratio (among many others) to help them make decisions about buying or selling stocks. Additionally, some generalizations can be made in a relative sense about this ratio. Firms with very high P/E ratios are generally considered companies with good prospects for strong growth in future earnings. Companies with lower P/E ratios are generally considered to have lower prospects for future earnings growth. It is also important to remember that although investors look for future earnings growth, they also recognize that *value is based on future cash flows, not accrual basis earnings.*

The next two ratios relate to the dividend policy of the firm. The dividend payout ratio measures the percentage of earnings that is paid to the owners in the form of dividends. The calculation is as follows.

$$\frac{\text{Dividend per common share}}{\text{Earnings per share}} = \text{Dividend payout ratio}$$

$$\frac{\$1.67}{\$7.28} = .2294 \text{ or } 22.94\%$$

In general, more stable and well-established firms will pay out a larger proportion of their earnings as dividends. On the other hand, high-growth companies tend to retain their earnings to reinvest in assets. Outback Steakhouse is a fast-growing restaurant company. As of this writing, they have yet to declare a dividend for their shareholders. They prefer to retain these earnings to finance their growth. Additionally, once firms begin to pay a dividend, they do not want to decrease it because of the potential impact on the stock price in the financial markets.

The final investor ratio is the dividend yield, which is the expected dividend for the coming year divided by the current stock price. The calculation for the Jamestown Hotel is

$$\frac{\text{Annual dividend per common share}}{\text{Market price per share}} = \text{Dividend yield}$$

$$\frac{\$1.67}{\$92.00} = .0182 \text{ or } 1.82\%$$

In general, dividend yields are inversely related to the firm's prospects for future growth. Therefore, a relatively low dividend yield implies high growth prospects. This appears to be the case for the Jamestown Hotel. It is important to remember that the dividend yield is not a true rate of return for holding the stock, which would be based on the dividends received plus any increase in the stock price.

3.9 PERSPECTIVES ON AND LIMITATIONS OF RATIO ANALYSIS

Now that we have reviewed a significant number of the important ratios used in the hospitality industry, we need to understand some of the differing viewpoints regarding the ratios. As previously discussed, the major parties interested in ratios are lenders, owners, and managers. Given that the ratio is calculated correctly, can these parties disagree about what makes a "good" ratio versus a "bad" one? Let us look at an example.

One of the most commonly used liquidity ratios is the current ratio. It measures a firm's ability to meet its current debt obligations. All else being the same, most lenders would prefer a high ratio to a low one. Lenders, often commercial banks, have investors who are concerned about receiving interest income and the repayment of principal. Accordingly, lenders hope that borrowers such as hotels will maintain a relatively high cash position to ensure repayment.

On the other hand, consider the perspective of the owners. Given the relatively fixed asset-intensive nature of a hotel company, it is these assets that produce the earnings and the cash flow—land, buildings, and equipment. Owners generally do not want their investment tied up in current assets like cash, accounts receivable, and inventory because these assets will not produce the return on equity desired by the owners. Therefore, all else being the same, the owners would prefer a low current ratio. Given that the lenders want a higher current ratio and the owners want a lower current ratio, what can management do?

In general, management must strike a balance. Although management works for the owners of the firm, they cannot ignore the needs of the lenders because of their importance to the hotel industry. Overall, management must work to satisfy the suppliers of both debt and equity capital. Although it may seem that lenders and owners have totally opposing viewpoints regarding this ratio, there is a reasonable range for management to work toward. Additionally, there are a number of ratios available (such as the number of times interest earned) when both lenders and owners are looking for a higher ratio.

It is important to understand that it is very difficult to say precisely what a particular ratio "should" be. We discussed earlier in the chapter that ratios are much more meaningful when they are compared to a standard, such as an industry average, actual performance from a prior period, or budgeted figure. Careful consideration must be given to each of these situations.

Moreover, even when a ratio is calculated correctly and a proper comparison is made, it doesn't tell you what the problem is. As an example, suppose our restaurant achieved a cost of food sold percentage of 45 percent for 2002. This figure is higher than 2001, higher than our budgeted amount of 42 percent, and higher than other comparable firms within our industry segment. So what's the problem?

This exemplifies the fact that ratio analysis is really just the beginning. Experience, judgment, and managerial skill must come into play to investigate the reasons for the high food cost. Some of the questions that could be asked include, Have we accounted for our employee and complimentary meals properly? Are our menu prices too low? Are we paying too much for our food? Is our sales mix too heavily weighted toward high-cost buffets? The overall point in this example is that ratios raise more questions than answers. Moreover, ratios don't solve problems; that's what hospitality managers are supposed to do.

A final caveat is also useful here. Some accounting textbooks and courses attempt to instruct about minimums and maximums for ratios. As an example, a current ratio is only "good" if it is greater than 1.0, with current assets exceeding liabilities. However, the student should ask if this rule is true for all firms across all industries. As an example, Marriott International is considered to be a very successful company by almost any standard. At the end of 1999, Marriott had current assets of $1.6 billion. On the other hand, they had current liabilities of $1.743 billion, indicating a current ratio of only .92. It appears that Marriott has violated the "rule" that current assets must exceed current liabilities. Does this mean that Marriott is in trouble with its creditors?

As previously discussed, the hotel business is fixed-asset intensive, and owners prefer firms to invest in assets that produce cash flows. Therefore, we cannot effectively compare current ratios of retail firms and hospitality firms.

Moreover, there may be some particular corporate policy that is affecting that ratio at that particular time. Ratio analysis can be more effective if the ratios are examined over a period of time.

3.10 SUMMARY

This chapter provided a review of the major financial statements: the income statement, balance sheet, statement of retained earnings, and statement of cash flows. The setup of the Uniform System of Accounts for both hotels and restaurants was examined as well as the important relationship between the income statement and the balance sheet. The calculation of the ending balance of retained earnings was also shown.

Ratio analysis was discussed in the framework of the different classes of ratios examined by different users. Furthermore, different users can have different viewpoints of the same ratio. It is important to remember that ratios are more valuable when appropriate comparisons are made. Finally, the limitations of ratios themselves were discussed. In general, ratios do not solve problems, and they raise more questions than answers. They are intended to help managers and other users begin a path of investigation (see Exhibit 3-12 on page 60).

KEY TERMS

Balance sheet
Income statement
Liquidity ratios
Solvency ratios
Statement of cash flows
Statement of retained earnings
Tax carryback
Tax carryforward
Uniform System of Accounts

DISCUSSION QUESTIONS

1. What are the four major types of financial statements?
2. What is the Uniform System of Accounts? What are the advantages of its use?
3. How is the income statement related to the balance sheet?
4. In general, are investors more concerned with earnings (i.e., net income) or cash flows? Why?
5. Discuss the Enron situation. Why did it have such a widespread impact?
6. Why must an analyst be careful when comparing ratios to industry averages?
7. What is the major difference between liquidity ratios and solvency ratios?
8. What is working capital? Where is it listed on the balance sheet?
9. What are the three major ratios used by investors? What does each of them measure?
10. Can parties disagree about the same ratio? Why? Give an example.

$$\frac{\text{Current assets}}{\text{Current liabilities}} = \text{Current ratio}$$

$$\frac{\text{Current assets} - \text{Inventories} - \text{Prepaid expenses}}{\text{Current liabilities}} = \text{Quick ratio}$$

$$\frac{\text{Cost of sales}}{\text{Average inventory}} = \text{Inventory turnover}$$

$$\frac{\text{Sales}}{\text{Total assets}} = \text{Asset turnover}$$

$$\frac{\text{Sales}}{\text{Fixed assets}} = \text{Fixed-asset turnover}$$

$$\frac{\text{Total debt}}{\text{Total assets}} = \text{Debt-to-assets ratio}$$

$$\frac{\text{Total debt}}{\text{Total equity}} = \text{Debt-to-equity ratio}$$

$$\frac{\text{Earnings before interest and taxes}}{\text{Interest expense}} = \text{Times interest earned}$$

$$\frac{\text{Net income}}{\text{Total revenue}} = \text{Net profit margin}$$

$$\frac{\text{Net income}}{\text{Total assets}} = \text{Return on investment (Assets)}$$

$$\frac{\text{Net income}}{\text{Total revenue}} \times \frac{\text{Total revenue}}{\text{Total assets}} = \text{Return on investment—DuPont (Assets)}$$

$$\frac{\text{Net income}}{\text{Stockholder's equity}} = \text{Return on equity}$$

$$\frac{\text{Occupied room nights}}{\text{Available room nights}} = \text{Occupancy percentage}$$

$$\frac{\text{Rooms revenue}}{\text{Occupied room nights}} = \text{Average daily rate}$$

$$\frac{\text{Rooms revenue}}{\text{Available room nights}} = \text{REVPAR}$$

or

$$\text{Occupancy percentage} \times \text{Average room rate} = \text{REVPAR}$$

$$\frac{\text{Food cost of sales}}{\text{Food revenue}} = \text{Food cost percentage}$$

$$\frac{\text{Beverage cost of sales}}{\text{Beverage revenue}} = \text{Beverage cost percentage}$$

$$\frac{\text{Market price of common shares}}{\text{Earnings per share}} = \text{Price-to-earnings ratio}$$

$$\frac{\text{Dividend per common share}}{\text{Earnings per share}} = \text{Dividend payout ratio}$$

$$\frac{\text{Annual dividend per common share}}{\text{Market price per share}} = \text{Dividend yield}$$

Exhibit 3-12   List of ratios discussed in the chapter.

PROBLEMS

1. You have been provided with the current assets and current liabilities section of the Pacifica Hotel.

PACIFICA HOTEL
Partial Balance Sheet
December 31, 2003

Current assets		Current liabilities	
Cash	$ 20,000	Wages payable	$ 10,000
Marketable securities	25,000	Accounts payable	20,000
Accounts receivable	35,000	Notes payable	70,000
Inventory	20,000		
Prepaid expenses	5,000		
Total	$105,000	Total	$100,000

a. Calculate the current ratio for the Pacifica Hotel.
b. Calculate the acid test ratio for the Pacifica Hotel.
c. Comment on these ratios from a lender's perspective and a shareholder's perspective.

2. Describe the effect on working capital under the following scenarios.
   a. A company decides to issue common stock
   b. A company generates revenue on account
   c. A company goes to a bank and gets a loan
3. John Q. Public is the Director of Sales for the Harbor Lights Hotel. In 2001, the hotel obtained an occupancy percentage of 70 percent and an average daily rate of $80. In 2002, he lowered rates in order to boost occupancy—the hotel had an occupancy percentage of 73 percent and an average daily rate of $76. Describe the effect of this strategy using a key ratio(s). Should he lower rates further in 2003?
4. Jones Restaurant Corporation has reported the following financial information as of December 31, 2003.

Total revenue	$4,000,000
Cost of goods sold	$2,300,000
Gross profit	$1,700,000
Operating expenses	$1,200,000
Fixed charges	$ 150,000
Income taxes	$ 100,000
Net income	$ 250,000
Total assets as of 12/31/03	$1,000,000

a. Calculate the return on assets for Jones Restaurant Corporation using DuPont Analysis.
b. What can we conclude about the two ratios comprising the return on assets?
5. Starbucks, a major seller of roasted coffees, currently has a market price of $22.15 per common share and a P/E ratio of 43. Diedrich Coffee, a competitor to Starbucks, has a market price of $3.84 per share and a P/E ratio of 6.
   a. Calculate the earnings of both companies.
   b. Compare the earnings growth prospects of the two companies.

6. You are provided with the following information about the Heartland Hotel Corporation.

Current Ratio	1.2
Current liabilities	$100,000
Debt/equity ratio	2.0
Acid test ratio	.8
Inventory turnover ratio (1)	4 times
Cost of goods sold	$160,000
Accounts receivable	$ 40,000
Net income	$ 90,000
Return on assets	10%

Calculate the balance sheet for the end of the year for Heartland Hotel Corporation.

Notes: **a.** Assume that average inventory is the same as end of year inventory.
  b. "Quick" assets only include cash and accounts receivable.

7. Dawn's Fruitcake Factory specializes in making Christmas fruitcakes. During the year, they had $3.0 million in food sales with a 40 percent food cost. Dawn takes inventory every quarter. The inventories for the past year are shown as follows.

End of 1st quarter	$300,000
End of 2nd quarter	$400,000
End of 3rd quarter	$600,000
End of 4th quarter	$200,000

a. Which quarter is Dawn using for her inventory turnover calculation?
b. Do you think this is the appropriate approach to calculate inventory turnover?

8. The following is the balance sheet for Sullivan Hotels Corporation as of December 31, 2002.

SULLIVAN HOTELS CORPORATION
Balance Sheet
December 31, 2002

Current Assets		Current Liabilities	
Cash	$ 50,000	Wages payable	$ 30,000
Marketable securities	30,000	Accounts payable	25,000
Accounts receivable	40,000	Notes payable	50,000
Inventory	60,000		
Prepaid expenses	15,000		
Total current assets	$ 195,000	Total current liabilities	$ 105,000
Fixed assets, net	$7,000,000	Long-term debt	$2,500,000
		Owner's equity	
		Common stock,	$3,000,000
		3,000,000 shares	
		outstanding ($1 par)	
		Paid in capital	$500,000
		Retained earnings	$1,090,000
		Total liabilities and	
Total assets	$7,195,000	owner's equity	$7,195,000

In 2002, the corporation generated a net income of $430,000.

a. Calculate the earnings per share in 2002.

b. Assume that in 2003 Sullivan Corporation issued 300,000 more shares of $1 par value common stock for a market price of $10 per share. Fifty percent of the proceeds will be used to pay down the long-term debt, 25 percent of the proceeds will be used to buy fixed assets, and the remainder will be deposited in the corporate bank account. Compile the balance sheet after the new stock issue.

c. Assume that Sullivan Corporation generates a net income of $450,000 in 2003 (after the new stock issue). Calculate the new earnings per share. How might the stockholders feel about the results of the new stock issue?

9. The following information pertains to the performance of the Williams Hotel for the year 2003, along with some pertinent industry averages.

Total revenue	$4,500,000
Net income	$ 256,000
Total assets, net	$3,000,000
Industry average profit margin	10%
Industry average for return on investment (Assets)	6.5%

a. Calculate the profit margin and return-on-investment ratios for the Williams Hotel. Is the hotel being managed effectively?

b. What could explain the conflicting information from the two ratios?

The Relationship Between Risk and Return | 4

Chapter Objectives

- To understand the concept of risk from a financial standpoint
- To understand the risk preferences of typical investors
- To be able to define risk aversion
- To be able to calculate mean return, variance, and standard deviation
- To understand the concept of the market portfolio
- To differentiate between systematic and unsystematic risk
- To understand and calculate the beta of a hospitality company
- To use the capital asset pricing model to estimate the rate of shareholder's required rate of return

4.1 INTRODUCTION

This chapter introduces students to the concepts of risk and return. We begin by developing an understanding of risk and basic human behavior. From there, we discuss how returns on investments are calculated, along with how risk can be measured. Additionally, the components of risk and their importance are discussed.

Once we develop a measure of the risk relevant to the investor, we discuss how combinations of assets can be used to reduce risk, as shown by the concept of the market portfolio. Furthermore, risk is broken down into components. Finally, we use a measure of risk to help determine the return we can expect from an asset.

4.2 HOW TYPICAL INVESTORS FEEL ABOUT RISK

Before we discuss how the typical investor feels about risk, let us define the term. **Risk** is the uncertainty that an outcome will vary from our expectations. In terms of investments, it translates into the notion that cash flows or percentage returns will be different than what we expect ahead of time. Although it is true that the outcome could always be better than what we expect, it could also be significantly worse. Typical investors do not merely look at the upside potential of an investment but the downside as well, considering all the possible outcomes. As the range of potential outcomes increases (widens), so does the risk.

We can examine how people feel about risk by watching the popular television show *Who Wants to Be a Millionaire*. The show features contestants who must answer a series of increasingly difficult questions for cash prizes. The first questions are fairly easy, and the money prizes are relatively small. However, the contestants usually get increasingly nervous as they approach the $1 million question. The reason for this is because if they answer a question incorrectly, they will lose a substantial portion of their winnings up to that point. Many opt to quit and keep their winnings rather than risk them by giving an incorrect answer.

So why don't most contestants take a chance and risk their existing winnings for bigger cash prizes? This decision relates to the declining marginal utility for money. The concept is best illustrated in Exhibit 4-1.

Let's assume you are a rational investor and you are participating in the game show previously described. You already have $1,000 and are preparing to answer the next question. The host informs you that if you answer the question correctly, you will win another $500. However, if you answer the question incorrectly, you will lose what you have and go back down to a total of $500. The horizontal axis measures the amount of money you have, and the vertical axis measures the happiness, or utility, you receive from winning the money. As shown in the graph, an increase from $1,000 to $1,500 will give you an extra 30 units of happiness. On the other hand, if you answer the question incorrectly and give up $500, you will lose 50 units of happiness. A rational investor will forego the opportunity to answer the next question and keep the money.

Are you just acting scared in this situation? You might be nervous, but you are actually exhibiting **risk-averse** behavior. Being risk averse does not mean that you do not take risks. Millions of investors take risks every day. Being risk averse simply means that for us to take risks, we must be compensated. Investors who take large risks must be compensated with large returns, or they would not take them.

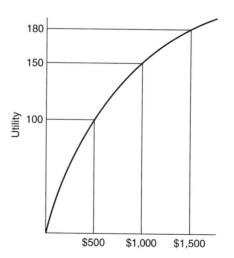

Exhibit 4-1 Declining marginal utility for money.

Does this example also apply to hospitality companies? Absolutely. McDonald's took a risk in opening a new restaurant in Russia after the collapse of the Soviet Union. Numerous risks involving political stability, currency translation, and even factors such as the ability to procure appropriate inventory presented significant challenges to the company. However, McDonald's carefully weighed the various risks against the potential benefits of being the first major American fast-food restaurant chain in Russia and came to the decision that the venture created value for the owners of the company. Thus, the McDonald's in Red Square is one of the most frequented restaurant locations in the world.

4.3 RETURNS AND DISTRIBUTIONS

Returns on investments can be expressed in monetary units as well as percentages. We will begin our discussion using monetary units of an investment in a hypothetical restaurant company in which we own a share of common stock.

4.3.1 Expected Return

Probably the most familiar situation for students regarding expected return, or mean value, is with exam scores. Many professors will give an exam and announce to the class the mean or class average. In most situations, the class average is known as a simple average. A simple average is calculated as

the sum of all observations/number of observations

This is the easiest type of average to calculate and is appropriate for test scores because each student represents the same proportion of the total class (one divided by the total number of students in the class). However, when we deal with prospective outcomes that have different probabilities, the calculation of expected value will change. Let us examine a financial example for a hospitality company.

Assume you purchase a share of stock in Joe's Restaurant Company that is expected to pay a dividend at the end of the year. As you well know, the payment of dividends is not guaranteed, nor is the amount of the dividend a certainty. Accordingly, we can say there is risk associated with the payment of the dividend. The potential payoffs and their associated probabilities are shown in Exhibit 4-2.

If you calculate a simple average of the potential dividends, you take $10 + $7 + $5 + $3 + $1 and divide that by 5 to get $5.40. However, that approach is incorrect. Why? This calculation assumes that each potential dividend has the same associated probability or likelihood of occurrence. This is clearly not the case. The

Dividend	Probability of dividend
$10	10%
$ 7	20%
$ 5	40%
$ 3	20%
$ 1	10%

Exhibit 4-2   Potential dividend distribution for Joe's Restaurant.

appropriate calculation is a weighted average, or **expected value** of the dividends. The expected value calculation involves each outcome being multiplied (or weighted) by the associated probability. This is done for each dividend, and then those products are added together. The proper calculation is as follows.

$$(\$10 \times .10) + (\$7 \times .20) + (\$5 \times .40) + (\$3 \times .20) + (\$1 \times .10) = \$5.10$$

This is the average amount of what we should expect our investment to generate. Notice the difference between this answer and the result using the simple average. Accordingly, the weighted average generates the correct value for the expected dividend.

4.3.2 The Normal Distribution

Although we now know what to expect from our investment, it is, after all, only an average. Although our weighted average calculation is correct, we know there is a range of potential outcomes, as shown in Exhibit 4-2. As shown in the exhibit, the different dividends have different probabilities associated with each of them. The probability is the "chance" of occurrence for each outcome. What the exhibit is really showing is a **probability distribution,** or a series of outcomes and probabilities associated with each. We can graph the dividend outcomes against each of the probabilities in a block diagram or histogram to get a visual depiction of this probability distribution. It is shown in Exhibit 4-3.

Exhibit 4-3 shows the boxes lower on box ends and larger in the middle. Now if we draw a line connecting the corners of the tops of the boxes and remove the boxes, we have the graphical representation shown in Exhibit 4-4.

This exhibit should be familiar to you. It is the famous bell-shaped curve, also known as the normal probability distribution. This is the "curve" that students may hear professors talk about before they adjust exam scores. The curve is normal because it indicates that half of the observations are to the right of the midpoint of the curve and half of the observations are to the left of the midpoint of the curve. However, not all distributions are normal. Some are "skewed" distributions in which one tail is larger than the other. This can be problematic when making inferences about the outcomes. Accordingly, if a distribution of exam scores is skewed, professors may change scores to make the distribution

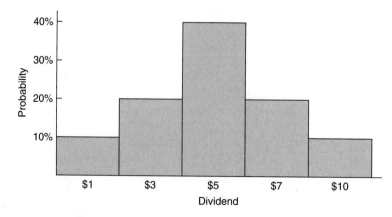

Exhibit 4-3   Probability distribution of dividends—histogram.

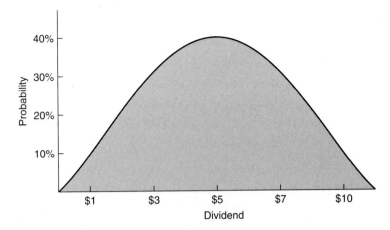

Exhibit 4-4 Probability distribution of dividends—bell curve.

more normal so that any statistical tests conducted on the scores will be more useful.

4.3.3 Variance and Standard Deviation

We have calculated the expected value of the potential dividend distribution from Joe's Restaurant. Although we know the average dividend, is there any way we can assess the risk associated with investment? By examining how each potential outcome differs or varies from the expected value, we can arrive at some conclusion about the risk of this investment. One measure is the **variance.** The variance represents the sum of the squared, weighted differences between each outcome and the expected value. The calculation in general form is

The sum of [(outcome 1 − expected value)^2 × probability of outcome 1]

+ [(outcome 2 − expected value)^2 × probability of outcome 2]

+ $\cdots$ [(outcome n − expected value)^2 × probability of outcome n]

The variance is a measure of the total risk of an investment. It is a positive number that can be expressed as a percentage or in currency values. It is also an absolute measure (as opposed to a relative measure that will be discussed later). In the Joe's Restaurant example, the variance is calculated as follows.

The sum of [($10 − $5.10)^2 × .10] + [($7 − $5.10)^2 × .20] + [($5.00 − $5.10)^2 × .40] + [($3 − $5.10)^2 × .20] + [($1 − 5.10)^2 × .10]. This reduces to $2.40 + $.72 + $.00 + $.88 + $1.68 = $5.68

Thus, the variance of the distribution of dividends for Joe's Restaurant is $5.68. However, in order to have the correct interpretation relative to the normal probability distribution, we need to find the **standard deviation** of the dividends. This is found by taking the square root of the variance, which is abbreviated with the lowercase of the Greek letter sigma (σ). The square root of $5.68 is $2.38. We can now further discuss the risk of this investment using standard deviation. Look at Exhibit 4-5.

Exhibit 4-5 shows the expected value under the center of the normal distribution curve. The portion of the arrow to the right of the expected value represents one standard deviation that is added to the expected value. The portion of

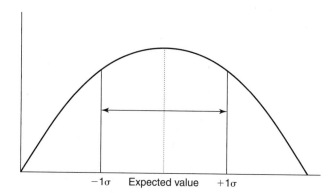

Exhibit 4-5   Bell curve and standard deviation.

the arrow to the left of the expected value is one standard deviation being sub-tracted from the expected value. In terms of our example, one standard deviation added to the expected value represents $5.10 + $2.38, or $7.48. One standard de-viation subtracted from the expected value indicates $5.10 − $2.38, or $2.72. The characteristics of the normal probability distribution are shown in Exhibit 4-6.

We can see that approximately 68 percent of the time we can expect an out-come to be within plus one and minus one standard deviation from the expected value. In our example, Joe's Restaurant should generate a dividend between $2.72 and $7.48 about two-thirds of the time. We now have developed some level of confidence regarding the payoff of this investment. Note that nearly all outcomes will be within plus or minus three standard deviations from the expected value.

4.3.4 Standard Deviation and Risk Aversion

Given an understanding of the risk of an investment, let us consider choosing be-tween two different hotel investments. The Avalon Hotel and the Brookside Hotel each have the potential for generating a wide variety of returns. Each of them, however, has the same expected return with normal return distributions. The dis-tribution of each of their returns is shown in Exhibit 4-7.

As shown in Exhibit 4-7, each hotel investment has the same expected return of 15 percent. However, the distribution of their returns is quite different. Al-though both return distributions are approximately normal, the Avalon Hotel has a much wider and flatter distribution of returns. On the other hand, the Brookside Hotel has a much narrower distribution. Which do we prefer? Given that most people are risk averse, the Brookside Hotel would be a better investment. Why?

Number of standard deviations from expected value	% of observations within range
-1σ and $+1\sigma$	68.3
-2σ and $+2\sigma$	95.4
-3σ and $+3\sigma$	99.7

Exhibit 4-6   Percentage of observations within range of standard deviations.

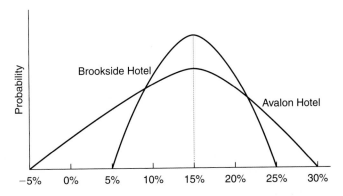

Exhibit 4-7 Comparison of two return distributions.

The reason is because of the greater level of certainty (or lower level of uncertainty) associated with the Brookside. As you may have guessed, the Brookside has a smaller deviation associated with its return distribution. Given that both hotel investments have the same expected value, we feel much more comfortable with a tighter distribution than a wider one. Some students will focus on the fact that the Avalon Hotel has some potentially high returns. However, it also has potential for some disastrous returns as well. Remember the declining marginal utility of money illustrated in Exhibit 4-1 to think of how people feel about uncertainty and gaining extra wealth.

Additionally, it is important to note that if the standard deviations are different, then we cannot compare them without standardizing them by their returns. The standard deviation is an absolute measure of total risk of an investment. To better evaluate the potential of two or more investments, we can use a relative measure—the ratio of standard deviation to return. This ratio is called the **coefficient of variation** and is shown in Exhibit 4-8.

Which hotel is the better investment from a risk-return perspective? Calculate the coefficient of variation as follows.

$$ABC \; Hotel = .12/.18 = .67$$
$$Benson \; Hotel = .15/.16 = .94$$

In this ratio, we seek the lowest amount of risk for the largest return. In this case, ABC Hotel has the highest return (182) and the lowest total risk. This would lead us to choose the ABC Hotel from the two hotels listed.

As we consider the risk and return profiles of different investments, it is a good time to reconsider some information from Chapter 2. Is there any investment that gives you a return without any standard deviation? Indeed there is. It is a risk-free investment such as a treasury bill that is guaranteed by the U.S. government.

Investment	Standard deviation	Expected return
ABC Hotel	12%	18%
Benson Hotel	15%	16%

Exhibit 4-8 Standard deviations and expected returns of two investments.

Because the return is always provided as advertised, there is no variety of returns, and the standard deviation of this investment is zero.

4.4 DIVERSIFICATION

Up to this point, we have discussed the case where investors choose which asset to hold. We have also shown how to decide between two assets when you know the risk and return profile of these assets using the coefficient of variation. However, rational investors rarely hold only a single asset. In this section we will discuss why investors want to hold more than one asset.

4.4.1 Benefits of a Portfolio

When we use the term *portfolio*, we mean a group of investments (at least two) that investors choose to own. Why own more than one asset? You may have heard the expression "Don't put all your eggs in one basket." This means that if you put all your money (and your hopes) in one plan, idea, or investment, you could easily be disappointed if something bad happens. Accordingly, most wise investors will own more than one type of asset.

The reason for this is quite simple. Investors want to guard against the possibility of a single asset declining in value. The idea is that even if one asset declines, another asset will gain in value to balance against the lower return on the first asset. This principle remains the same whether investors have two assets or hundreds of assets. This is the main idea of **diversification,** or holding what is known as a diversified portfolio. This type of portfolio attempts to maximize the return and minimize the risk (or standard deviation of returns) by being constructed based on how the assets within it relate to one another over time.

4.4.2 Correlation Coefficient

The **correlation coefficient,** called *rho*, is abbreviated as ρ. Although it has a wide variety of applications, it is often used in finance to measure how returns of assets are related to one another. A nonfinancial example would be to compare the amount of rainfall in cities around the world to umbrella sales. We would expect to find a positive relationship between rainfall and umbrella sales. Therefore, we could say these two variables are positively correlated. On the other hand, we could measure the days of sunshine in cities around the world and umbrella sales. Here we would expect to find these two variables to be negatively correlated.

The correlation coefficient is also handy because of its limited range. The coefficient ranges from negative 1 to positive 1. These are the extremes, of course, meaning that two variables that are moving exactly opposite of each other all the time are perfectly negatively correlated and have a rho of -1. Two variables moving together in perfect lockstep have a rho of $+1$. Note that these two situations are fairly rare, particularly in a financial context. If there is no relationship between the two variables, the correlation coefficient between them is zero.

Let's return to our portfolio example. The reason investors hold more than one asset in a portfolio is to maximize return and minimize risk. However, as we have learned, most assets (excluding risk-free assets) have a standard deviation of return. Additionally, if we put two or more assets into a portfolio, the portfolio

Asset	Return	% in portfolio (weight)	Weighted return
Restaurant A	12%	66.67	8%
Restaurant B	8%	33.33	2.67
Total	—	100	10.67%

Exhibit 4-9 Risk of two restaurants when held in a portfolio.

itself will have a standard deviation of return (similar to the standard deviation of an individual asset). The return on a portfolio is relatively easy to calculate: it is the return of each asset multiplied by its weight in the portfolio. Let's look at the return profile of Restaurant A and Restaurant B shown in Exhibit 4-9.

As shown in Exhibit 4-9, the overall return in the portfolio is the weighted average of the returns of the assets within the portfolio. Therefore, if we hold two-thirds of our money in Restaurant A stock and one-third in Restaurant B stock, the average return on our portfolio will be 10.67 percent (rounded). It is important to remember that this is only an expected value; there is a distribution of returns around this expected value, and our actual return could be higher or lower and vary from period to period. Now we can examine how to measure the risk of a portfolio.

The formula for the standard deviation of a two-asset portfolio is as follows.

$$\sigma_p = \sqrt{W_A^2 x \sigma_A^2 + W_B^2 x \sigma_B^2 + 2W_A W_B \rho_{AB} \sigma_A \sigma_B}$$

where W_A represents the proportion of asset A in the portfolio, W_B represents the proportion of asset B in the portfolio, and ρ_{AB} is the correlation coefficient for the returns of asset A and asset B. Let's add some risk to the example so we can calculate the standard deviation of a portfolio of Restaurant A and Restaurant B.

Given the information in Exhibit 4-10, we can calculate the standard deviation of the portfolio of these two assets. Furthermore, assume that the returns are perfectly correlated. The calculation is shown as:

$$\sigma_p = \sqrt{(.6667^2 x 4^2) + (.3333^2 x 8^2) + 2(.6667)(.3333)(1.0)(4)(8)}$$
$$= \sqrt{7.11 + 7.11 + 14.22} = 5.333 \text{ or } 5.333\%$$

As shown in the preceding example, the correlation coefficient between the two assets is $+1.0$, which, as previously discussed, is perfect positive correlation. The 5.333 percent (rounded) standard deviation is merely the weighted average of the two standard deviations of the two assets in the portfolio. Therefore, are we better off by combining these two assets into a portfolio? The answer is no. When two assets are perfectly positively correlated, we can only reduce the risk by weighting the portfolio with a greater percentage of the asset with the lower standard deviation. But this does not give us the benefits of diversification. We would

Asset	Weight in portfolio	Standard deviation of return
Restaurant A	66.67%	4%
Restaurant B	33.33%	8%

Exhibit 4-10 Risk profile of two restaurants.

like to be able to combine two assets and have the risk of the combined assets be less than either of the two individually.

Let's look at another example, which assumes the returns of the two restaurant assets have a correlation coefficient of -1.0, or perfect negative correlation (we will assume the same weights of the assets in the portfolio). Let's recalculate the standard deviation of the portfolio.

$$\sigma_p = \sqrt{(.6667^2 \times 4^2) + (.3333^2 \times 8^2) + 2(.6667)(.3333)(-1.0)(4)(8)}$$
$$= \sqrt{7.11 + 7.11 - 14.22} = 0.000 \text{ or } 0\%$$

Notice how the standard deviation is now zero, and risk is eliminated. This shows that if we can find two assets that are perfectly negatively correlated, we can create a portfolio that has no risk. It should be noted that we have used the appropriate proportion (two-thirds of asset A and one-third of asset B in this example) to completely eliminate risk. If we alter the weights of these assets in the portfolio, the standard deviation will not be zero. However, as long as the two assets of interest have returns that have a correlation coefficient of less than $+1.0$, we can find numerous combinations that have the same return with lower risk than when we combined the two assets that are perfectly positively correlated.

Let us look at one more example. Assume we wish to combine the same two assets in the same proportion into a portfolio. The only parameter we will change is the correlation coefficient of their returns. Let us assume that there is no correlation between them—in other words, the correlation coefficient is zero. Here is the calculation for the standard deviation of such a portfolio.

$$\sigma_p = \sqrt{(.6667^2 \times 4^2) + (.3333^2 \times 8^2) + 2(.6667)(.3333)(0)(4)(8)}$$
$$= \sqrt{7.11 + 7.11 + 0} = 3.77 \text{ or } 3.77\%$$

We can summarize the risk profiles of the different portfolios we have examined showing their different correlation coefficients in Exhibit 4-11.

There are two important considerations here before we consider which portfolio is best. First, the return of each of the portfolios is the same. If you recall the discussion on risk aversion and declining marginal utility for money, we know we would like to have the greatest return for a given level of risk. Accordingly, the ideal portfolio would be the one with the negative correlation coefficient between the assets (and with the assets in the right proportion) such that standard deviation (and risk) is zero.

Unfortunately, the chance of finding two assets that are perfectly negatively correlated is practically impossible. Therefore, the potential to eliminate *all* risk is extremely rare. However, this does not mean we do not obtain benefits from diversification. As you can see from Exhibit 4-11, if we can just find two assets that

Correlation coefficient	Standard deviation of portfolio	Return on portfolio
+1.0	5.33%	10.67%
0	3.77%	10.67%
−1.0	0.00%	10.67%

Exhibit 4-11   Standard deviation of portfolios with different correlation coefficients between assets.

are *less than perfectly positively correlated*, we can reduce risk and obtain some benefits of diversification through the construction of a portfolio.

4.5 THE MARKET PORTFOLIO

After the discussion on the construction of portfolios, you may be wondering how investors decide which assets to hold in their portfolios. As we learned in Chapter 2, a number of financial assets are available to invest in, and more are being developed every year. In addition to deciding which assets to include in a portfolio, is it possible to afford all the assets necessary to construct such a portfolio?

As previously discussed, investors have a number of choices about the construction of their portfolios. If we want to invest in a portfolio of three or more assets, we can calculate the expected return of the portfolio as well as its total risk (it is more complicated than a two-asset portfolio, so we will not show the formula here). After we calculate these statistics for a number of hypothetical portfolios, we plot risk and return as shown in Exhibit 4-12.

Exhibit 4-12 shows the risk/return profile of a sample of ten different portfolios. All of them have different levels of return for a given level of risk. Which one do we choose? Given the previous discussion about correlation coefficients, we know that most people are risk averse and want the highest level of return for a given level of risk. This means people are seeking a portfolio that is efficient, which in a general sense means the most output for a given input. In a financial context, the most **efficient portfolio** is the one that provides the highest level of return for a given level of risk. Unfortunately, at this point, we don't quite have enough information to decide which portfolio is best.

An important factor to consider is that although most people are risk averse, they do have different risk preferences. Some investors may want to invest only in a risk-free asset, whereas others are willing to invest in portfolios of risky assets as long as they are compensated with a higher return. An important assumption in portfolio selection is the notion that investors can borrow or lend money at the risk-free rate of interest. If you choose to do so, you can invest in treasury bills alone and thus lend money to the U.S. government. On the other hand, you can

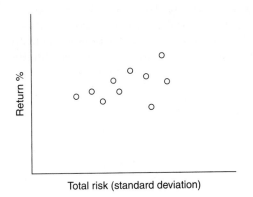

Exhibit 4-12   Set of hypothetical portfolios.

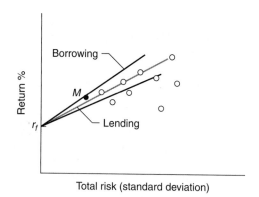

Exhibit 4-13   Capital market line.

borrow money from a broker (called "trading on margin") and invest in a variety of assets. If we add the risk-free asset to our set of hypothetical portfolios, we can perhaps select the best portfolio. This is shown in Exhibit 4-13.

Now that we have placed the risk-free asset on our graph (designated r_f), we can draw a line connecting the risk-free asset and a few of the hypothetical portfolios. Recall that a line is an infinite series of points; therefore, the lines we have drawn indicate an infinite variety of combinations of the risk-free asset and a portfolio of assets. These lines are called borrowing-lending lines because as previously stated, investors can put some of their money into a portfolio and lend the rest to the government; on the other hand, they can use borrowed money to invest in a portfolio to increase their return (but bear more risk).

You may recall from math classes that the equation for a straight line involves slope. The slope of the line is the rise (increase in y-axis) over the run (increase in x-axis). In our case, the rise indicates the return above the risk-free rate of return, or a return premium. The run is the total risk of the investment. As a risk-averse investor, we would prefer to hold the portfolio with the greatest level of a return for a given level of risk. This means we would like to invest in the portfolio that is tangent to the line with the steepest slope connecting it with the risk-free asset. In Exhibit 4-13, this is labeled as Portfolio M.

You will notice the portion of the line between Portfolio M and the risk-free asset is labeled the lending line. The portion of the line beyond Portfolio M is called the borrowing line. Earlier we mentioned that different people have risk preferences. How does this affect our portfolio selection? Interestingly enough, it doesn't here. If you compare the slope of the top line with the other two lines, you can see it has a higher slope. Therefore, no matter what our risk preferences are, every point along the top line that intersects point M dominates the points on the other two lines. In other words, no matter which combination of Portfolio M and the risk-free asset you hold, it is superior to the combinations used to comprise the other two lines.

Portfolio M has a special name—it is called the **market portfolio,** which is a theoretical portfolio of all the assets of value in the world held in the appropriate proportions to yield the highest level of return for the least amount of risk. Therefore, it is the most efficient portfolio to hold. Additionally, the borrowing–lending line that connects the risk-free asset with the market portfolio is called the

capital market line. The equation for the capital market line, which can be used to predict a required level of return, will be discussed in greater detail later in this chapter.

4.5.1 What Makes the Market Portfolio Unique

Because we have shown that the market portfolio is the best in terms of yielding a return for a given level of risk, then who wouldn't want to hold this portfolio? The answer is nobody. Rational investors who are placing their capital at risk want to get the highest level of return possible. Therefore, we assume every investor holds the market portfolio.

Investors not only want the highest return, they also want the lowest level of risk. The risk becomes lowered as more and more assets (with less-than-perfect correlation) are added to the portfolio. Therefore, adding all the assets in existence to the portfolio provides the ultimate diversified portfolio. And, most important, if everyone wants to hold the market portfolio, then we must assume investors are diversified.

4.5.2 The Market Portfolio and Risk Composition

The only problem is that holding every asset in existence would be impossible. Even the richest people in the world could not have every type of tradeable asset—including commodities, real estate, stocks, bonds, and many other investments. However, the good news is that holding all the assets is not necessary to obtain the benefits of the market portfolio.

We have only discussed the concept of total risk—the standard deviation of return. However, total risk is actually divided into two separate components:

$$\text{Systematic risk} + \text{Unsystematic risk} = \text{Total risk}$$

Systematic risk is the type of risk that is involved in all assets that do not have a guaranteed return. These involve characteristics of the general economy such as interest rates and inflation rates. This type of risk cannot be diversified away even as more assets are added to a portfolio. **Unsystematic risk** is the component of total risk related to a specific business or industry. This type of event may be a work stoppage or a new piece of legislation that only affects a particular industry. These circumstances do not impact the economy as a whole, and thus, this type of risk can be diversified away by adding assets to a portfolio.

The story of diversification has good news and bad news for investors. The good news is that investors do not actually need to hold every asset in the world to obtain the same benefits of diversification as the market portfolio. We can see the benefits of risk reduction in Exhibit 4-14.

Notice what happens to the standard deviation of the portfolio as we add more assets to it. The initial reduction of risk is very great. However, as we add more assets to a portfolio, the amount of risk reduction begins to decrease. Research has shown that as we accumulate approximately 25 to 50 assets in a portfolio, no further risk reduction is achieved.

In other words, we can emulate the benefits of the market portfolio by having only about 25 or 30 assets in a portfolio. Thus, we do not have to hold every asset in the world. However, have we completely eliminated risk at this point? Certainly not. We have eliminated the unsystematic, but we cannot eliminate the systematic risk. The curve flattens out at the level of systematic risk

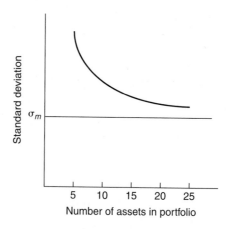

Exhibit 4-14   Risk reduction through the inclusion of assets.

that is designated as σ_m in the graph. This is the level of risk contained in the market portfolio or other similar portfolios we can construct or purchase.

What investments are available for investors to gain the benefits of holding the market portfolio? Investors have many choices. Some will buy a group of individual stocks. However, long ago the market recognized the benefits of holding a diversified portfolio. Therefore, many mutual funds are available that invest in a wide variety of assets to maintain a diversified portfolio for investors. Many mutual fund companies offer investments in stock indices such as the Standard & Poor's 500 index (although there are other indices as well). The mutual fund company will invest in these 500 different companies in the same proportion as they are held in the index itself. This yields two advantages to the investor: (1) the portfolio is well diversified, and (2) this means the mutual fund manager does not actively buy or sell stocks too often, thereby reducing the cost of fund management to the investor. Although some criticize this approach because returns can be reduced from taxes and fees, they are some of the largest and most popular mutual funds in existence today. Furthermore, it is relatively inexpensive to hold this diversified portfolio. Some mutual fund companies will allow an individual to open an Individual Retirement Account (IRA) fund for only $100.

Overall, not only should investors hold a diversified portfolio because it is efficient, but it is also relatively inexpensive for an investor to obtain the benefit of diversification. This conclusion has important implications for how investors examine risk and returns of assets. It also affects how hospitality managers select capital improvement projects for their owners.

4.6 THE MARKET PORTFOLIO AND BETA

Now that we understand why investors want to hold (and can hold) a portfolio of assets similar to the market portfolio, we now must assume the shareholders of the firm we work for are diversified. If investors are diversified, they are no longer concerned with an investment's unsystematic risk. This is because once the investment is added to the investors' well-diversified portfolio, unsystematic risk will be removed because of the effects of diversification. Therefore, analyzing investments from a total risk standpoint (standard deviation) is inappropriate.

A better measure would be one that measures the relevant risk to the diversified investor. The tool to do this is called **beta.** Beta measures the risk of an investment relative to the market portfolio. Because it is a relative measure, it makes use of a correlation coefficient as follows.

$$\text{Beta} = \frac{\rho_{xm}\sigma_x}{\sigma_m}$$

The formula shows rho, the correlation coefficient of the returns from any asset (asset x in this example) and the market portfolio. This is multiplied by the standard deviation of the returns of asset x. This product is then divided by the standard deviation of the returns of the market portfolio.

One of the features of beta is that it measures risk relative to a unit of one. The market portfolio, for example, has a beta of 1.0. This basically means the overall market is as risky as itself. If an asset has a beta of 2.0, then that asset is twice as risky as the market. If an asset has a beta of 0.5, then the asset is only half as risky as the market.

There are a number of ways to obtain betas for hospitality companies. One way would be to get historical stock returns (usually daily) for the company of interest and an asset representing the market portfolio (the S&P 500 index, for example). Regressing the two sets of returns would yield a beta. If you do not feel like calculating them yourself, they are also available on the World Wide Web. One source is the Yahoo! Finance Web site; other sources include various brokerage firms. A sample of the betas of selected hospitality companies is shown in Exhibit 4-15.

As shown in Exhibit 4-15, betas can vary significantly from company to company. Most of the betas of these randomly selected hospitality companies are relatively low. A word of caution about using betas from sources on the Web: It is not always clear how the betas were calculated. There is no magic number in terms of the number of years of returns to be used in the calculation, and this

Firm	Beta
California Pizza Kitchen	.58
Cheesecake Factory	1.21
Choice Hotels	.36
Harrah's Entertainment	.66
Hilton	.65
Jack in the Box	.47
Landry's	.37
Marriott	.79
McDonald's	.83
Outback Steakhouse	.87
Park Place Entertainment	.81
Starbucks	1.08
Yum	.41

Source: Yahoo! Finance Web site.

Exhibit 4-15 Betas for selected hospitality firms.

could have a significant impact on the beta. Some betas are calculated using three years of returns; some may use five years. Which years are chosen could also have an impact on the calculation. Additionally, some of the betas you may find don't make a lot of sense—either they are unusually large or unusually small. Sometimes they may even be negative, which does not make much economic sense as we will discuss in the next section.

4.7 BETA, EXPECTED RETURN, AND THE SECURITY MARKET LINE

This is a good time to be reminded of a basic principle in finance: Risk and return go together. In other words, a higher return is coupled with high risk. Up until the discussion on beta, we measured this risk in terms of total risk and standard deviation. However, once we introduced the concept of the diversified investor, the total risk measure is no longer the best measure to use. We can use beta as a predictive measure to understand the relationship between the risk investors bear and the return they expect.

In a previous section we discussed a special borrowing–lending line called the capital market line. It measured the return on a portfolio against the risk of the portfolio, as measured by standard deviation. We are now going to introduce another special borrowing–lending line called the security market line (SML), shown in Exhibit 4-16.

As shown in Exhibit 4-16, the SML is drawn from the risk-free rate of return through point M, which represents the market portfolio. The graph is measuring the systematic risk of an investment (beta) against the expected return. The beta of the market portfolio is 1.0, whereas the beta of the risk-free asset is 0. The return on the market portfolio is designated R_m. Notice how the slope of the line is positive; in other words, the higher the relevant (systematic) risk of an asset,

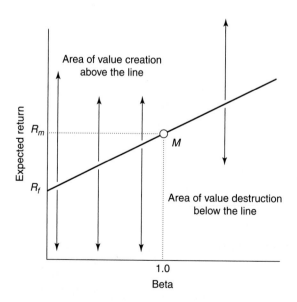

Exhibit 4-16 Security market line.

the higher its expected return. This has important implications for value creation and decision criteria in capital budgeting.

The SML actually represents a *minimum standard of return*, given the relevant risk of a project. Once again, we are assuming investors are diversified and want to hold (and do hold) a well-diversified portfolio. Therefore, investors can lend to the government or borrow against their portfolio and move up and down the line, depending on their risk preferences. However, at every level of risk there should be a minimum return generated. This is the standard by which we can measure asset returns. In other words, if a stock investment or a new capital asset does not at least generate a return as predicted by the SML, it is a value-destroying project and should be rejected.

Although we have discussed the SML in general graphic terms, we can calculate specifically the rate of return an asset should generate. The equation for the SML is

$$\text{Expected return} = R_f + (R_m - R_f) \times \beta$$

where R_f is the rate of return on the risk-free asset, R_m is the rate of return on the market portfolio, and β is the beta of the asset. This equation is also known as the **capital asset pricing model** (CAPM) and is used to predict the expected rate of return on an equity investment. Basically, the equation states that shareholders putting their capital at risk should get the risk-free rate of return plus a risk premium. The risk premium is the difference between the return on the market portfolio and the risk-free rate of return (this is also the slope of the SML shown in the graph). The risk premium is then adjusted by the systematic risk profile of the asset as compared to the market portfolio. In other words, if an asset is twice as risky as the market, the investor should be rewarded with twice the risk premium in terms of return.

Let us assume the risk-free rate of return is 4 percent, and the return on the market portfolio is 12 percent. Additionally, the beta of an investment is 1.5. What return should the investment generate? The calculation is shown as:

$$4\% + [(12\% - 4\%) \times 1.5] = 16\%$$

The investment should generate a return of 16 percent.

The SML can help us determine whether or not a project creates value. We can plot the return on equity (ROE) of a project against its systematic risk. If the ROE exceeds the required rate of return as shown by the SML, then the project is value creating and would plot above the line as noted on Exhibit 4-16. If the ROE of the project is below the minimum as shown by the SML, this project destroys value and would be below the line on Exhibit 4-16. We will discuss this in the context of value creation criteria later in the textbook.

4.7.1 The Limitations of the CAPM

The CAPM is arguably one of the most significant developments in finance in the last 50 years. It is a tool frequently used to help assess the viability of a capital budgeting project. Nevertheless, the ability of the CAPM to effectively predict expected returns has been questioned in recent years. Therefore, we will discuss a few limitations of the model.

First, the market portfolio is a theoretical concept. Although there are many proxies for this portfolio, there is no consensus on which one is best. A number of indices (Dow Jones Industrials and the S&P 500, just to name two) are frequently used. However, none of these indices are an exact replica of the market portfolio. Second, betas are calculated based on *historical* returns. These betas are then used to forecast *future* returns. Research has shown that betas are more useful for predicting returns for certain time periods, but not in all. The time period that encompasses the analyzed returns can have a significant impact on the accuracy of the predicted returns.

A significant amount of academic research has been conducted in an attempt to find other variables (other than systematic risk) to forecast expected returns. During certain periods, firm size has been more useful in predicting returns. Nevertheless, a definitive set of significant variables that accurately predicts all the variance in stock returns has yet to be established. The search continues for important variables that can consistently and accurately predict stock returns over time.

In the final analysis, the CAPM and beta have been shown to have some limitations. On the other hand, CAPM remains popular today because of the fundamental intuition of the model: The return of an asset is positively related to its relevant risk. It also was largely responsible for getting average investors to consider risk and its components and to begin thinking of risk in a different way than they did before.

4.7.2 Betas for Hospitality Assets

It is a relatively simple task to use the CAPM to predict returns on common stock investments of companies. Risk-free rates of return are published in newspapers, and betas can be found on the World Wide Web. Information on proxies for the market portfolio (such as the S&P 500 index) can also be found on the Web. But what should the expected return be for a new restaurant investment?

We know that because it can produce a cash flow and is not guaranteed, it must yield a return greater than the risk-free rate. We could use the CAPM if we could only calculate a beta. However, because it is a prospective project with no historical returns, this could not be done. How should we proceed?

This is a fairly common problem for new hospitality ventures. One of the simplest methods would be to find betas of publicly traded corporations that are similar to the project under consideration. If you are building a gourmet coffee store, you might consider using the beta of Starbucks. If you are considering a seafood house, examining the beta of Landry's might be helpful. Remember that the beta is an estimate based on past returns and is being used to predict future equity returns. Although it is an important component in the assessment of a capital budgeting project, the process of estimating the shareholder return is not an exact science and needs to be considered with other important components in the analysis such as cash flows, the return expected by lenders, tax rates, and other considerations discussed later in the textbook.

IS THE RESTAURANT BUSINESS RISKY?

In this chapter we learned about the systematic risk of an investment, called beta. Exhibit 4-15 shows the betas for a small sample of hospitality companies. One of the companies, Landry's, has a beta of only .37, the second-lowest beta in the sample. This means that their common stock only has about one-third of the risk of the overall market. Landry's is a diversified restaurant company with a number of different restaurant brands, including The Crab House, Joe's Crab Shack, Chart House Restaurants, Landry's Seafood House, and Rainforest Café. The Rainforest Café acquisition was completed in December 2000.

Traditionally, the restaurant business has been thought to be risky. Why, then, does Landry's have such a low beta? Does this mean the restaurant business is not risky after all? Not necessarily. Remember, the beta is only an indication of systematic or market-related risk. This is only a portion of the risk of an investment. It may be such that the risk of the restaurant business is unrelated to the market and more specific to the local operations. However, these unsystematic factors can be reduced substantially when placed in a well-diversified portfolio. That is why many restaurant stocks such as Landry's, McDonald's, Darden, and many others make logical investment choices for many investors.

4.8 SUMMARY

This chapter focused on risk and return. We first discussed why most investors do not like risk and then the behavioral characteristic of risk aversion. Risk was subsequently considered in a statistical context using expected return, variance, and standard deviation. We also demonstrated the relevance and use of the normal distribution.

Another important topic in the chapter is the concept of diversification and how investors can become diversified. Nevertheless, even a well-diversified portfolio cannot completely eliminate risk. Total risk discussed in terms of its two components: systematic and unsystematic risk. The concept of the market portfolio was introduced along with beta, a measure of systematic risk.

Finally, the concept of the capital asset pricing model (CAPM) was introduced as a way to help forecast expected return on investment for shareholders. The limitations of the model were also presented. In Chapter 5, we relate the concept or risk to one of the most important principles of finance: the time value of money.

KEY TERMS

√ Beta
√ Capital asset pricing model (CAPM)
Capital market line
√ Coefficient of variation
√ Correlation coefficient
Diversification
Efficient portfolio
Expected value
Market portfolio
Probability distribution
Risk
Risk aversion

√ **Standard deviation**
√ **Systematic risk**
√ **Unsystematic risk**
√ **Variance**

DISCUSSION QUESTIONS

1. Why are rational investors risk averse?
2. Define risk aversion.
3. Define expected value.
4. Why is a simple average calculation usually not appropriate when calculating expected values?
5. Define variance and standard deviation.
6. If two assets have the same expected return but different standard deviations, which one would we prefer?
7. What is the coefficient of variation?
8. What would you expect the correlation coefficient between a college football team's winning percentage and the following year's home game ticket sales to be?
9. What is the main objective of diversification?
10. What is the market portfolio? What makes it unique?
11. Define the components of total risk, and describe how they differ.
12. Define beta.
13. How do we know if a project creates value for its owners?

PROBLEMS

Problems designated with **Excel** *can be solved using* **Excel** *spreadsheets accessible at* http://www.prenhall.com/chatfield.

1. The Clayton Hotel is expected to generate different returns based on the state of the economy. These are shown in the following figure.

State of the economy	Probability of each state	Return
Recession	10%	–5%
Moderate growth	60%	6%
Boom	30%	18%

   a. Calculate the expected return for the Clayton Hotel using a *simple* average.
   b. Calculate the expected return for the Clayton Hotel using a *weighted* average.

2. Based on the information from Problem 1, complete the following for the Clayton Hotel.
   a. Calculate the variance.
   b. Calculate the standard deviation.
   c. Interpret the standard deviation relative to the normal distribution.

3. You are given the following information about three potential hotel investments.

Hotel	Return	Risk (standard deviation)
Hotel X	12%	7%
Hotel Y	20%	19%
Hotel Z	14%	10%

If could only choose one, which of these investments would you choose?

4. You are given the following information.   **EXCEL**

Hotel	Return	Weight (proportion of portfolio)	Risk (standard deviation of return)
Hotel X	10%	75%	3%
Hotel Y	20%	25%	9%

a. Calculate the expected return of the portfolio.
b. Calculate the standard deviation of the portfolio with a ρ of +1.0.
c. Calculate the standard deviation of the portfolio with a ρ of 0.
d. Calculate the standard deviation of the portfolio with a ρ of −1.0.

5. Given that the standard deviation of returns on the market is 10 percent, the standard deviation of the Hotel Lockhart is 20 percent, and the correlation coefficient of their returns is .5, calculate the beta for the Hotel Lockhart.

6. If the standard deviation of returns for the Lafayette Restaurant is 15 percent, the standard deviation of returns for the market portfolio is 12 percent, and the beta of the Lafayette Restaurant is .75, what is the correlation coefficient for the returns of the Lafayette Restaurant and the market portfolio?

7. If the risk-free rate of return is 4 percent, the return on the market portfolio is 12 percent, and the beta of the Hotel Norwood is 1.5, calculate the expected rate of return for the Hotel Norwood.

8. If the expected return for the Park Hotel is 20 percent, the risk-free rate of return is 6 percent, and the return on the market portfolio is 16 percent, what is the beta of the Park Hotel?

Time Value of Money 5

Chapter Objectives

- To understand the future value and present value computations of a single lump sum
- To know what an annuity is and understand the difference between an ordinary annuity, an annuity due, a deferred annuity, and a perpetuity
- To understand the future value and present value computations of an annuity
- To understand the present value computations for a perpetuity, a deferred annuity, and a series of nonconstant cash flows
- To understand annual compounding and compounding other than annual
- To understand and be able to compute effective annual rates
- To understand an amortization table

5.1 INTRODUCTION

This chapter introduces the topic of financial mathematics, which we also call the time value of money (TVM). Although this topic may be intimidating to many at first glance, give it a chance, and you may be surprised how much you enjoy solving financial problems. After all, this topic is based on common sense and is very logical. Also, learning financial mathematics will enable you to perform important functions, such as being able to calculate mortgage payments on a home loan, monthly payments on an automobile loan, or how much you need to save for retirement.

The TVM is a foundation topic in hospitality finance because it is relevant to many finance decisions in the hospitality industry, such as capital budgeting decisions, cost of capital estimation, and pricing a bond issuance. We will discuss these in later chapters as we present the additional information necessary to consider these topics. For now, we need to develop our ability to use TVM analytical procedures. The orientation of this chapter will be personal finance, as this is a rich and interesting context for presenting TVM concepts. Once we understand TVM concepts, we will then develop the context for applying these concepts in a hospitality industry framework in forthcoming chapters.

TVM is the concept that a set amount of money has different values at different points in time. In other words, $1.00 today is not worth $1.00 one year from now. A simple example to illustrate this concept is to think in terms of how the value of something changes over time. For example, whereas your parents could purchase the nicest house in the neighborhood in 1970 for $42,000, you may have to pay $145,000 for that same house today. In the early 1970s a basic economy car could be purchased for less than $3,000. Today there are very few new cars available for less than $10,000. Of course, when you consider the salaries of 1970 compared to today, proportionally your cost of purchasing this house or car may be relatively the same.

Performance of financial mathematics requires the use of interest rates, which reflect the change in the value of money from time period to time period. For example, if you deposit $10,000 into a bank account today, you expect to have more than $10,000 one year later. How much more? It depends on the interest rate. If the interest rate is 5.5% annually, then you expect to have $550 more ($10,000 times 5.5%) for a total of $10,550.

This is the time value of money. The preceding example is simple with limited usefulness. However, as you go through this chapter, you will learn more complex ways to find the value of money at different points in time. After you have mastered this chapter, you will be able to apply your newfound skills to all sorts of problems that you will find quite useful. In fact, many of the future chapters rely on the TVM concept. So be careful and diligent. Mastering this chapter will allow you to successfully handle future chapters. Conversely, if you do not understand the TVM concept, chances are you will not be able to successfully complete your study of financial management.

As we move through this chapter, you will learn how to find the value of a sum of money in the future at a given rate of interest. We refer to this as calculating the future value of a lump sum. You will also be able to calculate how much money must be invested today at a given **interest rate** to provide a given future amount. This is called *calculating the present value of a lump sum*. In addition, you will learn how to calculate the present and future values of a series of payments, known as annuity payments. All other concepts will follow from these four basic concepts.

5.2 FUTURE VALUE—COMPOUNDING

The first TVM concept we present is how to calculate the future value of a lump sum. In other words, what is a certain sum of money worth in the future at a particular rate of interest? The term **compounding** refers to the process of a present value earning interest and growing to a future value.

For example, say you deposit $1,000 into a bank account today. The account pays interest at a rate of 5 percent annually. An example of this type of account is a certificate of deposit (CD). Let us now calculate the future value of this lump sum of $1,000 one year from now at the 5 percent annual interest rate.

We start by modeling this problem on a timeline. Timelines are a useful way to keep your numbers organized to avoid making mistakes and to help visualize the problem more clearly.

$$\begin{array}{lcr}
0 & & 1 \\
\vdash & \rule{6cm}{0.4pt} & \dashv \\
PV = \$1{,}000 & & FV_1 = ?
\end{array}$$

Before formally solving the problem, let us consider the logic. One year from today your bank account will have a balance of $1,000 plus any interest earned. At an interest rate of 5 percent, your interest earned amounts to $50. Therefore, the balance in your account one year from today will be $1,050.

$$FV_1 = PV + \text{Interest}$$
$$= \$1,000 + \$1,000 \times 0.05 \ (5\% = 0.05)$$
$$= \$1,000 + 50 = \$1,050$$

Now, what if we leave this money in the bank account for a second year, and it earns the same 5 percent rate of interest over this second year? Again, model this problem on a timeline.

```
0                         1                          2
├─────────────────────────┼──────────────────────────┤
PV = $1,000              $1,050                     FV₂ = ?
                          └──────────────────────►  52.50
                                                   1,050.00
                                                   $1,102.50
```

As you can see, your balance will increase to $1,102.50 by the end of the second year. You have earned interest of $52.50 during this second year. Fifty dollars of this interest is earned on the original deposit of $1,000, and the other $2.50 is earned on the first year's interest of $50. In other words, the amount of interest earned in year two can be calculated as $1,050 times 5 percent, which is $52.50. We refer to this concept of earning interest on interest as **compound interest**. To calculate the future value of any sum for any interest rate over any period of time, we use the following equation.

$$(1) \ FV_n = PV \times (1 + i)^n = \$1,000 \times (1.05)^2 = \$1,102.50$$

FV_n is the future value of a lump sum at time n

PV is the present value

i is the interest rate

n is the number of compounding periods between the future value and the present value

There are several ways to solve the preceding equation and find the future value of $1,102.50. One is to work through the math. Another is to use a business calculator programmed to perform financial mathematics. And last is to use financial mathematics tables.

If using a calculator to perform the calculation, be sure the calculator is properly set up to perform the financial mathematics calculation (see Appendix 5.1). Then enter the three known variables.

$$PV = \$1,000 \quad n = 2 \quad i = 5\% \quad \text{then compute } FV = \$1,102.50$$

Appendix 5.1 provides some guidance for using two of the more popular business calculators to solve TVM problems.

The last method is to use financial mathematics tables that are designed to save the user from working through the mathematics (Exhibit 5-1). For this type of problem, the table provides a factor that we multiply by the known present value to solve for the **future value.** In this case, because we are solving for a future value, the factor is called a future value interest factor (FVIF). $FVIF_{i,n}$ is equal to $(1 + i)^n$ so that the equation

$$FV_n = PV \times (1 + i)^n \text{ can also be written as } FV_n = PV \times (FVIF_{i,n})$$

where the $(FVIF_{i,n})$ is the FVIF for a given interest rate (i) and a given number of periods (n).

To solve the preceding problem, we can write the equation as

$$FV_n = \$1,000 \times (FVIF_{5\%,2})$$

where $(FVIF_{5\%,2}) = 1.1025$ from Exhibit 5-1. Thus the answer is

$$FV_n = \$1,000 \times 1.1025 = \$1,102.50$$

Now let us practice what we have just learned. Calculate the future value in the following example using each of the three methods: (1) work through the mathematics of the equation, (2) use a business calculator programmed for financial mathematics, and (3) use the financial mathematics tables. For another example, suppose you deposit $12,000 into an account paying 7 percent annual interest. How much will you have in this account 14 years from now?

We strongly suggest you draw a timeline when solving financial mathematics problems. This will greatly assist in learning the time value of money concept and help to avoid errors. A properly labeled timeline helps you to visualize the problem and helps to keep everything organized.

Now let us solve the problem using each of the three methods. Of course you get the same answer regardless of the method used. Do you understand why?

Equation: $FV_{14} = \$12,000 \times (1.07)^{14} = \$30,942.41$

calculator use ← **Calculator:** $PV = \$12,000 \quad n = 14 \quad i = 7\% \quad$ then compute $FV = \$30,942.41$

Exhibit 5-1: $FV_{14} = \$12,000 \times (FVIF_{7\%,14}) = \$12,000 \times (2.5785) = \$30,942.00$

Notice when you look up the $FVIF_{7\%,14}$ you find the factor of 2.5785. This $FVIF_{7\%,14}$ is calculated as $(1 + i)^n$, or $(1.07)^{14}$, which is 2.5785. In other words, $FVIF_{i,n} = (1 + i)^n$ for a given interest rate, i, over a specified period of time, n. Therefore, using the factor is the same as working through the mathematical equation, except the tables round the factors to four decimal places.

Next, consider your calculator. If you enter $PV = 1$, $n = 14$, $i = 7\%$, and then solve for FV, you notice the same answer you calculated for the $FVIF_{7\%,14}$ or $(1.07)^{14}$, which is 2.5785. Thus the calculator is just a shortcut, efficient method for working through the mathematical equation. Whether you work through the mathematical equation yourself or use a business calculator programmed for financial mathematics or use the tables, all three methods really use the same mathematical equation. These are all alternative methods to solve for the same answer. You should obtain a FV equal to $30, 942.41 solving the mathematical equation or

Value of $1 Earning *i*% per Period for *n* Periods

Periods	1%	2%	3%	4%	5%	6%	7%	8%	9%	10%
1	1.0100	1.0200	1.0300	1.0400	1.0500	1.0600	1.0700	1.0800	1.0900	1.1000
2	1.0201	1.0404	1.0609	1.0816	1.1025	1.1236	1.1449	1.1664	1.1881	1.2100
3	1.0303	1.0612	1.0927	1.1249	1.1576	1.1910	1.2250	1.2597	1.2950	1.3310
4	1.0406	1.0824	1.1255	1.1699	1.2155	1.2625	1.3108	1.3605	1.4116	1.4641
5	1.0510	1.1041	1.1593	1.2167	1.2763	1.3382	1.4026	1.4693	1.5386	1.6105
6	1.0615	1.1262	1.1941	1.2653	1.3401	1.4185	1.5007	1.5869	1.6771	1.7716
7	1.0721	1.1487	1.2299	1.3159	1.4071	1.5036	1.6058	1.7138	1.8280	1.9487
8	1.0829	1.1717	1.2668	1.3686	1.4775	1.5938	1.7182	1.8509	1.9926	2.1436
9	1.0937	1.1951	1.3048	1.4233	1.5513	1.6895	1.8385	1.9990	2.1719	2.3579
10	1.1046	1.2190	1.3439	1.4802	1.6289	1.7908	1.9672	2.1589	2.3674	2.5937
11	1.1157	1.2434	1.3842	1.5395	1.7103	1.8983	2.1049	2.3316	2.5804	2.8531
12	1.1268	1.2682	1.4258	1.6010	1.7959	2.0122	2.2522	2.5182	2.8127	3.1384
13	1.1381	1.2936	1.4685	1.6651	1.8856	2.1329	2.4098	2.7196	3.0658	3.4523
14	1.1495	1.3195	1.5126	1.7317	1.9799	2.2609	2.5785	2.9372	3.3417	3.7975
15	1.1610	1.3459	1.5580	1.8009	2.0789	2.3966	2.7590	3.1722	3.6425	4.1772
16	1.1726	1.3728	1.6047	1.8730	2.1829	2.5404	2.9522	3.4259	3.9703	4.5950
17	1.1843	1.4002	1.6528	1.9479	2.2920	2.6928	3.1588	3.7000	4.3276	5.0545
18	1.1961	1.4282	1.7024	2.0258	2.4066	2.8543	3.3799	3.9960	4.7171	5.5599
19	1.2081	1.4568	1.7535	2.1068	2.5270	3.0256	3.6165	4.3157	5.1417	6.1159
20	1.2202	1.4859	1.8061	2.1911	2.6533	3.2071	3.8697	4.6610	5.6044	6.7275
25	1.2824	1.6406	2.0938	2.6658	3.3864	4.2919	5.4274	6.8485	8.6231	10.8347
30	1.3478	1.8114	2.4273	3.2434	4.3219	5.7435	7.6123	10.0627	13.2677	17.4494
40	1.4889	2.2080	3.2620	4.8010	7.0400	10.2857	14.9745	21.7245	31.4094	45.2593
50	1.6446	2.6916	4.3839	7.1067	11.4674	18.4202	29.4570	46.9016	74.3575	117.3909

Periods	11%	12%	13%	14%	15%	16%	17%	18%	19%	20%
1	1.1100	1.1200	1.1300	1.1400	1.1500	1.1600	1.1700	1.1800	1.1900	1.2000
2	1.2321	1.2544	1.2769	1.2996	1.3225	1.3456	1.3689	1.3924	1.4161	1.4400
3	1.3676	1.4049	1.4429	1.4815	1.5209	1.5609	1.6016	1.6430	1.6852	1.7280
4	1.5181	1.5735	1.6305	1.6890	1.7490	1.8106	1.8739	1.9388	2.0053	2.0736
5	1.6851	1.7623	1.8424	1.9254	2.0114	2.1003	2.1924	2.2878	2.3864	2.4883
6	1.8704	1.9738	2.0820	2.1950	2.3131	2.4364	2.5652	2.6996	2.8398	2.9860
7	2.0762	2.2107	2.3526	2.5023	2.6600	2.8262	3.0012	3.1855	3.3793	3.5832
8	2.3045	2.4760	2.6584	2.8526	3.0590	3.2784	3.5115	3.7589	4.0214	4.2998
9	2.5580	2.7731	3.0040	3.2519	3.5179	3.8030	4.1084	4.4355	4.7854	5.1598
10	2.8394	3.1058	3.3946	3.7072	4.0456	4.4114	4.8068	5.2338	5.6947	6.1917
11	3.1518	3.4785	3.8359	4.2262	4.6524	5.1173	5.6240	6.1759	6.7767	7.4301
12	3.4985	3.8960	4.3345	4.8179	5.3503	5.9360	6.5801	7.2876	8.0642	8.9161
13	3.8833	4.3635	4.8980	5.4924	6.1528	6.8858	7.6987	8.5994	9.5964	10.6993
14	4.3104	4.8871	5.5348	6.2613	7.0757	7.9875	9.0075	10.1472	11.4198	12.8392
15	4.7846	5.4736	6.2543	7.1379	8.1371	9.2655	10.5387	11.9737	13.5895	15.4070
16	5.3109	6.1304	7.0673	8.1372	9.3576	10.7480	12.3303	14.1290	16.1715	18.4884
17	5.8951	6.8660	7.9861	9.2765	10.7613	12.4677	14.4265	16.6722	19.2441	22.1861
18	6.5436	7.6900	9.0243	10.5752	12.3755	14.4625	16.8790	19.6733	22.9005	26.6233
19	7.2633	8.6128	10.1974	12.0557	14.2318	16.7765	19.7484	23.2144	27.2516	31.9480
20	8.0623	9.6463	11.5231	13.7435	16.3665	19.4608	23.1056	27.3930	32.4294	38.3376
25	13.5855	17.0001	21.2305	26.4619	32.9190	40.8742	50.6578	62.6686	77.3881	95.3962
30	22.8923	29.9599	39.1159	50.9502	66.2118	85.8499	111.0647	143.3706	184.6753	237.3763
40	65.0009	93.0510	132.7816	188.8835	267.8635	378.7212	533.8687	750.3783	1051.6675	1469.7716
50	184.5648	289.0022	450.7359	700.2330	1083.6574	1670.7038	2566.2153	3927.3569	5988.9139	9100.4382

Exhibit 5-1   Future value interest factor.

using the calculator. Using Exhibit 5-1 you should obtain an *FV* equal to $30,942.00 because Exhibit 5-1 rounds off the factors at four decimal places (2.5785).

5.3 PRESENT VALUE—DISCOUNTING

What if we know the value of a lump sum of money at some point of time in the future and want instead to calculate the appropriate **present value** today at some specified rate of interest? In other words, what is a future sum of money worth today? For example, what is $1,320 worth today at a 10 percent annual rate? In other words, how much do you have to invest today at a 10 percent annual rate to end up with $1,320 in one year? **Discounting** is the process of computing the present value of a future value.

```
0                                                    1
├──────────────────────────────────────────────────┤
PV = ?                                   FV₁ = $1,320
```

Just as with the previous future value problem, this problem can be solved in several different ways. We can work through the math, use a business calculator, or use financial mathematics tables. First, we will work through the math.

$$(2)\ PV = \frac{FV_n}{(1 + i)^n} = \frac{\$1,320}{(1 + 10\%)^1} = \$1,200$$

Using a business calculator, enter the three known variables:

$$FV = 1,320 \quad n = 1 \quad i = 10\% \quad \text{then compute } PV = \$1,200$$

When using financial mathematics tables to solve for present value, the table provides a factor that we multiply by the known future value to solve for the present value. Because we are solving for the present value, the factor in this case is called a *present value interest factor (PVIF)*. $PVIF_{i,n}$ is equal to $1/(1 + i)^n$ so that the equation

$$PV = \frac{FV_n}{(1 + i)^n}$$ can also be written as $PV = FV_n \times (PVIF_{i,n})$

To solve the preceding problem, we can write the equation as

$$PV = \$1,320 \times (PVIF_{10\%,1})$$

where $(PVIF_{10\%,1}) = 0.9091$ from Exhibit 5-2. Thus, the answer is

$$PV = \$1,320 \times 0.9091 = \$1,200.01$$

Notice once again, the answer obtained from the financial mathematics tables is slightly different than the answer obtained by working through the mathematics or by using the calculator. This is again because the factors in the financial mathematics tables are rounded to four decimal places.

Now let us practice what we have just learned. Calculate the present value in the following problem using each of the three methods. Your grandmother promises to deposit a lump sum into an account today to pay for the first year's tuition of your newborn child. Assume your child's first year of tuition will have to be paid 18 years from now and will be in the amount of $30,000. How much will

Value of $1 Discounted at *i*% per Period for *n* Periods

Periods	1%	2%	3%	4%	5%	6%	7%	8%	9%	10%
1	0.9901	0.9804	0.9709	0.9615	0.9524	0.9434	0.9346	0.9259	0.9174	0.9091
2	0.9803	0.9612	0.9426	0.9246	0.9070	0.8900	0.8734	0.8573	0.8417	0.8264
3	0.9706	0.9423	0.9151	0.8890	0.8638	0.8396	0.8163	0.7938	0.7722	0.7513
4	0.9610	0.9238	0.8885	0.8548	0.8227	0.7921	0.7629	0.7350	0.7084	0.6830
5	0.9515	0.9057	0.8626	0.8219	0.7835	0.7473	0.7130	0.6806	0.6499	0.6209
6	0.9420	0.8880	0.8375	0.7903	0.7462	0.7050	0.6663	0.6302	0.5963	0.5645
7	0.9327	0.8706	0.8131	0.7599	0.7107	0.6651	0.6227	0.5835	0.5470	0.5132
8	0.9235	0.8535	0.7894	0.7307	0.6768	0.6274	0.5820	0.5403	0.5019	0.4665
9	0.9143	0.8368	0.7664	0.7026	0.6446	0.5919	0.5439	0.5002	0.4604	0.4241
10	0.9053	0.8203	0.7441	0.6756	0.6139	0.5584	0.5083	0.4632	0.4224	0.3855
11	0.8963	0.8043	0.7224	0.6496	0.5847	0.5268	0.4751	0.4289	0.3875	0.3505
12	0.8874	0.7885	0.7014	0.6246	0.5568	0.4970	0.4440	0.3971	0.3555	0.3186
13	0.8787	0.7730	0.6810	0.6006	0.5303	0.4688	0.4150	0.3677	0.3262	0.2897
14	0.8700	0.7579	0.6611	0.5775	0.5051	0.4423	0.3878	0.3405	0.2992	0.2633
15	0.8613	0.7430	0.6419	0.5553	0.4810	0.4173	0.3624	0.3152	0.2745	0.2394
16	0.8528	0.7284	0.6232	0.5339	0.4581	0.3936	0.3387	0.2919	0.2519	0.2176
17	0.8444	0.7142	0.6050	0.5134	0.4363	0.3714	0.3166	0.2703	0.2311	0.1978
18	0.8360	0.7002	0.5874	0.4936	0.4155	0.3503	0.2959	0.2502	0.2120	0.1799
19	0.8277	0.6864	0.5703	0.4746	0.3957	0.3305	0.2765	0.2317	0.1945	0.1635
20	0.8195	0.6730	0.5537	0.4564	0.3769	0.3118	0.2584	0.2145	0.1784	0.1486
25	0.7798	0.6095	0.4776	0.3751	0.2953	0.2330	0.1842	0.1460	0.1160	0.0923
30	0.7419	0.5521	0.4120	0.3083	0.2314	0.1741	0.1314	0.0994	0.0754	0.0573
40	0.6717	0.4529	0.3066	0.2083	0.1420	0.0972	0.0668	0.0460	0.0318	0.0221
50	0.6080	0.3715	0.2281	0.1407	0.0872	0.0543	0.0339	0.0213	0.0134	0.0085

Periods	11%	12%	13%	14%	15%	16%	17%	18%	19%	20%
1	0.9009	0.8929	0.8850	0.8772	0.8696	0.8621	0.8547	0.8475	0.8403	0.8333
2	0.8116	0.7972	0.7831	0.7695	0.7561	0.7432	0.7305	0.7182	0.7062	0.6944
3	0.7312	0.7118	0.6931	0.6750	0.6575	0.6407	0.6244	0.6086	0.5934	0.5787
4	0.6587	0.6355	0.6133	0.5921	0.5718	0.5523	0.5337	0.5158	0.4987	0.4823
5	0.5935	0.5674	0.5428	0.5194	0.4972	0.4761	0.4561	0.4371	0.4190	0.4019
6	0.5346	0.5066	0.4803	0.4556	0.4323	0.4104	0.3898	0.3704	0.3521	0.3349
7	0.4817	0.4523	0.4251	0.3996	0.3759	0.3538	0.3332	0.3139	0.2959	0.2791
8	0.4339	0.4039	0.3762	0.3506	0.3269	0.3050	0.2848	0.2660	0.2487	0.2326
9	0.3909	0.3606	0.3329	0.3075	0.2843	0.2630	0.2434	0.2255	0.2090	0.1938
10	0.3522	0.3220	0.2946	0.2697	0.2472	0.2267	0.2080	0.1911	0.1756	0.1615
11	0.3173	0.2875	0.2607	0.2366	0.2149	0.1954	0.1778	0.1619	0.1476	0.1346
12	0.2858	0.2567	0.2307	0.2076	0.1869	0.1685	0.1520	0.1372	0.1240	0.1122
13	0.2575	0.2292	0.2042	0.1821	0.1625	0.1452	0.1299	0.1163	0.1042	0.0935
14	0.2320	0.2046	0.1807	0.1597	0.1413	0.1252	0.1110	0.0985	0.0876	0.0779
15	0.2090	0.1827	0.1599	0.1401	0.1229	0.1079	0.0949	0.0835	0.0736	0.0649
16	0.1883	0.1631	0.1415	0.1229	0.1069	0.0930	0.0811	0.0708	0.0618	0.0541
17	0.1696	0.1456	0.1252	0.1078	0.0929	0.0802	0.0693	0.0600	0.0520	0.0451
18	0.1528	0.1300	0.1108	0.0946	0.0808	0.0691	0.0592	0.0508	0.0437	0.0376
19	0.1377	0.1161	0.0981	0.0829	0.0703	0.0596	0.0506	0.0431	0.0367	0.0313
20	0.1240	0.1037	0.0868	0.0728	0.0611	0.0514	0.0433	0.0365	0.0308	0.0261
25	0.0736	0.0588	0.0471	0.0378	0.0304	0.0245	0.0197	0.0160	0.0129	0.0105
30	0.0437	0.0334	0.0256	0.0196	0.0151	0.0116	0.0090	0.0070	0.0054	0.0042
40	0.0154	0.0107	0.0075	0.0053	0.0037	0.0026	0.0019	0.0013	0.0010	0.0007
50	0.0054	0.0035	0.0022	0.0014	0.0009	0.0006	0.0004	0.0003	0.0002	0.0001

Exhibit 5-2 Present value interest factor.

your grandmother have to deposit into this account that promises to pay 8 percent annual interest?

Let us start out with a timeline to help organize and visualize the problem:

```
0                                                            18
├──────────────────────────────────────────────────────────┤
PV = ? ←─────────────────────────────────── FV₁₈ = $30,000
              8% interest for 18 years
```

Now solve the problem using each of the three methods.

Equation: $PV = \dfrac{\$30,000}{(1 + 8\%)^{18}} = \$7,507.47$

Calculator: $FV = \$30,000 \quad n = 18 \quad i = 8\%$ then compute $PV = \$7,507.47$

Exhibit 5-2: $PV = \$30,000 \times (PVIF_{8\%,18}) = \$30,000 \times (0.2502) = \$7,506.00$

All three methods arrive at the same answer, except the answer from Exhibit 5-2 is a bit lower. Factors from the tables are rounded to four decimal places, and as a result problems solved using the tables will not be quite as accurate as answers obtained by solving the mathematics equation or answers obtained by using the programmed financial functions of a business calculator.

In August of 1982 McDonald's Corporation issued two money multiplier notes. The first sold for $250 and promised to return $1,000 twelve years later. The second sold for $500 and promised to return $1,000 six years later. When McDonald's sold these notes, they were essentially borrowing money from the investors who purchased them.

What is McDonald's cost of borrowing $250 for twelve years or the return to the investor lending McDonald's $250 for twelve years? Financial mathematics can be used to answer this question. The $250 selling price of the first money multiplier note is a present value (*PV*) and the $1,000 paid back at the end of twelve years is a future value (*FV*). The interest cost to McDonald's or the interest return to the investor is computed as follows.

$PV = \dfrac{FV}{(1 + i)^n}$ where the $PV = \$250$, $FV = \$1,000$, and $n = 12$, so we have

$\$250 = \dfrac{\$1,000}{(1 + i)^{12}}$ where $i = 12.25\%$

We can also compute McDonald's cost of borrowing the $500 for six years or the return to the investor lending McDonald's $500 for six years in a similar manner using financial mathematics. The $500 selling price of the second money multiplier note is a present value (*PV*), and the $1,000 paid back at the end of six years is a future value (*FV*). The interest cost to McDonald's or the interest return to the investor is computed as follows.

$PV = \dfrac{FV}{(1 + i)^n}$ where the $PV = \$500$, $FV = \$1,000$, and $n = 6$, so we have

$\$500 = \dfrac{\$1,000}{(1 + i)^6}$ where $i = 12.25\%$

So the interest cost to McDonald's or the interest return to the investor is the same on both money multiplier notes.

Exhibit 5-3   The time value of money in the hospitality industry.

5.4 FUTURE VALUE OF AN ANNUITY

Instead of finding the future value of a single lump sum, we are now going to find the future value of a series of payments called annuity payments. An **annuity** is defined as a *series* of payments of a *fixed amount* for a specified number of *periods of equal length*. We are faced with annuities often in our everyday life. Examples include the car payments you make to pay off a car loan, the mortgage payments made to pay off a home mortgage, or even the lease payments you make on an apartment rental to fulfill a rent contract. Of course, these examples call for monthly payments, but for the time being we will look at solving problems with annual payments. Later, we will explain how to solve problems with monthly payments or other periodic payments.

All annuities consist of a series of equal, periodic payments and a single lump sum. If the single lump sum follows after the payments, then it will be a future value of an annuity. For example, suppose you plan to deposit $1,000 annually into an account at the end of each of the next five years. If the account pays 12 percent annually, what is the value of the account after five years? This can be viewed on a timeline as follows.

The timeline shows five annual payments of $1,000 each, and "$FVA_5$ = ?" indicates we are looking for the future value of the five payments at the end of five years. The FVA_5, the future value of the annuity, is the single lump sum associated with the annuity. Because this lump sum follows the payments in time, this is a future value of an annuity problem. How do we solve this type of problem? We will show you four methods to solve this problem.

1. Compute the future value of each payment individually and then add them up. In other words, view the problem as the sum of the future value of five lump sums.
2. Work through the mathematics of the future value of an annuity equation.
3. Use a calculator programmed for financial mathematics.
4. Use Exhibit 5-4.

Each of these four methods will generate the same answer to the problem.

First, we will compute the future value of each payment and then add. Let us revisit the timeline with some additional detail to help explain this method.

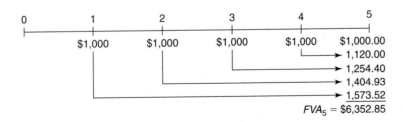

Future Value of $1 per Periods for *n* Periods Earning *i*% Interest per Period

Periods	1%	2%	3%	4%	5%	6%	7%	8%	9%	10%
1	1.0000	1.0000	1.0000	1.0000	1.0000	1.0000	1.0000	1.0000	1.0000	1.0000
2	2.0100	2.0200	2.0300	2.0400	2.0500	2.0600	2.0700	2.0800	2.0900	2.1000
3	3.0301	3.0604	3.0909	3.1216	3.1525	3.1836	3.2149	3.2464	3.2781	3.3100
4	4.0604	4.1216	4.1836	4.2465	4.3101	4.3746	4.4399	4.5061	4.5731	4.6410
5	5.1010	5.2040	5.3091	5.4163	5.5256	5.6371	5.7507	5.8666	5.9847	6.1051
6	6.1520	6.3081	6.4684	6.6330	6.8019	6.9753	7.1533	7.3359	7.5233	7.7156
7	7.2135	7.4343	7.6625	7.8983	8.1420	8.3938	8.6540	8.9228	9.2004	9.4872
8	8.2857	8.5830	8.8923	9.2142	9.5491	9.8975	10.2598	10.6366	11.0285	11.4359
9	9.3685	9.7546	10.1591	10.5828	11.0266	11.4913	11.9780	12.4876	13.0210	13.5795
10	10.4622	10.9497	11.4639	12.0061	12.5779	13.1808	13.8164	14.4866	15.1929	15.9374
11	11.5668	12.1687	12.8078	13.4864	14.2068	14.9716	15.7836	16.6455	17.5603	18.5312
12	12.6825	13.4121	14.1920	15.0258	15.9171	16.8699	17.8885	18.9771	20.1407	21.3843
13	13.8093	14.6803	15.6178	16.6268	17.7130	18.8821	20.1406	21.4953	22.9534	24.5227
14	14.9474	15.9739	17.0863	18.2919	19.5986	21.0151	22.5505	24.2149	26.0192	27.9750
15	16.0969	17.2934	18.5989	20.0236	21.5786	23.2760	25.1290	27.1521	29.3609	31.7725
16	17.2579	18.6393	20.1569	21.8245	23.6575	25.6725	27.8881	30.3243	33.0034	35.9497
17	18.4304	20.0121	21.7616	23.6975	25.8404	28.2129	30.8402	33.7502	36.9737	40.5447
18	19.6147	21.4123	23.4144	25.6454	28.1324	30.9057	33.9990	37.4502	41.3013	45.5992
19	20.8109	22.8406	25.1169	27.6712	30.5390	33.7600	37.3790	41.4463	46.0185	51.1591
20	22.0190	24.2974	26.8704	29.7781	33.0660	36.7856	40.9955	45.7620	51.1601	57.2750
25	28.2432	32.0303	36.4593	41.6459	47.7271	54.8645	63.2490	73.1059	84.7009	98.3471
30	34.7849	40.5681	47.5754	56.0849	66.4388	79.0582	94.4608	113.2832	136.3075	164.4940
40	48.8864	60.4020	75.4013	95.0255	120.7998	154.7620	199.6351	259.0565	337.8824	442.5926
50	64.4632	84.5794	112.7969	152.6671	209.3480	290.3359	406.5289	573.7702	815.0836	1163.9085

Periods	11%	12%	13%	14%	15%	16%	17%	18%	19%	20%
1	1.0000	1.0000	1.0000	1.0000	1.0000	1.0000	1.0000	1.0000	1.0000	1.0000
2	2.1100	2.1200	2.1300	2.1400	2.1500	2.1600	2.1700	2.1800	2.1900	2.2000
3	3.3421	3.3744	3.4069	3.4396	3.4725	3.5056	3.5389	3.5724	3.6061	3.6400
4	4.7097	4.7793	4.8498	4.9211	4.9934	5.0665	5.1405	5.2154	5.2913	5.3680
5	6.2278	6.3528	6.4803	6.6101	6.7424	6.8771	7.0144	7.1542	7.2966	7.4416
6	7.9129	8.1152	8.3227	8.5355	8.7537	8.9775	9.2068	9.4420	9.6830	9.9299
7	9.7833	10.0890	10.4047	10.7305	11.0668	11.4139	11.7720	12.1415	12.5227	12.9159
8	11.8594	12.2997	12.7573	13.2328	13.7268	14.2401	14.7733	15.3270	15.9020	16.4991
9	14.1640	14.7757	15.4157	16.0853	16.7858	17.5185	18.2847	19.0859	19.9234	20.7989
10	16.7220	17.5487	18.4197	19.3373	20.3037	21.3215	22.3931	23.5213	24.7089	25.9587
11	19.5614	20.6546	21.8143	23.0445	24.3493	25.7329	27.1999	28.7551	30.4035	32.1504
12	22.7132	24.1331	25.6502	27.2707	29.0017	30.8502	32.8239	34.9311	37.1802	39.5805
13	26.2116	28.0291	29.9847	32.0887	34.3519	36.7862	39.4040	42.2187	45.2445	48.4966
14	30.0949	32.3926	34.8827	37.5811	40.5047	43.6720	47.1027	50.8180	54.8409	59.1959
15	34.4054	37.2797	40.4175	43.8424	47.5804	51.6595	56.1101	60.9653	66.2607	72.0351
16	39.1899	42.7533	46.6717	50.9804	55.7175	60.9250	66.6488	72.9390	79.8502	87.4421
17	44.5008	48.8837	53.7391	59.1176	65.0751	71.6730	78.9792	87.0680	96.0218	105.9306
18	50.3959	55.7497	61.7251	68.3941	75.8364	84.1407	93.4056	103.7403	115.2659	128.1167
19	56.9395	63.4397	70.7494	78.9692	88.2118	98.6032	110.2846	123.4135	138.1664	154.7400
20	64.2028	72.0524	80.9468	91.0249	102.4436	115.3797	130.0329	146.6280	165.4180	186.6880
25	114.4133	133.3339	155.6196	181.8708	212.7930	249.2140	292.1049	342.6035	402.0425	471.9811
30	199.0209	241.3327	293.1992	356.7868	434.7451	530.3117	647.4391	790.9480	966.7122	1181.8816
40	581.8261	767.0914	1013.7042	1342.0251	1779.0903	2360.7572	3134.5218	4163.2130	5529.8290	7343.8578
50	1668.7712	2400.0182	3459.5071	4994.5213	7217.7163	10435.6488	15089.5017	21813.0937	31515.3363	45497.1908

Exhibit 5-4   Future value interest factor for an annuity.

The timeline on page 95 shows the first, second, third, and fourth $1,000 payments earning 12 percent interest for 4, 3, 2, and 1 years, respectively. The fifth payment is already a future value in five years and thus earns no interest. We would have the following:

$$FVA_5 = \$1,000 \times (1.12)^4 + 1,000 \times (1.12)^3 + 1,000 \times (1.12)^2$$
$$+ 1,000 \times (1.12) + 1,000$$
$$= \$1,573.52 + 1,404.93 + 1,254.40 + 1,120.00 + 1,000 = \$6,352.85$$

The preceding equation summing the future value of five lump sum payments to obtain the future value of an annuity can be simplified to the following equation.

$$FVA_5 = \$1,000 \times \left[\frac{(1 + 12\%)^5 - 1}{12\%} \right] = \$6,352.85$$

Thus we have just solved the future value of an annuity with the second method. We have worked through the mathematics of the future value of an annuity equation. This equation can be expressed more generally as

$$FVA_n = PMT \times \left[\frac{(1 + i)^n - 1}{i} \right]$$

We can also solve the problem using a business calculator. Enter the three variables we know:

$$PMT = \$1,000 \quad n = 5 \quad i = 12\% \quad \text{then compute } FV = \$6,352.85$$

We can also solve the problem using Exhibit 5-4. The table provides a factor that we multiply by the known annuity payment to solve for the future value. Because we are solving for the future value of an annuity, the factor in this case is called a future value interest factor for an annuity (FVIFA).

The $FVIFA_{i,n}$ is equal to $\left[\dfrac{(1 + i)^n - 1}{i} \right]$ so that the equation

$FVA_n = PMT \times \left[\dfrac{(1 + i)^n - 1}{i} \right]$ can also be written as $FVA_n = PMT \times (FVIFA_{i,n})$

To solve the problem using Exhibit 5-4 we can write the equation as

$$FVA_5 = PMT \times (FVIFA_{12\%,5})$$

where $(FVIFA_{12\%,5}) = 6.3528$ from Exhibit 5-4. Thus the answer is

$$FVA_5 = \$1,000 \times 6.3528 = \$6,352.80$$

Notice again, the answer obtained from the financial mathematics tables is slightly different than the answer obtained by working through the mathematics or by using the calculator. This is again because the factors in the financial mathematics tables are rounded to four decimal places.

Contracts calling for annuity payments can stipulate that either the payment is made at the end of each period, or the payment is made at the beginning of each period. The first type of annuity, in which the payment is made at the end of each period, is called an ordinary annuity. The second type, in which the payment is made at the beginning of each period, is called an annuity due. The example we just worked through is an ordinary annuity. When dealing with the future value of an annuity it can be quite tricky to properly identify an annuity as either an ordinary annuity or annuity due. We naturally tend to look at the first payment and when it is paid. This works fine for present value of annuities, which we will consider later, but it doesn't always work for future value of annuities. To properly classify the future value of an annuity as an ordinary annuity or an annuity due, we need to consider whether the last payment is at the beginning of the period or the end of the period. If the *last* annuity payment is at the *end* of the *last* period, then it is a future value of an ordinary annuity. If the *last* annuity payment is at the *beginning* of the *last* period, then it is a future value of an annuity due. Consider the timeline for the preceding example.

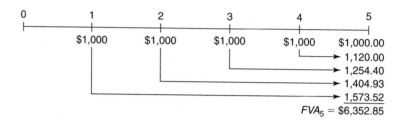

This is an ordinary annuity because the last payment is at the end of the last year, not because the first payment is at the end of the first year. The following timeline should help to clearly see the difference.

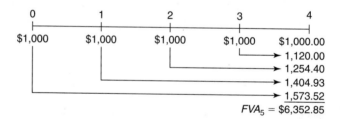

In the immediately preceding timeline, the first payment is at the beginning of the first year, but the first, second, third, and fourth payments still earn interest for 4, 3, 2, and 1 years, respectively. The last payment is already a future value at the appropriate time and earns no interest. With a 12 percent annual interest rate, the future value of the annuity is the same as before. The distinguishing characteristic is that the last payment is still at the end of the last year. This is still an ordinary annuity.

To change the example to the future value of an annuity due, we need to solve for the future value one period after the last payment. The timeline will be as follows.

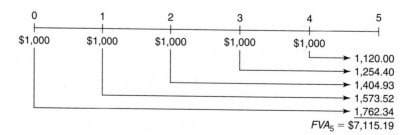

We can see in the preceding timeline that the last payment comes at the beginning of the last year. The first payment at the beginning of the first year does not make this an annuity due. Instead, the last payment at the beginning of the last year distinguishes this as an annuity due. In this future value of an annuity due, each payment earns one more period of interest than in the otherwise equivalent ordinary annuity. If each payment earns an extra 12 percent for one period, then the entire future value of the annuity due will earn an extra 12 percent for one period. Thus we can solve this problem using the following equation.

$$FVAD_5 = \$1,000 \times \left[\frac{(1 + 12\%)^5 - 1}{12\%} \right] \times (1 + 12\%)$$
$$= \$6,352.85 \times (1 + 12\%) = \$7,115.19$$

We can express the equation for a future value of an annuity due more generally as

$$FVAD_n = PMT \times \left[\frac{(1 + i)^n - 1}{i} \right] \times (1 + i)$$

Thus, the future value of an annuity due is always greater than an otherwise equivalent ordinary annuity by the amount of the interest rate for one period.

To practice what we have just learned, let us say you wisely decide to plan for your retirement when you graduate. You plan to open an Individual Retirement Account (IRA) and deposit $2,000 into this account every year until you retire 40 years from now. Assume you make 40 deposits in the form of an ordinary annuity (deposits at the end of each year). If your IRA earns 11 percent per year, how much will you have in your account when you retire in 40 years?

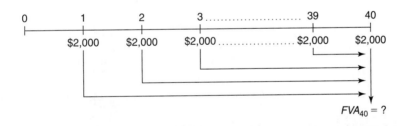

We can solve this by working through the mathematics of the future value of an annuity equation.

$$FVA_{40} = \$2,000 \times \left[\frac{(1 + 11\%)^{40} - 1}{11\%} \right] = \$1,163,652.13$$

When solving the problem using a business calculator, we need to enter the three known variables:

$PMT = \$2,000 \quad n = 40 \quad i = 11\% \quad$ then compute the $FV = \$1,163,652.13$

We can also solve the problem using Exhibit 5-4.

$$FVA_{40} = 2,000 \times FVIFA_{11\%,40}$$

where $(FVIFA_{11\%,40}) = 581.8261$ from Exhibit 5-4. Thus the answer is

$$FVA_{40} = \$2,000 \times 581.8261 = \$1,163,652.20$$

where this answer is slightly different than the other two answers due to rounding in the tables.

Are you surprised? After investing only $80,000 (40 times $2,000), you retire as a millionaire! The power of compound interest can often surprise. Investing $2,000 annually over a long period of time and earning 11 percent interest over this long period of time can create immense wealth.

How much more will the investment be worth if you invest the $2,000 payments at the beginning of each year, changing the problem to an annuity due calculation? Remember, the future value of the annuity will be higher by the amount of the interest rate earned on the entire future value for one year.

$$FVAD_{40} = \$2,000 \times \left[\frac{(1 + 11\%)^{40} - 1}{11\%} \right] \times (1 + 11\%)$$
$$= \$1,163,652.13 \times (1 + 11\%)$$
$$FVAD_{40} = \$1,291,653.87$$

Now let us consider an alternative investment in which instead of starting your IRA now, you wait for 20 years. In this case you only plan to make 20 deposits, so you will double the amount of these deposits to $4,000 annually at the end of each year. What is the future value of your retirement annuity at the end of the 20 years if you still earn 11 percent annually? Will the answer be the same as we calculated previously? After all, you are depositing twice as much money for one-half the number of years. Wrong! It turns out to be far less.

$$FVA_{20} = \$4,000 \times \left[\frac{(1 + 11\%)^{20} - 1}{11\%} \right] = \$256,811.33$$

Why is there such a huge difference? With 40 payments of $2,000 each, you end up with a future value of $1,163,652.13. With 20 payments of $4,000 each you end up with less than one-fourth as much. This illustrates the immense power of compound interest. In one case you are earning interest on interest for 40 years and in the other case you are earning interest on interest for only 20 years. So do not delay. Start saving for retirement as soon as possible.

5.5 PRESENT VALUE OF AN ANNUITY

Remember, all annuities consist of a series of equal, periodic payments and a single lump sum. If the single lump sum is before the payments, then it will be a present value of an annuity. For example, suppose you plan to withdraw $1,000 annually from an account at the end of each of the next five years. If the account pays 12 percent annually, what must you deposit today to have just enough to cover the five withdrawals? This can be viewed on a timeline as follows.

The timeline shows five annual payments of $1,000 each and "*PVA* = ?" indicates we are looking for the present value of the five payments. The *PVA*, the present value of the annuity, is the single lump sum associated with the annuity.

Because this lump sum is before the payments, this is a present value of an annuity problem. How do we solve this type of problem? We will show you four methods.

1. Compute the present value of each payment individually and then add them up. In other words, view the problem as the sum of the present value of five lump sums.
2. Work through the mathematics of the present value of an annuity equation.
3. Use a calculator programmed for financial mathematics.
4. Use Exhibit 5-5.

Each of these four methods will generate the same answer to the problem.

First we will compute the present value of each payment and then add. Let us revisit the timeline with some additional detail to help explain this method.

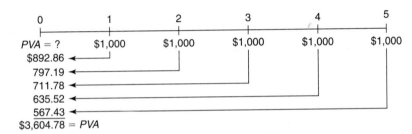

The preceding timeline shows the first, second, third, fourth, and fifth $1,000 withdrawals discounted at a 12 percent interest rate for 1, 2, 3, 4, and 5 years, respectively. This will give us the following present value of an annuity.

$$PVA = \frac{\$1,000}{(1 + 12\%)^1} + \frac{\$1,000}{(1 + 12\%)^2} + \frac{\$1,000}{(1 + 12\%)^3} + \frac{\$1,000}{(1 + 12\%)^4} + \frac{\$1,000}{(1 + 12\%)^5}$$

$$= \$892.86 + 797.19 + 711.78 + 635.52 + 567.43 + \$3,604.78$$

The preceding equation summing the present value of five lump sum payments to obtain the present value of an annuity can be simplified to the following equation.

$$PVA = \$1,000 \times \left[\frac{1 - \dfrac{1}{(1 + 12\%)^5}}{12\%} \right] = \$3,604.78$$

Thus we have just solved the present value of an annuity with the second method. We have worked through the mathematics of the present value of an annuity equation. This equation can be expressed more generally as

$$PVA = PMT \times \left[\frac{1 - \dfrac{1}{(1 + i)^n}}{i} \right]$$

We can also solve the problem using a business calculator. Enter the three variables we know:

$$PMT = \$1,000 \quad n = 5 \quad i = 12\% \quad \text{then compute } PV = \$3,604.78$$

Present Value of $1 per Period for *n* Periods Discounted at *i*% Interest per Period

Periods	1%	2%	3%	4%	5%	6%	7%	8%	9%	10%
1	0.9901	0.9804	0.9709	0.9615	0.9524	0.9434	0.9346	0.9259	0.9174	0.9091
2	1.9704	1.9416	1.9135	1.8861	1.8594	1.8334	1.8080	1.7833	1.7591	1.7355
3	2.9410	2.8839	2.8286	2.7751	2.7232	2.6730	2.6243	2.5771	2.5313	2.4869
4	3.9020	3.8077	3.7171	3.6299	3.5460	3.4651	3.3872	3.3121	3.2397	3.1699
5	4.8534	4.7135	4.5797	4.4518	4.3295	4.2124	4.1002	3.9927	3.8897	3.7908
6	5.7955	5.6014	5.4172	5.2421	5.0757	4.9173	4.7665	4.6229	4.4859	4.3553
7	6.7282	6.4720	6.2303	6.0021	5.7864	5.5824	5.3893	5.2064	5.0330	4.8684
8	7.6517	7.3255	7.0197	6.7327	6.4632	6.2098	5.9713	5.7466	5.5348	5.3349
9	8.5660	8.1622	7.7861	7.4353	7.1078	6.8017	6.5152	6.2469	5.9952	5.7590
10	9.4713	8.9826	8.5302	8.1109	7.7217	7.3601	7.0236	6.7101	6.4177	6.1446
11	10.3676	9.7868	9.2526	8.7605	8.3064	7.8869	7.4987	7.1390	6.8052	6.4951
12	11.2551	10.5753	9.9540	9.3851	8.8633	8.3838	7.9427	7.5361	7.1607	6.8137
13	12.1337	11.3484	10.6350	9.9856	9.3936	8.8527	8.3577	7.9038	7.4869	7.1034
14	13.0037	12.1062	11.2961	10.5631	9.8986	9.2950	8.7455	8.2442	7.7862	7.3667
15	13.8651	12.8493	11.9379	11.1184	10.3797	9.7122	9.1079	8.5595	8.0607	7.6061
16	14.7179	13.5777	12.5611	11.6523	10.8378	10.1059	9.4466	8.8514	8.3126	7.8237
17	15.5623	14.2919	13.1661	12.1657	11.2741	10.4773	9.7632	9.1216	8.5436	8.0216
18	16.3983	14.9920	13.7535	12.6593	11.6896	10.8276	10.0591	9.3719	8.7556	8.2014
19	17.2260	15.6785	14.3238	13.1339	12.0853	11.1581	10.3356	9.6036	8.9501	8.3649
20	18.0456	16.3514	14.8775	13.5903	12.4622	11.4699	10.5940	9.8181	9.1285	8.5136
25	22.0232	19.5235	17.4131	15.6221	14.0939	12.7834	11.6536	10.6748	9.8226	9.0770
30	25.8077	22.3965	19.6004	17.2920	15.3725	13.7648	12.4090	11.2578	10.2737	9.4269
40	32.8347	27.3555	23.1148	19.7928	17.1591	15.0463	13.3317	11.9246	10.7574	9.7791
50	39.1961	31.4236	25.7298	21.4822	18.2559	15.7619	13.8007	12.2335	10.9617	9.9148

Periods	11%	12%	13%	14%	15%	16%	17%	18%	19%	20%
1	0.9009	0.8929	0.8850	0.8772	0.8696	0.8621	0.8547	0.8475	0.8403	0.8333
2	1.7125	1.6901	1.6681	1.6467	1.6257	1.6052	1.5852	1.5656	1.5465	1.5278
3	2.4437	2.4018	2.3612	2.3216	2.2832	2.2459	2.2096	2.1743	2.1399	2.1065
4	3.1024	3.0373	2.9745	2.9137	2.8550	2.7982	2.7432	2.6901	2.6386	2.5887
5	3.6959	3.6048	3.5172	3.4331	3.3522	3.2743	3.1993	3.1272	3.0576	2.9906
6	4.2305	4.1114	3.9975	3.8887	3.7845	3.6847	3.5892	3.4976	3.4098	3.3255
7	4.7122	4.5638	4.4226	4.2883	4.1604	4.0386	3.9224	3.8115	3.7057	3.6046
8	5.1461	4.9676	4.7988	4.6389	4.4873	4.3436	4.2072	4.0776	3.9544	3.8372
9	5.5370	5.3282	5.1317	4.9464	4.7716	4.6065	4.4506	4.3030	4.1633	4.0310
10	5.8892	5.6502	5.4262	5.2161	5.0188	4.8332	4.6586	4.4941	4.3389	4.1925
11	6.2065	5.9377	5.6869	5.4527	5.2337	5.0286	4.8364	4.6560	4.4865	4.3271
12	6.4924	6.1944	5.9176	5.6603	5.4206	5.1971	4.9884	4.7932	4.6105	4.4392
13	6.7499	6.4235	6.1218	5.8424	5.5831	5.3423	5.1183	4.9095	4.7147	4.5327
14	6.9819	6.6282	6.3025	6.0021	5.7245	5.4675	5.2293	5.0081	4.8023	4.6106
15	7.1909	6.8109	6.4624	6.1422	5.8474	5.5755	5.3242	5.0916	4.8759	4.6755
16	7.3792	6.9740	6.6039	6.2651	5.9542	5.6685	5.4053	5.1624	4.9377	4.7296
17	7.5488	7.1196	6.7291	6.3729	6.0472	5.7487	5.4746	5.2223	4.9897	4.7746
18	7.7016	7.2497	6.8399	6.4674	6.1280	5.8178	5.5339	5.2732	5.0333	4.8122
19	7.8393	7.3658	6.9380	6.5504	6.1982	5.8775	5.5845	5.3162	5.0700	4.8435
20	7.9633	7.4694	7.0248	6.6231	6.2593	5.9288	5.6278	5.3527	5.1009	4.8696
25	8.4217	7.8431	7.3300	6.8729	6.4641	6.0971	5.7662	5.4669	5.1951	4.9476
30	8.6938	8.0552	7.4957	7.0027	6.5660	6.1772	5.8294	5.5168	5.2347	4.9789
40	8.9511	8.2438	7.6344	7.1050	6.6418	6.2335	5.8713	5.5482	5.2582	4.9966
50	9.0417	8.3045	7.6752	7.1327	6.6605	6.2463	5.8801	5.5541	5.2623	4.9995

Exhibit 5-5 Present value interest factor for an annuity.

We can also solve the problem using Exhibit 5-5, which provides a factor that we multiply by the known annuity payment to solve for the present value. Because we are solving for the present value of an annuity, the factor in this case is called a "present value interest factor for an annuity" (PVIFA).

The $PVIFA_{i,n}$ is equal to $\left[\dfrac{1 - \dfrac{1}{(1+i)^n}}{i}\right]$, so the equation

$PVA = PMT \times \left[\dfrac{1 - \dfrac{1}{(1+i)^n}}{i}\right]$ can also be written as $PVA = PMT \times (PVIFA_{i,n})$

To solve the problem using Exhibit 5-5, we can write the equation as

$$PVA = PMT \times (PVIFA_{12\%,5})$$

where $(PVIFA_{12\%,5}) = 3.6048$ from Exhibit 5-5. Thus the answer is

$$PVA = \$1,000 \times 3.6048 = \$3,604.80$$

Notice again, the answer obtained from the financial mathematics tables is slightly different than the answer obtained by working through the mathematics or by using the calculator. This is again because the factors in the financial mathematics tables are rounded to four decimal places.

Let us consider annuity dues once again but now in the context of the present value of an annuity. Remember that an annuity due occurs when the annuity payments are made at the beginning of each year. The example we just worked through is an ordinary annuity. When dealing with the present value of an annuity, it is generally easy to properly identify an annuity as an ordinary annuity or annuity due. We naturally tend to look at the first payment and when it is paid. This works fine for present value of annuities. To properly classify the present value of an annuity as an ordinary annuity or an annuity due, we need to consider whether the first payment is at the beginning of the period or the end of the period. Consider the timeline for the preceding example.

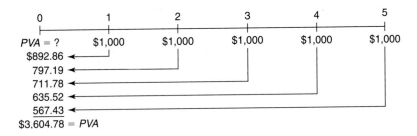

This is an ordinary annuity because the first payment is at the end of the first year. To change the example to the present value of an annuity due, we need to solve for the present value on the same date as the first payment. The timeline will be as follows.

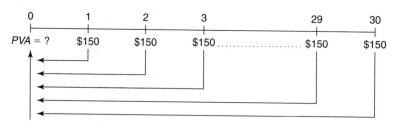

We can see in the preceding timeline that the first payment comes at the beginning of the first year. We can also see that the present value of the annuity due and the first payment coincide on the same date. In this present value of an annuity due, each payment is discounted one less period of time than in the otherwise equivalent ordinary annuity. If each payment is discounted for one less period at a 12 percent interest rate, then the entire present value of the annuity due will be 12 percent higher. Thus we can solve this problem using the following equation.

$$PVAD = \$1{,}000 \times \left[\frac{1 - \dfrac{1}{(1 + 12\%)^5}}{12\%} \right] \times (1.12) = \$3{,}604.78 \times (1.12) = \$4{,}037.35$$

We can express the equation for a present value of an annuity due more generally as

$$PVAD = PMT \times \left[\frac{1 - \dfrac{1}{(1 + i)^n}}{i} \right] \times (1 + i)$$

Thus, the present value of an annuity due is always greater than an otherwise equivalent ordinary annuity by the amount of the interest rate for one period.

Once again, time for some practice, which is the only way you will master the subject. Let us go back to thinking about your retirement, but now consider what will happen once you retire. Say you expect to live for another 30 years after you retire. To live as you desire in your "golden years," you will need $150,000 annually. If you expect to receive these payments at the end of each year from an account earning 6 percent annually, what lump sum must you have invested in this account one year before your first payment (withdrawal from the account)? Once again, we use a timeline to visualize this problem.

We can solve this by working through the mathematics of the present value of an annuity equation.

$$PVA = \$150{,}000 \times \left[\frac{1 - \dfrac{1}{(1 + 6\%)^{30}}}{6\%} \right] = \$2{,}064{,}724.67$$

Solving the problem using a business calculator, we need to enter the three known variables:

$PMT = \$150,000 \quad n = 30 \quad i = 6\% \quad$ then compute the $PV = \$2,064,724.67$

We can also solve the problem using Exhibit 5-5.

$$PVA = \$150,000 \times (PVIFA_{6\%,30})$$

where $(PVIFA_{6\%,30}) = 13.7648$ from Exhibit 5-5. Thus the answer is

$$PVA = \$150,000 \times 13.7648 = \$2,064,720$$

where this answer is slightly different than the other two answers due to rounding in the tables.

How much more will be needed if you withdraw the $150,000 payments at the beginning of each year, changing the problem to an annuity-due calculation? Remember, the present value of the annuity will be higher by the amount of the interest rate earned on the entire present value for one year.

$$PVAD = \$150,000 \times \left[\frac{1 - \dfrac{1}{(1 + 6\%)^{30}}}{6\%} \right] \times (1.06) = \$2,064,724.67 \times (1.06)$$

$$= \$2,188,608.15$$

Thus you will need a greater amount saved if you want to make the retirement withdrawals at the beginning of each year.

5.6 PERPETUITY—AN INFINITE ANNUITY

Our next concept is to find the present value of an infinite series of uniform, future payments. First, let us examine this concept to see if it even makes sense to proceed. Why would someone be willing to pay a set payment year after year, forever? This may best be examined through an example. It is probably easiest to understand this by first considering what is the interest rate of return on a **perpetuity.** We will look at this first and then move on to the present value of a perpetuity. Suppose a bond is contracted to pay $90 per year forever. The bond has no maturity; it continues forever. Also, assume you are willing to pay $900 for this bond today. What is the rate of return on this bond? In other words, what interest rate will equate the present value of the $90 annual cash flows with the $900 price you are willing to pay?

If you invest $900 today, you receive in return $90 annually forever. What is your rate of return? You will receive $90 each year, or a 10 percent return each year.

$$\text{Rate of return} = \$90/\$900 = 10\% \text{ annually}$$

We can write this equation more generally as

$$i = \frac{PMT}{PV}$$

where the rate of return is the interest rate, how much you are willing to pay today is the present value, and the $90 each year is the perpetuity payment. If instead we know the amount of the perpetuity payment and the interest rate, then we can rearrange the terms to solve for the present value.

$$PV = \frac{PMT}{i}$$

If an investment promises to pay $90 annually forever and the interest rate is 10 percent, then the present value can be readily calculated as follows.

$$PV = \frac{\$90}{10\%} = \$900$$

Are these types of perpetuity contracts actually available? Yes; for example, British Consul bonds are set up as perpetuity contracts. In addition, many corporations issue common stock paying a consistent dividend, and remember, common stock does not have a maturity date. This would be similar to perpetuity.

Let us practice some more by solving the following problem. Roadside Motels, Incorporated pays a $1.00 per share dividend on its common stock. This company is not expected to grow or shrink in the future. The only form of return you expect to receive if you buy a share of this common stock is the dividend. Because Roadside's common stock has no maturity date, your best guess is that the dividend will continue forever at $1.00 per year. If you believe a fair rate of return on Roadside common stock is 8 percent per year, how much will you be willing to pay for a share of Roadside common stock?

The present value of Roadside's future dividends based on the 8 percent rate of return is the most you should be willing to pay for a share of Roadside. We will discuss the valuation of common stock more in Chapter 7. The answer to the problem is

$$PV = \frac{\$1.00}{8\%} = \$12.50$$

5.7 PRESENT VALUE OF A DEFERRED ANNUITY

When calculating the present value of an annuity, it is vital to know if it is an annuity due, an ordinary annuity, or a deferred annuity. When the first annuity payment is made today, then it is an annuity due. When the first payment is made one period from today, then it is an ordinary annuity. We have already discussed how to calculate the present value for these annuities. When the first payment is made more than one period in the future, we call this a deferred annuity because the first payment is deferred more than one year into the future. For example, an investment promises to pay you $100 annually beginning at the end of year 5 and continuing until the end of year 10. If you decide 7 percent is an appropriate rate of return, what is the present value of these cash flows? Let us visualize this on a timeline.

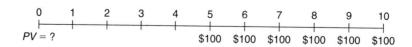

As you can see from the preceding timeline, this is an annuity. The first $100 payment is deferred until the end of year 5, so we call it a deferred annuity because the first payment is deferred more than one year. The first step in finding the present value of this deferred annuity is to calculate the present value of an ordinary annuity.

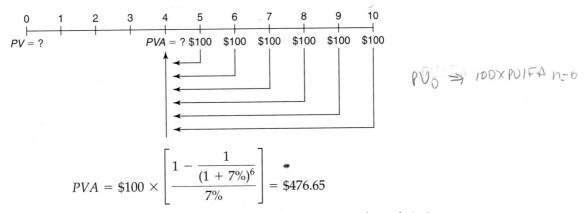

$$PVA = \$100 \times \left[\frac{1 - \dfrac{1}{(1 + 7\%)^6}}{7\%} \right] = \$476.65$$

Notice the exponent in the present value of an ordinary annuity formula is 6 because there are six payments. Also, the present value of an ordinary annuity is one period before the first payment; therefore, the $476.65 is at the end of year four as indicated on the timeline. To obtain a present value of the six cash flows today, there is still one more step, as shown by the next timeline.

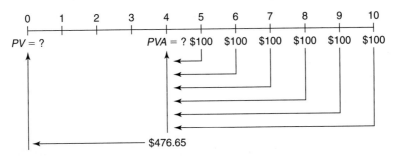

We must take the $476.65 at year four and discount this lump sum at 7 percent for four more years to obtain a present value today.

$$PV = \frac{\$476.65}{(1 + 7\%)^4} = \$363.63$$

We did the computation as two calculations, but the formula for the present value of a deferred annuity can be written as one formula.

$$PV = \$100 \times \left[\frac{1 - \dfrac{1}{(1 + 7\%)^6}}{7\%} \right] \times \frac{1}{(1 + 7\%)^4} = \$363.63$$

This formula can be written generally as follows.

$$PV = PMT \times \left[\frac{1 - \dfrac{1}{(1 + i)^n}}{1} \right] \times \frac{1}{(1 + i)^m} \qquad \text{where}$$

> *PMT* = deferred annuity payment
>   *i* = interest rate
>   *n* = number of deferred annuity payments
>   *m* = number of periods the first payment is deferred minus one

To use a business calculator to compute this present value of a deferred annuity, follow these steps.

1. *PMT* = $100   *n* = 6   *i* = 7%   then compute the *PVA* = $476.65
2. Clear the time value registers
3. *FV* = $476.65 (the previously computed *PVA*)   *n* = 4 (this is the "*m*" in the above equation but is input as "*n*" on the calculator)   *i* = 7%   then compute *PV* = $363.63

Let us do some more practice with another deferred annuity problem. Suppose you want to provide $25,000 annually for your daughter's college education. You will need the first $25,000 at the end of 15 years, and there will be four total payments of $25,000 each. If you can earn 8 percent annually, what lump sum do you need to invest today to provide for your daughter's college education? The following timeline helps to visualize this problem and shows how we will solve it.

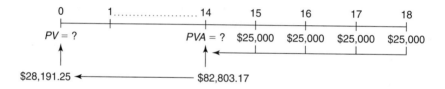

Because there are four annual payments and the first is at the end of year 15, then the other three payments must be at the end of years 16, 17, and 18. We first find the present value of an ordinary annuity, which is the $82,803.17 one year before the first $25,000 payment. This is year 14. Then we discount the lump sum of $82,803.17 back 14 years to arrive at the present value of $28,191.25 today! The computation is as follows.

$$PV = \$25{,}000 \times \left[\frac{1 - \dfrac{1}{(1 + 8\%)^4}}{8\%}\right] \times \frac{1}{(1 + 8\%)^{14}}$$

$$= \$82{,}803.17 \times \frac{1}{(1 + 8\%)^{14}} = \$28{,}191.25$$

We can now answer this present value of a deferred annuity several different ways. This should offer more insight into solving for the present value of a deferred annuity as well as help to understand ordinary annuities and annuities due better. First, let us solve the problem by computing the present value of an annuity due and then discounting this lump sum back 15 years to arrive at a present value today.

```
 0      1 .................. 14      15       16       17       18
 ├──────┼──────────────────┼───────┼────────┼────────┼────────┤
PV = ?                            $25,000  $25,000  $25,000  $25,000
                                  PVAD = ?  ◄──────────────────┘

$28,191.25 ◄───────────────── $89,427.42
```

$$PV = \$25,000 \times \left[\frac{1 - \dfrac{1}{(1 + 8\%)^4}}{8\%}\right] \times (1.08) \times \frac{1}{(1 + 8\%)^{15}}$$

$$= \$89,427.42 \times \frac{1}{(1 + 8\%)^{15}} = \$28,191.25$$

We can also solve the problem by computing the future value of an ordinary annuity and then discounting this lump sum back 18 years to arrive at a present value today.

```
 0      1 .................. 14      15       16       17       18
 ├──────┼──────────────────┼───────┼────────┼────────┼────────┤
PV = ?                            $25,000  $25,000  $25,000  $25,000
                                      └────────┴────────┴──────► FVA = ?

$28,191.25 ◄────────────────────────────────────── $112,652.80
```

$$PV = \$25,000 \times \left[\frac{(1 + 8\%)^4 - 1}{8\%}\right] \times \frac{1}{(1 + 8\%)^{18}}$$

$$= \$112,652.80 \times \frac{1}{(1 + 8\%)^{18}} = \$28,191.25$$

Finally, we will solve the problem by computing the future value of an annuity due and then discounting this lump sum back 19 years to arrive at a present value today.

```
 0      1 .................. 15      16       17       18       19
 ├──────┼──────────────────┼───────┼────────┼────────┼────────┤
PV = ?                      $25,000 $25,000  $25,000  $25,000
                                └────────┴────────┴────────► FVAD = ?

$28,191.25 ◄────────────────────────────────────── $121,665.02
```

$$PV = \$25,000 \times \left[\frac{(1 + 8\%)^4 - 1}{8\%}\right] \times (1.08) \times \frac{1}{(1 + 8\%)^{19}}$$

$$= \$121,665.02 \times \frac{1}{(1 + 8\%)^{19}} = \$28,191.25$$

There is always more than one way to solve a time value of money problem. Understanding the preceding four methods for solving the present value of a deferred annuity will lead to a much firmer grasp of the nature of annuities and how to work with them in time value of money problems.

5.8 PRESENT VALUE OF A SERIES OF NONCONSTANT CASH FLOWS

Now it is time to investigate how to value a complex stream of cash flows. Obviously not all cash flow streams meet the definition of an annuity. In this section, we will show you how to value a stream of cash flows that are not constant.

Let us start with an example. Say you are considering new kitchen equipment for your restaurant that is expected to save you $1,000 the first year, $500 a year for years 2 through 5, and $750 in the sixth year. If you believe 10 percent is a fair discount rate, what is the present value of this nonconstant stream of cash flow savings? We will start by visualizing the problem on a timeline.

Now let us solve this problem using the skills we have learned in this chapter. To solve in this manner, we need to break the problem into separate parts.

Step 1 Find the present value of the $1,000 lump sum to be received one year from now.

$$PV_0 = \frac{\$1,000}{(1 + 10\%)^1} = \$909.09$$

Step 2 Find the present value of the four-payment $500-a-year deferred annuity.

$$PVA = \$500 \times \left[\frac{1 - \dfrac{1}{(1 + 10\%)^4}}{10\%} \right] \times \frac{1}{(1 + 10\%)^1} = \$1,440.85$$

Step 3 Find the present value of the $750 lump sum to be received six years from now.

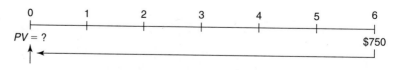

$$PV_0 = \frac{\$750}{(1 + 10\%)^6} = \$423.36$$

Step 4 Because all cash flows are now restated in present value terms, we can add these present values together.

$$\text{Total } PV_0 = \$909.09 + 1,440.85 + 423.36 = \$2,773.30$$

5.9 COMPOUNDING PERIODS OTHER THAN ANNUAL

Now let us relax the assumption we have been using regarding the length of the compounding period. Remember, to this point we have assumed annual compounding and annual payments. Yet there are many real-world applications using compounding and payments that are not annual. But do not worry; this will not be too difficult if you pay attention to the logic.

As an example, say you have $100 to invest for a year and have narrowed down your choices to two banks. The Third Bank of New York pays 10 percent annually, compounded annually, or the Second California Bank pays 10 percent annually, compounded semiannually (every six months). Is there really a difference between these two banks if you deposit your money for one year? The timelines show what will happen and the difference between the two.

On the first timeline, $100 earns 10 percent interest for one year:

$$FV_1 = \$100 \times (1.10) = \$110$$

On the second timeline, $100 first earns 5 percent (half of 10 percent) for six months:

$$FV_{0.5} = \$100 \times (1.05) = \$105$$

And then $105 earns another 5 percent for the second half year.

$$FV_1 = \$105 \times (1.05) = \$110.25$$

In the second half year, 5 percent interest was earned not only on the original $100 invested but also on the $5 interest earned in the first half year. The interest earned on interest in the second half year has contributed an extra $0.25 to the future value. The $110.25 answer could have been computed in one equation. The general equation for computing the future value when compounding is not annual is as follows.

$$FV_n = PV \times \left(1 + \frac{i_{nom}}{m}\right)^{mxn}$$

where i_{nom} is the **nominal annual interest rate,** m is the number of compounding periods in one year, and n is the number of years. Applying this equation to this example, we obtain

$$FV_1 = \$100 \times \left(1 + \frac{10\%}{2}\right)^{2\times1} = \$100 \times (1.05)^2 = \$110.25$$

Let us practice with an example you may find useful in your personal financial life someday. Say you are interested in a new car and venture down to your local car dealership to consider what they have to offer. Often the salesperson will want to quickly move the negotiation away from the total price you will pay to the monthly payment that will put you behind the wheel. They might be trying to take the intimidation out of buying the car, and they also might be trying to enhance the total price they can charge by masking the price through small monthly payments. A good tactic is to negotiate price first before you discuss financing.

So when you go to buy a car, bring your financial calculator along. Once you have settled on a price, use the financial calculator to be sure you obtain the best financing deal. Let us work through some numbers to illustrate.

You have found a car with a Blue Book value of $22,800. You have checked with your local bank and know you can obtain a five-year, 60-payment car loan at a 9 percent annual rate. You proceed to the dealership and are offered your dream car for less than $500 a month (by the dealership, not the bank). Actually the offer is for $498 a month for five years to be exact. To make the deal even more attractive, the salesperson says you can drive the car off the lot for no money down and the first payment is not due for one month. What do you think?

Let us analyze this deal. We can calculate the present value of this 60-month, ordinary annuity of $498 per month to obtain the implied price. Because we can obtain a car loan at a 9 percent annual rate, this should be our **discount rate.** Remember, the annuity payments are monthly. The interest rate and number of payments must be consistent with a monthly payment. The interest rate will be 0.75% or 0.0075 (9%/12) per month, and the number of payments will be 60 monthly payments in five years. With this information, we can obtain the present value of our payments and thus the price we are really paying for the car.

$$PVA_0 = \$498 \times \left[\frac{1 - \dfrac{1}{(1 + 0.75\%)^{60}}}{0.75\%} \right] = \$23,990.34$$

Surprised? You should not be. If the car should be priced at $22,800 or less, then the salesperson is trying to hide the higher price behind the monthly payments. If you bought the car for $22,800 and financed the purchase through the bank at 9 percent, then each of your 60 monthly payments would be as follows.

$$\$22,800 = PMT \times \left[\frac{1 - \dfrac{1}{(1 + 0.75\%)^{60}}}{0.75\%} \right] \qquad PMT = \$473.29$$

Learn time value of money concepts, and this is one area where you can save some money.

5.10 EFFECTIVE ANNUAL RATES

When compounding periods are not annual, the actual annual interest rate paid or received is referred to as the **effective annual rate.** Go back and consider the initial example in the last section. Remember, if you deposit $100.00 in an account earning 10 percent annually, compounded annually, then you will have a future value of $110.00 after one year. However, when the compounding is changed to 10 percent annually, compounded semiannually, then you will have a slightly greater future value of $110.25 after one year. We already know this greater future value is due to earning interest on interest during the year. So instead of earning 10 percent interest over one year, when the compounding is semiannual, 10.25 percent interest is earned over one year ($10.25/$100.00 = 10.25%). In other words, 10 percent annual, compounded semiannually, provides an effective annual interest rate of 10.25%. A general equation for calculating an effective rate is

$$\text{Effective Annual Rate} = \left(1 + \frac{i_{\text{nom}}}{m}\right)^m - 1$$

where i_{nom} is the nominal annual rate, and m is the number of compounding periods in one year. Applying the equation to this example we obtain

$$\text{Effective annual rate} = \left(1 + \frac{10\%}{2}\right)^2 - 1 = (1 + 5\%)^2 - 1$$

$$= (1.05)^2 = 0.1025 = 10.25\%$$

Appendix 5.2 shows an alternate way to compute effective annual rates using a business calculator.

When comparing interest rates that are compounded differently, convert the interest rates to effective annual rates, and then you can compare to determine which rate is effectively the lowest or highest.

5.11 AMORTIZED LOANS

Amortized loans are paid off in equal payments over a set period of time. In other words, an amortized loan is just an ordinary annuity in which the original loan amount borrowed is the present value of the future contracted payments. The terms of amortized loans are defined as follows.

PV = loan amount
PMT = contracted payment per period
n = number of payments
i = contracted interest rate
$FV = 0$

The future value is zero because you pay off the entire loan amount with the contracted payments over the life of the loan.

As an example, we will use a home mortgage with the following contract terms. The mortgage calls for borrowing $120,000 for 30 years with a contract interest rate of 9 percent annually ($\frac{9\%}{12} = 0.75\%$ monthly), and payments are due monthly with the first payment at the end of the first month. What is the monthly payment?

$$\$120,000 = PMT \times \left[\frac{1 - \frac{1}{(1 + 0.75\%)^{360}}}{0.75\%}\right] \qquad PMT = \$965.55$$

Month	Payment	Interest	Principal	Balance
0				$120,000.00
1	$965.55	$900.00	$65.55	119,934.45
2	965.55	899.51	66.04	119,868.41
3	965.55	899.01	66.53	119,801.88
4	965.55	898.51	67.03	119,734.85
357	965.55	28.43	937.12	2,853.73
358	965.55	21.40	944.14	1,909.58
359	965.55	14.32	951.23	958.36
360	965.55	7.19	958.36	0.00

Exhibit 5-6 Amortization table.

Notice that if you work out annual payments, they are more than twelve times the monthly payment.

$$\$120,000 = PMT \times \left[\frac{1 - \dfrac{1}{(1 + 9\%)^{30}}}{9\%} \right] \qquad PMT = \$11,680.36$$

Twelve times the monthly payment: $12 \times \$965.55 = 11,586.60$. The actual monthly payment will be $93.76 less on an annual basis than paying once a year. Why is this? Earlier we showed that compounding interest more frequently in the course of a year equates to a higher future value due to interest being earned on interest. The opposite holds true for discounting. More frequent compounding periods will reduce the total interest paid as the loan balance is paid down more frequently, and thus less interest is owed.

An **amortization table** is shown in Exhibit 5-6. When you finance a home with a mortgage, an amortization table for your loan is often provided. It shows the amount of each payment, how much of each payment is allocated to interest and how much is allocated to repayment of the **principal** balance, and your remaining principal balance owed at the end of each month assuming you make your payments on time.

Look at the first month of the amortization table. You see at the beginning that you owe $120,000. At the end of the first month, you will make your first payment in the amount of $965.55. First, calculate how much of this payment is allocated to interest. Remember, to this point you owe interest for one month at the rate of 9 percent annually, or 0.75% monthly on $120,000. Take the beginning balance of $120,000 times the monthly interest rate of 0.75 percent to obtain $900.00 owed in interest at the end of the first month. The remainder of your first month's payment is allocated to repayment of the principal balance ($965.55 − 900.00 = $65.55).

That is correct! You are making a payment of $965.55, and only $65.55 is allocated to repayment of the principal balance from the first payment. After paying $965.55, you owe $65.55 less. You still owe $119,934.45 at the end after making your first payment. The good news is that each subsequent month, less and less of your payment is allocated to paying interest and more and more of your payment is allocated to the repayment of the principal balance.

To be sure you understand the logic of an amortization table, let us consider what happens with the second monthly payment. During the second month, interest is accruing at the 0.75 percent monthly rate on the end of the first month's balance of $119,934.45. So interest from the second monthly payment is $119,934.45 × 0.75% = $899.51. The remainder of the second monthly payment is allocated to repayment of the principal balance ($965.55 − 899.51 = $66.04). Thus, the principal balance owed after the second monthly payment is $119,868.41. This is $66.04 less than the balance at the end of the first month ($119,934.45 − 66.04 = $119,868.41).

Notice what happens by the last payment. Only $7.19 of the $965.55 payment is allocated to interest, and the remaining $958.36 is allocated to principal to finish off the loan. So at the beginning of a typical 30-year monthly mortgage loan, most of each monthly payment is allocated to interest. But with each payment made, the principal balance continues to decline, and thus the interest allocation from each payment decreases, and the repayment of principal allocation increases. By the time you reach the last year of the loan, most of each payment is allocated to principal with just a small portion allocated to interest.

Now, let us consider how the preceding mortgage example would change if we still borrow $120,000 at 9 percent but repay the loan with monthly payments over 15 years instead of 30 years.

$$\$120{,}000 = PMT \times \left[\frac{1 - \dfrac{1}{(1 + 0.75)^{180}}}{0.75\%} \right] \qquad PMT = \$1{,}217.12$$

It may surprise you to see that the monthly payment does not double in size but only increases by a little more than $250. Actually, 15-year mortgages usually have a slightly lower interest rate than 30-year mortgages. This would cause the 15-year mortgage payment to be slightly less than calculated here. This does not mean the 15-year mortgage is necessarily the better deal. The preferred mortgage maturity depends on your financial situation, your willingness to accept risk, and investment opportunities available. However, now you have the ability to compare the various mortgage options to each other.

5.12 SUMMARY

The time value of money (TVM) concept was introduced in this chapter. A good working knowledge of time value of money concepts is crucial to an overall understanding of finance. Also, a good working knowledge of TVM concepts can be extremely helpful to your personal financial life. We have covered many TVM topics in this chapter. The major topics covered were

- The future value and present value of a lump sum
- The future value and present value of an annuity, an ordinary annuity, or an annuity due and the present value of a deferred annuity
- Solving for the present value or interest rate on a perpetuity
- Finding the present value of nonconstant cash flows
- Computations with nonannual compounding including the use and calculation of effective annual rates
- Understanding and computing a loan amortization schedule

KEY TERMS

Amortization table or schedule
Annuity
Compound interest
Compounding
Discounting
Discount rate
Effective annual rate
Future value
Interest rate
Nominal annual interest rate
XPerpetuity
Present value
Principal

DISCUSSION QUESTIONS

1. You are investing money at a 7 percent annual nominal interest rate. Would you prefer the rate be compounded more frequently or less frequently?
2. You are borrowing money at a 9 percent annual nominal interest rate. Would you prefer the rate be compounded more frequently or less frequently?
3. What happens to the future value of a single cash amount as the interest rate increases?
4. What happens to the future value of an annuity as the interest rate increases?
5. What happens to the present value of a single cash amount as the interest rate increases?
6. What happens to the present value of an annuity as the interest rate increases?
7. What are some examples of ordinary annuities?
8. What are some examples of annuity dues?
9. Why are effective annual rates generally greater than equivalent nominal annual rates?
10. What does a loan amortization schedule show?

PROBLEMS

Problems designated with **Excel** *can be solved using* **Excel** *spreadsheets accessible at* http://www.prenhall.com/chatfield.

1. What is the future value of $1,000 invested for five years at the following interest rates?
   a. 5%
   b. 8%
   c. 10%
2. What is the future value of $1,000 invested at a 7 percent rate for the following length of time?
   a. 2 years
   b. 5 years
   c. 10 years

3. What is the present value of $10,000 to be received in four years at the following interest rates?
   a. 4%
   b. 7%
   c. 12%

4. Using an 8 percent interest rate, what is the present value of $10,000 to be received in the following number of years?
   a. 3 years
   b. 6 years
   c. 12 years

5. A bond issued by Fried's Restaurants pays no interest but will return $1,000 in 15 years. If you buy the bond for $326.39 today, what will be your interest rate of return on the investment?

6. If you invest $4,000 in a certificate of deposit today, a bank promises the certificate of deposit will be worth $5,000 in five years. What is your interest rate return on this investment?

7. Brewer Resorts is considering the purchase of a piece of real estate for the future site of a new project. The real estate costs $5 million. A bank has offered to finance the purchase at a 7 percent interest rate with a 10 percent down payment. The loan would be repaid with 15 equal, annual, end-of-year payments. If Brewer borrows the $4.5 million (90 percent of $5 million), what is the amount of each payment?

8. Grace turned 25 years old today and would like to retire by the time of her 60th birthday. In addition to social security and her company pension plan, she plans to invest $3,000 annually into an investment that promises to return 9 percent annually. If her first $3,000 payment is on her 26th birthday and her last $3,000 payment is on her 60th birthday, what will be the value of this investment on her 60th birthday?

9. Andy wants to take out a loan to purchase a new home. He is willing to pay up to $10,000 at the end of each of the next 30 years to repay the loan. If the loan interest rate is 6 percent, what is the most he can borrow?

10. An investment costs $20,000 today and will return $3,000 at the end of each of the next 10 years. What is the interest rate of return on this investment?

11. Carl would like to save $100,000 by his 40th birthday to pay for a special midlife crisis vacation. He plans to achieve this by investing equal annual amounts each year beginning on his 24th birthday and ending and including a payment on his 40th birthday. If the investment pays an 11 percent interest rate, what is the size of each annual payment Carl needs to invest?

12. An investment of $1,000 annually at the end of each year for the next 15 years will be worth $30,000 at the end of 15 years. What is the interest rate return on this investment?

13. A $20,000 loan requires equal annual end-of-year payments for four years. **EXCEL** The interest rate is 10 percent.
   a. What is the amount of each loan payment?
   b. Construct a loan amortization schedule to include the amount of interest and principal paid each year as well as the remaining balance at the end of each year.

14. A $100,000 loan requires equal annual end-of-year payments of $38,803.35 **EXCEL** for three years.
   a. What is the annual interest rate?

b. Construct a loan amortization schedule to include the amount of interest and principal paid each year as well as the remaining balance at the end of each year.

15. An investment promises to return $2,000 at the end of each of the next 10 years and then $5,000 at the end of each of the next five years (years 11 through 15). What is the value of this investment today at a 7 percent interest rate?

16. An investment promises to return $8,000 at the end of each of the next eight years and then $3,000 at the end of each of the remaining seven years (years 9 through 15). What is the value of this investment today at a 9 percent interest rate?

17. You plan to invest $10,000 into a bank certificate of deposit for three years. The certificate of deposit pays a 12 percent annual nominal rate. What is the value of your investment in three years if the 12 percent rate is compounded at the following periods?
    a. annually
    b. semiannually (every six months)
    c. quarterly (every three months)
    d. monthly

18. You plan to invest $5,000 into a bank certificate of deposit for five years. The certificate of deposit pays a 6 percent annual nominal rate. What is the value of your investment in five years if the 6 percent rate is compounded at the following periods?
    a. annually
    b. semiannually (every six months)
    c. quarterly (every three months)
    d. monthly

19. An investment promises to return $1,000 annually with the first $1,000 to be received at the end of 10 years and the last $1,000 to be received at the end of 25 years. What is the value of this investment today at a 7 percent rate of return?

20. An investment promises to return $1,500 annually with the first $1,500 to be received at the end of 5 years and the last $1,500 to be received at the end of 12 years. What is the value of this investment today at a 5 percent rate of return?

21. Andy just won a lottery. The prize is 20 annual payments of $100,000 each with the first payment to be today. What is the value of this prize (the 20 payments of $100,000 each) today at an 8 percent interest rate?

22. You just celebrated your 25th birthday today. You plan to invest $1,000 annually, with the first $1,000 invested today and the last invested on your 59th birthday.
    a. What is the value of this investment on your 60th birthday if all invested funds earn 6 percent annually?
    b. What interest rate do you need to earn for the investment to be worth $150,000 on your 60th birthday?

23. You just celebrated your 25th birthday today. You plan to invest $2,000 annually, with the first $2,000 invested on your 26th birthday and the last invested on your 60th birthday.
    a. What is the value of this investment on your 61st birthday if all invested funds earn 6 percent annually?
    b. What interest rate do you need to earn for the investment to be worth $300,000 on your 61st birthday?

24. Mike is planning to provide for his son's future college tuition. He expects to need $40,000 in 15 years, $42,000 in 16 years, $45,000 in 17 years, and $50,000 in 18 years for this purpose. If he can earn 10 percent annually, what single amount does he need to invest today to provide for his son's future college tuition?

25. Mike is planning to provide for his son's future college tuition. He expects to need $40,000 in 15 years, $42,000 in 16 years, $45,000 in 17 years, and $50,000 in 18 years for this purpose. He plans to provide for this by investing equal annual end-of-year payments for the next 15 years. If he can earn 10 percent annually, what is the required amount of each payment?

26. Ted and Carol are planning to provide for their two daughters' future college tuition. The oldest daughter is expected to need $8,000 in 8 years, $9,000 in 9 years, $10,000 in 10 years, and $11,000 in 11 years. The youngest daughter is expected to need $14,000 in 14 years, $15,000 in 15 years, $16,000 in 16 years, and $17,000 in 17 years. If Ted and Carol can earn 8 percent annually, what single amount do they need to invest today to provide for their daughters' future college tuition?

27. Ted and Carol are planning to provide for their two daughters' future college tuition. The oldest daughter is expected to need $8,000 in 8 years, $9,000 in 9 years, $10,000 in 10 years, and $11,000 in 11 years. The youngest daughter is expected to need $14,000 in 14 years, $15,000 in 15 years, $16,000 in 16 years, and $17,000 in 17 years. Ted and Carol plan to provide for this by investing equal annual end-of-year payments for the next 8 years. If they can earn 8 percent annually, what is the required amount of each payment?

28. Larry plans to retire in his 60s. In addition to social security and his company pension plan, he has a supplemental retirement investment plan. All funds invested in this plan will earn 12 percent annually. From this supplemental investment plan, he hopes to make 20 annual withdrawals of $100,000, with the first withdrawal on his 66th birthday and the last on his 85th birthday.
   a. What single amount does Larry need to invest on his 30th birthday to provide for the 20 withdrawals of $100,000 each?
   b. What equal annual payment does Larry need to invest in order to provide for the 20 withdrawals? The first payment will be on his 31st birthday, and the last payment will be on his 65th birthday.

29. Larry plans to retire in his 60s. In addition to social security and his company pension plan, he has a supplemental retirement investment plan. All funds invested in this plan will earn 12 percent annually. From this supplemental investment plan, he hopes to withdraw $500,000 on his 66th birthday and also make 20 annual withdrawals of $100,000, with the first withdrawal on his 66th birthday and the last on his 85th birthday.
   a. What single amount does Larry need to invest on his 30th birthday to provide for these withdrawals?
   b. What equal annual payment does Larry need to invest to provide for these withdrawals? The first payment will be on his 31st birthday, and the last payment will be on his 65th birthday.

30. Larry plans to retire in his 60s. In addition to social security and his company pension plan, he has a supplemental retirement investment plan. All funds invested in this plan will earn 12 percent annually. Currently (assume today is Larry's 30th birthday), Larry has $15,000 invested in this plan. From this supplemental investment plan, he hopes to withdraw $500,000 on his 66th birthday and also make 20 annual withdrawals of $100,000, with the first withdrawal on his 66th birthday and the last on his 85th birthday.

a. To provide for these withdrawals, what single amount does Larry need to invest on his 30th birthday in addition to the $15,000 already there?

b. To provide for these withdrawals, what equal annual payment does Larry need to invest in addition to the $15,000 already there? The first payment will be on his 31st birthday, and the last payment will be on his 65th birthday.

APPENDIX 5.1   USING A BUSINESS CALCULATOR PROGRAMMED FOR FINANCIAL MATHEMATICS

Using a business calculator programmed to perform financial mathematics is a fast, efficient way to solve time value of money (TVM) problems, and most of you will probably depend on these calculators for this course. The Hewlett-Packard hp 10BII and the Texas Instruments BA II PLUS are both excellent financial calculators. In this section we will provide three rules to prepare your calculator for the computation of TVM problems. Also we will offer some tips for using, understanding, and getting the most out of your calculator. Understanding the information in this appendix will help you avoid making mistakes.

Rule #1: Clear the Financial Registers

The financial registers consist of five keys (keys are represented by [ ]): [N] for n number of periods or n number of annuity payments, [I/YR] or [I/Y] for the i interest rate per period, [PV] for the present value of a lump sum or the present value of an annuity, [PMT] for the annuity payment (this is not relevant for lump sum calculations), and [FV] for the future value of a lump sum or the future value of an annuity. The basic clear key on your calculator only clears the display; it does not clear the financial registers. It is important to clear the financial registers because the last value entered into any financial register key (n, i, PV, PMT, or FV) is stored until cleared. You may not use all five financial register keys for every problem. Thus, mistakes are likely to happen as you move from one problem to the next unless you clear the financial registers as explained.

Hewlett-Packard hp 10BII

[orange], [C All]   [C ALL] is the secondary function for the [C] key

Texas Instruments BA II PLUS

[2nd], [CLR TVM]   [CLR TVM] is the secondary function for the [FV] key

Rule #2: Set the Number of Periods per Year

Many business calculators allow the user to preset the number of compounding periods to something other than once per year. However, as a general rule, it is usually easiest to set compounding periods to once per year. This will help you to avoid mistakes and provide a uniform, consistent method of solving TVM problems. Many business calculators default to 12 compounding periods a year when a new battery powers up the calculator. We will show you how to set the calculators to one compounding period per year.

Hewlett-Packard hp 10BII

[1], [orange], [P/YR]   [P/YR] is the secondary function for the [PMT] key

Texas Instruments BA II PLUS

[2nd], [P/Y], [1], [ENTER], [CE/C]   [P/Y] is the secondary function for the [I/Y] key

Rule #3: Set Begin or End Mode

When computing problems that call for annuity payments, setting your calculator for ordinary annuity or annuity due is imperative. An ordinary annuity is one with payments at the end of each period. An annuity due is one with payments at the beginning of each period. This is explained more thoroughly later in this appendix. Setting the calculator for ordinary annuity or annuity due is only necessary when solving annuity problems. When solving lump sum problems, it does not matter.

Hewlett-Packard hp 10BII

If BEGIN is displayed on the bottom of the calculator screen (slightly left of center), then the calculator is in the *annuity due* mode and is set for an annuity due calculation. If BEGIN is not displayed on the calculator screen as noted, then the calculator is in the *ordinary annuity* mode and is set for an ordinary annuity. To change from one mode to the other, enter the following key strokes.

[orange], [BEG/END]   [BEG/END] is the secondary function for the [MAR] key

It does not matter if the calculator is in the BEGIN mode or the END mode; [orange], [BEG/END] will change it to the other mode.

Texas Instruments BA II PLUS

If BGN is displayed on the top, right-hand side of the calculator screen, then the calculator is in the annuity due mode and is set for an annuity due calculation. If BGN is not displayed on the calculator screen as noted, then the calculator is in the ordinary annuity mode and is set for an ordinary annuity. To change from one mode to the other, enter the following key strokes.

[2nd], [BGN], [2nd], [SET], [CE/C]   [BGN] is the secondary function for the [PMT] key and [SET] is the secondary function for the [ENTER] key

It does not matter if the calculator is in the BEGIN mode or the END mode, [2nd], [BGN], [2nd], [SET], [CE/C] will change it to the other mode.

Additional Tips on Calculator Use

Let us illustrate a basic calculation on each calculator. Consider an earlier example where $1,000 is invested for two years at 5 percent annually. Let us calculate the future value on each calculator. The last step for each calculator is **bold-faced** to indicate the step that computes the final answer.

Hewlett-Packard hp 10BII

[orange], [C ALL],   [1,000], [PV],   [2], [N],   [5], [I/YR],   **[FV]** and −**1,102.50** should appear on the screen.

Texas Instruments BA II PLUS

[2nd], [CLR TVM],   [1,000], [PV],   [2], [N],   [5], [I/Y],   **[CPT], [FV]** and **FV = −1,102.50** should appear on the screen.

The order of entering the input information (present value, number of period, etc.) does not matter if the proper key ([PV], [N], etc.) is hit after the information is entered. Notice the future value actually comes out to a negative number (–1,102.50) on both calculators. Does this suggest you now owe the bank money? Of course, you do not owe the bank money. This negative answer is simply an artifact of how the calculator was programmed. The logic is as follows. By placing a positive number in the [PV] register, you are receiving this money. When you solve for future value, the negative number computer for [FV] is saying this is the amount you need to pay back. Thus negative numbers indicate payments or cash outflows, and positive numbers indicate receipts or cash inflows. If the input dollar value is a payment (receipt), then the computed number must be a receipt (payment). Because the $1,000 is a payment by you to the bank, the intent of the calculator for this problem is that the $1,000 should be entered as a negative [PV]. The computed number will be a positive [FV] because it is a receipt to you from the bank. Negative numbers can be entered to the calculator by using the [+/−] key to change a number from positive to negative.

We suggest you generally ignore the sign in front of numbers when computing a dollar value. This will be the case when solving for [PV], [FV], or [PMT]. But when solving for the interest rate ([I/YR] or [I/Y]), or the [N], you will generally be entering two dollar values to the calculator as some combination of [PV], [FV], and [PMT]. In this case, you will need to enter one of the dollar values as a positive number and the other dollar value as a negative number. Let us illustrate this with an example. Suppose you plan to invest $1,000 today and leave it invested for eight years. What interest rate is required to end up with a future value of $2,000 in eight years?

Hewlett-Packard hp 10BII
[orange], [C ALL],   [1,000], [PV],   [2,000], [+/−], [FV]   [8], [N], [I/YR] and **9.05** should appear on the screen, indicating a 9.05 percent return will grow $1,000 to $2,000 in eight years. But try the calculation again without converting the $2,000 future value to a negative number (leave out the [+/−] after the [2,000]). **no Solution** will show on the screen. It does not matter if the [1,000] or the [2,000] is made negative. As long as the other is positive, the calculator will properly compute the answer.

Texas Instruments BA II PLUS
[2nd], [CLR TVM],   [1,000], [PV],   [2,000], [+/−], [FV]   [8], [N], [CPT], [I/Y] and **I/Y = 9.05** should appear on the screen. If both the [1,000] and [2,000] are entered as positive numbers or both are entered as negative numbers, then **Error 5** will show on the screen. Again, just be sure one of the two is positive and the other is negative, and the calculator will properly compute the answer.

APPENDIX 5.2   USING A FINANCIAL CALCULATOR TO COMPUTE EFFECTIVE ANNUAL RATES

A financial calculator can be used very quickly and simply to compute annual interest rates. Compute the future value of a lump sum for one year at the interest rate that is not compounded annually. If you use an easy number to work with as the present value lump sum, then the effective annual rate will be obvious from your computed future value. For example, in section 5.9 we invested $100 for one year at a 10 percent annual rate, compounded semiannually. Our future value was $110.25. Because we started out with $100, clearly the effective annual rate must be 10.25 percent because we earned $10.25 on a $100 investment ($10.25/$100.00 = 10.25%).

Let us try another example. Invest $100 for one year at a 6 percent annual rate, compounded monthly.

$$FV_1 = \$100 \times \left(1 + \frac{6\%}{12}\right)^{12 \times 1} = \$100 \times (1.005)^{12} = \$106.17$$

This can be obtained on your financial calculator with the following steps.

1. Be sure to properly clear out your calculator and prepare it for a new time value of money problem.
2. Enter PV 5 $100.
3. Enter $i = 0.50\%$ (the interest rate per monthly compounding period: $\frac{6\%}{12}$).
4. Enter $n = 12$ (12 monthly compounding periods in one year).
5. Compute $FV = \$106.17$.

Because you have earned $6.17 on a $100 investment in one year, the effective annual rate is 6.17%.

Fixed-Income Securities: Bonds and Preferred Stock | 6

Chapter Objectives

- To understand why bonds and preferred stock are generally classified as fixed income securities
- To understand basic bond terminology
- To understand basic bond features as detailed in a bond indenture
- To understand bond ratings
- To understand and know how to compute the value and yield to maturity on a bond
- To understand basic preferred stock terminology and understand basic preferred stock features
- To understand and know how to compute the value and yield to maturity on a preferred stock

6.1 INTRODUCTION

Corporations issue securities as a means of raising money. Investors buy securities because they hope to receive more back in the future than they paid for the securities today. Securities are generally classified as bonds, preferred stock, or common stock. We consider bonds and preferred stock together in this chapter because they are both considered fixed-income securities. In other words, if you invest in bonds or preferred stock, the cash you hope to receive back in the future is fixed and is not expected to vary. Investor return on bonds and preferred stock generally does not depend on the financial success of the corporation. Of course, if a corporation is a failure and has cash flow difficulties, this is likely to reduce your return on bonds and preferred stock. But if a bond promises to pay interest of $80 annually or preferred stock promises to pay a $5 dividend per share annually, it does not matter how successful the corporation is. The most the bond will pay is $80 annually, and the most the preferred stock will pay is $5 per share annually. Thus the upside return on bonds and preferred stock is limited to the fixed return contractually agreed on, and the return on the downside, in times of financial difficulty, could be as little as zero. Common stock is quite different than bonds and preferred stock in that the upside and downside returns are very much dependent on the financial success of the corporation. Common stock will be discussed in detail in Chapter 7.

Bonds and preferred stock are both considered fixed-income securities but differ from each other in several ways. The bond interest owed an investor is a legally binding contractual obligation, whereas preferred dividends owed an investor are not. As a result, the ramifications for failure to pay bond interest are more serious than for failure to pay preferred dividends. Also, bond interest is a tax-deductible cost to the paying corporation, whereas preferred dividends are paid out of after-tax income and thus have no tax-shelter value. Corporate bonds have a specific maturity; preferred stock is generally considered perpetual. In fact, these differences between corporate bonds and preferred stock show that preferred stock is a hybrid security. Preferred stock shares some of the characteristics of bonds and also shares some of the characteristics of common stock. The fixed-income characteristic shared by both bonds and preferred stock is why we consider these two securities in the same chapter, and it makes the valuation methodology for these two securities similar. The first half of this chapter will focus on bonds and the second half on preferred stock.

6.2 BASIC BOND TERMINOLOGY

When an investor buys a corporate bond, the investor is essentially lending money to the corporation. The investor is the creditor, and the corporation is the borrower. Bonds generally promise to pay back the principal at maturity and interest every six months until maturity. The principal is usually called the **par value** or the face value. Par values are usually $1,000, and bond prices are quoted as a percent of par value. Thus a bond selling for $970 would be quoted at a price of "97" (97% of $1,000 is $970). The interest rate on a bond is usually called the **coupon rate,** and the interest payment is called the coupon payment. The coupon rate is an annual rate multiplied times the par value to obtain the annual coupon payment. Most coupon payments are paid every six months. Divide the annual coupon payment by two to obtain the actual six-month coupon payment. Thus a bond with a 9 percent coupon rate will pay $90 annually (9% times the $1,000 par value), but the actual payments will be $45 every six months.

The term **bond** generally denotes any type of long-term debt security. If specific physical assets, such as equipment or real estate, collateralize a bond, it is called a **mortgage bond.** If a bond is not secured by collateral, it is called a **debenture.** Both mortgage bonds and debentures are backed by the cash flow of the issuing company, but mortgage bonds are safer because specific physical assets also back them.

Bonds also differ by seniority. **Seniority** refers to the order in which a corporation would pay off its obligations in case of financial difficulty. A senior obligation is paid before an obligation lacking seniority. Seniority among a corporation's bonds is often denoted by the terms *senior, junior, unsubordinated,* and **subordinated.** A senior debenture is paid before a junior debenture, as is an unsubordinated debenture before a subordinated debenture. A senior, unsubordinated debenture would have the highest seniority ranking and be paid first, whereas a junior, subordinated debenture would have the lowest seniority ranking.

6.3 BOND FEATURES

An investor in a corporate bond is essentially acting as a lender to the corporate bond issuer. Thus the investor and issuing corporation have essentially entered into a credit agreement that is covered by a credit contract, called an **indenture.**

Since 1990, firms in the hospitality and tourism* industry have issued more than 1,600 debt securities. These debt issues raised more than $360 billion to be invested in the hospitality and tourism industry by these firms. Numerous well-known firms have issued debt securities over this period of time, including

- Wendy's International Incorporated
- Venetian Casino Resort Group
- Carnival Corporation
- Hilton Hotels Corporation
- Landry's Restaurants
- Harrah's Operating Company
- Marriott International Incorporated
- Six Flags Entertainment Corporation
- Mandalay Resort Group

Some of the specific debt securities issued recently (2002) include

- A $338 million issue by Wynn Las Vegas LLC, owner and operator of the future Le Reve Casino in Las Vegas
- A $750 million issue by LaQuinta Corporation
- A $375 million issue by Park Place Entertainment Corporation
- A $140 million issue by Intrawest Corporation, an owner and operator of ski and golf resorts
- Eights issued totaling more than $2.8 billion by McDonald's Corporation
- A $150 million issue by Darden Restaurants Incorporated

As you can see, debt securities provide a significant amount of capital for firms in the hospitality and tourism industry.

*The phrase *hospitality and tourism industry* is used as defined by John R. Walker in **Introduction to Hospitality Management** (Prentice Hall, 2004).

Exhibit 6-1   Bonds in the hospitality and tourism industry.

The bond indenture is usually an extensive contract and often can be hundreds of pages long. It will describe the characteristics of the bond and also include a number of restrictions on the issuing corporation. These are called restrictive covenants and often include dividend payment limits, additional debt limitations, and restrictions on firm activities that might increase risk to the bond investors.

Bond characteristics are specifically explained by the indenture. Details include the nature of the interest rate and maturity. The interest rate on corporate bonds is usually fixed over the life of the bond, but sometimes bonds have an adjustable or floating interest rate. In this case, the rate adjusts to a predetermined market interest rate.

The maturity on most corporate bonds is fixed, but some features can cause a bond to be paid off before maturity. One is the **call feature.** If a bond is callable, the corporation can repay the bond early if it so wishes. The repayment amount is usually the bond's par value. Call features often come with a call deferment. For instance, a 20-year maturity, callable bond with a five-year call deferment cannot be called in the first five years of its life. Over the remaining 15 years of its life, the corporation can pay it off early. Many callable bonds also have a call premium that requires the corporation to pay an extra premium to an investor, in addition to the par value, if the bond is called prior to maturity. Call premiums usually start out at one year's worth of interest and then decline with time. For example, suppose the preceding bond had a 7.5 percent coupon rate and initially a 7.5 percent call premium. If the bond is called immediately at the end of the five-year deferment, the corporation would pay the $1,000 par value plus $75 (7.5% times $1,000 par value) to the investor for every $1,000 denomination owned. If the bond is called later, the call premium will decline 0.5 percent (7.5% call premium divided by the remaining 15 years to maturity) for each year after five years. So if the bond is called after six years, the call premium will be 7.0 percent, or $70.

There are two basic reasons why a corporation may call a bond prior to maturity. The first is to save on interest expense if market interest rates decline. The coupon rates on corporate bonds are generally fixed over the life of the bond. If market interest rates have declined, the only way to save interest expense is to call a fixed-rate bond early and refund with a new lower-interest rate bond. A second reason is to escape the restrictive covenants included in the bond indenture. For example, a large restaurant chain may want to acquire a smaller chain of restaurants, but restrictive covenants in a bond indenture may prevent this. The large restaurant chain could call this bond early and release itself from compliance with the indenture's restrictive covenants.

Another feature that can cause a bond to be repaid prior to maturity is the **put feature.** This is sort of the opposite of the call feature. A put feature allows an investor to demand the corporation repay the bond prior to maturity. This provides a measure of protection to the investor. Should the investor want repayment prior to maturity and the bond's market value has declined, a put feature will allow the investor to require repayment from the issuing corporation. Repayment is usually at par value. This protects the investor against an increase in the general level of interest rates and also against other events that would negatively affect the value of the particular bond.

A **sinking fund** feature may also cause early repayment of a bond. Without a sinking fund, a corporation would only pay bond interest each year and no principal. At maturity, the entire principal would then be due. This is similar to taking out a five-year car loan for $25,000 and paying only interest each month for 60 months. Imagine having to pay $25,000 all at once at the end of five years. This is sometimes called a "crisis at maturity" due to the possible difficulty of repaying a large sum of money all at once. A sinking fund eliminates this possible crisis at maturity by requiring the corporation to "sink" a certain sum of money into a fund for the partial early retirement of the bond. In the preceding example, suppose the 20-year bond had a total par value of $100 million. The sinking fund might require the corporation to redeem $6 million per year beginning at the end of year 5. After 15 years of early redemptions, only $10 million of bonds are left to retire at maturity ($100 million − 15 × $6 million). The redemption can usually be through open market purchases or through the use of a call feature. If the call feature is used, a lottery generally determines which bonds are called each year.

Bonds can have many other features in addition to those just discussed. For example, a bond can be linked to the corporation's common stock through a conversion feature or the issuance of warrants with a bond. Bonds can also have poison-pill features to discourage a takeover attempt. We have discussed some of the basic features affecting the return and redemption of corporate bonds and will not try to cover all possible bond features.

6.4 BOND RATINGS

Several companies rate bonds for default risk. These include Moody's Investors Service and Standard & Poor's Corporation. Bonds rated high for low-default risk will have lower interest expense. Bonds rated low for high-default risk will pay higher interest rates. The **bond ratings** and definitions are given in Exhibit 6-2 for Moody's Investors Service and in Exhibit 6-3 for Standard & Poor's Corporation. Exhibit 6-4 provides some current ratings for a few hospitality firms.

Aaa

The best quality bonds and preferred stock with the smallest amount of risk.

Aa

High-quality bonds and preferred stock. Their long-term risk is a little higher than Aaa-rated securities. Aa- and Aaa-rated bonds are generally known as high-grade bonds.

A

Upper-medium-grade bonds and preferred stock. Considered to have adequate safety but with possible problems in the future.

Baa

Medium-grade bonds and preferred stock. Currently considered to have adequate safety but with possible problems in the future. These securities have speculative characteristics.

Ba

Bonds and preferred stock with only moderate safety and having speculative characteristics. Their future is uncertain.

B

Bonds and preferred stock with only small safety and lacking desirable investment characteristics.

Caa

Bonds and preferred stock of poor standing. The level of safety may be dangerous.

Ca

Bonds and preferred stock are highly speculative and may be in default.

C

Bonds and preferred stock in the lowest rating class with poor prospects.

Note: Moody's applies qualifiers "1," "2," and "3" in each rating classification from Aa through Caa. The qualifier "1" indicates the higher end of its rating category, the qualifier "2" indicates the midrange, and the qualifier "3" indicates the low range.

Exhibit 6-2 Moody's investors service bond ratings.

AAA

Securities with the highest rating and considered extremely strong.

AA

Securities just slightly riskier than those rated AAA and considered very strong.

A

Securities with moderately more risk than those rated AAA and AA but still considered strong securities.

BBB

Securities with adequate safety, but more susceptible to changing conditions than those securities rated more highly.

All securities rated lower than BBB are considered to have speculative characteristics.

BB

The strongest of the speculative securities but still has speculative elements.

B

These securities are more risky than those rated BB but currently are likely to pay their obligations.

CCC

These securities have current safety problems, and continued success is dependent on favorable conditions.

CC

These securities have large current safety problems.

C

These securities are currently making payments, but this is likely to change soon. Issuing firm may have already filed for bankruptcy.

D

Indicates a default has already occurred.

Note: Standard & Poor's applies qualifiers "+" and "−" in each rating classification from AA through CCC to show a security's position with a rating classification.

Exhibit 6-3   Standard & Poor's corporation bond ratings.

6.5 VALUING CORPORATE BONDS

Remember, corporate bonds pay interest semiannually. The annual interest amount is equal to the coupon rate times the par value, which is the principal amount repaid at maturity. Bond par values are usually $1,000, and we will use this for the remainder of the chapter. To determine the value of a corporate bond, we will simply find

Company name	Moody's most senior bond issue rating (As of 7/21/03)	Standard & Poor's issuer rating (As of 7/21/03)
Avado Brands	Caa1	CC
Hilton Hotels	Ba1	BBB−
Mandalay Resort Group	Ba1	BB+
MGM Mirage	Ba1	BBB−
Royal Caribbean Cruises	Ba2	BB+
Six Flags	B2	BB−

Exhibit 6-4

the present value of the future cash flows an investor expects to receive. Again, there are two separate cash flows to value: (1) the coupon payments, and (2) the principal amount or par value. Although coupon payments are usually paid semiannually, for introduction purposes we will assume coupon payments are paid annually.

To illustrate how to value a corporate bond, let us consider an example. Suppose Sullivan Resorts Incorporated is looking to issue a 15-year corporate bond. The bond contractually promises to pay a 10 percent coupon rate and pay a par value of $1,000 at maturity. Assume a fair market rate of return on bonds of this risk class is 10% annually. Investors consider the market rate of interest as their required rate of return and will use this value as the discount rate to value these bonds. What is the value of one Sullivan Resorts' corporate bond?

First, we define our terms.

C = Coupon payment = Coupon rate × Par value = 10% × $1,000 = $100 annually

M = Maturity value = Par value = $1,000

n = The number of payments to maturity = 15

i_b = The investor's required rate of return on corporate bonds = 10%

V_b = The value of the corporate bond

The following timeline illustrates the cash flows on the Sullivan Resorts' bond.

```
   0      1       2       3 ............................ 14       15
   ├──────┼───────┼───────┼─────────────────────────────┼────────┤
   V_b   $100    $100    $100 ...........................$100    $100
                                                                 $1,000
```

Notice there are two separate cash flows here. We want to find (1) the present value of an ordinary annuity (the $100 annually), and (2) the present value of a future lump sum (the $1,000 at maturity). Once we find the present value of each part in today's dollars, we can add these together. The sum of the two present values will be the value of the corporate bond today.

V_b = PV of coupon payments annuity + PV of lump sum maturity value

Using our equations from Chapter 5, we can express this as follows.

$$V_b = C \times \left[\frac{1 - \frac{1}{(1 + i_b)^n}}{i_b} \right] + \frac{\$1,000}{(1 + i_b)^n}$$

We will use $1,000 for the maturity value in this generalized equation since the maturity value is usually $1,000 for corporate bonds. The equation for the above example is

$$V_b = \$100 \times \left[\frac{1 - \dfrac{1}{(1 + 10\%)^{15}}}{10\%} \right] + \frac{\$1,000}{(1 + 10\%)^{15}}$$

$$V_b = \$760.61 + 239.39 = \$1,000.00$$

Now think of the logic of this valuation. Our answer suggests it is fair to pay $1,000 for a contract that promises to pay us $100, or 10 percent per year, and give us our $1,000 back at maturity. Is this fair? Yes, if our required rate of return is 10 percent. We receive the 10 percent rate of return per year, and we got our investment back at the end of the contract. (See Appendix 6-1 for using a business calculator to solve for the value of a corporate bond.)

Note in the preceding example that the value of the corporate bond equals the par value. This happens because the coupon rate equals the investor's required rate of return. Whenever the coupon rate equals the investor's required rate of return, the bond value and par value will be equal. Bond investors say these types of corporate bonds sell at par. Many corporations try to issue bonds at par value, but not all. In addition, market interest rates change through time, so even those bonds issued at par will change in value over time as market rates of interest change. Therefore, let us explore the valuation of corporate bonds when the market rate of interest does not equal the coupon rate.

First, we consider how to value a corporate bond when the market rate of interest is less than the coupon rate. We will use the same example of the Sullivan Resorts' corporate bond. Remember the coupon rate is 10 percent, the maturity value is $1,000, and the years to maturity is 15 years. Again, for simplicity, assume the coupon payments are annual. However, now assume the market rate of interest is 8 percent. What is now the value of this corporate bond?

$$V_b = \$100 \times \left[\frac{1 - \dfrac{1}{(1 + 8\%)^{15}}}{8\%} \right] + \frac{\$1,000}{(1 + 8\%)^{15}}$$

$$V_b = \$855.95 + 315.24 = \$1,171.19$$

Does this make sense? Could the corporate bond sell for $1,171.19? Let us explore the logic. The bond is paying 10 percent interest per year, but you require only 8 percent. This is a good thing, right? Well, other investors will also see the advantageous coupon rate that is paid by this bond. Therefore, investors will bid the price up to $1,171.19, which is the price at which an investor will get back exactly 8 percent if they hold the bond to maturity. Therefore, as in this case, when the market rate of interest is less than the contracted coupon rate, the value of the bond is greater than the par value. When the value of the bond is greater than the par value, we say the bond is selling at a premium. The premium in this example is the $171.19 over and above the $1,000 par value.

Now, alternatively, let's look at the case of how to value a corporate bond when the market rate of interest is greater than the coupon rate. We will use the same example of the Sullivan Resorts' corporate bond. Remember the coupon rate is 10 percent, the coupon is paid annually, the maturity value is $1,000, and the bond matures in 15 years. Now, if we assume the market rate of interest is 12 percent, what is the fair value of this corporate bond?

$$V_b = \$100 \times \left[\frac{1 - \dfrac{1}{(1 + 12\%)^{15}}}{12\%} \right] + \frac{\$1,000}{(1 + 12\%)^{15}}$$

$$V_b = \$681.09 + 182.70 = \$863.78$$

Notice $681.09 + 182.70$ only equals 863.78 if you carry out your answers to more than two decimal places and then round back to two decimal places.

Does this make sense? Could the corporate bond sell for $863.78? Let us explore the logic. The bond is paying 10 percent interest per year, but you require 12 percent. This does not look good initially. Other investors will also see the disadvantageous coupon rate that is paid by this bond. Therefore, investors will bid the price down to $863.78, which is the price at which investors will get back exactly 12 percent if they hold the bond to maturity. Therefore, as in this case, when the market rate of interest is more than the contracted coupon rate, the value of the bond is less than the par value. When the value of the bond is less than the par value, we say the bond is selling at a discount. The discount in this example is the $136.22 under the $1,000 par value ($1,000 − $863.78).

The following are some rules about corporate bonds to keep in mind:

1. If i_b = coupon rate, then the bond sells for par value.
2. If i_b > coupon rate, then the bond sells for a discount (less than par value).
3. If i_b < coupon rate, then the bond sells for a premium (more than par value).
4. If i_b increases, then bond value decreases (inverse relationship between i and PV).
5. If i_b decreases, then bond value increases (inverse relationship between i and PV).

6.6 COMPUTING YIELD TO MATURITY ON CORPORATE BONDS

We can also compute the investor's **yield to maturity** for a given bond price with our valuation equation. Yield to maturity is the investor's rate of return if the investor buys the bond and holds it to maturity. Let us use the same example. Remember, Sullivan Resorts' corporate bond has a 10 percent coupon rate, a $1,000 par value, and 15 years to maturity. Compute the yield to maturity for an investor buying this bond for $900.00. The following timeline illustrates the cash flows on this Sullivan Resorts' bond:

0	1	2	3	14	15
($900)	$100	$100	$100	$100	$100
					$1,000

We can use the bond valuation equation to solve for the investor's yield to maturity.

$$V_b = PV \text{ of coupon payments annuity} + PV \text{ of lump sum maturity value}$$

$$V_b = C \times \left[\frac{1 - \frac{1}{(1 + i_b)^n}}{i_b} \right] + \frac{\$1,000}{(1 + i_b)^n}$$

In this case we are not solving for the bond's value. We know the bond can be purchased for $900 so we use this for the bond value and solve for the interest return.

$$\$900 = \$100 \times \left[\frac{1 - \frac{1}{(1 + i_b)^{15}}}{i_b} \right] + \frac{\$1,000}{(1 + i_b)^{15}}$$

$$i_b = 11.42\%$$

If the investor buys the bond for $900 and holds the bond until maturity, the rate of return will be 11.42 percent. Solving for the interest rate in the preceding equation is more difficult than solving for the bond value. When solving for the bond value, the present value of the annuity (coupon payments) can be solved separately from the present value of the lump sum (maturity value), and then the two present values can be added together. But to solve for the interest rate that equates the two present values to the bond value of $900, you must solve the whole equation simultaneously. The easiest way to do this is with a business calculator. Appendix 6-1 shows the easiest way to solve for the bond value is to solve the whole equation simultaneously on the business calculator. Similarly, Appendix 6-2 shows you how to solve for a bond's yield to maturity on the business calculator.

6.7 BONDS WITH SEMIANNUAL COUPON PAYMENTS

Most corporate bonds actually pay coupon payments semiannually, meaning every six months. We used an *annual* coupon payment to introduce you to the concept of bond valuation, but now we consider how things change when we allow the coupon payment to be paid semiannually. Let us once again use the Sullivan Resorts' corporate bond with a 10 percent coupon rate, a $1,000 par value, and 15 years to maturity. The 10 percent coupon rate is expressed as an annual rate, but it is paid semiannually. What is the value of this bond to an investor requiring a 12 percent rate of return? The complete equation should look as follows.

$$V_b = \$50 \times \left[\frac{1 - \frac{1}{(1 + 6\%)^{30}}}{6\%} \right] + \frac{\$1,000}{(1 + 6\%)^{30}}$$

$$V_b = \$688.24 + 174.11 = \$862.35$$

Notice the coupon payment is $50 because the coupon is paid every six months. If the payment is a six-month payment, then i and n in the present value of an annuity equation must be consistent with the six-month payment. Thus the interest rate must be a six-month rate ($12\%/2 = 6\%$), and the number of payments is 30, six-month payments in 15 years. An implied assumption is that the 12 percent required rate of return is a nominal annual rate, compounded semiannually. This allows us to simply divide the 12 percent by 2 and use the resulting

The following are typical quotations for bonds as listed in the *Wall Street Journal* for Thursday, November 14, 2002.

Bonds	Cur yld	Vol	Close	Net chg
AMR 9s16	20.0	325	45	−7.63
Hilton 5s06	cv	98	95	−0.75
McDnl 7.05s25	6.8	5	103.50	2.25

First, under the title BONDS, we see the company name abbreviated, the coupon rate, and the maturity. The "s" is just a separator, providing spacing between each bond's coupon rate and its maturity. The second column is the current yield expressed as a percent. This is calculated by dividing the bond's coupon payment by the closing price. The third column is the volume of $1,000 denomination bonds traded on November 14, 2002. The fourth column is the closing price of a bond expressed as a percent of par value. The fifth and last column is the net change in price from the previous trading day.

The first bond is issued by American Airlines, has a 9 percent coupon rate, matures in 2016, and has a current yield of 20 percent. The 9 percent coupon rate along with a $1,000 par value tells us the annual coupon payment is $90. Because the closing price is $450 (45% of $1,000), the current yield is $90/$450 = 20 percent. On November 14, 2002, 325 bonds were traded, and the price declined by 7.63 percent of the $1,000 par value, or $76.30 from the day before. Thus the closing price of the bond on November 13, 2002, was $526.30 ($450 + 76.30).

Notice the Hilton bond lists *cv* under current yield. This means the Hilton bond is convertible into common stock at a predetermined exchange rate at the discretion of the investors.

Exhibit 6-5   Corporate bond quotations.

6 percent as our six-month required rate of return. Because we are using a 12 percent nominal annual rate, compounded semiannually for the present value of the annuity, we must also use this for present value of the maturity value. So we have to use 6 percent for i and 30 for n in the entire equation. This simply implies the investor requires the same consistent rate of return for all bond cash flows, both the coupon payments and the maturity value.

Now, let us consider how to compute yield to maturity for the preceding bond if the bond is selling for $900. Again, we use the same basic equation.

$$\$900 = \$50 \times \left[\frac{1 - \frac{1}{(1 + i_b)^{30}}}{i_b} \right] + \frac{\$1,000}{(1 + i_b)^{30}}$$

$i_b = 5.70\%$, but this is a semiannual rate of return because both the payment and number of payments are expressed in semiannual terms. Multiply the 5.70 percent semiannual rate by two, and we have an 11.40 percent nominal annual rate of return, compounded semiannually for the investor's yield to maturity.

6.8 BASIC PREFERRED STOCK TERMINOLOGY

Preferred stock has seniority relative to common stock. A corporation must pay preferred stock dividends before paying common stock dividends, and in the case of financial difficulty, preferred stock has a claim on the firm's assets prior to

Since 1990, more than 104 firms in the hospitality and tourism* industry have issued preferred stock. These preferred stock issues raised more than $13 billion to be invested in the hospitality and tourism industry by these firms. Numerous well-known firms have issued preferred stock over this period of time, including

- McDonald's Corporation
- Royal Caribbean International
- MGM Grand Hotels Incorporated
- Wyndham International Incorporated
- Station Casinos Incorporated
- Motels of America Incorporated
- Marriott International Incorporated
- Country Harvest Buffet
- Rubio's Restaurant Incorporated

Recently, Six Flags Incorporated issued $250 million of preferred stock in 2001, and Sydran Group LLC, an owner and operator of restaurants, issued $110 million of preferred stock in 2000. Although not nearly as prevalent as debt securities, preferred stock, nonetheless, is a significant source of capital for some firms in the hospitality and tourism industry.

*The phrase *hospitality and tourism industry* is used as defined by John R. Walker in **Introduction to Hospitality Management** (Prentice Hall, 2004).

Exhibit 6-6   Preferred stock in the hospitality and tourism industry.

common stock's claim. It is called *preferred* stock because it has a *preference* over and above common stock when it comes to the firm's cash flows and assets.

Preferred stock usually has a **par value** of $25, $50, or $100. It pays a quarterly dividend, but the dividend is expressed as an annual amount. In fact, the annual preferred dividend amount is usually expressed as part of a corporation's preferred stock name. For example, "Six Flags $1.81 preferred" would most likely be the way investors would refer to Six Flags class B preferred stock that pays a $1.81 annual dividend.

We have previously discussed in section 6.1 how preferred stock is a hybrid security. By that we mean it shares some of the characteristics of bonds and some of the characteristics of common stock. We discuss preferred stock in the same chapter with bonds because both securities are considered fixed-income securities. In other words, unless a firm has financial difficulty, the cash return paid by bonds and preferred stock (coupon payments and dividends, respectively) are known with certainty.

6.9 PREFERRED STOCK FEATURES

Preferred stock typically promises to pay a fixed dividend. There is adjustable-rate preferred stock in which the dividend adjusts along with market interest rates. There is also participating preferred stock in which the preferred investors share, to a limited extent, in the firm's earnings. But most preferred stock pays a fixed dividend. Although preferred stock has no stated maturity, it is often redeemed at some point in the future through the provisions of a **sinking fund** or a call feature. A sinking fund on preferred stock works much as it does on a bond. A preferred stock sinking fund will generally require a certain percentage of the total preferred stock be redeemed each year. If the percentage redeemed each year is 2.5 percent, then the preferred stock will have a maximum maturity of 40 years (100%/2.5%). Some preferred stock is perpetual, meaning it will never be redeemed. In this case, the preferred stock is expected to pay dividends forever.

Most preferred stock is cumulative. If a corporation misses a **dividend** on **cumulative** preferred stock, then the missed dividend accumulates. The corporation can never again pay a common stock dividend until all missed accumulated preferred dividends have been paid. This provides a powerful incentive for a successful firm to always pay its preferred dividends. Owners of preferred stock generally have no voting rights. However, most preferred stock provides voting rights if two or more quarterly preferred dividends are missed.

6.10 VALUING PREFERRED STOCK

Preferred stock pays dividends quarterly, but we will simplify this for introductory purposes and assume preferred dividends are paid once a year. To determine the value of preferred stock, we will simply find the present value of the future cash flows an investor expects to receive. If the preferred stock is perpetual, there is only one type of cash flow, the same fixed preferred dividend each year,

---

The following are typical quotations for preferred stock as listed in the *Wall Street Journal* (November 15, 2002) for Thursday, November 14, 2002.

Stock	Cur div	Yld	Close	Net chg
HsptlyProp pfA	2.38	9.0	26.35	–0.07
Innkeepers pfA	2.16	9.5	22.75	–0.24
SixFlgs pfB	1.81	11.6	15.60	0.05
WinstonHtl pfA	2.31	10.4	22.11	0.11

First, under the title STOCK, we see the company name abbreviated. The "pf" is an abbreviation indicating preferred stock. The "A" or the "B" after the "pf" indicates either class A or class B preferred stock. The second column is the annual dividend. The third column is the dividend yield. This is calculated by dividing the preferred stock dividend by the closing price (second column divided by fourth column). The fourth column is the closing price of the preferred stock at the end of the day. The fifth and last column is the net change in price from the previous trading day.

The first list shows a class "A" preferred stock issued by Hospitality Properties Trust. It pays a $2.38 annual dividend and has a 9.0 percent dividend yield ($2.38/26.35 = 9.0%). The closing price of this preferred stock at the end of the day is $26.35, and this is down $0.07 from the $26.42 closing price the day before.

Exhibit 6-7   Preferred stock quotations.

forever. We call this cash flow a perpetuity, and we developed an equation for computing the present value of a perpetuity in Chapter 5.

To illustrate how to value preferred stock, let us consider an example. Suppose Sullivan Resorts Incorporated has issued preferred stock. We will call it Sullivan Resorts $2.50 preferred. The preferred stock promises to pay a fixed dividend of $2.50 annually, forever. Assume a fair market rate of return on preferred stock of this risk class is 11 percent annually. What is the value of one Sullivan Resorts $2.50 preferred?

First, we define our terms.

V_p = value of a share of preferred stock

d_p = preferred annual dividend per share = $2.50

i_p = required rate of return on preferred stock = 11%

The formula for the value of a share of preferred stock is the same as the present value of a perpetuity. The present value of the perpetuity is the value of the preferred stock (V_p), the perpetual payment is the preferred dividend payment (d_p), and the interest rate is the investor-required rate of return on the preferred stock (i_p).

$$V_p = \frac{d_p}{i_p} = \frac{\$2.50}{11\%} = \$22.73$$

The value of Sullivan Resorts $2.50 preferred at an 11 percent rate of return is $22.73.

The preceding equation can also be used to compute the investor's rate of return on preferred stock when purchased at a given price. For example, suppose Sullivan Resorts' $2.50 preferred is actually selling for $20 per share. What is your rate of return if you buy this preferred stock for $20? We can take the equation for the value of preferred stock and solve it for i_p.

$$i_p = \frac{d_p}{V_p} = \frac{\$2.50}{\$20} = 12.50\%$$

If you buy Sullivan Resorts' $2.50 preferred for $20 per share, your rate of return is expected to be 12.50 percent. This rate of return on preferred stock may be called the **yield to maturity.**

6.11 SUMMARY

The concept of security valuation was introduced in this chapter. The value of a security is the present value of the security's expected future cash flows discounted at the investor's required rate of return. We showed how to apply this concept to the valuation of bonds and preferred stock. Additionally, this chapter explained the following.

- The computation of yield to maturity for bonds and preferred stock
- Bonds and preferred stock are considered fixed-income securities because their return is generally fixed and does not increase with the earnings of the issuing corporation

- A bond's indenture details the covenants restricting future actions of the is-suing firm and also explains the various features of the bond
- Preferred stock is a hybrid security, sharing some of the characteristics of bonds and some of the characteristics of common stock

KEY TERMS

Bond
Bond rating
Call feature
Coupon rate
Cumulative dividends
Debenture
Indenture
Mortgage bond
Par value on a bond
Par value on preferred stock
Preferred stock
Put feature
Seniority
Sinking fund on bonds
Sinking fund on preferred stock
Subordinated
Yield to maturity

DISCUSSION QUESTIONS

1. What is the difference between a mortgage bond and a debenture?
2. What is the difference between a call feature and a put feature?
3. Why are bonds and preferred stocks considered fixed-income securities?
4. Why is preferred stock considered a hybrid security?
5. What is the difference between a bond's yield to maturity and its coupon rate?
6. How does a sinking fund feature reduce an investor's risk on a bond?
7. Why do corporations prefer a high-bond rating to a lower bond rating on their debt securities?
8. Why is it important to an investor that preferred stock dividends be cumulative?
9. What is the general procedure for estimating the value of a security?
10. What is a bond indenture?

PROBLEMS

1. McDonald's Corporation's $1,000 par value zero-coupon notes mature in six years. What is the yield to maturity to an investor buying one of these notes for $250?

2. Mann Corporation's $1,000 par value zero-coupon debentures mature in 30 years. If they are priced to return 9 percent to the investor, what is the market price of one Mann Corporation zero-coupon debenture?

3. McDonald's Corporation has $8\frac{7}{8}$ percent (8.875%) bonds that mature in 15 years. What is the value of a $1,000 par value McDonald's Corporation bond for each of the following required rates of return, assuming the investor will hold the bond to maturity? Assume the coupon is paid annually.

$1,000 × 8.875%

a. 10%
b. 8.875%
c. 6%

4. What is the yield to maturity on a $1,000 par value $8\frac{7}{8}$ percent McDonald's Corporation bond if the investor buys the bonds at the following market prices? Assume the coupon is paid annually and the bond matures in 15 years.

a. $1,175
b. $1,000
c. $850

5. What is the value of a $1,000 par value $8\frac{7}{8}$ percent McDonald's Corporation bond for each of the following required rates of return, assuming the investor will hold the bond to maturity? Assume the coupon is paid semiannually (every six months) and the bond matures in 15 years.

a. 10%
b. 6%

6. Marriott Corporation originally issued a $9\frac{3}{8}$ percent (9.375%) bond in 1987. These $1,000 par value bonds mature in three years. What is the value of a Marriott Corporation bond at each of the following required rates of return, assuming the investor will hold the bond to maturity? Assume the coupon is paid annually.

a. 7%
b. 9.375%
c. 12%

7. What is the yield to maturity on a $1,000 par value $9\frac{3}{8}$ percent Marriott Corporation bond if the investor buys the bonds at the following market prices? Assume the coupon is paid annually and the bond matures in three years.

a. $1,025
b. $1,000
c. $950

8. What is the value of a $1,000 par value $9\frac{3}{8}$ percent Marriott Corporation bond for each of the following required rates of return, assuming the investor will hold the bond to maturity? Assume the coupon is paid semiannually (every six months) and the bond matures in 3 years.

a. 7%   13.37
b. 12%

9. What is the value of a share of Six Flags B $1.81 preferred stock to an investor requiring the following rates of return? Assume dividends are paid annually.

a. 12%
b. 10%
c. 9%

10. What is the yield to maturity on a share of Six Flags B $1.81 preferred stock if an investor buys the stock at the following market prices. Assume dividends are paid annually.
    a. $30
    b. $25
    c. $19

11. What is the value of a share of Hospitality Properties Trust B $2.22 preferred stock to an investor requiring the following rates of return? Assume dividends are paid annually.
    a. 11%
    b. 9%
    c. 7%

12. What is the yield to maturity on a share of Hospitality Properties Trust B $2.22 preferred stock if an investor buys the stock at the following market prices. Assume dividends are paid annually.
    a. $35
    b. $25
    c. $17

APPENDIX 6.1 USING A BUSINESS CALCULATOR TO SOLVE THE VALUE OF A CORPORATE BOND

When using a business calculator to solve time value of money problems in Chapter 5, we always were dealing with four variables. We entered the information for three variables into the calculator, and the calculator would compute the value of the fourth unknown variable. Using the business calculator to efficiently calculate bond value is quite similar, but different in one significant way. We are now dealing with five variables. The five variables are (1) the present value of the bond, (2) the coupon payment, (3) the maturity value, (4) the number of coupon payments to maturity, and (5) the investor's required rate of return. We will enter four known variables (2 through 5) and solve for the value of the bond (variable 1). It is important to enter the coupon payment and the maturity value with the same sign because they are both cash flows to be received by the investor. Let us compute the value for the Sullivan Resorts' corporate bond example used in this chapter. The annual coupon payment is $100, the maturity value is $1,000, the number of years to maturity is 15, and the investor's required rate of return is 10%.

Hewlett-Packard hp 10BII
[orange], [C ALL], [100], [PMT], [1,000], [FV], [15], [N], [10], [I/YR], **[PV]** and **−1,000.00** should appear on the screen.

Texas Instruments BA II PLUS
[2nd], [CLR TVM], [100], [PMT], [1,000], [FV], [15], [N], [10], [I/Y], **[CPT],** **[PV]** and **PV = −1,000.00** should appear on the screen.

Notice that the answer provided by the calculator has a negative sign in front of the 1,000.00. As we explained in Chapter 5, this negative sign can be ignored when simply computing the present value of a bond.

APPENDIX 6.2 USING A BUSINESS CALCULATOR TO COMPUTE A BOND'S YIELD TO MATURITY

Using the business calculator to calculate the yield to maturity on a bond is quite similar to solving for the bond value. Once again, we are dealing with five variables: (1) the present value of the bond, (2) the coupon payment, (3) the maturity value, (4) the number of coupon payments to maturity, and (5) the investor's rate of return. We will enter four known variables (1 through 4) and solve for the investor's rate of return (variable 5). This investor's rate of return is actually the yield to maturity. One key difference here is that we are now entering into the calculator three known cash values. The three cash values are the bond value (*PV*), the bond's coupon payment (*PMT*), and the bond's maturity value (*FV*). It is crucial to use the proper signs on these three variables; otherwise an incorrect yield to maturity will result. If you consider the logic of each of the cash values, it is not too difficult to understand the correct signs for each number. The bond value (*PV*) is what the investor pays to invest in the bond, and thus it should have a negative sign. The coupon payment (*PMT*) and maturity value (*FV*) are both cash flows the investor receives and should thus have positive signs. It is important to enter the coupon payment and the maturity value with the same sign because they are both cash flows to be received by the investor. Let us compute the yield to maturity for the Sullivan Resorts' corporate bond example used in this chapter. The bond can be purchased for $900, the annual coupon payment is $100, the maturity value is $1,000, and the number of years to maturity is 15.

Hewlett-Packard hp 10BII
[orange], [C ALL],   [900], [+ / −], [PV],   [100], [PMT],   [1,000], [FV],   [15], [N],
  [I/YR] and **11.42** should appear on the screen, indicating the yield to maturity is
11.42 percent.

Texas Instruments BA II PLUS
[2nd], [CLR TVM],   [900], [+ / −], [PV],   [100], [PMT],   [1,000], [FV],   [15], [N],
  [CPT], [I/Y] and **I/Y = 11.42** should appear on the screen, indicating the yield to
maturity is 11.42 percent.

Common Stock 7

Chapter Objectives

- To understand how common stock represents a residual ownership claim on a corporation
- To understand why it is more difficult to estimate the value of common stock than bonds
- To understand basic common stock features
- To understand and be able to compute four basic dividend valuation models
- To understand how investor rate of return and a firm's earnings and dividends growth affect common stock value

7.1 INTRODUCTION

Corporations issue securities as a means of raising money. Investors buy securities because they hope to receive more back in the future than they paid currently for the securities. Fixed-income securities, bonds, and preferred stock were discussed in the last chapter. Common stock, another security that corporations may issue to raise funds, is quite different than bonds and preferred stock in that the upside and downside returns are very much dependent on the financial success of the corporation.

Common stock gives the investor ownership in the underlying corporation and provides a residual claim on both the firm's assets and the firm's cash flows. However, unlike corporate bonds, common stock does not represent a contractual obligation on the part of the corporation, nor does it have a stated maturity. The residual claim on assets implies the owners of common stock have a residual (leftover) claim on assets after other claim holders are paid. Common stockholders also have ownership rights to cash flows remaining after all other claimants are paid. For successful companies, this can be a very significant claim. The amount of this claim is typically equated with a company's earnings as shown on its income statement. Part of these earnings may be paid directly to the common stockholders in the form of a dividend. However, earnings not paid to common stockholders in the form of dividends still belong to the common stockholders.

Therefore, we must consider both parts of the company's earnings stream when valuing common stock. The two parts of earnings are dividends and the addition to retained earnings. The task of valuing common stock is not as clear-cut as valuing corporate bonds. The cash flows from corporate bonds, which consist of stated, periodic coupon payments and payment of a known par value at maturity, are generally easy to forecast. Common stock cash flows consist of dividend payments and a price should the investor sell the common stock at some point in the future. Future common stock dividends and future common stock price are generally difficult to forecast accurately. Despite the difficulty of forecasting future common stock cash flows, we will introduce some basic models used to estimate the value of common stock.

7.2 COMMON STOCK FEATURES

When an investor buys common stock, the investor is buying ownership in the corporation. The defining features of common stock include (1) a residual claim on assets, (2) a residual claim on cash flows, (3) variable return, (4) voting rights, and (5) no set maturity.

The residual claim on assets implies the owners of common stock have a residual (leftover) claim on assets after other claim holders are paid. Other claim holders include employees, creditors, and the government. This residual claim can be worth a great deal if a successful company is sold. But in the case of bankruptcy, this residual claim is generally worth very little, if anything. Common stockholders also have ownership rights to cash flows remaining after all other claimants are paid. This is typically viewed as a claim on a company's earnings as shown on its income statement. Owners of common stock share equally in any payment of corporate dividends. Corporate dividends are generally paid quarterly.

A corporation's stockholders elect the corporation's board of directors, which has the ultimate control over the corporation. The board has the power to hire, fire, and set the compensation for the corporation's executives. The board also sets long-term policy and makes major corporate decisions. And on occasion, the stockholders may also vote on other important corporate matters.

Sometimes a corporation has more than one class of stock, in which case, typically, class A common stock has one vote per share or no votes per share. Class B common stock typically has superior voting power. An example would be class B stock with four votes per share. A corporation will typically create two classes of common stock when the controlling owners want to raise additional outside equity funding but not give up control of the company. Even though class B common stock typically has superior voting rights, dividend rights typically remain the same.

Common stock financing provides lower risk to the corporation than bond or preferred stock financing. Although corporations do not want to cut common stock dividends, the lack of a fixed dividend on common stock provides greater flexibility versus the use of bonds or preferred stock. Also the use of debt financing places many restrictions on the firm as specified in the debt contract (an indenture in the case of bond financing). Not only does common stock financing not come with restrictions on the firm, but also by expanding the equity base of the corporation, it is typically easier to increase debt financing. For example, if a firm typically has a debt to equity ratio of 2 to 1, then every one dollar of additional equity will allow the firm to borrow an additional two dollars of debt and still stay within their targets for debt financing.

Common stock financing comes with a downside as well as an upside. Investors view common stock as a riskier investment than bonds or preferred stock. As a result, investors in common stock require higher expected rates of return. This translates into a higher cost of common stock financing than bond or preferred stock financing for the corporation. Also, the costs involved with issuing common stock are much higher than the costs involved with issuing bonds and preferred stock.

7.3 VALUING COMMON STOCK

We now introduce four basic models that can be used to value common stock in some basic cases. These models are generally not used in the simplified form presented here by analysts to value stocks. Analysts use more complex versions of these models or a type of earnings multiple methodology to value stocks. Although the models presented only apply in simple situations, they illustrate the underlying principles of common stock valuation. These models provide insight into the determinants of common stock value. Also these models provide the basis for a method for estimating the cost of equity, which is presented in Chapter 8. The four models are

1. General valuation model
2. Zero-growth model
3. Constant-growth model
4. Multiple growth rates ending in constant growth model

First, we introduce the concept of growth of a company's earnings and a method that allows us to approximate this growth rate. Managers of a company have two choices of what to do with company earnings. Remember, these earnings belong to the common stockholders, who are the owners. Managers, acting as agents for the owners, decide whether to distribute earnings back to the owners or keep these earnings in the company. Earnings paid to owners are called *dividends*. Earnings kept within the company are called *retained earnings*.

In theory, managers will pay out earnings as dividends when the company does not have profitable projects in which to invest earnings. Conversely, managers will retain earnings when the company does have profitable projects in which to invest. Therefore, when earnings are retained and reinvested into profitable projects, the company and its earnings will grow in the future. The scale of this growth depends on the amount of earnings retained and on the return earned by the assets in which the retained earnings are invested. Therefore, to calculate the growth rate of a company's earnings, take the percentage of earnings retained (retention ratio) and multiply by the return on equity.

$$g = \text{Growth rate} = r \times ROE$$
$$r = \text{Retention ratio} = 1 - \text{Dividend payout ratio}$$
$$ROE = \text{Return on equity}$$

The following are typical quotations for common stock as listed in the Wall Street Journal for common stock trading on the New York Stock Exchange (December 17, 2002) for Monday, December 16, 2002.

Ytd % chg	52-Week Hi	Lo	Stock (sym)	Div	Yld %	Pe	Vol 100s	Close	Net chg
15.1	36.75	25.80	HsptlyProp **HPT**	2.88	8.5	16	2709	33.95	0.44
−20.6	11.95	6.42	Innkeepers **KPA**	.32a	4.1	78	684	7.78	0.42
−61.2	18.69	3	SixFlags **PKS**		...	dd	5045	5.97	−0.13
2.5	9.76	5.78	WinstonHtl **WXH**	.60	7.6	cc	345	7.93	0.18

First, under the title "YTD %CHG," we see the percentage change in the value of the company over the last one year. Winston Hotels common stock value has increased 2.5 percent over the last year, whereas Six Flags common stock value has declined 61.2 percent over the last year. Next, located under "52-WEEK HI LO" are the highest and lowest selling prices of each company's common stock during the last year. From the preceding table, during the past one year, Hospitality Properties Trust's common stock's highest price has been $36.75 and its lowest price has been $25.80. Innkeepers USA Trust's common stock's highest price has been $11.95 and its lowest $6.42.

Under "STOCK (SYM)," the company name and its ticker symbol is listed. In the table from top to bottom we have Hospitality Properties Trust (HPT), Innkeepers USA Trust (KPA), Six Flags (PKS), and Winston Hotels (WXH).

Under "DIV" the latest dividend is expressed as an annual dollar amount. Notice Innkeepers USA Trust has .32a for a dividend. This means its latest dividend is $0.32 on an annual basis, and the "a" indicates that this includes an extra in addition to the regular dividend. Under "YLD %" is the company's **dividend yield** calculated by dividing the annual dividend by the company's latest or closing stock price. We can check the accuracy of this percentage ourselves by dividing the annual dividend by the closing price under "CLOSE." For example, Hospitality Properties Trust's dividend yield can be calculated as follows.

$$\text{Latest annual dividend} = \$2.88$$
$$\text{Closing price} = \$33.95$$
$$\text{Dividend yield} = \frac{\$2.88}{\$33.95} = 8.48\%$$

Hospitality Properties Trust's dividend yield of 8.48 percent is about 8.5 percent, as listed in the table under "YLD %." Notice Six Flags pays no dividend, so a dividend yield is not calculated for it.

Under "PE" is each company's price–earnings ratio. This is each company's latest or closing stock price divided by their latest annual earnings per share. Hospitality Properties Trust and Innkeepers USA Trust have price–earnings ratios of 16 and 78, respectively. The "dd" for Six Flags indicates Six Flags has lost money in the last year and has no earnings per share, and thus the price–earnings ratio is not calculated. The "cc" next to Winston Hotels indicates its price–earnings ratio is over 100.

Under "VOL" is the volume of common stock shares traded for the day. For example, Six Flags had 504,500 shares traded on December 16, 2002. "CLOSE" indicates the market closing price. For example Six Flags and Winston Hotels closed at $5.97 and $7.93, respectively, at the end of the day, December 16, 2002. "NET CHG" indicates the change in price from the previous trading day's closing price. For example, Hospitality Properties Trust common stock price increased $0.44 from the previous trading day to $33.95 on December 16, 2002. Therefore, the previous trading day's closing price for Hospitality Properties Trust was

$$\text{Previous day's price} = \$33.95 - 0.44 = \$33.51$$

Six Flags common stock price decreased $0.13 from the previous day to $5.97 on December 16, 2002. Therefore, the previous trading day's closing price for Six Flags was

$$\text{Previous day's price} = \$5.97 + 0.13 = \$6.10$$

Exhibit 7-1 Common stock quotations.

For example, let us say Feinstein's MicroBrew Incorporated pays out 40 percent of earnings as dividends. Thus the other 60 percent of earnings (one minus the portion of earnings paid out as dividends) must be reinvested in the firm and increase the firm's retained earnings. This 60 percent is the retention ratio. Suppose the earnings retained can be invested to earn 20 percent (return on equity). What is the growth rate (g)? In this example, the growth rate in the company's earnings is 60 percent multiplied by 20 percent, which equals 12 percent. We also use this as our best approximation of a company's growth rate in dividends.

$$g = 0.60 \times 0.20 = 0.12 = 12\%$$

We expect earnings and dividends to grow at a 12 percent rate per year into the foreseeable future.

For companies that maintain consistency in their retention and payout ratios and earn a consistently stable return on equity, the growth rate will approximate a constant. In these cases, we will use the constant-growth model. If a company's retention and payout ratios are not consistent or its return on equity is not stable, then we must use a nonconstant-growth model.

7.4   GENERAL DIVIDEND VALUATION MODEL

Remember that the value of a security is the present value of the future expected cash flows paid by the security. If an investor is considering the purchase of common stock and plans to hold the common stock for n years, then the value of the common stock can be expressed as follows.

$$P_0 = \frac{d_1}{(1 + k_e)} + \frac{d_2}{(1 + k_e)^2} + \cdots + \frac{d_n}{(1 + k_e)^n} + \frac{P_n}{(1 + k_e)^n}$$

where P_i = the value of common stock at the end of year i

d_i = the common stock dividend at the end of year i

k_e = the investor's required rate of return on equity or common stock,

Because this is an introductory treatment of common stock valuation, we will assume, for simplicity, that common stock pays dividends once a year. If you continue to study finance, it will not be difficult to advance to more realistic quarterly dividend models once you understand the annual dividend models. We will also assume the investor is buying common stock right after it pays a dividend, and therefore the investor will have to wait for one year before receiving the first dividend.

The equation shows the value of common stock is the present value of the expected dividends to be received plus the present value of the expected price you sell the stock for in the future. Thus, if an investor plans to buy common stock and hold it for three years and then sell it at the end of year three ($n = 3$), the valuation equation will look like

$$P_0 = \frac{d_1}{(1 + k_e)} + \frac{d_2}{(1 + k_e)^2} + \frac{d_3}{(1 + k_e)^3} + \frac{P_3}{(1 + k_e)^3}$$

Suppose the investor expects dividends to be $1.00, $1.05, and $1.10 at the end of years one, two, and three, respectively, and expects to sell the stock for

$15 at the end of three years. Also assume the investor requires a 15 percent rate of return.

$$P_0 = \frac{\$1.00}{(1 + 15\%)} + \frac{\$1.05}{(1 + 15\%)^2} + \frac{\$1.10}{(1 + 15\%)^3} + \frac{\$15.00}{(1 + 15\%)^3} = \$12.25$$

For ease of calculation, you can combine the last dividend with the selling price because they both occur in the last year.

$$P_0 = \frac{\$1.00}{(1 + 15\%)} + \frac{\$1.05}{(1 + 15\%)^2} + \frac{(\$1.10 + 15.00)}{(1 + 15\%)^3} = \$12.25$$

The common stock is worth $12.25 to the investor today. If the stock can be purchased for $12.25, then the investor expects to receive the 15 percent required rate of return. If the investor can buy the stock for less than $12.25, then the rate of return will be greater than 15 percent.

There are several obvious problems with using this model in practice. First, the investor must know how long he plans to hold the stock. Second, the investor needs to forecast the future expected dividends. And third, the investor needs to forecast the future expected selling price and the end of the holding period. However, as we consider other common stock valuation models, we will discover that the investor's holding period will not affect the value of common stock today. Also, we will consider how to use a company's expected growth rate in dividends and earnings to forecast a company's future expected dividends.

7.5 ZERO-GROWTH DIVIDEND VALUATION MODEL

Suppose a company's dividends are not growing; in other words, the company pays out a constant dividend every year. Investing in this type of company is similar to investing in a perpetuity, which is a periodic, constant cash flow. The present value of perpetuity is

$$PV = \frac{PMT}{i}$$

We can readily adapt this to estimate the value of common stock with constant dividends. Again, remember that the value of common stock is the present value of the future expected cash flows from the common stock.

$$P_0 = \frac{d}{k_e}$$

where d = the constant common stock dividend.

Let us take as an example Mature Hotels Incorporated, a hotel chain in the Northeast with older properties, that does not expect to grow in the future. Mature Hotels expects earnings per share of $5 over this coming year. Suppose investors believe a 10 percent required rate of return is appropriate. Because Mature Hotels does not expect to grow in the future, its managers have decided not to retain any earnings. Note that because Mature Hotels' management decides not to retain earnings, this company has a 100 percent payout. Therefore, we can best approximate the present value of a share of Mature Hotels with the zero-growth dividend valuation model. Because Mature Hotels' managers expect earnings of $5 per share and has decided to pay out 100 percent of earnings, the first annual dividend is also expected to be $5 per share. In addition, because the company is not expected to grow in the future due to the absence of new retained earnings, all future dividends are also expected to be $5 per share.

$$d_1 = d_2 = d_3 = \cdots d_\infty = \$5.00$$

If we apply our zero-growth formula, we find a present value of a share of Mature Hotels common stock to be $50.

$$P_0 = \frac{\$5.00}{10\%} = \$50.00$$

Our zero-growth formula is based on the present value of a perpetuity and would seem to imply an investor plans to never sell the common stock, but to hold on to it forever. What if the investor has a finite holding period, or in other words, plans to sell the stock in n years, rather than hold it forever? Let us consider the implications by combining the general dividend valuation model with the zero-growth dividend valuation model.

Suppose an investor plans to hold the preceding constant-growth stock for just one year and then sell it. We know what the investors expected dividend will be in one year. It will be $5.00. What is the expected selling price of the stock in one year? Let us assume that investors' required rate of return on the stock remains at 10 percent in the future. An investor considering the purchase of this stock in one year would expect to receive what future cash flows? Of course, the investor can expect a $5.00 annual dividend forever. Thus, the expected selling price of the stock one year from today is

$$P_1 = \frac{\$5.00}{10\%} = \$50.00$$

Therefore, an investor buying the stock today and planning to hold it for just one year expects to receive a $5.00 dividend in one year and also expects to sell the stock for $50 in one year. The value to this investor today is

$$P_0 = \frac{\$5.00}{(1 + 10\%)} + \frac{\$50.00}{(1 + 10\%)} = \$50.00$$

This is the same as the investor planning to hold the stock forever. What about an investor planning to buy the stock and hold it for two years? Again, we know expected dividends are $5.00 in each of year 1 and year 2. What is the expected selling price at the end of year 2? Again, just like for year 1, investors considering buying the stock in two years expect a $5.00 annual dividend. Thus, the expected selling price of the stock two years from today is

$$P_2 = \frac{\$5.00}{10\%} = \$50.00$$

In fact, for zero-growth common stock, the price will not change in the future as long as the required rate of return remains constant. In other words

$$P_0 = P_1 = P_2 = \cdots P_n$$

Therefore, an investor buying the stock today and planning to hold it for two years expects to receive a $5.00 dividend at the end of each of the first two years and also expects to sell the stock for $50 in two years. The value to this investor today is

$$P_0 = \frac{\$5.00}{(1 + 10\%)} + \frac{\$5.00}{(1 + 10\%)^2} + \frac{\$50.00}{(1 + 10\%)^2} = \$50.00$$

We could continue this pattern over and over again, and we would continue to get the same result. If the investor bought the stock and planned to hold it for three years, or four years, or more, the present value of the expected dividends and expected future stock price will still be $50. This illustrates that how long the investor plans to hold the stock should not affect the value of the stock to the investor. We will show this result one more time when we present the constant-growth dividend valuation model.

7.6 CONSTANT-GROWTH DIVIDEND VALUATION MODEL

For our next example, let's look at Dynamic Hotels Incorporated. This hotel is in the Southwest with an expanding portfolio of properties, and the managers expect significant growth in the future. Dynamic Hotels expects earnings per share of $5 in the coming year. Suppose investors believe a 10 percent required rate of return is appropriate. Because Dynamic Hotels expects to grow in the future, its managers have decided to retain 60 percent of future earnings. Based on this retention rate, this company will have a 40 percent dividend payout ratio. Also, Dynamic Hotels expects it can earn 12 percent on earnings reinvested in the firm (return on equity), and it expects this 12 percent return on equity and the 60 percent retention ratio to remain constant in the future. Therefore, we can best approximate the present value of a share of Dynamic Hotels with the constant-growth dividend valuation model.

First, what do you think will be the dividend paid to shareholders of Dynamic Hotels one year from now? Of course, the dividend will be $2.00 per share because 40 percent of earnings are forecast to be paid out to shareholders (40% x $5.00 = $2.00).

Second, what will be the expected growth rate of Dynamic Hotels in the future? Assume the managers of Dynamic Hotels expect to keep a constant retention ratio of 60 percent to fund growth in projects that are expected to consistently earn a 12 percent return on equity. Given these assumptions, the future growth rate of Dynamic Hotels is

$$g = 12\% \times 0.60 = 7.2\%$$

The constant-growth dividend valuation model is

$$P_0 = \frac{d_1}{(k_e - g)}$$

Applying this to Dynamic Hotels common stock,

$$P_0 = \frac{\$2.00}{(10\% - 7.2\%)} = \frac{\$2.00}{2.8\%} = \$71.43$$

Stop for a minute and think about the valuation of these two companies—Mature Hotels and Dynamic Hotels. Both expect earnings over the next year of

$5.00 per share, and investors of each have a 10 percent required rate of return, so why do they have different stock prices? It is due to the assumption of growth. Because Dynamic Hotels expects earnings and dividends to grow and Mature Hotels does not, Dynamic Hotels is worth more. Our models let us determine a reasonable estimate of the relative values of the common stock for each company.

The constant-growth dividend valuation model provides good estimates of common stock value as long as a company's future earnings retention ratio and return on equity and thus its growth rate are roughly stable. If it is difficult to forecast these variables accurately or we expect large systematic differences year to year, then the model provides less-accurate estimates, and other procedures for estimating common stock value are more appropriate.

Notice in the preceding analysis of the constant-growth stock that we made no assumptions about the holding period. Let us now make some holding period assumptions and use the general dividend valuation model to estimate value based on different holding periods. First, assume an investor plans to buy the stock today and hold it for just one year. This investor expects to receive just two cash flows from an investment in this stock. One cash flow is the dividend in one year (d_1), and the other is the price the stock can be sold for in one year (P_1). Remember, we estimated a 7.2 percent growth rate in earnings and dividends for Dynamic Hotels. Let us also assume Dynamic Hotels' stock price will grow at 7.2 percent. This can be expected if the company's retention ratio remains at 60 percent, its return on equity at 12 percent, and investors' required rate of return at 10 percent. Therefore, if the company's stock price is currently $71.43 (from the preceding calculation) and is growing at 7.2 percent annually, the stock price in one year will be $76.57 ($71.43 $\times$ 1.072). The investor planning to buy and hold the stock for just one year can expect to receive a dividend of $2.00 (d_1) and sell the stock for $76.57 (P_1). The value to this investor is just the present value of these two cash flows at the 10% required rate of return:

$$P_0 = \frac{\$2.00}{(1 + 10\%)} + \frac{\$76.57}{(1 + 10\%)} = \$71.43$$

And we can see the value to this investor is the same as from our constant-growth dividend valuation model with no assumption about holding period. Let us continue and consider the value of Dynamic Hotels common stock to an investor planning to buy the stock and hold it for just two years. In this case, two dividends are expected. The first is $2.00, and the second is $2.14 $(d_2 = \$2.00 \times 1.072)$. Also, the investor expects to sell the stock in the second year for $82.08 (P_2). This is 7.2 percent higher than the expected stock price at the end of year 1 $(P_2 = \$76.57 \times 1.072)$. The value to this investor is just the present value of these three cash flows at the 10 percent required rate of return:

$$P_0 = \frac{\$2.00}{(1 + 10\%)} + \frac{\$2.14}{(1 + 10\%)^2} + \frac{\$82.08}{(1 + 10\%)^2} = \$71.43$$

And again, we see the value to the investor is the same as previously calculated (actually the preceding calculation comes out to $71.42, but if we do not round off d_2 and P_2 to two decimal places, the calculation does work out to $71.43). We could continue this pattern over and over again, and we would continue to get the same result. If the investor bought the stock and planned to hold it for three years, or four years, or more, the present value of the expected dividends and expected future stock price will still be $71.43. This illustrates once again that how long the investor plans to hold the stock should not affect the value of the stock to the investor.

7.7 VALUING COMMON STOCK WITH MULTIPLE GROWTH RATES

We have considered how to estimate the value of common stock in general and how to value when there is no growth and when there is constant growth. The general model is logical and provides insights into common stock valuation. But the general model is also difficult to apply in practice. The no-growth and constant-growth models work well when the assumptions of the models are met. In this section we consider how to estimate the value of common stock in which several different growth rates are expected and can be forecast with some degree of accuracy.

Let us reconsider the case of Spectacular Hotels Incorporated. This hotel chain is located in the high-growth areas of Las Vegas, Nevada, and Phoenix, Arizona, with an expanding portfolio of properties that their managers expect to continue into the future. Suppose Spectacular Hotels expects a very high 15 percent growth rate for the next two years and thereafter expects a constant 7.2 percent growth rate. Because of the higher growth rate, Spectacular Hotels now expects higher earnings over the next year and thus a higher dividend of $2.15 to be paid in one year (d_1). The dividend in year two should grow 15 percent from year 1 and equal $2.47 [$d_2 = \$2.15 \times (1 + 15\%)$]. We can picture the cash flows and growth rates as follows.

```
0      g = 15%    1     g = 15%    2  ─────────→   g = 7.2%   ─────────→
├──────────────────┼───────────────┼────────────────────────────────────
           $2.15                 $2.47
```

What is the value of this common stock to an investor requiring a 10 percent rate of return? Remember, we showed in the last two sections that the investor's holding period does not affect the value of the common stock. We showed this by example in the case where first, growth was zero, and then second, where growth was constant. The investor's holding period does not affect common stock value regardless of growth. This means, in the preceding example, we can make any assumption we want about holding period, and we should obtain the same estimate of common stock value. In order to make the estimate calculation as easy as possible, we will assume the investor will buy this stock and hold it for two years and expect to receive three cash flows. The three cash flows are two dividends (d_1 and d_2) and the selling price of the common stock in two years (P_2). We already have estimated the two dividends. If we can obtain an estimate of the common stock selling price in two years, then we can estimate the value of the common stock today with the general dividend valuation model as follows:

$$P_0 = \frac{d_1}{(1 + 10\%)} + \frac{d_2}{(1 + 10\%)^2} + \frac{P_2}{(1 + 10\%)^2}$$

We will estimate the common stock selling price in two years (P_2) by recognizing the growth rate after two years is constant at 7.2%. This will allow us to adapt the constant-growth dividend valuation model to estimate P_2. The model as developed earlier is

$$P_0 = \frac{d_1}{(k_e - g)}$$

This can be written in a more general form as follows.

$$P_n = \frac{d_{n+1}}{(k_e - g)}$$

where the price of common stock at the end of any year "n" (P_n) is equal to the expected dividend one year later (d_{n+1}) divided by the difference between the required rate of return and the growth rate. The growth rate used in this calculation must be the constant growth rate expected after "n" years. Adapting this to our example, we can estimate the selling price of Spectacular Hotels common stock at the end of year 2 by

$$P_2 = \frac{d_3}{(k_e - g)}$$

We can estimate d_3 by letting d_2 grow at the 7.2 percent growth rate.

$$d_3 = \$2.47 \times (1 + 7.2\%) = \$2.65$$

We can now use this to estimate the expected selling price in two years. Be sure to use the growth rate expected after 2 years (7.2%, not 15%).

$$P_2 = \frac{\$2.65}{(10\% - 7.2\%)}$$

$$P_2 = \frac{\$2.65}{2.8\%} = \$94.64$$

Now we can use the expected selling price in year 2 along with the expected dividends in the first two years to estimate the value today.

$$P_0 = \frac{\$2.15}{(1 + 10\%)} + \frac{\$2.47}{(1 + 10\%)^2} + \frac{\$94.64}{(1 + 10\%)^2} = \$82.21$$

Therefore, the value of Spectacular Hotel common stock in this case is $82.21. We assumed a two-year holding period, but this was only to make the calculation easier. Assuming any other holding period would not change the answer, but only change how difficult and tedious the calculation is. For example if we assume a three-year holding period, we will estimate value as follows.

$$P_0 = \frac{d_1}{(1 + 10\%)} + \frac{d_2}{(1 + 10\%)^2} + \frac{d_3}{(1 + 10\%)^3} + \frac{P_3}{(1 + 10\%)^3}$$

We already have an estimate for the first three dividends (d_1, d_2, and d_3). We need to estimate P_3 using constant-dividend growth model.

$$P_3 = \frac{d_4}{(k_e - g)}$$

We can estimate d_4 by letting d_3 grow at the 7.2 percent growth rate.

$$d_3 = \$2.65 \times (1 + 7.2\%) = \$2.84$$

We can now use this to estimate the expected selling price in three years. Be sure to use the growth rate expected after three years (7.2%, not 15%).

$$P_3 = \frac{\$2.84}{(10\% - 7.2\%)}$$

$$P_3 = \frac{\$2.84}{2.8\%} = \$101.43$$

Now we can use the expected selling price in year three along with the expected dividends in the first three years to estimate the value today.

$$P_0 = \frac{\$2.15}{(1 + 10\%)} + \frac{\$2.47}{(1 + 10\%)^2} + \frac{\$2.65}{(1 + 10\%)^3} + \frac{\$101.43}{(1 + 10\%)^3} = \$82.21$$

Therefore, the value of Spectacular Hotel common stock is still $82.21 (the preceding value actually comes out to $82.19, but this is due to rounding differences). The assumption of holding period does not affect the value. It only affects the amount of work involved in the estimation calculation. In a case such as this, the easiest computation is to assume the holding period is equal to the point at which the growth rate becomes constant. In our example of Spectacular Hotels, the growth rate is expected to become constant after two years. Therefore, using a two-year holding period makes for the easiest computation to estimate the value of the common stock.

Let us look at another example to be sure we know how to use the multiple-growth dividend valuation model. Consider the example of Fantastic Casinos, Incorporated. Fantastic Casinos operates in the same geographic region as Spectacular Hotels. Fantastic Casinos expects a $2.24 dividend one year from now and a 20 percent growth rate for the second year, followed by a 12 percent growth rate in the third year and a 7.2 percent growth rate thereafter. Investors require a 10 percent rate of return once again. The dividend in years 2 and 3 should be as follows.

$$d_2 = \$2.24 \times (1 + 20\%) = \$2.69$$
$$d_3 = \$2.69 \times (1 + 12\%) = \$3.01$$

We can picture the cash flows and growth rates as follows.

What is the value of this common stock to an investor requiring a 10 percent rate of return? Remember, we can make any assumption we want about holding period, and we should obtain the same estimate of common stock value. In order to make the estimate calculation as easy as possible, we will assume the investor will buy this stock and hold it until the growth rate becomes constant. This will be three years for this example. With a three-year holding period, the investor expects to receive four cash flows. The four cash flows are three dividends (d_1 d_2, and d_3) and the selling price of the common stock in three years (P_3). We already have estimated the three dividends. Now we need to obtain an estimate of the common stock selling price in three years, then we can estimate the value of the common stock today with the general dividend valuation model as follows.

$$P_0 = \frac{d_1}{(1 + 10\%)} + \frac{d_2}{(1 + 10\%)^2} + \frac{d_3}{(1 + 10\%)^3} + \frac{P_3}{(1 + 10\%)^3}$$

We will estimate the common stock selling price in three years (P_3) by recognizing the growth rate after three years is constant at 7.2 percent. This will allow us to adapt the constant-growth dividend valuation model to estimate P_3.

$$P_3 = \frac{d_4}{(k_e - g)}$$

We can estimate d_4 by letting d_3 grow at the 7.2 percent growth rate.

$$d_4 = \$3.01 \times (1 + 7.2\%) = \$3.23$$

We can now use this to estimate the expected selling price in three years. Be sure to use the growth rate expected after three years (7.2%, not 12% or 20%).

$$P_3 = \frac{\$3.23}{(10\% - 7.2\%)}$$

$$P_2 = \frac{\$3.23}{2.8\%} = \$115.36$$

Now we can use the expected selling price in year 3 along with the expected dividends in the first three years to estimate the value today.

$$P_0 = \frac{\$2.24}{(1 + 10\%)} + \frac{\$2.69}{(1 + 10\%)^2} + \frac{\$3.01}{(1 + 10\%)^3} + \frac{\$115.36}{(1 + 10\%)^3} = \$93.19$$

Therefore, the value of Fantastic Casinos common stock in this case is $93.19. We assumed a three-year holding period, but this was only to make the calculation easier. Assuming any other holding period would not change the answer, but only change how difficult and tedious the calculation is.

7.8 COMMON STOCK VALUE, INVESTOR'S RATE OF RETURN AND GROWTH

Let us consider the impact of a change in the investor's required rate of return or a change in a firm's expected future growth rate on common stock value. First, if the general level of interest rates increases, investors will require a higher rate of return because their opportunity cost will have increased. If a common stock's future expected cash flows (future dividend and future selling price) have not changed, then the stock value must decline to the investor. The only way for an investor to receive a higher rate of return if the future expected cash flows remain the same is to pay less for the stock. Let us illustrate this with the Dynamic Hotel example and the constant-growth dividend valuation model from section 7.6. Previously we estimated Dynamic Hotels common stock value at $71.43 using the following equation.

$$P_0 = \frac{\$2.00}{(10\% - 7.2\%)} = \frac{\$2.00}{2.8\%} = \$71.43$$

This is based on an expected dividend of $2 in one year, a 10 percent required rate of return, and a 7.2 percent growth rate in future dividends. Let us assume the general level of interest rates increases, and as a result investors require a 12 percent return on Dynamic Hotels common stock. The value of the common stock will decline as follows.

$$P_0 = \frac{\$2.00}{(12\% - 7.2\%)} = \frac{\$2.00}{4.8\%} = \$41.67$$

We have illustrated the inverse relationship between rates of return and stock value using the constant-growth dividend model for ease of exposition. The same relationship will hold for all the models of common stock valuation presented in this chapter.

Now let us consider the impact of a change in a firm's expected dividend growth rate on common stock value. If a firm's dividends are expected to increase more rapidly in the future, this means dividends are expected to be larger than the initial expectation. Of course, if the rate of return remains the same, the value of the common stock will increase. Let us once again illustrate this relationship with the Dynamic Hotel example and the constant-growth dividend valuation model. In an earlier section of this chapter (section 7.6), we estimated Dynamic Hotel's common stock value at $71.43 using the following equation.

$$P_0 = \frac{\$2.00}{(10\% - 7.2\%)} = \frac{\$2.00}{2.8\%} = \$71.43$$

Now assume Dynamic Hotels return on equity increases, causing the firm's expected dividend growth rate to increase to 8 percent. The value of Dynamic Hotels common stock will increase as follows.

$$P_0 = \frac{\$2.00}{(10\% - 8\%)} = \frac{\$2.00}{2\%} = \$100.00$$

Actually, the stock value would go up to more than $100 because d_1 would increase to more than $2.00 with a higher growth rate (P_0 would equal $101, see Exhibit 7-2). This illustrates the positive relationship between a firm's expected dividend growth rate and common stock value. Again, the same relationship will hold for all the models of common stock valuation presented in this chapter, not just the constant-growth dividend valuation model.

7.9 SUMMARY

Common stocks and the estimation of common stock value were introduced in this chapter. The value of a security is the present value of the security's expected future cash flows discounted at the investor's required rate of return. Applying this concept to common stock is much more difficult than to bonds and preferred stock. We showed how to apply this concept to the valuation of common stock, recognizing that the resulting values calculated are approximations. Additionally, this chapter explained the following.

- Common stock provides the investor with a residual claim on the assets and cash flow of the corporation.

In the example from section 7.6, we estimated Dynamic Hotel's common stock value at $71.43 using the following equation.

$$P_0 = \frac{\$2.00}{(10\% - 7.2\%)} = \frac{\$2.00}{2.8\%} = \$71.43$$

This implied a growth rate of 7.2 percent. Let us show what will happen if growth increases to 8 percent. The dividend expected in one year (d_1) was previously expected to be $2.00. This implies the current dividend (d_0) was previously a bit less than $1.87 as follows.

$$d_1 = d_0 \times (1 + g)$$

$$\$2.00 = d_0 \times (1 + 7.2\%)$$

$$d_0 = \frac{\$2.00}{(1 + 7.2\%)} = \$1.87$$

But now we have an 8 percent growth rate, causing the dividend expected in one year (d_1) to be $2.02, as follows.

$$d_1 = \$1.87 \times (1 + 8\%) = \$2.02$$

The value of Dynamic Hotel's common stock will increase as follows.

$$P_0 = \frac{\$2.02}{(10\% - 8\%)} = \frac{\$2.02}{2\%} = \$101.00$$

Exhibit 7-2   The impact of higher growth on common stock value.

- A variable return, voting rights, and no set maturity are characteristics of common stock.
- An investor's holding period does not affect the value of common stock.
- An inverse relationship exists between investor's rate of return and common stock value.
- There is a positive relationship between the dividend growth rate and common stock value.

KEY TERMS

Common stock
Dividend yield

DISCUSSION QUESTIONS

1. What is meant when it is said that common stock is a form of residual ownership?
2. Why is valuing common stock more difficult and less precise than valuing bonds?
3. One of the features differentiating common stock from bonds and preferred stock is voting rights. What do owners of common stock have the right to vote for?

4. Why do some corporations have more than one class of common stock?
5. Why is common stock financing a lower risk to the corporation than financing with bonds or preferred stock?
6. Why is common stock financing a higher cost than financing with bonds or preferred stock?
7. How does the investor's required rate of return affect common stock value?
8. How is the valuation of common stock with zero growth similar to the valuation of preferred stock?
9. The constant-growth dividend valuation model may provide a reasonably good estimate of common stock value, even if a firm's future growth is not expected to be perfectly constant. Explain why.
10. How does a firm's future growth rate affect common stock value?

PROBLEMS

Problems designated with **Excel** *can be solved using* **Excel** *spreadsheets accessible at http://www.prenhall.com/chatfield.*

1. Sullivan's International Tours Incorporated currently (d_0) pays a $3.00 common stock dividend. Dividends have been recently growing at a 4 percent annual rate and are expected to continue growing at this rate for the foreseeable future. Sam is considering an investment in Sullivan's International Tours and plans to hold the stock for just one year, at which time he expects to sell the stock for $45. What is the current value of Sullivan's International Tours' common stock to Sam if he requires a 14 percent rate of return?

2. Christianson's Hearty Restaurants currently (d_0) pays a $2.00 common stock dividend. Dividends have been recently growing at a 5 percent annual rate and are expected to continue growing at this rate for the foreseeable future. What is the current value of Christianson's Hearty Restaurants' common stock to an investor who requires the following rates of return?
   a. 18%
   b. 12%
   c. 7%

3. Lucas Hotels Incorporated currently (d_0) pays a $4.00 common stock dividend. Dividends have been recently growing at a 6 percent annual rate. What is the current value of Lucas Hotels' common stock to an investor requiring a 15 percent rate of return and expecting the following growth rate?
   a. 3%
   b. 6%
   c. 9%

EXCEL 4. Feinstein's Breweries currently (d_0) pays a $1.00 common stock dividend. Dividends have been recently growing at a 10 percent annual rate and are expected to continue growing at this rate for the next three years. Thereafter the growth rate is expected to be 5 percent for the foreseeable future. What is the current value of Feinstein's Breweries' common stock to an investor requiring a 13 percent rate of return?

EXCEL 5. Brookman's High Roller Casinos currently (d_0) pays a $5.00 common stock dividend. Dividends have been recently growing at a 12 percent annual rate and are expected to continue growing at this rate for the next four years.

Thereafter, the growth rate is expected to be 6 percent for the foreseeable future. What is the current value of Brookman's High Roller Casinos common stock to an investor requiring a 15 percent rate of return?

6. Shoemakers Business Hotels currently (d_0) pays a $2.20 common stock dividend. Dividends have been recently growing at a 3 percent annual rate and are expected to continue growing at this rate for the next two years. Thereafter, the growth rate is expected to be 0 percent for the foreseeable future. What is the current value of Shoemakers Business Hotels' common stock to an investor requiring a 17 percent rate of return? **EXCEL**

7. Jay's Outdoor Wilderness Outfitters currently (d_0) pays a $4.50 common stock dividend. Jennifer is considering an investment in Jay's Outdoor Wilderness Outfitters and plans to hold the stock for four years, at which time she expects to sell the stock for $70. She expects the dividend to increase to $5.00 one year from now and then to grow at an 8 percent rate for the next five years. What is the current value of Jay's Outdoor Wilderness Outfitters' common stock to Jennifer if she requires a 15 percent rate of return? **EXCEL**

8. Park's Asian Markets Restaurants currently (d_0) pays a $1.50 common stock dividend. Robert is considering an investment in Park's Asian Markets Restaurants and plans to hold the stock for three years, at which time he expects to sell the stock for $50. Robert expects the dividend to increase to $2.00 one year from now, $2.75 in two years, and $3.75 in three years. What is the current value of Park's Asian Market Restaurants' common stock to Robert if he requires a 12 percent rate of return? **EXCEL**

9. Hames Conventioneers Incorporated currently (d_0) pays a $2.40 common stock dividend. Dividends have been recently growing at a 15 percent annual rate and are expected to continue growing at this rate for the next three years, then at a 10 percent rate for the next two years, and thereafter at a 5 percent rate into the foreseeable future. What is the current value of Hames Conventioneers' common stock to an investor requiring an 18 percent rate of return? **EXCEL**

10. White Waters Amusement Parks currently (d_0) pays a $4.10 common stock dividend. Dividends have been recently growing at a 14 percent annual rate and are expected to continue growing at this rate for the next two years, then at a 9 percent rate for the next one year, and thereafter at a 4 percent rate into the foreseeable future. What is the current value of White Waters Amusement Parks' common stock to an investor requiring a 16 percent rate of return? **EXCEL**

Cost of Capital | 8

8.1 INTRODUCTION

One of the key finance functions in a firm is to make investments and acquire assets. It is crucial to the long-term success of the firm that investments earn a sufficient rate of return, called the **cost of capital.** It is the rate of return required to keep investors satisfied, and therefore the cost of capital is really an average rate of return reflecting the rates of return required by various investors in the firm. It takes into account the cost of funds for new investments raised from debt, preferred stock, retained earnings, and common stock.

It is well accepted that not only is measuring a firm's cost of capital often difficult, but also that estimating the cost of capital is crucial to a firm's decision making. This chapter offers an introduction to the concept of cost of capital as well as the basic means used to approximate a firm's cost of capital.

8.2 THE WEIGHTED AVERAGE COST OF CAPITAL

A firm's **weighted average cost of capital** is essentially the firm's minimum required rate of return on investments. The cost of capital is measured as a percentage rate. As the name implies, the weighted average cost of capital is an average cost of the various sources of capital employed by a firm. We will call these different sources of capital the "capital components." The capital components may include funds raised by debt, preferred stock, retained earnings, and common stock.

The weighted average cost of capital is a marginal measurement, meaning it is concerned with the cost of new funds used to finance new investments. We are not concerned with the cost of funds already raised and previously invested in the firm. The cost of funds previously raised is certainly important, but the weighted average cost of capital is to be used in the evaluation of new investment proposals. Therefore, we should measure the cost of new funds to be used to finance new investments.

The weighted average cost of capital is measured on an after-tax basis. Investors care about cash flows after all relevant costs have been paid. Taxes are certainly a real and relevant cost. If a firm is to maximize its value, then the cost of capital should take into account taxes, and all costs should be measured on an after-tax basis.

In measuring the weighted average cost of capital, we consider only long-term sources of capital. Short-term sources of funds such as a short-term bank loan are generally not used to make long-term investments. As such, the weighted average cost of capital should only consider short-term sources of funds if they are used to finance long-term investments. An example would be a short-term bank loan that is refunded and rolled over every six months. Generally, the weighted average cost of capital measures the cost of long-term sources of funds to include long-term debt, preferred stock, retained earnings, and common stock.

The weighted average cost of capital is an average cost of a firm's various components of capital. The weights in the average cost of capital are a measurement of a firm's target capital structure, which is simply the proportion of various capital components a firm plans to use to fund investments. For example, gaming companies generally have a capital structure heavily weighted toward debt. For example, as of June 30, 2001, MGM-Mirage obtained 74.3 percent of capital from long-term debt and 25.7 percent of capital from equity. This was MGM-Mirage's actual capital structure as of June 30, 2001, but it may not be their target capital structure. The target might be to obtain 70 percent of capital from long-term debt and 30 percent from equity, in which case MGM-Mirage plans to lower the proportion of debt and increase the proportion of equity in the actual capital structure over time. Another firm's target capital structure might be to obtain 40 percent of capital from long-term debt, 10 percent from preferred stock, and 50 percent from equity. The weights in the weighted average cost of capital are measures of a firm's **target capital structure.** Throughout this chapter we assume we know a firm's target capital structure. This topic will be discussed again in Chapter 12.

The basic weighted average cost of capital (k_a) equation is as follows.

$$k_a = w_d \times k_d + w_p \times k_p + w_e \times k_e$$

where the w's represent the firm's target capital structure and are measured as proportions. All the w's must add up to 100 percent.

$$w_d + w_p + w_e = 100\%$$

The terms of the equation are defined as follows.

w_d = the proportion of debt in the capital structure

w_p = the proportion of preferred stock in the capital structure

w_e = the proportion of equity in the capital structure

k_d = the after-tax cost of debt

k_p = the cost of funds raised from preferred stock

k_e = the cost of funds raised from equity

Many firms do not employ preferred stock, and for these firms the weighted average cost of capital equation will break down more simply to the following.

$$k_a = w_d \times k_d + w_e \times k_e$$

If a firm does not use preferred stock, then the weighted average cost of capital is a weighted average of the cost of debt and the cost of equity.

Next, we consider how to estimate the cost of various capital components. This, along with a firm's target capital structure, allows us to approximate a firm's weighted average cost of capital and therefore have a measure of a firm's minimum required rate of return on new investments.

8.3 ESTIMATING THE COST OF CAPITAL COMPONENTS

The possible components of a firm's capital structure include long-term debt, preferred stock, retained earnings, and common stock. If short-term debt is used for long-term financing by continual refunding, then this is also a component of a firm's capital structure. For the remainder of this chapter we will not consider short-term debt as an element of a firm's capital structure.

Many firms do not use preferred stock as part of their capital structure. Like bonds, preferred stock generally pays a fixed return to investors. But unlike the interest cost of bonds, the dividend cost of preferred stock is not tax deductible for the issuing corporation. Thus, for most firms, the after-tax cost of debt is much less than the after-tax cost of preferred stock. This may explain why bonds are a much more popular fixed-income security than preferred stock.

The U.S. government is considering eliminating the double taxation of corporate dividends. Proposals to make dividend income on both preferred and common stock tax free to the investor may make preferred stock a much more popular financing method in the future.

The cost of a capital component is a reflection of the investor-required rate of return. For example, suppose my company borrows $1,000 from you and pays you back $1,000 plus 10 percent interest in one year. What is your rate of return on the loan? Of course it is 10 percent. What is my company's cost for borrowing $1,000 from you? Of course it is also 10 percent. But what if I had to pay $10 for a standard boilerplate legal contract to satisfy you with legal evidence of the loan? Then my company's cost for borrowing $1,000 from you is 10 percent plus $10. This raises my company's cost on the loan to 11 percent as follows.

$$\text{Interest} = 10\% \times \$1,000 = \$100$$
$$\text{Legal fee} \qquad\qquad = \underline{\$\ 10}$$
$$\text{Total loan cost} \qquad = \$110$$

$$\text{Cost of borrowing one thousand dollars} = \frac{\$110}{\$1,000} = 11\%$$

So we can see a component cost of capital is the investor-required rate of return plus an adjustment for any transaction costs the issuing corporation may have to pay. These transaction costs are called **issuance** or **flotation costs** because they are costs paid to "issue" or "float" securities to investors. Issuance costs consists of fees paid to investment bankers and lawyers who assist a corporation issue bonds, preferred stock, or common stock.

The three possible types of securities issued by corporations differ in seniority and thus risk. Bonds have higher seniority than preferred stock and common stock and are first to be paid in the case of financial difficulty. Preferred stock has higher seniority than common stock and will be paid before common stock in case of financial difficulty. Common stock, which ranks last in terms of seniority, is the riskiest of the three securities from the investor's point of view because an investor in common stock has residual claims on the cash flows and assets of the corporation. Common stock dividends are paid from cash, only after interest on debt and dividends on preferred stock are paid. Thus, from the investor's point of view, common stock is the riskiest corporate security and bonds are the lowest risk security, with preferred stock in between. As a result, investors demand the lowest returns on bonds and the highest returns on common stock. On top of this, the cost of bonds is tax deductible, but the cost of preferred stock and common stock is not. Therefore, there is a clear hierarchy of cost of capital components for a corporation. The cost of bonds is the lowest due to the relatively low risk of bonds and the tax deductibility of interest on bonds to the issuing corporation. The cost of common stock is the highest due to its relatively high risk to investors. And of course, the cost of preferred stock falls between bonds and common stock.

Next, we will consider how to estimate the components' cost of capital. In doing so, we will build on the models for estimating investor returns from Chapters 6 and 7.

8.4 THE COST OF DEBT

The interest cost of debt is a tax-deductible cost, and we must take this into consideration. Therefore, the interest cost of debt expressed as a percentage rate will be multiplied by one minus the firm's marginal tax rate to compute the firm's effective after-tax cost of debt.

$$k_d = k_{dbt} \times (1 - t)$$

where k_d is still the after-tax cost of debt,

k_{dbt} = the before-tax interest rate cost of debt, and
t = the firm's marginal tax rate

If a firm issues bonds to raise funds, then the before-tax interest rate can be calculated using the same basic equation from Chapter 6 for the calculation of yield to maturity on corporate bonds. There is one difference in the application of the equation here. In Chapter 6 we used the market value of the bond. Here we will use the net proceeds to the company after issuance costs are paid. The equation used to calculate the before-tax interest cost on a bond is

$$V_{net} = C \times \left[\frac{1 - \frac{1}{(1 + k_{dbt})^n}}{k_{dbt}} \right] + \frac{M}{(1 + k_{dbt})^n}$$

where V_{net} is the net proceeds from the bond issuance after issuance costs are paid, and

C = Coupon payment
M = Maturity value or the par value = $1,000
n = Number of payments until maturity

Do not forget that once you obtain the before-tax interest rate on the bond (k_{dbt}), you still need to compute the after-tax interest cost as

$$k_d = k_{dbt} \times (1 - t)$$

Let us illustrate the computation of the cost of debt with an example. Suppose Mayers Dazzling Resorts Incorporated is considering the issuance of a bond in the near future. Investment bankers provide information about the likely selling price, coupon rate, and issuance costs. They believe a 20-year bond will sell at a market price of $1,000, with a 9 percent coupon rate, and issuance costs will be $5 for each $1,000 bond denomination. Also, let us assume Mayers's marginal tax rate is 40 percent. What is the after-tax cost of debt from this bond issue for Mayers Dazzling Resorts Incorporated? First we need to compute the net proceeds from the bond issuance. It is just the $1,000 market price minus the $5 issuance cost per bond.

$$V_{net} = \$1,000 - 5 = \$995$$

Then we need to compute the before-tax interest rate on the bond to Mayers.

$$\$995 = \$90 \times \left[\frac{1 - \frac{1}{(1 + k_{dbt})^{20}}}{k_{dbt}} \right] + \frac{\$1,000}{(1 + k_{dbt})^{20}}$$

The easiest way to solve the preceding equation is with a business calculator as illustrated in Appendix 6.2. Using this procedure we obtain

$$PV = V_{net} = -\$995$$
$$PMT = C = \$90$$
$$N = n = 20$$
$$FV = M = \$1,000$$

And then compute I/Y or I/YR to obtain the before-tax interest cost.

$$I/Y = I/YR = k_{dbt} = 9.05\%$$

Then we can compute the after-tax cost of funds raised by the bond issuance.

$$k_d = 9.05\% \times (1 - 0.40) = 5.43\%$$

You can see the issuance costs do not make a heavy impact on the before-tax interest rate. The before-tax return to an investor buying this bond at the $1,000 market price is the 9 percent coupon rate. The investor before-tax rate of return and coupon rate are the same in this case because the bond is selling at par value. The $5 per bond issuance costs only raise the cost slightly to 9.05 percent. The issuance costs on bonds are usually low, not having a large impact on the interest cost to the issuing corporation. As such, ignoring the issuance costs on bonds will not cause a very large error and would still generally provide a good approximate cost of debt. For instance, in our example here, ignoring the issuance costs will give us the following after-tax cost of debt.

$$k_d = 9\% \times (1 - 0.40) = 5.40\%$$

This is just 0.03 percent less than our calculation when considering issuance costs.

The preceding procedure works well when a corporation has just sold bonds or is currently in the process of selling bonds. Then all the information to use in the equation will be readily available. If this is not the case, then information can be used from bonds the firm currently has outstanding in the marketplace. By using the coupon rate, remaining maturity, and current market price on the outstanding bonds, the before-tax cost (k_{dbt}) can be computed and used as an estimate for the before-tax cost on new bonds to be issued by the firm. The only thing this method doesn't provide is an estimate of issuance costs. But issuance costs could be estimated independently, or as suggested earlier, a close estimate of before-tax cost can still be obtained while ignoring issuance costs.

Consider the following example for Mayers Dazzling Resorts Incorporated. Suppose Mayers does not have any information on a current bond issuance but has an outstanding 30-year bond with a 12 percent coupon rate issued 10 years ago. Currently this bond is selling for $1,280 and has 20 years remaining to maturity. We can estimate the before-tax interest rate on a new bond issued by Mayers by computing the before-tax yield on this bond.

$$\$1,280 = \$120 \times \left[\frac{1 - \dfrac{1}{(1 + k_{dbt})^{20}}}{k_{dbt}} \right] + \frac{\$1,000}{(1 + k_{dbt})^{20}}$$

$$PV = V_{net} = -\$1,280$$
$$PMT = C = \$120$$
$$N = n = 20$$
$$FV = M = \$1,000$$

And then compute I/Y or I/YR to obtain the before-tax interest cost.

$$I/Y = I/YR = k_{dbt} = 8.94\%$$

The estimate of after-tax interest cost on a new bond for Mayers is

$$k_d = 8.94\% \times (1 - 0.40) = 5.37\%$$

But what if Mayers has not recently sold any bonds, is not in the process of selling bonds, and has no bonds outstanding? Or possibly Mayers may have bonds outstanding, but a good market price of the bonds cannot be obtained because they do not trade very often or trade privately. If Mayers has a relationship with an investment banker, that person can most likely provide good estimates of all the information needed to estimate the after-tax interest cost on a new bond. Even if this fails, then Mayer can get a rough estimate of after-tax interest costs by considering the yields on bonds issued by companies with similar financial and risk characteristics.

8.5 THE COST OF PREFERRED STOCK

The use of preferred stock to raise funds is not nearly as common as the use of bonds. Nevertheless, a number of firms do use this method of raising capital. Some preferred stock is issued as a perpetuity, but many preferred stock issues have a call feature or a sinking fund, as described in Chapter 6. This complicates the valuation of preferred stock and also the computation of the cost of funds raised with preferred stock. We will show how to compute the cost of preferred stock funds, assuming the preferred stock is a perpetuity, and also how to compute the cost in the case of a known, stated ending date for the preferred stock.

Computing the cost of funds raised with preferred stock is similar to computing the investor's rate of return on preferred stock, as shown in Chapter 6. Instead of using the market price, we will use the net proceeds from the preferred stock issuance after issuance costs are paid. The following equation is used when the preferred stock is a perpetuity.

$$k_p = \frac{d_p}{V_{net}}$$

where V_{net} is the net proceeds from the preferred stock issuance after issuance costs are paid and

d_p = the preferred annual dividend per share
k_p = the cost of funds raised by the issuance of preferred stock

k_p is the final cost of funds raised by the issuance of preferred stock, as preferred dividends are not a tax-deductible cost, as is interest expense.

Let us illustrate the computation of the cost of preferred stock with an example. Suppose Mayers Dazzling Resorts Incorporated is considering the issuance of preferred stock in the near future. Investment bankers provide information about the likely selling price, dividend rate, and issuance costs. They believe a perpetual preferred stock issue will sell at a market price of $100, the same as the par value. They expect a 10 percent dividend rate, and issuance costs will be $3 per share. What is the cost of preferred stock to Mayers Dazzling Resorts for this issue? First we need to compute the net proceeds from the preferred stock issuance. It is just the $100 market price minus the $3 issuance cost per share.

$$V_{net} = \$100 - 3 = \$97$$

The cost of funds raised by issuing preferred stock is

$$k_p = \frac{\$10}{\$97} = 10.31\%$$

You can see the issuance costs do make a more significant impact on the before-tax cost for this preferred stock example than for our earlier bond example. The before-tax return to an investor buying this preferred stock at the $100 market price is the 10 percent dividend rate. The $3 per share issuance costs raises the cost slightly to 10.31 percent. The issuance costs are usually a greater percentage of the market price for preferred stock than for bonds. As such, the issuance costs on preferred stock are usually taken into account because ignoring them will generate a larger error than ignoring issuance costs for bonds.

Also notice we do not make any adjustments to our computation for taxes. Preferred stock dividends are not tax deductible, and therefore the issuing firm's marginal tax rate does not affect the firm's cost of raising funds with preferred stock.

Now suppose Mayers Dazzling Resorts Incorporated decided to issue preferred stock with an ending date in 10 years. In other words, Mayers will call all the preferred stock back in 10 years, paying each investor the par value of $100 at that time. Let us assume Mayers' preferred stock is still expected to sell at a $100 market price with a 10 percent dividend rate and $3 issuance costs per share. How do we figure out the cost of raising funds with this particular preferred stock issue? We compute the cost similar to how we did for bonds, except taxes do not affect this cost. The net proceeds from the preferred stock are still $97 per share. The dividends are still $10 per share. But now the $10 dividends are a 10-payment annuity instead of a perpetuity without end. And in addition to the dividends, investors will receive $100 (par value) in 10 years. The preferred dividends are treated as coupon payments on a bond, and the $100 par value is treated just as the $1,000 par value on bond.

$$\$97 = \$10 \times \left[\frac{1 - \frac{1}{(1 + k_p)^{10}}}{k_p} \right] + \frac{\$100}{(1 + k_p)^{10}}$$

$$PV = V_{net} = -\$97$$
$$PMT = d_p = \$10$$
$$N = n = 10$$
$$FV = \text{Par value} = \$100$$

And then compute I/Y or I/YR to obtain the cost for this preferred stock.

$$I/Y = I/YR = k_p = 10.50\%$$

Thus, the cost for Mayers Dazzling Resorts Incorporated to raise funds with preferred stock is 10.50 percent in this example.

8.6 INTERNAL COMMON EQUITY—NEW RETAINED EARNINGS

Capital provided from a firm's common equity actually has two possible sources. New capital provided by the reinvestment of a firm's profits is called *additions to retained earnings* or *new retained earnings*. In the cost of capital context, this is called *internal equity* because the firm itself, through reinvestment of profits, provides these funds internally. The other source of common equity capital is from the sale of new common stock shares to investors. The proceeds of these sales (after issuance costs) are available for investment by the firm. We call this *external equity* because these funds come from outside the firm from external investors.

The cost of internal equity may at first appear to be zero because internal equity is just the firm's own profits reinvested in the firm. But nothing could be further from the truth. Investors in a firm's bonds are paid by interest payments. Investors in a firm's preferred stock are paid by dividends. The remaining profit belongs to investors in common stock. This profit can be paid out as dividends to common shareholders or can be reinvested in the firm. If part of the profit is reinvested, there is an opportunity cost to the common shareholders. The shareholders could have used this money to make further investments on their own. Therefore, profits should only be reinvested if the firm can earn as much as common shareholders could earn on their own. How much is this? We propose that a minimum expected rate of return on reinvested profits is the rate of return that investors expect when they buy the firm's common stock at its current price. If the firm does not expect to earn this rate of return on reinvested profits, then the profits should be paid out as dividends to the common shareholders. We will use this rate of return as the cost of using internal equity.

How do we measure the rate of return investors expect when they buy a firm's common stock? Measuring investor return on bonds and preferred stock is fairly straightforward because all the expected cash flows are stated. But the expected cash flows on common stock are not stated, and thus investor return on common stock is difficult to estimate. In the next three sections we will present three different methods for estimating the cost of using internal equity. These are (1) the dividend valuation model method, (2) the capital asset pricing model method, and (3) the bond yield plus risk premium method. None of these methods is perfectly or necessarily superior to the other methods. They all provide an estimate subject to error of the cost of using internal equity. A company's final estimate for the cost of internal equity could be based on any one of these three methods or it could be an average of the three methods. There is not one method that dominates the other methods.

8.7 DIVIDEND VALUATION MODEL METHOD FOR ESTIMATING THE COST OF INTERNAL EQUITY

One of the commonly used procedures to estimate the cost of internal equity is the dividend valuation model. Remember that in Chapter 7 we showed the value of common stock can be expressed as follows.

$$P_0 = \frac{d_1}{(1 + k_e)} + \frac{d_2}{(1 + k_e)^2} + \cdots + \frac{d_n}{(1 + k_e)^n} + \frac{P_n}{(1 + k_e)^n}$$

where P_i = the value of common stock at the end of year i
d_i = the common stock dividend at the end of year i
k_e = the investor's **required rate of return** on equity or common stock

Given the current market price of the common stock (P_0) and forecasts for future dividends (d_i's) and future stock price (P_n), we could solve for the investors' required rate of return on equity (k_e) and thus the cost of using funds generated from internal equity. The problem is that future common dividends and future common stock price cannot be estimated with the same amount of accuracy as bond coupon payments and preferred stock dividends. But, if the company's future dividends are expected to grow at a stable rate in the future, the constant-growth version of the dividend valuation model will provide good estimates of either the stock value or the investor-required rate of return.

We used the constant-growth dividend valuation model in Chapter 7 to estimate the value of common stock (P_0) given a known investor-required rate of return (k_e), growth rate (g), and expected dividend in one year (d_1).

$$P_0 = \frac{d_1}{(k_e - g)}$$

But now we want to use this model to estimate the investor-required rate of return for a given market value, growth rate, and expected dividend in one year. So we need to rearrange the terms algebraically to solve for investor-required rate of return (k_e).

$$k_e = \frac{d_1}{P_0} + g$$

It is much easier to see the intuition behind the constant-growth dividend valuation equation in this form than in the form used in Chapter 7. Basically, the preceding equation shows the return to an investor in common stock is equal to the **dividend yield** (d_1/P_0) plus stock price appreciation (g).

Let us illustrate this model with an example. Suppose Mayers Dazzling Resorts Incorporated common stock is selling for $40 per share, pays a current dividend (d_0) of $3.50 per share, and is expected to grow at a 4 percent rate into the foreseeable future. The cost of internal equity estimate is

$$k_e = \frac{\$3.64}{\$40.00} + 4\%$$
$$= 9.10\% + 4\%$$
$$= 13.10\%$$

where we calculated $d_1 = d_0 \times (1 + g) = \$3.50 \times (1.04) = \$3.64$.

The investor-required rate of return on Mayers Dazzling Resorts' common stock is estimated at 13.10 percent. This would also be the dividend valuation model estimate of the cost of internal equity for Mayers Dazzling Resorts Incorporated.

The difficulty in applying this model is in obtaining an estimate of the future growth rate (g). The actual market price of the common stock (P_0) can be obtained easily enough, as can next year's expected dividend (d_1). Research supports the use of analysts' forecasts of growth as the most accurate forecasts, and also analysts' forecasts work best to explain market prices of common stock. Analysts' forecasts can be obtained from Value Line, investment advisory services, and the larger brokerage houses.

8.8 CAPITAL ASSET PRICING MODEL METHOD FOR ESTIMATING THE COST OF INTERNAL EQUITY

We presented the Capital Asset Pricing Model (CAPM) in Chapter 5 as a way to relate a firm's risk to the investor-required rate of return on the firm's common stock. And of course, once we have a measure of investor-required rate of return on common stock, then we also have a measure of cost of using funds generated from internal equity.

The CAPM defines investor-required rate of return as a risk-free rate (k_r) plus a risk premium that increases with the amount of the firm's systematic risk as measured by beta (β_j). The risk premium is compensation to the investor for bearing systematic risk. Higher systematic risk increases the risk premium and increases the required rate of return, and lower systematic risk decreases the risk premium and decreases the required rate of return. This relationship is expressed mathematically by the security market equation

$$k_j = R_f + (R_m - R_f) \times \beta_j$$

where k_j = the investor-required rate of return on firm j's common stock.

R_f = the expected risk-free rate of return

β_j = the beta or measure of systematic risk for company j's common stock

R_m = the expected market return

$(R_m - R_f) \times \beta_j$ = the risk premium for firm j's common stock

$(R_m - R_f)$ = expected risk premium on an average risk $(\beta_j = 1.0)$ firm's common stock

The security market line equation is explained thoroughly in Chapter 4, but let us do a brief recap here. The preceding equation shows the investor-required rate of return (k_j) is equal to a risk-free rate of return (R_f) plus a risk premium $[(R_m - R_f) \times \beta_j]$ for firm j's common stock. The risk premium is equal to an expected risk premium on an average-risk common stock $[(R_m - R_f)]$ multiplied by firm j's measure of systematic risk (β_j). So firm j's risk premium is essentially the average risk premium scaled up or down according to the level of firm j's systematic risk. If firm j is riskier than average, then we scale the average risk premium up for firm j. If firm j is less risky than average, then we scale the average risk premium down for firm j.

The expected risk-free rate of return (R_f) is usually measured by a U.S. Treasury bill rate. Beta (β_j) can be estimated on your own if you have the proper data and statistical ability, but Value Line and major brokerage firms also regularly compute the beta for major corporations. The expected market return (R_m) is the average return investors expect to receive on common stocks in the future. It should be the expected return on an average risk $(\beta_j = 1.0)$ common stock. Measuring the expected market return can be quite complex. Ibbotson Associates study market returns over long periods of time and provide information on past market returns that can be used to estimate future market returns. Also, financial service companies provide estimates of future market returns that can be used as an estimate of the expected market return in the CAPM.

Let us illustrate the use of the CAPM to estimate a firm's cost of internal equity with an example. Suppose Mayers Dazzling Resorts Incorporated has a beta (β_M) estimated at 1.20, the expected risk-free rate of return (R_f) is 5 percent, and the expected market return (R_m) is 12 percent. Use the security market line equation to compute the investor-required rate of return for Mayers Dazzling Resorts (k_M).

$$
\begin{aligned}
k_M &= R_f + (R_m - R_f) \times \beta_M \\
&= 5\% + 1.20 \times (12\% - 5\%) \\
&= 5\% + 1.20 \times 7\% \\
&= 5\% + 8.4\% \\
&= 13.4\%
\end{aligned}
$$

Notice in the preceding equation that the expected risk premium on an average risk common stock is 7 percent [$(R_m - R_f)$], and the risk premium for Mayers Dazzling Resorts is 8.4 percent [$\beta_M \times (R_m - R_f)$]. The investor-required rate of return for Mayers Dazzling Resorts common stock is 13.4 percent, and this is also an estimate for the cost of using funds from internal equity. Notice the required rate of return for Mayers (13.4%) is higher than the expected market rate of return (12.0%) because the Mayers beta (1.2) is higher than the average beta (1.0).

8.9 THE BOND YIELD PLUS RISK PREMIUM METHOD FOR ESTIMATING THE COST OF INTERNAL EQUITY

The bond yield plus risk premium method is probably the easiest of the three methods used to estimate the cost of internal equity. Its application requires an estimate of a firm's own bond yield on a before-tax basis. This is generally pretty easy to come by. Then you add a risk premium to the bond yield to estimate the cost of internal equity. The difficulty in applying this method is to estimate an appropriate risk premium. There is evidence supporting risk premiums as low as 2 percent and in some cases in excess of 7 percent, depending on the general level of interest rates and the riskiness of the firm. There is also evidence that the risk premium over and above the bond yield is larger when the general level of interest rates is low and smaller when the general level interest rates is high. Also companies with low systematic risk ($\beta_j < 1.0$) will tend to have a smaller risk premium, and companies with a high systematic risk ($\beta_j > 1.0$) will tend to have a larger risk premium.

Let us illustrate the use of the bond yield plus risk premium method for estimating the cost of internal equity with an example. Mayers Dazzling Resorts Incorporated has bonds trading at an 8.5 percent yield. Suppose the typical risk premium over bond yield for an average company ($\beta_j = 1.0$) is 4 percent. But remember from our previous example that Mayers Dazzling Resorts Incorporated has a beta of 1.20. As such, we will use a higher risk premium of 5 percent. So Mayers Dazzling Resorts' cost of internal equity using the bond yield plus risk premium method is

$$k_e = 8.5\% + 5.0\% = 13.5\%$$

8.10 EXTERNAL COMMON EQUITY—NEW ISSUES OF COMMON STOCK

When common equity funds are provided by growth in retained earnings, the cost of internal equity as estimated in the previous sections is the correct cost to use. But if retained earnings growth is not sufficient to meet a firm's need for equity funding, then new shares of common stock may be sold to raise capital. Capital generated by the sale of new common stock is called external equity. External equity has issuance costs as do bonds and preferred stock. Because internal equity is just the investment of firm's own profits back into the firm, it involves no issuance costs. The issuance costs with external equity will raise its cost above that for internal equity. The issuance costs on common stock involve several different cost items. They include investment banker and legal costs as well as the negative impact on the firm's common stock price usually caused by a new issuance of common stock.

The same general approach to handling issuance costs with bonds and preferred stock is used to adjust the cost of equity. We simply reduce the market price of the common stock by the amount of the issuance costs per share. But there is only one method used to estimate the cost of equity that uses the market price of common stock in the equation. The market price per share of common stock can be adjusted for issuance costs in the dividend valuation model. Using the same equation from section 8.7,

$$k_{ne} = \frac{d_1}{P_0} + g$$

where k_{ne} = the cost of new equity or the cost of external equity.

Replace the common stock market price (P_0) with the per share net proceeds from the sale of common stock after issuance costs are paid.

$$k_{ne} = \frac{d_1}{P_{net}} + g$$

Let us use the same example of Mayers Dazzling Resorts Incorporated that we used in section 8.7 to show how this works. Remember Mayers' common stock sells for $40 per share, is expected to pay a dividend of $3.64 at the end of the year, and is expected to grow at a 4 percent rate into the foreseeable future. The cost of *internal* equity as computed previously is

$$k_e = \frac{\$3.64}{\$40.00} + 4\%$$
$$= 9.10\% + 4\%$$
$$= 13.10\%$$

The cost of *external* equity for Mayers Dazzling Resorts requires an estimate of issuance costs. This estimate could be provided by Mayers' investment banker. Suppose in this case issuance costs are expected to be $6 per share. Then the cost of external equity using the dividend valuation model is

$$k_{ne} = \frac{\$3.64}{(\$40 - \$6)} + 4\%$$
$$= \frac{\$3.64}{\$34} + 4\%$$
$$= 10.71\% + 4\%$$
$$= 14.71\%$$

The dividend valuation model is the only model generally used to estimate the impact of issuance costs on the cost of *external* equity, but there are three different methods generally used for estimating the cost of *internal* equity. A firm might use all three methods to generate a cost of internal equity estimate, or it might just use one of the three methods. What if a firm does not use the dividend valuation model to estimate the cost of *internal* equity? Does the firm have to use the dividend valuation model to estimate the cost of *external* equity? No, the dividend valuation model can be used to estimate the cost adjustment for external equity, and then this cost adjustment can be used in conjunction with any other method to derive a final cost estimate for external equity. Let us illustrate this by looking back at our Mayers Dazzling Resorts example. Using the dividend valuation model, the cost of internal equity is 13.10 percent and the cost of external equity is 14.71 percent. The adjustment for issuance costs is 1.61 percent. In other words, issuance costs add 1.61 percent to the cost of Mayers' *internal* equity to arrive at Mayers' cost of *external* equity.

$$\text{adjustment for issuance costs} = 14.71\% - 13.10\% = 1.61\%$$

This adjustment can then be added to any cost of *internal* equity the firm decides to use. If the firm uses a 13.4 percent cost of *internal* equity from the CAPM method, then the cost of *external* equity is 15.01 percent.

$$k_{ne} = 13.40\% + 1.61\% = 15.01\%$$

If the firm uses a 13.5 percent cost of *internal* equity from the bond yield plus risk premium method, then the cost of *external* equity is 15.11 percent.

$$k_{ne} = 13.50\% + 1.61\% = 15.11\%$$

Suppose the firm uses a 13.33 percent cost of *internal* equity from averaging the three model estimates together as

$$k_e = \frac{(13.10\% + 13.40\% + 13.50\%)}{3} = 13.33\%$$

Adjusting this 13.33 percent cost of *internal* equity for issuance costs gives us a 14.94 percent cost of *external* equity.

$$k_{ne} = 13.33\% + 1.61\% = 14.94\%$$

8.11 COMPUTATION OF THE WEIGHTED AVERAGE COST OF CAPITAL

Now that we know how to compute the components' cost of capital, we are ready to complete the weighted average cost of capital estimation. In section 8.2, we presented the equation for weighted average cost of capital as

$$k_a = w_d \times k_d + w_p \times k_p + w_e \times k_e$$

In addition to the components' cost of capital, we need to know the target capital structure to calculate the weighted average cost of capital for a firm. Let us assume Mayers Dazzling Resorts Incorporated has a target capital structure of 40 percent long-term debt (w_d), 10 percent preferred stock (w_p), and 50 percent common equity (w_e). Let us also assume Mayers expects sufficient growth in retained earnings to meet the firm's needs for common equity funding.

Using the calculations for Mayers Dazzling Resorts from the previous sections, we have a 5.44 percent cost of long-term debt (k_d), a 10.31 percent cost of raising funds with preferred stock (k_p), and several estimates for the cost of internal equity (k_e). The cost of internal equity is estimated to be 13.10 percent using the dividend valuation model, 13.40 percent using the CAPM, and 13.50 percent using the bond yield plus risk premium method. We also computed a 13.33 percent cost of internal equity by averaging the three model estimates. Use 13.33 percent as

Mayers' cost of internal equity. Now we have all the inputs we need to estimate the weighted average cost of capital.

$$k_a = w_d \times k_d + w_p \times k_p + w_e \times k_e$$
$$k_a = 0.40 \times 5.44\% + 0.10 \times 10.31\% + 0.50 \times 13.33\%$$
$$= 9.87\%$$

Therefore, Mayers Dazzling Resorts should use 9.87 percent as the minimum required rate of return when evaluating investments. An investment should be expected to return at least this amount before Mayers considers committing funds to an investment. An average return of 9.87 percent is required to pay off the firm's contractual obligations on bonds and preferred stock and still have enough left over to satisfy common shareholders with a sufficient return. Exhibit 8.1 summarizes this computation of the weighted average cost of capital, including the initial estimation of the component costs.

In the preceding weighted average estimation, we assumed Mayers expects sufficient growth in retained earnings to meet the firm's needs for common equity funding. What if this is not the case? How does this change the estimation of Mayers' weighted average cost of capital? Let us assume Mayers is considering investing up to $100 million in new projects for the coming year and thus needs the following amounts of funding from debt, preferred, stock and common equity.

$$\text{Long-term debt funding} = 0.40 \times \$100 \text{ million} = \$40 \text{ million}$$
$$\text{Preferred stock funding} = 0.10 \times \$100 \text{ million} = \$10 \text{ million}$$
$$\text{Common equity funding} = 0.50 \times \$100 \text{ million} = \$50 \text{ million}$$

What if Mayers expects to have only $20 million of new retained earnings to help finance this growth. This will not meet Mayers' needs for equity funding and will leave a shortfall of $30 million in common equity. What can be done? Of course, Mayers Dazzling Resorts Incorporated can raise the other $30 million by selling new shares of common stock. Remember, we call this external equity. In section 8.10 we computed a 14.94 percent cost of external equity for Mayers using the average estimate for internal equity and then adding an adjustment for issuance costs. To estimate Mayers' weighted average cost of capital, we must adapt our equation to this different situation. Remember, 50 percent, or $50 million, of common equity is expected to be needed. Mayers expects to have $20 million of new retained earnings, and this will provide 20 percent of the $100 million investment budget. The other $30 million of common equity will be provided externally through the sale of new common stock. This will provide 30 percent of the $100 million investment budget. The estimate of the new weighted average cost of capital is

$$k_a = w_d \times k_d + w_p \times k_p + w_e \times k_e + w_{ne} \times k_{ne}$$
$$k_a = 0.40 \times 5.44\% + 0.10 \times 10.31\% + 0.20 \times 13.33\% + 0.30 \times 14.94\%$$
$$= 10.36\%$$

What we have done is broken up the 0.50 weight for common equity into two components. Internal equity is weighted at 0.20 ($20 million of the $100 million investment budget), and external equity is weighted at 0.30 ($30 million of the $100 million investment budget). Of course, the use of external equity raises

The weighted average cost of capital is computed using the following equation.

$$k_a = w_d \times k_d + w_p \times k_p + w_e \times k_e$$

Remember the k_d, k_p, and k_e are the after-tax cost of funds raised from long-term debt, the cost of funds raised from preferred stock, and the cost of funds raised from common equity, respectively. Also, w_d, w_p, and w_e represent a firm's target for the proportion of funds raised from long-term debt, preferred stock, and common equity, respectively. These proportions represent a firm's target capital structure. Mayers Dazzling Resorts Incorporated has the following target capital structure.

$$w_d = 40\% \quad \text{(Long-term debt)}$$
$$w_p = 10\% \quad \text{(Preferred stock)}$$
$$w_e = 50\% \quad \text{(Common equity)}$$

Next let us estimate Mayers's after-tax cost of debt (k_d). Mayers believes one of its own 20-year bonds will sell at a market price of $1,000, with a 9 percent coupon rate and issuance costs of $5 for each $1,000 bond denomination. Also, Mayers's marginal tax rate is 40 percent. First, we need to compute the net proceeds from the bond issuance. It is just the $1,000 market price minus the $5 issuance cost per bond.

$$V_{net} = \$1,000 - 5 = \$995$$

Then we need to compute the before-tax interest rate on the bond to Mayers.

$$\$995 = \$90 \times \left[\frac{1 - \dfrac{1}{(1 + k_{dbt})^{20}}}{k_{dbt}} \right] + \frac{\$1,000}{(1 + k_{dbt})^{20}}$$

The easiest way to solve the preceding equation is with a business calculator as illustrated in Appendix 6.2. Using this procedure, we obtain

$$PV = V_{net} = -\$995$$
$$PMT = C = \$90$$
$$N = n = 20$$
$$FV = M = \$1,000$$

And then compute I/Y or I/YR to obtain the before-tax interest cost.

$$I/Y = I/YR = k_{dbt} = 9.05\%$$

Then we can compute the after-tax cost of funds raised by the bond issuance.

$$k_d = 9.05\% \times (1 - 0.40) = 5.43\%$$

Next let us estimate Mayers' cost of raising funds with preferred stock. Mayers believes a perpetual preferred stock issue will sell at a market price of $100, the same as the par value. They expect a 10 percent dividend rate and issuance costs of $3 per share. First, we need to compute the net proceeds from the preferred stock issuance. It is just the $100 market price minus the $3 issuance cost per share.

$$V_{net} = \$100 - 3 = \$97$$

The cost of funds raised by issuing preferred stock is

$$k_p = \frac{\$10}{\$97} = 10.31\%$$

The last component cost of capital we need to estimate is the cost of internal equity. Three different basic methods are used to estimate the cost of internal equity: the dividend valuation model, the CAPM, and the bond yield plus risk premium.

Let us first consider estimating Mayers' cost of internal equity using the dividend valuation model. Suppose Mayers Dazzling Resorts Incorporated's common stock is selling for $40 per share, pays a current dividend (d_0) of $3.50 per share, and is expected to grow at a 4 percent rate into the foreseeable future. The dividend one year from today (d_1) is expected to be $3.64.

$$d_1 = d_0 \times (1 + g) = \$3.50 \times (1.04) = \$3.64$$

The cost of internal equity estimate is

$$k_e = \frac{\$3.64}{\$40.00} + 4\%$$
$$= 9.10\% + 4\%$$
$$= 13.10\%$$

Now let us estimate Mayers cost of internal equity using the CAPM. Suppose Mayers Dazzling Resorts Incorporated has a beta (β_M) estimated at 1.20, the expected risk-free rate of return (k_r) is 5%, and the expected market return (k_m) is 12%. Use the security market line equation to compute the investor-required rate of return for Mayers Dazzling Resorts (k_M).

$$k_M = R_f + (R_m - R_f) \times \beta_M$$
$$= 5\% + 1.20 \times (12\% - 5\%)$$
$$= 5\% + 1.20 \times 7\%$$
$$= 5\% + 8.4\%$$
$$= 13.4\%$$

For a third estimate of Mayers' internal cost of equity, we will use the bond yield plus risk premium method. Mayers Dazzling Resorts Incorporated has bonds trading at an 8.5 percent yield. Suppose the typical risk premium over bond yield for an average company ($\beta_j = 1.0$) is 4 percent. But remember from our previous example that Mayers Dazzling Resorts Incorporated has a beta of 1.20. As such, we will use a higher risk premium of 5 percent. We have not used a precise method to raise the risk premium to 5 percent. We know Mayers has above-average systematic risk from its beta ($\beta_M > 1.0$). We have just used our judgment to estimate a higher-than-average risk premium of 5 percent versus a 4 percent average risk premium. So Mayers Dazzling Resorts' cost of internal equity using the bond yield plus risk premium method is

$$k_e = 8.5\% + 5.0\% = 13.5\%$$

We could use any one of the three estimates for the cost of Mayers' internal cost of equity, or we could use an average of the three estimates as follows:

$$k_e = \frac{(13.10\% + 13.40\% + 13.50\%)}{3} = 13.33\%$$

We can now complete the weighted average cost of capital computation for Mayers Dazzling Resorts.

$$k_a = w_d \times k_d + w_p \times k_p + w_e \times k_e$$
$$k_a = 0.40 \times 5.43\% + 0.10 \times 10.31\% + 0.50 \times 13.33\%$$
$$= 9.87\%$$

Therefore, Mayers Dazzling Resorts' weighted average cost of capital is 9.87%, and Mayers should use 9.87% as the minimum required rate of return when evaluating investments.

Exhibit 8-1 Computing the weighted average cost of capital.

the cost of capital because now Mayers Dazzling Resorts is paying issuance costs for part of the common equity. Now Mayers Dazzling Resorts should use 10.24 percent as the minimum required rate of return when evaluating investments.

8.12 USING THE WEIGHTED AVERAGE COST OF CAPITAL

A weighted average cost of capital is estimated for a period of time. Typically, a firm will use a time frame of six months or a year to estimate its **marginal cost of capital.** Suppose a year is used. A firm will estimate its cost of new funds (cost of debt, preferred stock, and equity) over the coming year and use the estimates to compute a weighted average cost of capital. This weighted average cost of capital is then used as a minimum required rate of return to evaluate possible investments over the next year. If capital costs change significantly during the year, then the weighted average cost of capital should be computed once again with the new estimates. This new weighted average cost of capital would then be used to evaluate any projects from this time forward.

It might be attractive to take a simpler approach to using the cost of capital. For example, suppose Mayers Dazzling Resorts plans to build a new hotel in the coming year at a cost of $40 million, entirely funded with proceeds from a bond sale. It is tempting to evaluate this project at the 5.44 percent after-tax cost of debt we estimated in section 8.4. It is much easier to compute just the after-tax cost of debt than the entire weighted average cost of capital. Also, all funding for this project comes from the bond sale, so would it not be appropriate to use just the cost of debt to evaluate this project? No, this is not correct. Let us consider the possible consequences of making investment decisions in this fashion.

If the after-tax cost of debt is the minimum required rate of return for the new hotel, then any expected return above 5.44 percent makes the new hotel project an acceptable investment. If this hotel project is accepted and financed with a $40 million bond issue, then Mayers Dazzling Resorts will need to use preferred stock and common equity financing for later projects. Remember, only 40 percent of Mayers's capital is targeted to come from debt, whereas the other 60 percent should be raised from preferred stock issuance and common equity. Thus, later investment projects would need to be financed with preferred stock costing 10.31 percent, internal equity costing 13.10 percent, or external equity costing 14.71 percent. Using the same method of analysis, later investment projects will need to return a minimum of 10.31 percent, 13.10 percent, or 14.71 percent, depending on the source of funds used to finance the projects. If some projects are evaluated with a 5.44 percent minimum required rate of return, other projects at 10.31 percent, another set of projects at 13.10 percent, and still other projects at 14.71 percent, depending on the source of funds, the firm will have dysfunction investment decision making. A project financed with debt would be acceptable with only a 6 percent expected rate of return, whereas another project financed with equity would be unacceptable with a 12 percent expected rate of return.

We advocate using a weighted average cost of capital, even if all components of capital are not used to finance an investment project. This notion is called separating the financing decision from the investment decision. In other words, as a firm evaluates investment projects, it should not consider the amount of funding from long-term debt, preferred stock, and equity. Instead, assume funds for the project are drawn from long-term debt, preferred stock, and equity in the same proportions as the firm's target capital structure. This means the firm can use its weighted average cost of capital to evaluate all projects, regardless of whether they are financed with long-term debt, preferred stock, common equity, or some combination of the three components.

8.13 SUMMARY

Firms need to know their minimum required rate of return when evaluating possible investment projects. The weighted average cost of capital provides an estimate of a firm's minimum required rate of return. It is essentially a reflection of the average rate of return necessary to keep all of the firm's investors satisfied. A firm's investors include purchasers of bonds, preferred stock, and common stock. Also, the following concepts were explained in this chapter.

- A firm's weighted average cost of capital is based on investors' required rates of return on a firm's securities and target capital structure.
- The cost of capital used to evaluate new investments needs to be a marginal cost, not an historical cost.
- The cost of capital is concerned with the cost of long-term, not short-term, sources of funds.
- Issuance costs cause the cost of funds from securities to be higher than the investor return.
- A cost of capital estimate is for a given period of time, such as for the next six months or for the next one year.
- Evaluate all projects as if they are financed with long-term debt, preferred stock, and common equity in accordance with the firm's target capital structure, even if a project is financed with just one component of capital.

KEY TERMS

Cost of capital
Dividend yield
Flotation costs
Issuance costs
Marginal cost of capital
Required rate of return
Target capital structure
Weighted average cost of capital

DISCUSSION QUESTIONS

1. What is riskier from an investor's point of view, a firm's bonds, preferred stock, or common stock?
2. Why do a firm's retained earnings have a cost?
3. How are retained earnings different from funds raised by the issuance of bonds, preferred stock, or common stock?

4. Which is better for evaluating a firm's new investment proposals, the marginal cost of capital or the historical cost of capital?

5. There are two reasons why the cost of debt is less than the cost of funds raised from preferred stock or common stock. What are the two reasons?

6. Explain what is meant by the concept of separating the financing decision from the investment decision.

7. Why is the cost of external equity greater than the cost of internal equity?

8. Why is computing a firm's cost of debt just like computing the investor's yield to maturity, as we learned in Chapter 6?

9. Is a firm's amount of retained earnings shown on its current balance sheet a good measure of the amount of internal equity available for new investments?

10. What are the three alternative methods used to estimate the cost of internal equity?

PROBLEMS

Problems designated with **Excel** *can be solved using* **Excel** *spreadsheets accessible at* http://www.prenhall.com/chatfield.

 1. Bowen's Casinos recently sold an issue of 15-year maturity bonds. The bonds were sold at $955 each. After issuance costs, Bowen received $948 each. The bonds have a $1,000 maturity value and a 7 percent coupon rate. The coupon is paid annually. What is the after-tax cost of debt for these bonds if Bowen's effective tax rate is 40 percent?

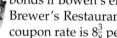 2. Brewer's Restaurants expects to sell a new bond issue at its par value. The coupon rate is $8\frac{3}{8}$ percent, and the coupon is paid annually. Because issuance costs are so small Brewer plans to ignore their impact on the after-tax cost. What is the after-tax cost of these $1,000 par value bonds if Brewer's effective tax rate is 40 percent?

3. Annette's Travel Incorporated plans to issue preferred stock at a price of $50 per share. The dividend will be $4.30 per share, and issuance costs are expected to be $3.00 per share. What is the cost to Annette's Travel of raising funds with preferred stock?

4. Shama's Tours Incorporated plans to issue a 20-year bond. Shama's Tours expects the $1,000 par value bonds to sell for $995 each. Issuance costs are expected to be $5 per $1,000 bond, and the coupon rate is $11\frac{7}{8}$ percent. If the effective tax rate is 40 percent, what is the after-tax cost of debt to Shama's Tours?

5. Norman Entertainment Corporation recently sold an issue of preferred stock at $45 per share. The dividend is $7.55, and the issuance costs are $4 per share. What is the cost to Norman Entertainment of raising funds with preferred stock?

6. Grace Fine Dining Trust is financed 100 percent with equity and intends to remain this way. Grace's common stock beta is 1.20, the expected market return (average market return) is 12 percent, and the risk-free rate is 5 percent. What are the cost of equity and the weighted average cost of capital for Grace?

7. Sullivan & Associates expects to pay a common stock dividend of $2.00 per share next year (d_1). Dividends are expected to grow at a 5 percent rate for

Introduction to Capital Budgeting and Cash Flow Estimation | 9

Chapter Objectives

- To understand capital budgeting and why good capital budgeting decisions are crucial to the long-term success of a hospitality firm
- To understand the different types of capital budgeting decisions
- To understand the basic principles for estimating the cash flows associated with a capital budgeting project
- To understand and know how to estimate a capital budgeting project's net investment
- To understand and know how to estimate a capital budgeting project's net cash flows
- To understand and know how to compute the after-tax cash flow from the sale of a depreciable asset
- To understand depreciation and its impact on a capital budgeting project's net cash flows

9.1 INTRODUCTION

Capital budgeting is generally viewed as the decision-making process used in the acquisition of long-term physical assets. Long-term assets are those with economic lives of more than one year. Capital budgeting decisions lead to capital investments in various capital projects. A capital investment is a cash expenditure to acquire a long-term asset or a cash expenditure that is expected to generate a long-term positive cash flow. This could include a hotel's investment in a new fire alarm system. This might not generate a future cash flow, but it is a long-term asset satisfying legal requirements and ethical goals. An employee-training program is also a capital investment. It does not entail the acquisition of a physical asset, but it is expected to generate a long-term positive cash flow through more-productive employees. Therefore, investments in capital budgeting projects are capital investments, but not all capital investments are investments in capital budgeting projects, such as the employee-training program described previously.

Traditional capital budgeting projects include capital investments in a new hotel, a casino expansion, an addition of a new restaurant to a hotel, an addition of new laundry facilities to a hotel, a new bar added to a restaurant, the replacement of a sprinkler system with a new updated fire suppression system, and the list could go on and on. In this chapter, we introduce the concept of capital budgeting decisions and also discuss the information needed to proceed with a capital budgeting decision.

Capital budgeting decisions are crucial to most firms' long-term success because they require large investments of cash, and the decisions have a long-lasting impact on a firm's cash flows. If a firm makes good capital budgeting decisions, then it will have good hotels, resorts, restaurants, or bars generating a positive cash flow for a long period of time. If a firm makes bad capital budgeting decisions, then the firm is shackled with bad projects and has invested cash that does not generate a sufficient return. Once a bad capital budgeting decision has been made, it is usually costly to reverse. What does one do with an unsuccessful hotel, restaurant, or bar? Continue to operate it with cash losses, or sell it at a significant loss.

A firm's capital budgeting decisions determine its future course by determining what services will be offered, how they will be offered, and where they will be offered. A firm's future long-term cash flow and health is dependent on good capital budgeting decisions, and as a result, firms should have good,

---

In July 1999 the Resort at Summerlin opened in the suburbs of Las Vegas at a cost of $366 million. By November of 2001, this casino resort was sold in a U.S. Bankruptcy Court auction for $80 million to Hotspurs Resorts. Swiss Casinos of America "failed to generate enough business to make interest payments on $366 million in debt" on the property. Swiss Casinos of America was the original owner of the property.

Under new operators, the property is apparently doing much better. Some of this improvement is explained by "A new, intensive marketing approach . . ." and other operating changes. And certainly these changes may have improved the operations of the casino.

This example illustrates the importance of good capital budgeting decisions and good execution of the decisions. Swiss Casinos of America, the original investor in the resort, ended up with a failed capital budgeting project. They could continue operating at a loss, if they could afford to continue losing money. Or they could sell the resort at a significant loss. They were eventually forced to sell at a loss. A property originally costing more than $350 million to open was sold for only $80 million.

Why is the property apparently so successful now? It may be that the new management has improved the operations significantly. But, it has to be much easier to generate sufficient cash flow from the casino resort to justify an $80 million investment than it does to justify a more than $350 million investment.

Good capital budgeting decisions will create projects returning positive cash flows for a long period of time. Poor capital budgeting decisions will create projects that lose money for a long period of time or create a large one-time loss when the failed project is sold for a loss.

*The information and quotes in this exhibit come from an article in *Las Vegas Review Journal* (November 30, 2002, section D, page 1).

Exhibit 9-1   Capital budgeting and financial health in the hospitality industry.

sound procedures in place to evaluate capital budgeting projects and all capital investments.

9.2 CLASSIFYING CAPITAL BUDGETING PROJECTS

Capital budgeting projects can be classified according to their purpose. A firm might take on a project in order to grow, to reduce costs, to replace assets, or to meet legal requirements and ethical goals. Replacement capital budgeting decisions often come under the classification of cost reduction, and we will treat it as one category.

Many capital budgeting projects are clearly for the purpose of growing the firm and increasing the firm's future cash flows. This would include the expansion of facilities or an investment in new, additional facilities.

Capital budgeting projects may also be mainly motivated to decrease future operating costs. This could include new, more energy efficient, air-conditioning units, new kitchen equipment requiring less maintenance, or new hotel laundry facilities to replace a more expensive outside vendor. These capital budgeting decisions will usually, but not always, be a decision to replace inefficient or old assets. And sometimes a replacement decision will not be motivated by cost considerations but simply required if a firm wants to continue in a certain business.

Some capital budgeting projects may not be motivated by growth or cost reduction considerations but required by government regulation or by ethical considerations. These would include fire alarm and fire suppression systems, equipment to minimize pollution, and other investments to promote the safety of employees, customers, and the community.

It is also useful to classify capital budgeting projects by the type of decision being made as well as by purpose. All capital budgeting decisions can be classified as independent decisions or mutually exclusive decisions. Classification of a project as independent or mutually exclusive impacts the method of capital budgeting analysis, as we will see later in the chapter.

Independent capital budgeting decisions are stand-alone decisions. The capital budgeting project is analyzed in isolation and is not compared to other projects. The decision on whether to build a new hotel or not is independent. The decision to build a new hotel in either Anaheim or Los Angeles is not independent but mutually exclusive because you will build one or the other, but not both. If you decide to build one, then you exclude the other. The distinction between independent and mutually exclusive decisions is important. An **independent project** is analyzed to determine if it will increase the value of the firm or not, whereas the analysis of **mutually exclusive projects** must go one step further. Not only must we ask if a new hotel in Anaheim will increase the value of the firm, we must also question if a new hotel in Los Angeles will increase the value of the firm. If the answer is yes to both questions, then we must also decide which of the two projects increases the value of the firm the most because the projects are mutually exclusive, and we can only invest in one or the other.

Many capital budgeting projects are naturally mutually exclusive. The decision to replace kitchen equipment may include a choice of new kitchen equipment from three different companies. Now, one must not only decide if this

Classification by purpose:

1. Growth projects, such as expanding the hotel from 200 rooms to 300 rooms
2. Cost reduction projects to increase efficiency, such as replacing old air conditioners with new air conditioners to save energy and maintenance costs
3. Projects required by government regulation or motivated by ethical considerations, such as adding a new fire alarm and fire suppression system to a hotel or restaurant

Classification by type of decision:

1. Independent project decisions, such as should Sullivan's Bar & Grille open a new business in downtown Las Vegas or not
2. Mutually exclusive project decisions, such as should Sullivan's Bar & Grille open a new business in downtown Las Vegas or in Henderson. If the decision is to do one or the other, but not both, then it is a mutually exclusive decision.

Exhibit 9-2   Classification of capital budgeting projects.

investment will increase the value of the firm, but also which company's kitchen equipment will increase the value of the firm the most.

9.3 THE CAPITAL BUDGETING DECISION AND CASH FLOW ESTIMATION

How a capital budgeting project impacts a firm's future cash flows should be estimated prior to making an investment decision. The information required to evaluate a large project of a major corporation would need to come from many sources. Information about future product demand, pricing, and competition is needed from marketing personnel to estimate future revenues. Information about material costs is needed from purchasing personnel, employee expenses from human resources, and any other information required to estimate future operating costs. If the evaluation is of a significant project for a small firm, then all this information may need to be provided by one person or a few personnel. And if a project is sufficiently small or obviously beneficial to a firm's health, it may not be worth performing a formal capital budgeting analysis. The proposal by a restaurant to add a new toaster for several hundred dollars or the proposal by a hotel to buy a new computer monitor for its front desk operations almost certainly does not require a formal capital budgeting process for a management decision.

Capital budgeting decision methods are based on cost/benefit analysis. The cost of starting a project is quantified and called the **net investment.** The benefit of a project is the increased future cash flow. This is quantified on an annual basis and called the **net cash flows.** Different capital budgeting methods then compare the net investment to the net cash flows to decide if a project is worthy of investment. When forecasting cash flows in the process of estimating a project's net investment and net cash flows, some basic principles should be followed.

Cash flows should be estimated on an incremental basis, not on a total basis. *Incremental basis* means the change in cash flows caused by an investment in a project. If a hotel is considering an investment to expand one of its restaurants,

---

1. Estimate cash flows on an incremental basis. Consider the change in cash flows brought about by a capital budgeting project, not the total cash flows.
2. Cash flows should be estimated on an after-tax basis. Taxes are a real cost and require a real commitment of cash. Be sure to always consider tax impacts.
3. The impact of indirect effects should be estimated. If a project will bring in more customers to your other business lines or cannibalize your other business lines, this will change overall firm cash flow.
4. Sunk costs are irrelevant cash flows; opportunity costs are relevant cash flows.

Exhibit 9-3   Basic principles for estimating cash flows.

then only the expected change in sales revenue caused by the expansion should be considered in the capital budgeting analysis. Incremental sales revenue means the change in sales revenue. The total sales revenue would not be the relevant number because a portion of total sales revenue will exist with or without the expansion.

Always consider the impact of taxes on cash flow. Taxes are a real cost. But of course, only consider incremental taxes caused by a capital budgeting investment.

The indirect effects of a project on cash flows, in addition to the direct effects, should always be taken into account. Suppose a casino is considering an investment to add a new restaurant to the several restaurants already operating in the casino. Not only does one need to consider the cash flow directly generated by the new restaurant but also any reduction in cash flow at the casino's other restaurants resulting from competition with the new restaurant. Also relevant is any new cash flow at the casino generated from new customers attracted to the new restaurant. All firm cash flows resulting from a project, either negative or positive, are relevant.

Last, but not least, costs need to be estimated on an **opportunity cost** basis, not based on historical or sunk costs. **Sunk costs** are costs that have been paid in the past and are thus irrelevant because the costs have been paid whether a project is accepted or rejected. Suppose a corporation is considering building a new restaurant on land purchased years ago for $100,000, but the land is worth $500,000 today net of taxes and brokerage fees. The relevant cost to use in the capital budgeting analysis is the $500,000, not the $100,000. This is the opportunity the corporation is truly giving up if they invest in the new restaurant. The $100,000 was paid years ago, and this will not change whether the corporation builds the new restaurant or not. The $100,000 is a sunk cost and is no longer relevant.

9.3.1 Net Investment Estimation

The *net investment* is the cash outflow at the beginning of a project's economic life. Sometimes it is called the *initial outlay* or the *initial investment*. It is just another project cash flow, but because it is a net outflow and occurs at the beginning, it is usually differentiated from other project cash flows. Sometimes the net investment is defined as the cash outflow occurring at the single point in time that the project's life begins. Yet many projects require cash flows over several months or even years before the project is ready to start generating cash inflows. We will define the net investment cash flows as the net cash outflows required to ready a project for its basic function or operation. For many projects, this will take place at virtually a single point in time, such as a new computer for a hotel's front desk operations or a new toaster for a restaurant. But for many projects, the net investment will cover a period of time, such as the building of a new restaurant or hotel or the remodeling of an existing restaurant or hotel. In such a situation, capital expenditures will take place over several months or years before the project is finished and ready for operation.

Any cash flow required to start a project or caused by a project is relevant to the project analysis. If the cash flow occurs before the project is ready for operation, we label it as part of the net investment. Most of these cash flows will be obvious, including the cost of the asset, any installation cost, any delivery cost, and any tax effects. Possibly not so obvious is the investment required in net working capital and the after-tax salvage value from assets being replaced.

Some capital budgeting projects are expected to grow the firm through increased future sales and cash flows. These projects generally require an increase in current assets to support this growth. This might include more cash to handle a greater number of transactions, more accounts receivable as more credit is granted to customers to generate more sales, and more inventory to support the increased sales. Often, growth will spontaneously generate greater current liabilities, including more accounts payable as increased inventory is purchased on credit, and more accruals as increased wages are generated and additional taxes are owed on greater income.

Net working capital is current assets minus current liabilities, and thus the expected increase in net working capital measures the dual impact of increased current assets and increased current liabilities. Growth-oriented capital budgeting projects generally increase net working capital because current assets are likely to increase more than current liabilities. If a project is expected to need increased net working capital prior to commencing operations, then this increased net working capital needs to be estimated and included as a cash outflow in the net investment estimation.

Some capital budgeting decisions are replacement decisions in which the firm is considering the replacement of old assets with new assets. In these cases, the old assets usually still have some value and can be salvaged for a positive cash flow. This cash flow needs to be estimated on an after-tax basis and included in the net investment as a cash inflow. Because net investment is defined as a cash outflow, the after-tax salvage value from replaced assets will decrease a project's net investment.

The tax impact on replaced assets depends on the market value of the assets relative to the book value. An asset's book value is the remaining asset acquisition cost that has not yet been depreciated. If an asset's market value is equal to its book value, there is no tax effect. If an asset's market value is greater than the book value but less than the acquisition cost, the excess of the market value over the book value is taxed as ordinary income. If an asset's market value is greater than the acquisition cost, the excess above the acquisition cost is taxed as a **capital gain,** and the amount of the market value equal to the difference between the acquisition cost and the book value is taxed as ordinary income. If the market value is less than the book value, the difference is treated as a tax-deductible expense that will cause less taxes to be paid than otherwise. The effect for most firms will be like a tax refund equal to the difference (book value minus market value) times the marginal tax rate.

The Takeoka Japanese Restaurant is considering adding a new line of food to their menu. Takeoka has already spent $1,000 to survey customers about their acceptance and interest in this new food choice. At this point the decision is whether to invest in the additional kitchen equipment and working capital required to proceed with the new venture. The new equipment will cost $30,000, freight for the equipment is $500, and installation cost is $1,500. The new equipment will replace the functions of some old kitchen equipment as well as allowing the preparation of new menu items. The old kitchen equipment can be salvaged for $4,000 after-tax. Also, Takeoka will need to carry an additional $2,000 in food inventory to offer the new menu items. What is the net investment for this project?

$$NINV = \$30,000 + \$500 + \$1,500 + \$2,000 - \$4,000 = \$30,000$$

Notice the $1,000 survey cost is not included in the net investment. The $1,000 has been paid, and it will stay paid, whether the project is accepted or not. Therefore, it is no longer relevant to the decision at this point. Notice the $2,000 for additional inventory is included. This $2,000 is not an expense because it has just been exchanged for another asset. Instead of $2,000 in cash, Takeoka will have $2,000 in inventory. But it is an opportunity cost. The opportunity to use the $2,000 is lost as long as Takeoka retains the extra $2,000 in inventory. Therefore, it is appropriate to show it as a cash outflow in the net investment.

Exhibit 9-4   A net investment example.

A project's net investment estimation can be expressed as follows:

NINV = Asset cost + Delivery cost + Installation cost + Incremental
net working capital − After-tax salvage value from replaced assets

Exhibit 9-4 illustrates the application of this equation in a net investment example.

9.3.2 Net Cash Flow Estimation

An estimate of project cash flows is needed for a capital budgeting analysis. The cash flows required at the beginning of a project's life to ready the project for basic operation are called the *net investment cash flows*. The cash flows after this point are called the *net cash flows*, or annual cash flows. The net cash flows are usually cash inflows, whereas the net investment cash flows are usually cash outflows. A project's net cash flows need to be estimated for each year of a project's expected economic life.

We begin a project's annual net cash flow estimation by projecting the expected change in a firm's net income. But we are interested in cash flow, not profit. We need to adjust net income to estimate cash flow. This is accomplished by adding depreciation to net income. Depreciation is properly considered in the net income calculation so as to estimate taxes correctly. But it needs to be added back in the net cash flow calculation to reflect that it is not an out-of-pocket expense.

If a project requires net working capital increases after the net investment period, then each year's net cash flow needs to be adjusted accordingly. Many times a project will not only cause immediate growth in a firm's sales, but also continue to grow the firm's sales over the life of the project. In this case, net working capital will likely continue to grow over the life of the project as well, so as to

Continuing with the example in Exhibit 9-4 in which Takeoka Japanese Restaurant is considering an investment to introduce a new menu line, the change in depreciation will need to be calculated to estimate the net cash flows for the project. Suppose the economic life of the project is five years, but the new equipment is to be depreciated straight-line over 8 years to a zero value. The old equipment being replaced has been fully depreciated to a zero value. Depreciable expense from the new equipment will include the cost of the asset, delivery cost, and installation cost.

$$\text{Depreciable expense} = \$30,000 + \$500 + \$1,500 = \$32,000$$

Annual depreciation on the new equipment will be $32,000 allocated evenly over the eight-year depreciable life.

$$\text{Annual depreciation} = \$32,000/8 = \$4,000 \text{ annually}$$

Takeoka expects sales to gradually increase for the first three years from this new menu line. The following table reflects the expected sales increase expected each year as well as the associated increase in cash expenses and increased investment in new working capital.

Year	ΔSales revenue	ΔCash expenses	ΔNet working capital
1	$ 20,000	$10,000	$ 500
2	$ 50,000	$25,000	$ 500
3	$100,000	$50,000	$1,000
4	$100,000	$50,000	
5	$100,000	$50,000	

Takeoka expects sales to increase until the third year. Naturally, costs will increase along with sales, and additional working capital, especially inventory, will be needed to support the increased sales. The net cash flows can now be calculated assuming a marginal tax rate of 40 percent and using the equation for net cash flow from earlier.

$NCF_1 = (\$20,000 - 10,000 - 4,000) \times (1 - 40\%) + 4,000 - 500 = \$7,100$

$NCF_2 = (\$50,000 - 25,000 - 4,000) \times (1 - 40\%) + 4,000 - 500 = \$16,100$

$NCF_3 = (\$100,000 - 50,000 - 4,000) \times (1 - 40\%) + 4,000 - 1,000 = \$30,600$

$NCF_4 = (\$100,000 - 50,000 - 4,000) \times (1 - 40\%) + 4,000 = \$31,600$

$NCF_5 = (\$100,000 - 50,000 - 4,000) \times (1 - 40\%) + 4,000 = \$31,600$

The cash flow for the fifth and last year will also include salvage value of the equipment plus the return of net working capital invested over the life of the project. Remember, there was a $2,000 investment in net working capital (inventory) at the very beginning from the calculation of the net investment in Exhibit 9-4. This additional cash flow at the end of the project life is the terminal, nonoperating cash flow. Suppose the equipment can be salvaged for $12,000 after tax.

$$\text{Terminal, Nonoperating Cash Flow} = \$12,000 + 2,000 + 500 + 500 + 1,000 = \$16,000$$

where the $12,000 is the salvage value, the $2,000 is the inventory investment in the beginning; the $500, $500, and $1,000 are the investments in net working capital in years 1, 2, and 3, respectively. The total cash flow for the fifth and last year is the net cash flow for year 5 plus the terminal, nonoperating cash flow.

$$\text{Total cash flow 5} = \$31,600 + 16,000 = \$47,600$$

The cash flows for the five years can also be summarized in table form.

	Year 1	Year 2	Year 3	Year 4	Year 5
ΔSales revenue	$20,000	$50,000	$100,000	$100,000	$100,000
ΔCash expenses	−10,000	−25,000	−50,000	−50,000	−50,000
ΔDepreciation	−4,000	−4,000	−4,000	−4,000	−4,000
ΔEarnings before taxes	$ 6,000	$21,000	$ 46,000	$ 46,000	$ 46,000
ΔTaxes	−2,400	−8,400	−18,400	−18,400	−18,400
ΔNet income	$ 3,600	$12,600	$27,600	$ 27,600	$ 27,600
ΔDepreciation	+4,000	+4,000	+4,000	+4,000	+4,000
ΔNet working capital	−500	−500	−1,000	0	0
Net cash flow	$ 7,100	$16,100	$ 30,600	$ 31,600	$ 31,600
After-tax salvage					+12,000
Net working capital return					+ 4,000
Total cash flow	$ 7,100	$16,100	$ 30,600	$ 31,600	$ 47,600

Exhibit 9-5   A net cash flow example.

support the growth in sales. This will need to be reflected in the project's net cash flow calculations. In the following explanation of net cash flow calculations, we will use the symbol Δ quite often. A Δ means the change in something. Thus, if a firm's net income increased from $100,000 to $115,000, then ΔNet income = $115,000 − $100,000 = $15,000. Also, t stands for the marginal tax rate. If a firm's taxable income increases by $100 and the firm's taxes increase by $40, then the firm's marginal tax rate (t) is 40 percent. The following equation shows the calculations of net cash flow more explicitly.

$$NCF = \Delta\text{Net income} + \Delta\text{Depreciation} - \Delta\text{Net working capital}$$

The ΔNet income can be estimated by forecasting the ΔEarnings before taxes and multiplying by one minus the marginal tax rate.

$$NCF = \Delta\text{Earnings before taxes} \times (1 - t) + \Delta\text{Depreciation}$$
$$- \Delta\text{ Net working capital}$$

The ΔEarnings before taxes can be estimated by forecasting the ΔSales revenue, the ΔCash expenses, and the ΔDepreciation and combining them to calculate the ΔEarnings before taxes.

$$NCF = (\Delta\text{Sales revenue} - \Delta\text{Cash expenses} - \Delta\text{Depreciation}) \times (1 - t)$$
$$+ \Delta\text{Depreciation} - \Delta\text{Net working capital}$$

Exhibit 9-5 continues with the net investment example begun in Exhibit 9-4 to illustrate the calculation of a project's net cash flows.

Essentially, the change in earnings before tax is first calculated. If a variable has a positive impact on profit, then it is added; if it has a negative impact on profit, it is subtracted. For instance, if a project is a growth project and leads to higher cash expenses, then the increased cash expenses have a negative impact on profits and are subtracted in the NCF calculation. Of course, hopefully the increased sales revenue more than offsets this. But if a project's motivation is reduced costs, then the resulting reduction in cash expenses has a positive impact on profits and is added (actually the negative change in cash expenses is subtracted for a net positive impact) in the NCF calculation.

The net cash flow calculations should not include additional interest expense generated by the financing of the project. Certainly all costs are relevant, including financial costs. Financial costs are generally taken into account by the use of a **required rate of return.** Most capital budgeting decision methods used to recommend acceptance or rejection of a project take this required rate of return account. Required rates of return are essentially a measure of the firm's cost of capital and therefore take into account the interest cost of debt and other financial costs as explained in the previous chapter. Thus there is no need to include financial costs at this stage of the analysis.

The end of a project's economic life often brings one-time cash flows in addition to the basic operating cash flow. We will call these terminal, nonoperating cash flows because they come at a project's termination, and they are not regular, recurring, operating cash flows. One possible terminal, nonoperating cash flow is the salvage value of assets acquired as a result of the project investment. If a project is truly finished, then we assume the firm will sell any remaining assets from the project. The after-tax salvage value of project assets should be added to the net cash flow for the last year. Also, all investments in net working capital (cash outflows) would generally be returned at the end of a project's life as cash inflows. An earlier investment to increase inventories and accounts receivable would probably be liquidated as the firm uses up the remaining inventory and collects its accounts receivable at the project's end. Often, though, the increased current assets would not be reduced because a successful project may be continued in the future by a replacement investment. But even in this case, the cost of the increased net working capital should be assigned to the replacement project and the value of the increased net working capital still credited to the initial project's final year net cash flow. If one does not assume the investments in net working capital are returned at the end of project life, this implies the increased net working capital is lost, and this is unlikely to be the case. A project's final year cash flow will often be modified as follows.

$$
\begin{aligned}
\text{Final year } NCF = \ & (\Delta\text{Sales revenue} - \Delta\text{Cash expenses} - \Delta\text{Depreciation}) \\
& \times (1 - t) + \Delta\text{Depreciation} + \Delta\text{Net working capital} \\
& + \text{After-tax salvage value}
\end{aligned}
$$

where the ΔNet working capital is the sum of all the previous net working capital investments made including those in the net investment cash flows. Exhibit 9-5 provides an example to illustrate this calculation along with a net cash flow calculation.

9.3.3 Estimation of After-Tax Salvage Values

Capital budgeting projects usually require large investments in depreciable assets. The salvage values of these depreciable assets often increase a project's cash flow at the end of the project's life. Also, replacement decision capital budgeting projects often can reduce the amount of the net investment at the beginning of the project's life by the salvage value of old assets being replaced. The tax effect from these salvage values are also an important input to the analysis, either reducing or increasing the salvage value on an after-tax basis. As an example, suppose the

Jameson Corporation is salvaging or selling an old asset for its market value, and the asset's book value is $10,000. An asset's book value is equal to its acquisition cost minus accumulated depreciation. An asset's acquisition costs include costs for installation and delivery. Suppose Jameson's old asset was originally acquired for $100,000, and $90,000 has been depreciated. Then the book value is $10,000. Acquisition cost of $100,000 minus accumulated depreciation of $90,000 equals $10,000. A later section in this chapter will discuss depreciation, and Exhibit 9-6 provides more detail on computing after-tax salvage values with an example. But for now let us continue with this example and consider the tax consequences to the Jameson Corporation from salvaging an old asset.

If an asset is sold for its book value, there is no tax effect. If the Jameson Corporation sells the asset for exactly the book value of $10,000, there are no taxes owed and no reduced taxes. The after-tax salvage value is $10,000 because there is no tax impact.

If an asset is sold for more than its book value but less than its original acquisition cost, taxes are owed on the gain over and above the book value. If the Jameson Corporation sells the asset for $15,000, then taxes are owed on the $5,000 received above the book value of $10,000. This $5,000 is calculated by subtracting the $10,000 book value from the $15,000 sale price. If we assume a 40 percent marginal tax rate, 40% × $5,000 = $2,000 would be owed in taxes, and the Jameson Corporation would receive $13,000 after-tax from the salvage value.

If an asset is sold for less than its book value, taxes are reduced on other corporate income by an amount equal to the loss times the marginal tax rate. If the Jameson Corporation sells the asset for $7,000, there is a $3,000 loss calculated by subtracting the $10,000 book value from the $7,000 sale price. This loss will lower taxes on other corporate income by $3,000 × 40% = $1,200. Because the Jameson Corporation will pay $1,200 less in taxes than otherwise, the net salvage value is actually $8,200. This is calculated by adding the $7,000 sale price to the $1,200 reduction in taxes.

If an asset is sold for more than its acquisition cost, ordinary income taxes are owed on the accumulated depreciation (acquisition cost minus book value), and capital gains taxes are owed on the gain over and above the original acquisition cost. If the Jameson Corporation sells the asset for $130,000, then ordinary income taxes are owed on the $90,000 accumulated depreciation at 40 percent equal to $36,000, and additional capital gains taxes are owed on the gain over the $100,000 original cost. If the capital gains rate is 40 percent, this would be $30,000 × 40% = $12,000 for a total of $48,000 in taxes owed, leaving a net salvage value of $82,000 ($130,000 minus $48,000). Depending on tax regulations, the capital gains tax rate has sometimes been the same as the ordinary income tax rate and has sometimes been below the ordinary income tax rate. This situation is rare. It is unusual for depreciable assets to appreciate in value, but it is possible.

9.3.4 Depreciation

Long-term physical assets are depreciated over time rather than expensed immediately. **Depreciation** is the allocation of a capital expenditure over several years. The exact length of time depends on the type of asset (see Appendix 9.1). Depreciation has two basic functions. One is for financial reporting purposes,

We will continue the example from Exhibits 9-4 and 9-5 to further illustrate the calculation of after-tax salvage values. Takeoka's new kitchen equipment will generate $32,000 in depreciable expenses including asset cost, delivery cost, and installation cost. Depreciation will be straight-line to a zero value over eight years for depreciation of $4,000 per year. But the economic life of the project is only five years, meaning Takeoka plans to finish with the new equipment in five years. At the end of five years, the book value of the new equipment will be $12,000. This is the amount of depreciation still remaining. It can be calculated as the depreciation still remaining after five years.

$$3 \text{ Years} \times \$4,000 \text{ Depreciation per year} = \$12,000 \text{ Book value}$$

or it can be calculated as the acquisition cost minus accumulated depreciation.

$$\$32,000 - 5 \text{ Years} \times \$4,000 \text{ Depreciation per year} = \$12,000 \text{ Book value}$$

When Takeoka disposes of the equipment in 5 years, the salvage price and the book value together determine the tax impact from the disposal as follows.

1. If the equipment is sold for its book value, there is no tax impact.

$$\text{After-tax salvage value} = \$12,000$$

2. If the equipment is sold for more than its book value but less than its acquisition cost, the sale price over and above the book value is a recapture of depreciation and taxed as ordinary income. Suppose the equipment is sold for $20,000.

$$\text{After-tax salvage value} = \$20,000 - (\$8,000 \times 40\%) = \$20,000 - 3,200 = \$16,800$$

where $8,000 is the recapture of depreciation.

3. If the equipment is sold for less than its book value, taxes on other firm income are reduced by an amount equal to this loss (the amount less than the book value) times the marginal tax rate. Suppose the equipment is sold for $7,000.

$$\text{After-tax salvage value} = \$7,000 + (5,000 \times 40\%) = \$7,000 + 2,000 = \$9,000$$

where $5,000 is the loss calculated as the book value minus the sale price.

and the other function is for calculating tax-deductible expenses and, subsequently, the income taxes owed by a firm. Depreciation is a legitimate tax-deductible expense. Different methods of calculating depreciation are used, depending on the purpose. For financial reporting purposes, an asset is generally depreciated to an estimated salvage value using one of several methods. For tax calculation purposes, an asset is generally depreciated to a zero value using the **Modified Accelerated Cost Recovery System (MACRS)** as explained in Appendix 9.1.

Net cash flows are an estimate of a project's impact on the firm's cash flows. Naturally, depreciation used for tax purposes (MACRS) is relevant in the estimation of net cash flows because we are interested in the impact on cash flow. MACRS is the depreciation that determines a firm's actual taxes paid and thus determines a firm's cash flows. This chapter on capital budgeting is introductory in nature, and we want to keep the depreciation calculation simple while focusing most of our time on cash flow estimation and various capital budgeting decision methods. Thus, instead of using MACRS depreciation to a zero value, this chapter's presentation will use straight-line depreciation to a zero value as follows.

4. If the equipment is sold for more than its book value and more than its acquisition, there are two different taxes to calculate. First is the recapture of depreciation calculated as the difference between the acquisition cost and the book value. This is taxed as ordinary income. Second is the capital gain calculated as the sale price minus the acquisition cost. This is taxed as a capital gain. Suppose the equipment is sold for $42,000, and the capital gains tax rate is 25 percent.

After-tax salvage value = $42,000 − (20,000 × 40%) − (10,000 × 25%)
After-tax salvage value = $42,000 − 8,000 − 2,500 = $31,500

Following is a summary of these calculations in one table. Keep in mind the original acquisition cost of the equipment is $32,000, and at the end of the five-year economic life, accumulated depreciation is $20,000 and the book value is $12,000.

	Equal book value	More than book value	Less than book value	More than acquisition cost
Sale price	$12,000	$20,000	$7,000	$42,000
Book value	12,000	12,000	12,000	12,000
Depreciation recapture	0	8,000	−5,000	20,000
Capital gain	0	0	0	10,000
Ordinary income taxes				
40% × Depreciation recapture	0	3,200	−2,000	8,000
Capital gains taxes				
25% × Capital gain	0	0	0	2,500
After-tax salvage value				
Sale price − Taxes	**$12,000**	**$16,800**	**$9,000**	**$31,500**

Exhibit 9-6   Estimating after-tax salvage values.

$$\text{Annual depreciation amount} = \frac{\text{Depreciable asset's acquisition cost}}{\text{Total number of years of depreciation}}$$

But in actual capital budgeting analysis, the relevant depreciation to use is MACRS.

Depreciation is a tax-deductible expense. But it is an expense allocation for a past cash outflow made in a previous period of time; it is not a cash outflow in the current period. Depreciation does reduce taxes in the current period. Because of the reduced taxes, depreciation causes current net cash flows to be higher than otherwise. For example, consider the net cash flow equation.

$$NCF = (\Delta\text{Sales revenue} - \Delta\text{Operating costs} - \Delta\text{Depreciation}) \times (1 - t) + \Delta\text{Depreciation} - \Delta\text{Net working capital}$$

Suppose a new project is expected to increase sales revenue by $100,000 a year, increase operating costs by $40,000 a year and depreciation by $20,000 a year, the marginal tax rate is 40 percent, and there is no expected change in net working capital. The net cash flow is $44,000 per year. If depreciation increases by $30,000 instead of $20,000 per year, the net cash flow is $48,000 per year! The impact of depreciation on a project's cash flows is further illustrated in Exhibit 9-7.

If a capital budgeting project is expected to increase sales revenue by $100,000 a year and increase cash expenses by $40,000 a year and depreciation by $20,000 a year, the net cash flow is

$$NCF = (\$100{,}000 - 40{,}000 - 20{,}000) \times (1 - 40\%) + 20{,}000 = \$44{,}000$$

The change in earnings after tax is $24,000 (earnings after tax is from the preceding equation before adding back the $20,000 depreciation).

If depreciation is expected to be $30,000 higher each year instead of $20,000, the net cash flow is

$$NCF = (\$100{,}000 - 40{,}000 - 30{,}000) \times (1 - 40\%) + 30{,}000 = \$48{,}000$$

The change in earnings after-tax is $18,000 (from the preceding equation before adding back the $30,000 depreciation). Following is a summary of these two calculations in one table.

	Depreciation = $20,000	Depreciation = $30,000
ΔSales revenue	$100,000	$100,000
ΔCash expenses	−40,000	−40,000
ΔDepreciation	−20,000	−30,000
ΔEarnings before taxes	$ 40,000	$ 30,000
ΔTaxes (40%)	−16,000	−12,000
ΔNet income	$ 24,000	$ 18,000
ΔDepreciation	+20,000	+30,000
Net cash flow	**$ 44,000**	**$ 48,000**

The impact of depreciation on firm profit and cash flow is summarized as follows.

	Profit	Cash flow
Depreciation increases	Decreases	Increases
Depreciation decreases	Increases	Decreases

Exhibit 9-7   The impact of depreciation on net cash flow.

9.4 SUMMARY

We have introduced the capital budgeting concept in this chapter and stressed its importance to a firm's long-term health. Capital budgeting decisions determine the future course a business takes. A firm making bad capital budgeting decisions will have projects that generate losses. The firm can continue to accept these losses for a long time or sell the assets, usually at a significant loss. A firm making good capital budgeting decisions will have assets generating positive cash flows for a long time. Thus, a firm's capital budgeting decisions determine its long-term health.

We have also discussed the information needed to make a capital budgeting decision. In estimating a project's cash flows, it is vital to consider only incremental cash flows and to measure costs as opportunity costs. A project's estimated cash flows are organized into one of three categories: (1) net investment, (2) net cash flows, and (3) terminal, nonoperating cash flow. A project's net investment is the cost of acquiring a project. The net cash flows and terminal, nonoperating cash flows are the benefits a project is expected to produce. The next chapter will show the several common methods used to compare a project's costs and benefits to generate a project decision—should a firm invest or not invest in a project?

KEY TERMS

Capital budgeting
Capital gain
Depreciation
Independent project
Modified accelerated cost recovery system (MACRS) depreciation
Mutually exclusive project
Net cash flow
Net investment
Opportunity costs
Required rate of return
Sunk costs

DISCUSSION QUESTIONS

1. Why are good capital budgeting decisions crucial to the long-term viability of a firm?
2. What is the difference between independent projects and mutually exclusive projects?
3. Explain why larger depreciation increases a capital budgeting project's net cash flow.
4. What is the difference between an opportunity cost and a sunk cost?
5. Define the net investment for a capital budgeting project. What is included in a capital budgeting project's net investment?
6. Define the net cash flows for a capital budgeting project. What is included in a capital budgeting project's net cash flows?
7. Capital budgeting projects can be classified according to the purpose of the project. List and explain the three categories for classifying projects according to their purpose.
8. The impact of indirect effects of a capital budgeting project should be included in cash flow estimation. Give some examples of indirect effects, and explain why they are important and should be considered in the capital budgeting decision process.
9. Explain how the net investment for a replacement capital budgeting project is likely to be different than the net investment for a pure growth-oriented capital budgeting project.
10. If a depreciable asset is sold for its book value, there are no tax consequences. But if a depreciable asset is sold for a value different than its book value, there are tax consequences. Explain the preceding statements.

PROBLEMS

1. Depot Casino Corporation is considering an expansion of their busiest casino. Depot Casino has already conducted and paid $50,000 for a marketing survey. The expansion will cost $2.5 million for the assets including delivery costs and all construction costs. In addition, $500,000 in net working capital will be needed immediately. Compute the net investment of this expansion project.

2. Kyoto Sushi Incorporated is considering the replacement of their sushi display cases. The current cases were purchased 3 years ago at a total cost of $40,000 and are being depreciated straight-line to a zero value over 8 years. If Kyoto Sushi sells these sushi display cases at the following prices, what are the after-tax cash flows to Kyoto Sushi? Use 40 percent for the effective tax rate.
   a. $25,000
   b. $30,000
   c. $35,000
   d. $10,000

3. Feinstein's Finest is considering opening a new pub in the southwest part of town. The building will cost $1.5 million, and fixtures such as bars, kitchen equipment, and so on, will cost another $200,000, including installation costs. Stocking the pub with inventory before it opens will cost another $100,000. Land for the building site cost Feinstein $300,000 several years ago, but now the land could be sold to net Feinstein $1,000,000 after-tax. Compute the net investment for Feinstein's Finest new pub.

4. Kilby's Casinos is considering replacing their craps tables. They were purchased 4 years ago for a total cost of $100,000 and are being depreciated straight-line to a zero value over 10 years. If these crap tables are sold at the following prices, what are the after-tax cash flows to Kilbys Casinos? Use 40 percent for the effective tax rate.
   a. $75,000
   b. $60,000
   c. $20,000

5. Bob's Outdoor Adventures is considering replacing his fleet of Hummers. A new fleet of specially configured Hummers will cost $800,000, including all shipping, dealer prep, documentation, and title costs. The old fleet can be sold for $200,000 and the remaining book value on the old fleet is $150,000. Compute the net investment for this replacement project. Use 40 percent for the effective tax rate.

6. A project is expected to increase a firm's sales revenues by $100,000 annually, increase its cash expenses by $45,000 annually, and increase its depreciation by $30,000 annually. The project has an expected economic life of 7 years. What is the net cash flow each year? Use 40 percent for the effective tax rate. Assume there is no working capital to be liquidated at the end of 7 years, and there is also no salvage value at the end of 7 years.

7. A project is expected to increase a firm's sales revenues by $20,000 annually, *decrease* its cash expenses by $25,000 annually, and increase its depreciation by $15,000 annually. The project has an expected economic life of 10 years. What is the net cash flow each year? Use 40 percent for the effective tax rate. Assume there is no working capital to be liquidated at the end of 10 years, and there is also no salvage value at the end of 10 years.

8. A project is expected to decrease a firm's cash expenses by $150,000 annually and increase its depreciation by $80,000 annually. The project has an expected economic life of 8 years. What is the net cash flow each year? Use 40 percent for the effective tax rate. Assume there is no working capital to be liquidated at the end of 8 years, and there is also no salvage value at the end of 8 years.

9. Lee's Fabulous Foods Incorporated is planning to add a new line of noodles that will require the acquisition of new processing equipment. The equipment will cost $1,000,000, including installation and shipping. It will be depreciated straight-line to a zero value over the 10-year economic life of the project. Interest cost associated with financing the equipment purchase is estimated to be $40,000 annually. The expected salvage value of the machine at the end of 10 years is $200,000.

   One year ago a marketing survey was performed to gauge the likely success of this new project. The survey cost $25,000 and was paid last year.

   If this new equipment is acquired, it will also allow the replacement of old equipment used for other food lines. This old equipment can be salvaged for $150,000 and has a book value of $200,000. The remaining depreciation on the old equipment is $40,000 annually for five more years.

   Additional net working capital of $85,000 will be needed immediately. When the project is terminated in 10 years, there no longer will be a need for this incremental working capital.

   Lee expects to sell $300,000 worth of this new pasta annually. The cost of producing and selling the pasta is estimated to be $50,000 annually (not including depreciation or interest expense). The marginal tax rate is 40 percent.
   a. Compute the net investment.
   b. Compute the net cash flow for the first year.
   c. Compute the net cash flow for the final year (year 10), including all terminal cash flows.

10. Nakatas Resorts is planning to expand. This will require the acquisition of new equipment. The equipment will cost $200,000, including delivery and installation. It will be depreciated straight-line to a zero value over the 5-year economic life of the project. Interest costs associated with financing the equipment purchase are estimated to be $15,000 annually. The expected salvage value of this new equipment at the end of 5 years is $25,000.

    Additional net working capital of $30,000 will be needed immediately. When the project is terminated in 5 years, there no longer will be a need for this incremental working capital. If new equipment is acquired, existing equipment can be salvaged for $10,000. The existing equipment has been completely depreciated.

    Nakatas expects the expansion to increase sales by $100,000 annually. Cash operating costs are expected to increase by $40,000 annually (not including depreciation or interest expense). The marginal tax rate is 40 percent.
    a. Compute the net investment.
    b. Compute the net cash flow for the first year.
    c. Compute the net cash flow for the last year (year 5), including all terminal cash flows.

Year	3-Year	5-Year	7-Year	10-Year	15-Year	20-Year
1	33.33%	20.00%	14.29%	10.00%	5.00%	3.75%
2	44.45%	32.00%	24.49%	18.00%	9.50%	7.219%
3	14.81%	19.20%	17.49%	14.40%	8.55%	6.677%
4	7.41%	11.52%	12.49%	11.52%	7.70%	6.177%
5		11.52%	8.93%	9.22%	6.93%	5.713%
6		5.76%	8.92%	7.37%	6.23%	5.285%
7			8.93%	6.55%	5.90%	4.888%
8			4.46%	6.55%	5.90%	4.522%
9				6.56%	5.91%	4.462%
10				6.55%	5.90%	4.461%
11				3.28%	5.91%	4.462%
12					5.90%	4.461%
13					5.91%	4.462%
14					5.90%	4.461%
15					5.91%	4.462%
16					2.95%	4.461%
17						4.462%
18						4.461%
19						4.462%
20						4.461%
21						2.231%

Exhibit A9-1 MACRS depreciation rates excluding realty property.

APPENDIX 9.1—MODIFIED ACCELERATED COST RECOVERY SYSTEM

Depreciation for tax purposes of assets placed into service since 1986 is prescribed by the Modified Accelerated Cost Recovery System (MACRS). This system does not take into account the expected useful life of an asset or the expected salvage value of an asset and therefore is generally not similar to depreciation used for financial accounting purposes. MACRS classifies all depreciable assets into six categories except real estate. The six classes are 3-, 5-, 7-, 10-, 15-, and 20-year categories. Probably the most used categories are 5- and 7-year. The 5-year class includes automobiles, computers, and other technology-oriented equipment. The 7-year class includes office furniture and equipment and many types of manufacturing equipment.

Assets in the 3-, 5-, 7-, and 10-year categories are depreciated using 200 percent declining balance depreciation using the half-year convention. You must switch to straight-line depreciation in the first year the straight-line rate exceeds the declining balance rate. The half-year convention means a half-year of depreciation is taken in the first year an asset is put in service, and a half-year of depreciation is taken at the end as well. Thus an asset in the 5-year category would receive a half-year of depreciation in the first year, a full year of depreciation for each of the next four years, and a half-year of depreciation for year 6. Assets in the 15- and 20-year categories are depreciated using 150 percent declining balance depreciation using the half-year convention and also switching to straight-line depreciation once it become greater than the declining balance rate. The depreciation rates are shown in Exhibit A9-1. The full cost of an asset is the basis that these rates are multiplied by to calculate depreciation.

Real estate property has separate categories and depreciation methods. Residential rental property has a 27.5-year recovery period, and nonresidential real property has a 39-year recovery period. Depreciation under both categories starts the month the property is placed into service and also uses the half-month convention. Suppose a new nonresidential building with a cost basis of $1 million is placed into service in October 2003. Straight-line depreciation for one year is 0.02564 (1 divided by 39) of $1,000,000, or $25,640. Because the half-month convention is used, 2.5 months of depreciation are allowed in 2003 (December, November, and a half-month for October). Depreciation for the first year will be $5,342 (2.5/12 × $25,640).

Capital Budgeting Decision Methods | 10

Chapter Objectives

- To understand and know how to compute a capital budgeting project's payback period, discounted payback period, net present value, profitability index, internal rate of return, and modified internal rate of return
- To understand how to use capital budgeting decision methods on independent capital budgeting projects
- To understand how to use capital budgeting decision methods on mutually exclusive capital budgeting projects
- To understand how to evaluate a capital budgeting project with cash flows that are not normal
- To understand the advantages and disadvantages of each of the capital budgeting decision methods

10.1 INTRODUCTION

In this chapter, we present the traditional methods used to evaluate capital budgeting projects. These methods can also be used to evaluate other capital investments besides traditional capital budgeting projects, which might include investments in employee training, advertising campaigns, a permanent increase in inventory, repayment of a bond to be funded with a new, lower interest rate bond, or research and development expenditures.

The cost of acquiring a project is measured as the project's **net investment,** and the benefits from a project are measured as the project's **net cash flows.** Once a project's net investment and net cash flows have been estimated, a decision method is used to recommend either acceptance or rejection of the project. The decision methods are based on a comparison of the project costs with the project benefits. Some capital budgeting decision methods perform the cost-benefit analysis by determining how long it takes for the project benefits to recover the project cost (payback period and discounted payback period). The discounted payback period considers the time value of money (TVM) in determining this period of time, whereas the payback period does not take into account the time value of money. Other methods perform a straight, forward comparison of the benefits and cost while taking into account the time value of money (net present value and profitability index). The **net present value** method is the difference between benefits and costs, and the **profitability index** is the ratio of benefits to costs. And finally, some methods determine the annual percentage rate of return a project's benefits provide to a project investment. These last methods are called the internal rate of return and the modified internal rate of return. The remainder of this chapter presents these six different capital budgeting decision methods and explains the strengths and weaknesses of each.

10.2 CAPITAL BUDGETING DECISION METHODS

To assist in the presentation of the six capital budgeting methods, two capital budgeting examples will be used. The Ramdeen Restaurant is considering two possible projects. The first is the expansion of his very successful restaurant. Ramdeen estimates the cash flows from the expansion will be as follows.

Ramdeen's Restaurant Expansion Project

Year	Cash flow
0	−$200,000
1	$ 70,000
2	$ 70,000
3	$ 70,000
4	$ 70,000
5	$ 70,000

The expansion project has a $200,000 net investment and positive net cash flows of $70,000 a year for 5 years, as estimated in the preceding table. The second project is to build a new restaurant on the other side of town. Ramdeen estimates the cash flows from the new restaurant as follows.

Ramdeen's New Restaurant Project

Year	Cash flow
0	−$300,000
1	$ 50,000
2	$ 70,000
3	$100,000
4	$120,000
5	$150,000

The new restaurant project has a $300,000 net investment and positive net cash flows of $50,000, $70,000, $100,000, $120,000, and $150,000, respectively for years 1 through 5, as estimated in the preceding table.

10.2.1 Payback Period

A project's **payback period** is the amount of time required for the net cash flows to recover the net investment. Generally, the quicker a project pays back, the better the project. It is quite simple to calculate the payback period for a project with net cash flows that are the same each year, such as Ramdeen's expansion project.

$$\text{Payback period} = \frac{\$200{,}000}{\$70{,}000} = 2.86 \text{ years}$$

But the calculation is a bit more difficult for a project with uneven net cash flows such as Ramdeen's new restaurant project. It is best calculated by constructing a cash flow table and adding a cumulative cash flow column.

Ramdeen's New Restaurant Project

Year	Cash flow	Cumulative cash flow
0	−$300,000	−$300,000
1	$ 50,000	−$250,000
2	$ 70,000	−$180,000
3	$100,000	−$ 80,000
4	$120,000	
5	$150,000	

Accumulating the cash flow column creates the new column, labeled "Cumulative Cash Flow." Year 0 is just the negative $300,000 net investment, the same as the "Cash Flow" column. Year 1 is −$300,000 plus $50,000, which equals a cumulative cash flow of negative $250,000 for year 1. Year 2 is −$250,000 plus $70,000, which equals a cumulative cash flow of negative $180,000. Year 3 is −$180,000 plus $100,000, which equals a cumulative cash flow of −$80,000. It is obvious the year 4 cash flow of $120,000 is more than enough to pay back the remaining −$80,000 of the net investment, and therefore we know the payback period is more than three years, but less than four years. Again, with −$80,000 of the net investment remaining after year 3, the payback period has to be more than three years. But with a cash flow of $120,000 in year 4, the payback period must be less than four years. Now it only remains to calculate what proportion of year 4 it will take to pay back the remaining −$80,000. This will be $\frac{\$80{,}000}{\$120{,}000} = 0.67$ of the fourth year, giving us a payback period of 3.67 years. Or we could show the calculation for the new restaurant as

$$\text{Payback period} = 3 + \frac{\$80{,}000}{\$120{,}000} = 3 + 0.67 = 3.67 \text{ years}$$

According to the payback period calculations, the expansion project is better because it pays back more than three-fourths of a year quicker (3.67 − 2.86 = 0.81 years) than the new restaurant project. But does this mean the expansion project is a better investment for Ramdeen? No, of course not. The payback period can be a useful measure of a project's liquidity risk. It is proper to say that Ramdeen expects to recoup his net investment more quickly on the expansion than the new restaurant, but it would be stretching logic to make much more out of the payback period calculation.

The payback period has several serious weaknesses. First, it does not take into account the time value of money. We learned in Chapter 4 that the time when money is received has a significant impact on the money's value. Thus, $100 received today is more valuable than $100 received in two years. In the payback calculation, this time value of money is not considered.

Major weaknes of payback ①

Second, there is no objective criterion for what is an acceptable payback period. Certainly a corporation can require all projects payback in less than three years or four years or some other finite number of years. But this is subjective because there is nothing objective about a certain number of years' cutoff point that maximizes firm value. Two analysts considering the same project with the same data could make different accept/reject decisions using the payback period. For example, one analyst could use a two-year cutoff for payback and reject the expansion project, and the other analyst could use a three-year cutoff for payback and accept the expansion project.

②

Third, cash flows after the payback period have no impact on the payback period calculation. For example, suppose the expansion project had a $100,000 expected net cash flow in year 5 instead of $70,000. This would clearly make the project more attractive, but the project's payback period does not reflect this. Because cash flows after the payback period are ignored, the payback period would still be 2.86 years.

③

The payback period can be a useful measure of a project's liquidity risk, but this method has three serious drawbacks as indicated. A better measure of liquidity risk is the discounted payback period.

10.2.2 Discounted Payback Period

The **discounted payback period** improves on the payback period by considering the time value of money. A project's discounted payback period is the amount of time required for the **net cash flows' present values** to recover the net investment. The present values are typically calculated by discounting the net cash flows at the required rate of return. Generally, the shorter a project's discounted payback, the better the project. If the **required rate of return** is known and a project's cash flows have been estimated, the first step in the discounted payback's calculation is to discount the project's cash flows at the required rate of return (calculate the present values of the cash flows). Then the discounted payback period is calculated the same as the regular payback period, except the present values of the cash flows are used.

Let us illustrate the discounted payback with examples from Ramdeen's Restaurant. Let the required rate of return equal 10 percent.

Ramdeen's Restaurant Expansion Project

Year	Cash flow	PV of cash flow	Cumulative
0	−$200,000	−$200,000	−$200,000
1	$ 70,000	$ 63,636	−$136,364
2	$ 70,000	$ 57,851	−$ 78,513
3	$ 70,000	$ 52,592	−$ 25,921
4	$ 70,000	$ 47,811	
5	$ 70,000	$ 43,464	

The "PV of cash flow" column is simply the cash flow discounted back at 10 percent rounded to the nearest dollar. For example, $70,000 discounted at 10 percent for one year equals $63,636 rounded to the nearest dollar. $70,000 discounted at 10 percent for two years equals $57,851, and so on for years 3, 4, and 5. The present value of the −$200,000 net investment is still −$200,000 because it is literally a present value at time zero (today). The "Cumulative" column is the accumulation of the "PV of cash flow" column. For example, the −$200,000 present value cash flow from year 0 plus the $63,636 present value cash flow from year 1 accumulate to −$136,364 (year 1 under "Cumulative"). The −$136,364 cumulative cash flow from year 1 plus the $57,851 present value cash flow from year 2 accumulate to −$78,513 (year 2 under "Cumulative). The −$78,513 cumulative cash flow from year 2 plus the $52,592 present value cash flow from year 3 accumulate to −$25,921 (year 3 under "Cumulative"). After year 3 there still remains $25,921 of the net investment not recovered from the present value of the net cash flows. Therefore, the discounted payback period must be more than 3 years. Because the $47,811 present value cash flow from year 4 is more than enough to recover the remaining net investment of $25,921, the discounted payback period for the expansion project will be more than 3 years but less than 4 years as follows.

$$\text{Discounted payback period} = 3 \text{ years} + \frac{\$25,921 \text{ not yet recovered after 3 years}}{\$47,811 \text{ PV of cash flow from year 4}}$$

$$= 3 + 0.54 = 3.54 \text{ years}$$

The calculation for Ramdeen's New Restaurant Project is similar to the calculation for the expansion project.

Ramdeen's New Restaurant Project

Year	Cash flow	PV of cash flow	Cumulative
0	−$300,000	−$300,000	−$300,000
1	$ 50,000	$ 45,455	−$254,545
2	$ 70,000	$ 57,851	−$196,694
3	$100,000	$ 75,131	−$121,563
4	$120,000	$ 81,962	−$ 39,601
5	$150,000	$ 93,138	

This table is constructed just like the table used to calculate the discounted payback period for Ramdeen's Restaurant Expansion Project. The third column, "PV of cash flow," is the present value of each cash flow discounted at the 10 percent required rate of return for the appropriate number of years. The "Cumulative" column accumulates the values from the "PV of cash flow" column. After four years, there is still $39,601 remaining from the net investment not yet recovered from the present value of the net cash flows. The present value of the cash flow from the fifth year is more than enough to pay back this remaining $39,601, and therefore the discounted payback period must be more than four years, but less than five years. The discounted payback period for the new restaurant project is

$$\text{Discounted payback period} = 4 + \frac{\$39,601}{\$93,139} = 4 + 0.43 = 4.43 \text{ years}$$

Again, the discounted payback period indicates Ramdeen's expansion project pays back quicker than the new restaurant project, even when considering the time value of money. The expansion project expects to recover the net investment in 3.54 years and the new restaurant project in 4.43 years. The shorter discounted payback still does not imply the expansion is a better project. It does imply the expansion recovers its net investment quicker and has less liquidity risk than the new restaurant project.

The discounted payback period is an improvement on the payback period. First, it does take into account the time value of money by discounting future cash flows back to the present. All cash flows are standardized by considering and accumulating only present values.

The discounted payback period improves on the second weakness of the payback period. This second weakness is the lack of an objective criterion for use with the payback period. The discounted payback period, however, has an objective criterion under certain circumstances. Consider the two projects just discussed. Both projects have only positive cash flows after the net investment. Projects with all positive net cash flows after the net investment are considered normal projects. The expansion project has a discounted payback period of 3.54 years, indicating the net investment is recovered in 3.54 years with the required 10 percent rate of return. If all the cash flows occur as expected for 3.54 years, Ramdeen has earned its 10 percent required rate of return. All cash flows after 3.54 years provide Ramdeen with a return over and above 10 percent because the project is normal, and all remaining cash flows are positive. A similar analysis can be applied to Ramdeen's new restaurant project. Its discounted payback period is 4.43 years, and it is a normal project. If cash flows occur as expected, the new restaurant project earns the 10 percent required rate of return in 4.43 years, and the positive cash flows continuing thereafter will provide additional returns over and above 10 percent.

A **normal capital budgeting project** with a discounted payback period less than its economic life is an acceptable project. It is expected to increase firm value. This is true for the two examples used previously. Both projects are expected to return more than the 10 percent required rate of return because their discounted payback periods are less than their five-year economic lives. If a project is not normal, we cannot use this decision rule to determine a project's acceptability. For example, suppose Ramdeen's expansion project expected a negative cash flow in the fifth year instead of a positive $70,000. Without doing some additional calculations, we could not say the project returned more than 10 percent just because the net investment was recovered in 3.54 years. The negative cash flow in the fifth year could cause the accumulated present values of the net cash flows to be less than the net investment. This would in turn lead to a rate of return less than 10 percent.

The discounted payback period can be used to determine the acceptability of normal projects, but it cannot be used to determine which project is best for the firm. Ramdeen's expansion project has a quicker discounted payback period than the new restaurant project. This does indicate better liquidity risk for the expansion project and a quicker recovery of the project's net investment. It does not indicate that the expansion project is better or that it will increase firm value more than the new restaurant project.

The discounted payback period offers a partial solution to the lack of an objective criterion to use with the payback period. To decide the acceptability of a project, there is an objective criterion to use with the discounted payback period on normal projects. A discounted payback period less than the economic life indicates an acceptable normal project. However, when comparing mutually exclusive projects to one another, there is no objective criterion to use with the discounted payback period.

Finally, the discounted payback period does not improve on the third weakness of the payback period. Cash flows after the discounted payback period have no impact on the discounted payback period. Again, suppose the expansion project had a $100,000 expected net cash flow in year 5 instead of $70,000. This would clearly make the project more attractive, but the project's discounted payback period would still be 3.54 years.

The discounted payback period is an improved measure of liquidity risk relative to the payback period. It can also be used to decide the acceptability of normal projects. But it should only be used in conjunction with other capital budgeting decision methods.

10.2.3 Net Present Value

A project's net present value (*NPV*) is the sum of the present values of the net cash flows discounted at the required rate of return minus the net investment. All capital budgeting decision methods are basically a form of cost-benefit analysis, but the net present value method is the most straightforward application of cost-benefit analysis. Net present value is simply the benefits, as measured by the sum of the present values of the net cash flows, minus the cost, as measured by the net investment. If a project's benefits exceed the cost, the net present value is positive, and the project is acceptable. If a project's benefits are less than the cost, the net present value is negative, and the project is unacceptable.

$$NPV = \text{Sum of present values of net cash flows} - \text{Net investment}$$

The net present value for Ramdeen's expansion project using the 10 percent required rate of return is

$$NPV = \$70,000 \times \left[\frac{1 - \frac{1}{(1 + 10\%)^5}}{10\%} \right] - \$200,000$$

Finding the present value of the $70,000 net cash flows each year for 5 years discounted as an annuity payment at a 10 percent required rate of return,

$$NPV = \$265,355 - \$200,000 = \$65,355$$

Ramdeen's expansion project has a positive net present value of $65,355, indicating the project is acceptable.

The net present value for Ramdeen's new restaurant project is

$$NPV = \frac{\$50,000}{(1 + 10\%)} + \frac{70,000}{(1 + 10\%)^2} + \frac{100,000}{(1 + 10\%)^3} + \frac{120,000}{(1 + 10\%)^4} + \frac{150,000}{(1 + 10\%)^5} - \$300,000$$

Finding the present value of the five uneven net cash flows at a 10 percent required rate of return,

$$NPV = \$353,537 - \$300,000 = \$53,537$$

Appendix 10.1 shows how to compute *NPV* with a business calculator.

Ramdeen's new restaurant project has a positive net present value of $53,537, indicating this project is also acceptable.

A positive net present value indicates a project is acceptable. A negative net present value indicates a project is unacceptable. Beyond a project's acceptability, a project's net present value imparts additional information. It is also an estimate of the change in firm value caused by investment in the project. In other words, the value of Ramdeen's Restaurant is expected to increase by $65,355 if an investment is made in the expansion project, and firm value is expected to increase by $53,537 if an investment is made in the new restaurant project.

Using net present value to make capital budgeting decisions is consistent with maximizing firm value because net present value is a measure of a project's contribution to firm value. Ramdeen's expansion project is expected to add $65,355 to firm value over and above a 10 percent return on the $200,000 net investment. The new restaurant project is expected to add $53,537 to firm value over and above a 10 percent return on the $300,000 net investment. Both projects are expected to provide more than the 10 percent required return to invested funds. The restaurant expansion project provides more value over and above the 10 percent required return ($63,355 expansion project *NPV* versus $53,537 new restaurant project *NPV*). Therefore, if there are no other significant differences between the two projects, the restaurant expansion increases firm value the most and is the better project. Other possible significant differences that could nullify this conclusion include different project risk levels not taken into account, or one project fits better into Ramdeen's long-term strategic plan. If the projects are independent, then both projects are acceptable and could be funded. If the projects are mutually exclusive, then the available information indicates the restaurant expansion project will increase firm value the most and should be accepted.

10.2.4 Profitability Index

A capital budgeting project's profitability index (*PI*) is similar to a project's net present value because both methods compare a project's cost to its benefits. The net present value achieves this by subtracting the cost (net investment) from the benefits (sum of present values of net cash flows). The profitability index is constructed by taking the ratio of the benefits to the cost. In other words, the sum of the present values of net cash flows is divided by the net investment.

$$PI = \frac{\text{Sum of present values of net cash flows}}{\text{Net investment}}$$

The profitability index for Ramdeen's restaurant expansion is

$$PI = \frac{\$70,000 \times \left[\dfrac{1 - \dfrac{1}{(1 + 10\%)^5}}{10\%}\right]}{\$200,000}$$

Find the present value of the $70,000 net cash flows each year for 5 years discounted as an annuity payment at a 10% required rate of return.

$$PI = \frac{\$265,355}{\$200,000} = 1.33$$

This can also be calculated by adding one to the ratio of the *NPV* and the net investment as follows.

$$PI = 1 + \frac{NPV}{\text{Net Investment}} = 1 + \frac{\$65,355}{\$200,000}$$

$$PI = 1 + .33 = 1.33$$

The profitability index for Ramdeen's new restaurant project is

$$PI = 1 + \frac{\$53,537}{\$300,000} = 1 + .18 = 1.18$$

A profitability index greater than one indicates an acceptable project and is consistent with a positive net present value. A profitability index less than one indicates an unacceptable project and is consistent with a negative net present value. Further, a profitability index of one indicates a project is expected to earn exactly the required rate of return. Ramdeen's expansion project's profitability index of 1.33 indicates it is expected to earn the 10 percent required rate of return, plus provide a net present value of $0.33 per $1.00 of net investment. The new restaurant project's profitability index of 1.18 indicates it is expected to earn the 10 percent required rate of return, plus provide a net present value of $0.18 per $1.00 of net investment.

The profitability index method is most useful when a firm faces capital rationing, which exists when a firm can invest only a limited amount in capital budgeting projects, regardless of the number, size, and expected returns of the capital budgeting projects available. When a firm faces capital rationing, it should choose the combination of capital budgeting projects to maximize the total net present value, or in other words, to maximize firm value. The higher a project's profitability index, the more net present value it provides per dollar invested. Under capital rationing it may not be possible to invest in all positive, net present value projects. Therefore, the firm needs to focus on projects providing the most net present value per dollar invested, and this is explicitly measured by a project's profitability index.

The profitability index is an appropriate indicator of a project's acceptability. In many circumstances, it can also be used to determine the preferred project in mutually exclusive comparisons. But this capital budgeting decision method is not used to a great extent, except in capital rationing situations.

10.2.5 Internal Rate of Return

A capital budgeting project's **internal rate of return** is the rate of return causing the project's net present value to equal zero. It is a project's true annual percentage rate of return based on the estimated cash flows. A project's internal rate of return is compared to the project's required rate of return. If the internal rate of return exceeds the required rate of return, the project is acceptable and is expected to increase firm value. If the internal rate of return is less than the required rate of return, the project is unacceptable and is expected to decrease firm value.

The equation used to compute internal rate of return (*IRR*) for Ramdeen's expansion project can be adapted from the *NPV* equation. The equation previously used to compute *NPV* is

$$NPV = \$70,000 \times \left[\frac{1 - \frac{1}{(1 + 10\%)^5}}{10\%} \right] - \$200,000$$

The internal rate of return is the interest rate that makes the *NPV* equal zero. Therefore, *IRR* is substituted for the 10 percent interest rate in the *NPV* equation, and the *NPV* is set equal to zero.

$$\$70{,}000 \times \left[\frac{1 - \dfrac{1}{(1 + IRR)^5}}{IRR} \right] - \$200{,}000 = 0$$

If the *NPV* is zero, then the sum of the present values of net cash flows exactly equals the net investment, and the equation for computing *IRR* can also be expressed as

$$\$70{,}000 \times \left[\frac{1 - \dfrac{1}{(1 + IRR)^5}}{IRR} \right] = \$200{,}000$$

Finding the internal rate of return for the expansion project is a matter of finding the interest rate that equates the present value of $70,000 a year for five years with $200,000. The expansion project's *IRR* is 22.11 percent. This is much higher than the 10 percent required rate of return, indicating the expansion project is acceptable.

The internal rate of return for Ramdeen's new restaurant project is

$$\frac{\$50{,}000}{(1 + IRR)} + \frac{70{,}000}{(1 + IRR)^2} + \frac{100{,}000}{(1 + IRR)^3} + \frac{120{,}000}{(1 + IRR)^4} + \frac{150{,}000}{(1 + IRR)^5}$$
$$- \$300{,}000 = 0$$

or

$$\frac{\$50{,}000}{(1 + IRR)} + \frac{70{,}000}{(1 + IRR)^2} + \frac{100{,}000}{(1 + IRR)^3} + \frac{120{,}000}{(1 + IRR)^4} + \frac{150{,}000}{(1 + IRR)^5} = \$300{,}000$$

If a project has uneven cash flows, as in this case, solving for the internal rate of return is tedious unless using a business calculator with a cash flow function or using a computer spreadsheet with an *IRR* function. The tedious method initially requires a guess at the *IRR*. Let us try 15 percent. Then, we need to calculate the preceding present values at a 15 percent interest rate, sum the present values, and compare to the $300,000 net investment. The sum of the present values equals $305,347, which is greater than the net investment. Next, choose a higher interest rate to lower the sum of the present values. Let us try 20 percent. At 20 percent, the sum of the present values equals $266,300. Now use these two guesses to close in on the answer. The difference between the two guesses is $39,047 ($305,347 minus $266,300). The first guess is $5,347 above the $300,000 present value we are trying to achieve. This is 13.69 percent of the gap between the two guesses ($5,347 divided by $39,047), so we should add to the 15 percent guess, 13.69% of 5% (20% minus 15%). *IRR* is approximately equal to 15% + 0.1369 × 5% = 15% + 0.68% = 15.68%.

Using the cash flow function on a calculator or a computer-based spreadsheet reveals a more accurate *IRR* of 15.63 percent. (Appendix 10.1 shows how to compute *IRR* with a business calculator.) This is higher than the 10 percent required rate of return, indicating the new restaurant project is acceptable. If the two projects are independent, then both projects should be accepted based on the internal rate of return evidence. If the projects are mutually exclusive, then *IRR* indicates the expansion project is better. This ranking is consistent with the projects' *NPV*s and therefore consistent with maximizing firm value. The internal rate of return will usually rank projects consistently with net present value, but not always. This will be discussed later in this chapter.

10.2.6 Modified Internal Rate of Return

The internal rate of return is a very popular capital budgeting decision method; however, the modified internal rate of return is a better measure of projects' relative profitability. The **modified internal rate of return** (*MIRR*) is the interest rate equating the present value of a project's investment costs with the terminal value of the project's net cash flows.

The present value of a project's investment costs is called a project's *beginning value*. The beginning value is the sum of the present values of all project investment outlays. If all investment outlays take place at the very beginning (time = 0), then the beginning value equals the net investment. If a project has investment outlays in the future, then the beginning value is the sum of the present values of the investment's outlays discounted at the project's required rate of return.

The terminal value of the project's net cash flows is the sum of the future values of the net cash flows at the end of the project's economic life. The terminal value assumes the net cash flows are invested at the project's required rate of return.

To calculate the modified internal rate of return for Ramdeen's expansion project, we first calculate the project's beginning and terminal values.

MIRR > required ✓

0	1	2	3	4	5
−200	$70	$70	$70	$70	$70

Beginning value

Terminal value

$BEG = \dfrac{Terminal}{(1 + MIRR)^N}$

Beginning value = $200,000

$$\text{Terminal value} = \$70,000 \times \left[\frac{(1 + 10\%)^5 - 1}{10\%}\right] = \$427,357$$

The modified internal rate of return is the interest rate equating the present value of the terminal value with the beginning value. The modified internal rate of return for Ramdeen's expansion project is

$$\$200,000 = \frac{\$427,357}{(1 + MIRR)^5} \qquad MIRR = 16.40\%$$

The modified internal rate of return of 16.40 percent is greater than the 10 percent required rate of return, indicating the expansion project is acceptable.

Next we calculate the beginning value, the terminal value, and the modified internal rate of return for Ramdeen's new restaurant project.

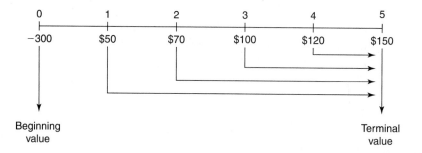

Beginning value = $200,000

Terminal value = $50,000 × (1 + 10%)^4 + 70,000 × (1 + 10%)^3
+ 100,000 × (1 + 10%)^2 + 120,000 × (1 + 10%) + 150,000

Terminal value = $569,375

The modified internal rate of return for Ramdeen's new restaurant project is

$$\$300,000 = \frac{\$569,375}{(1 + MIRR)^5} \qquad MIRR = 13.67\%$$

The modified internal rate of return of 13.67 percent is greater than the 10 percent required rate of return, indicating the expansion project is acceptable.

The six capital budgeting decision methods are summarized in Exhibit 10-1. To gain further understanding of how these methods are used in the hospitality industry, see Exhibit 10-2.

Payback Period is the number of years it takes for a project's net cash flows to recover the net investment. There is no objective criterion for deciding if a project is acceptable.

Discounted Payback Period is the number of years it takes for the present values of a project's net cash flows to recover the net investment. If the discounted payback period is less than the project's economic life, an independent, normal project is acceptable and is expected to increase the value of the firm.

Net Present Value is the sum of the present values of the net cash flows minus the net investment. A net present value greater than zero indicates an acceptable independent project.

Profitability Index is the sum of the present values of the net cash flows divided by the net investment. A profitability index greater than one indicates an acceptable independent project.

Internal Rate of Return is the interest rate at which a project's net present value equals zero. It is also the interest rate at which the sum of the present values of the net cash flows equal the net investment. If an independent, normal project's internal rate of return is greater than the required rate of return, the project is acceptable.

Modified Internal Rate of Return is the interest rate at which the project's present value of investment costs equal the project's terminal value of net cash flows. If the modified internal rate of return is greater than the required rate of return, the project is acceptable.

Exhibit 10-1 Capital budgeting decision methods.

Discounted cash flow techniques, such as internal rate of return and the net present value methods, are commonly used in the hospitality industry, as reported in two recent articles in *The Journal of Hospitality Financial Management.** One article surveyed firms in the hotel and gaming industry, and the other article surveyed firms in the restaurant industry. Both articles show the primary methods used for capital budgeting decisions were first the internal rate of return method and second the net present value method. Also, the payback method was the most commonly used secondary method in both the hotel and gaming industry and the restaurant industry.

If you plan a career in the hospitality industry, certainly knowledge of capital budgeting techniques could be helpful, and it could be crucial, depending on positions held. Even if you do not plan to be in a finance-related position, knowledge of capital budgeting techniques can help you or your manager make better asset acquisition decisions. The top managers of large hospitality firms are knowledgeable of capital budgeting techniques and use these techniques to make asset acquisition decisions as reported by these two studies.

* "A Survey of Capital-Budgeting Methods Used by the Hotel/Gaming Industry" by Stanley M. Atkinson and Stephen M. LeBruto, 5, no. 1 (1997), 23–31. Also "A Survey of Capital Budgeting Methods Used by the Restaurant Industry" by Robert A. Ashley, Stanley M. Atkinson, and Stephen M. LeBruto, 8, no. 1 (2000), 47–51.

Exhibit 10-2   Capital budgeting decision methods used in the hospitality industry.

10.3   INDEPENDENT PROJECTS AND CAPITAL BUDGETING DECISION METHODS

Independent capital budgeting decisions are stand-alone decisions. An investment in an **independent project** is analyzed to determine if it will increase the value of the firm or not. If a capital budgeting project is independent and normal, then any of the preceding capital budgeting decision methods besides the payback period can be used to determine the acceptability of the project. Following is a summary of the acceptability criteria for each of these five decision methods.

1. The discounted payback period is equal to or less than the economic life.
2. The net present value is equal to or greater than zero.
3. The profitability index is equal to or greater than one.
4. The internal rate of return is equal to or greater than the required rate of return.
5. The modified internal rate of return is equal to or greater than the required rate of return.

If a capital budgeting project is independent and normal, then the preceding five decision methods will provide consistent decisions regarding the project's acceptability. In other words, if one method indicates a project is acceptable, then all five methods will indicate the project is acceptable. If one method indicates a project is not acceptable, then all five methods will indicate the project is not acceptable.

10.4 MUTUALLY EXCLUSIVE PROJECTS AND CAPITAL BUDGETING DECISION METHODS

Mutually exclusive capital budgeting **projects** require a different decision process than independent projects. One must not only decide if a mutually exclusive capital budgeting project is acceptable and will increase the value of the firm, but one must also decide which one of the several acceptable mutually exclusive projects is expected to increase the value of the firm the most. In other words, when deciding between mutually exclusive projects, all acceptable projects need to be ranked, with only the best project accepted. The best project is expected to increase the value of the firm more than the other projects. The project with the highest net present value is, by definition, expected to increase the value of the firm the most. The mutually exclusive project with the highest profitability index, internal rate of return, and modified internal rate of return will usually be the project expected to increase the value of the firm the most, but this is not always true. There is no reason to expect the mutually exclusive project with the shortest payback period or discounted payback period to be the most valuable project. Short payback periods indicate lower liquidity risk, but not necessarily higher project value. So net present value, profitability index, internal rate of return, and modified internal rate of return will generally rank mutually exclusive projects consistently, but there are several situations in which they may not be consistent. The first situation is when projects have different size net investments (scale differences). The second is when projects' cash flows are timed differently. And the third situation is when projects have nonnormal cash flows.

10.4.1 Scale Differences

Scale differences between mutually exclusive projects will create ranking problems when using the profitability index, the internal rate of return, and the modified internal rate of return. Differences in scale means projects' net investments are different. For example, consider the following two mutually exclusive projects.

Year	Project A NCFs	Project B NCFs
0	−$1,000	−$1,500
1	700	1,000
2	700	1,000
3	700	1,000

Let the required rate of return equal 10 percent. The net present values for the two projects are as follows.

$$NPV_A = \$700 \times \left[\frac{1 - \frac{1}{(1 + 10\%)^3}}{10\%} \right] - \$1,000 = \$740.80$$

$$NPV_B = \$1,000 \times \left[\frac{1 - \frac{1}{(1 + 10\%)^3}}{10\%} \right] - \$1,500 = \$986.85$$

This indicates that project B is expected to increase the value of the firm the most and is the preferred project. The profitability index for each project is

$$\text{Profitability index}_A = 1 + \frac{\$740.80}{\$1,000} = 1.74$$

$$\text{Profitability index}_B = 1 + \frac{\$986.85}{\$1,500} = 1.66$$

Project A has a higher profitability index, even though project B is expected to increase the value of the firm the most. The project internal rates of return are

$$\$700 \times \left[\frac{1 - \dfrac{1}{(1 + IRR_A)^3}}{IRR_A}\right] = \$1,000 \qquad IRR_A = 48.72\%$$

$$\$1,000 \times \left[\frac{1 - \dfrac{1}{(1 + IRR_B)^3}}{IRR_B}\right] = \$1,500 \qquad IRR_B = 44.63\%$$

Similar to the profitability index, the internal rate of return is higher for the inferior project (project A). The project modified internal rates of return are

$$\text{Beginning value}_A = \$1,000$$

$$\text{Terminal value}_A = \$700 \times \left[\frac{(1 + 10\%)^3 - 1}{10\%}\right] = \$2,317$$

$$\$1,000 = \frac{\$2,317}{(1 + MIRR_A)^3} \qquad MIRR_A = 32.33\%$$

$$\text{Beginning value}_B = \$1,000$$

$$\text{Terminal value}_B = \$1,000 \times \left[\frac{(1 + 10\%)^3 - 1}{10\%}\right] = \$3,310$$

$$\$1,500 = \frac{\$3,310}{(1 + MIRR_B)^3} \qquad MIRR_B = 30.19\%$$

The modified internal rate of return ranks the two projects the same as the profitability index and internal rate of return. These rankings are inconsistent with the ranking of net present value. The net present value indicates project B will increase firm value by $246.05 more than project A. You might be tempted to choose project A as the best project because its net investment is $500 less than the net investment for project B, and you only lose $246.05 by choosing project A instead of project B. But keep the following in mind. Project B is expected to return 10 percent on the entire $1,500 net investment (including the extra $500 net investment relative to project A). Then over and above this 10 percent return, project B provides increased firm value of $986.85. So after providing the 10 percent required rate of return on the extra $500 net investment, it still provides an additional $246.05 in value. When mutually exclusive projects are different in terms of scale, the net present value is the only method that will always rank the projects correctly.

10.4.2 Cash Flow Timing Differences

The net cash flows in mutually exclusive projects may be timed quite differently. Some projects may have cash flows distributed evenly over their economic life, whereas other projects may have large cash flows early and small cash flows later, whereas still other projects may have small cash flows early and large cash flows later. Consider the following two mutually exclusive projects.

Year	Project A NCFs	Project C NCFs
0	−$1,000	−$1,000
1	700	0
2	700	0
3	700	2,500

Let the required rate of return equal 10%. The net present values for the two projects are as follows.

$$NPV_A = \$700 \times \left[\frac{1 - \dfrac{1}{(1 + 10\%)^3}}{10\%} \right] - \$1,000 = \$740.80$$

$$NPV_C = \frac{\$2,500}{(1 + 10\%)^3} - \$1,000 = \$878.29$$

This indicates that project C is expected to increase the value of the firm the most and is the preferred project. The profitability index for each project is

$$\text{Profitability index}_A = 1 + \frac{\$740.80}{\$1,000} = 1.74$$

$$\text{Profitability index}_C = 1 + \$878.29/\$1,000 \frac{\$878.29}{\$1,000} = 1.88$$

Project C has a higher profitability index and correctly ranks the two projects. The project internal rates of return are

$$\$700 \times \left[\frac{1 - \dfrac{1}{(1 + IRR_A)^3}}{IRR_A} \right] = \$1,000 \qquad IRR_A = 48.72\%$$

$$\frac{\$2,500}{(1 + IRR_C)^3} = \$1,000 \qquad IRR_C = 35.72\%$$

The internal rate of return is higher for the inferior project (project A) and therefore does not rank the projects correctly. The project modified internal rates of return are

$$\text{Beginning value}_A = \$1,000$$

$$\text{Terminal value}_A = \$700 \times \left[\frac{(1 + 10\%)^3 - 1}{10\%} \right] = \$2,317$$

$$\$1,000 = \frac{\$2,317}{(1 + MIRR_A)^3} \qquad MIRR_A = 32.33\%$$

$$\text{Beginning value}_C = \$1,000$$

$$\text{Terminal value} = \$2,500$$

$$\$1,000 = \frac{\$2,500}{(1 + MIRR_C)^3} \qquad MIRR_C = 35.72\%$$

Notice the modified internal rate of return is the same as the internal rate of return for project C. When a project has just two cash flows, a net investment and one cash flow at the end of the project's economic life, then modified internal rate of return equals the internal rate of return. The modified internal rate of return correctly ranks the two projects. When project cash flows are timed differently, the internal rate of return may not rank the projects correctly. But the net present value, the profitability index, and the modified internal rate of return do correctly select the best project under these circumstances.

10.5 NOT-NORMAL CASH FLOWS

Capital budgeting projects with not-normal cash flows are possible but not very common in the hospitality industry. Normal project cash flows include a cash outflow (a negative cash flow) at the beginning of a project's life. We call this cash outflow the *net investment*, and then, normal projects have positive cash flows (cash inflows) the remainder of their life. We call these *net cash flows* (NCF). A project with not-normal cash flows will have at least one negative cash flow (outflow) following at least one positive cash flow (inflow). The following is an example of a project with not-normal cash flows.

Year	Project NCFs
0	−$1,000
1	2,000
2	2,000
3	− 3,200

The project starts out with a negative cash flow and is followed by two positive cash flows. This is normal so far. But the project has not-normal cash flows because the positive cash flow in year 2 is followed by a negative cash flow in year 3. This creates problems for using the payback period and discounted pay back period methods. How can you calculate how long it takes to payback the investment cash flows when you still have investment cash flows continuing at the end of the project's life? Therefore, both payback methods cannot be used in this scenario.

The net present value, profitability index, and modified internal rate of return handle this situation easily. Assuming a 10 percent required rate of return, the net present value for the above project is

$$NPV = \frac{\$2,000}{(1 + 10\%)} + \frac{2,000}{(1 + 10\%)^2} - \frac{3,200}{(1 + 10\%)^3} - 1,000$$
$$NPV = \$66.87$$

The profitability index is

$$\text{Profitability index} = 1 + \frac{\$66.87}{\$1,000} = 1.07$$

The modified internal rate of return begins with the calculation of the beginning value. This is the sum of the present value of the investment cash outflows.

$$\text{Beginning value} = \$1,000 + \frac{3,200}{(1 + 10\%)^3} = \$3,404.21$$

Both projects have a similar net present value, but project D has much more room for error. If project D's net cash flows decline by more than 32 percent, from $3,000 annually to $2,011 annually, the project still recovers its net investment and earns the 10 percent required rate of return ($NPV > \$0$). But if project E's net cash flows decline by less than 5 percent, from $21,096 annually to $20,105 annually, the project will not earn its 10 percent required return on the $50,000 net investment ($NPV < \$0$). Additionally, project D only places $5,000 at risk, whereas project E places $50,000 at risk. Project D's higher profitability index, internal rate of return, and modified internal rate of return indicate project D's higher margin for safety.

The net present value is the best single indicator of a project's profitability, but it reveals nothing about the margin of safety. The profitability index, the internal rate of return, and the modified internal rate of return not only indicate both projects are profitable, but also their much higher levels for project D indicate a much higher margin for safety with project D versus project E. Exhibit 10-4 summarizes the advantages of the various capital budgeting decision methods. Appendix 10.2 works through a comprehensive "new hotel" capital budgeting example to arrive at the net present value for the project.

Payback Period provides a measure of liquidity and risk. The shorter the payback period, the quicker a project's net investment is expected to be recovered and the better the liquidity and the lower the risk. It provides no information on project profitability.

Discounted Payback Period is a better measure of risk and liquidity than payback period because it accounts for the time value of money. The shorter the discounted payback period, the quicker a project's net investment is expected to be recovered and the better the liquidity and lower the risk. If the discounted payback period is less than the economic life, it does indicate a normal, independent project is acceptable.

Net Present Value is the single best measure of project profitability. It does not provide much information about project risk unless it is evaluated in conjunction with other information. Net present value is consistent with value maximization.

Profitability Index is a relative measure of profitability and provides some information about project risk. The higher a project's profitability index, the greater the margin of safety. The profitability index may not rank mutually exclusive projects correctly when scale differences exist between projects.

Internal Rate of Return is a relative measure of profitability and provides some information about project risk. The higher a project's internal rate of return, the greater the margin of safety. The internal rate of return may not rank mutually exclusive projects correctly.

Modified Internal Rate of Return is a relative measure of profitability and provides some information about project risk. The higher a project's modified internal rate of return, the greater the margin of safety. The modified internal rate of return may not rank mutually exclusive projects correctly when scale differences exist between projects.

Exhibit 10-4 The advantages of capital budgeting decision methods.

10.7 SUMMARY

All the capital budgeting decision methods provide useful information. If one really wants to narrow down the methods used, we would recommend the net present value as the best indicator of profitability, the discounted payback period as the best indicator of liquidity and risk, and the modified internal rate of return as the best indicator of the margin for safety. In summary, we have covered the following major topics in this chapter.

- The definition and how to compute six different capital budgeting decision methods: payback period, discounted payback period, net present value, profitability index, internal rate of return, and modified internal rate of return
- Using capital budgeting decision methods with independent projects
- Using capital budgeting decision methods with mutually exclusive projects
- Using capital budgeting decision methods on projects with cash flows that are not normal
- The advantages and disadvantages of the six capital budgeting decision methods

KEY TERMS

Discounted payback period
Independent project
Internal rate of return
Modified internal rate of return
Mutually exclusive project
Net cash flow
Net investment
Net present value
Normal capital budgeting project
Payback period
Profitability index
Required rate of return

DISCUSSION QUESTIONS

1. How can a capital budgeting decision be viewed in the context of cost-benefit analysis?
2. How is the discounted payback period an improvement on the payback period?
3. Explain how using the net present value method to make a capital budgeting decision is consistent with the objective of maximizing a firm's value.
4. How are the net present value method, the profitability index, and the internal rate of return similar to one another?
5. How is the modified internal rate of return different than the internal rate of return? How is the modified internal rate of return an improvement on the internal rate of return?

6. Each of the following capital budgeting decision methods will provide a consistent decision on an independent capital budgeting project with normal cash flows. What is the decision criteria or rule for each of these methods?
   a. Discounted payback period
   b. Net present value
   c. Profitability index
   d. Internal rate of return
   e. Modified internal rate of return
7. Why is a capital budgeting decision involving mutually exclusive projects different than a decision involving independent projects?
8. What are the characteristics of mutually exclusive capital budgeting projects that may cause the net present value and internal rate of return methods to rank the projects differently?
9. What are the advantages of using the payback period or discounted payback period methods along with other methods when making a capital budgeting decision?
10. What is the advantage of using the internal rate of return method along with net present value when making a capital budgeting decision?

PROBLEMS

Problems designated with **Excel** *can be solved using* **Excel** *spreadsheets accessible at* http://www.prenhall.com/chatfield.

1. An independent capital budgeting project has a net investment of $100,000 and is expected to generate net cash flows of $40,000 annually for four years. The required rate of return is 12 percent.
   a. Compute the payback period.
   b. Compute the discounted payback period.
   c. Should the project be accepted? Explain your answer.
2. An independent capital budgeting project is expected to have the following cash flows.

Year	Cash flows
0	-$500,000
1	$100,000
2	$150,000
3	$250,000
4	$300,000

   a. Compute the payback period.
   b. Compute the discounted payback period using an 11 percent required rate of return.
   c. Should the project be accepted? Explain your answer.
3. An independent capital budgeting project has a net investment of $1 million and is expected to generate net cash flows of $300,000 annually for 5 years. The required rate of return is 18 percent.

a. Compute the net present value.

b. Compute the profitability index.

c. Should the project be accepted? Explain your answer.

4. An independent capital budgeting project is expected to have the following cash flows.

Year	Cash flows
0	−$225,000
1	$ 75,000
2	$125,000
3	$200,000

a. Compute the net present value at a 17 percent required rate of return.

b. Compute the profitability index at a 17 percent required rate of return.

c. Should the project be accepted? Explain your answer.

5. An independent capital budgeting project has a net investment of $4.5 million and is expected to generate net cash flows of $1.5 million annually for 5 years. The required rate of return is 14 percent.

a. Compute the internal rate of return.

b. Compute the modified internal rate of return.

c. Should the project be accepted? Explain your answer.

6. An independent capital budgeting project is expected to have the following cash flows.

Year	Cash flows
0	−$875,000
1	$400,000
2	$500,000
3	$600,000

a. Compute the internal rate of return.

b. Compute the modified internal rate of return using a 13 percent required rate of return.

c. Should the project be accepted? Explain your answer, assuming 13 percent is the required rate of return.

7. The following table shows the cash flows for two mutually exclusive capital budgeting projects. The required rate of return for both projects is 10 percent.

Year	Project X cash flows	Project Y cash flows
0	−$120,000	−$120,000
1	$100,000	$ 20,000
2	$ 40,000	$ 50,000
3	$ 10,000	$100,000

a. Compute the net present value for both projects.

b. Compute the internal rate of return for both projects.

c. Compute the modified internal rate of return for both projects.

d. Which project should be accepted? What causes net present value and internal rate of return to rank the projects differently?

8. The following table shows the cash flows for two mutually exclusive capital budgeting projects. The required rate of return for both projects is 13 percent.

Year	Project P cash flows	Project Q cash flows
0	−$250,000	−$250,000
1	0	$120,000
2	0	$120,000
3	0	$120,000
4	0	$120,000
5	$900,000	$120,000

a. Compute the net present value for both projects.

b. Compute the internal rate of return for both projects.

c. Compute the modified internal rate of return for both projects.

d. Which project should be accepted? What causes net present value and internal rate of return to rank the projects differently?

9. The following table shows the cash flows for two mutually exclusive capital budgeting projects. The required rate of return for both projects is 15 percent.

Year	Project A cash flows	Project B cash flows
0	−$300,000	−$500,000
1	$100,000	$200,000
2	$175,000	$250,000
3	$200,000	$300,000

a. Compute the net present value for both projects.

b. Compute the internal rate of return for both projects.

c. Compute the modified internal rate of return for both projects.

d. Which project should be accepted? What causes net present value and the internal rate of return to rank the projects differently? Does the modified internal rate of return rank the projects consistent with the net present value? Explain your answer.

10. Bernie's Restaurants is considering two mutually exclusive projects having the following cash flow streams.

Year	Project A NCF	Project B NCF
0	−$90,000	−$100,000
1	$40,000	$ 30,000
2	$40,000	$ 50,000
3	$40,000	$ 25,000
4	$40,000	$ 55,000

    a. Compute the net present value (*NPV*) for both projects using a 15 percent required rate of return.

    b. Compute the internal rate of return (*IRR*) for both projects.

    c. Which project should the firm accept and why?

11. Annie's Resorts is considering the acquisition of a new cruise boat for guests. **EXCEL** It is estimated to cost $400,000 including delivery. It will require an immediate increase of $50,000 in net working capital. The new boat will be depreciated straight-line to a zero value over the 10-year expected economic life. The salvage value of the new boat is expected to be $100,000 at the end of 10 years.

    Estimated annual additional revenues from the new boat are $150,000. Estimated annual additional costs are $80,000. The marginal tax rate is 40 percent.

    a. If Annie's Resorts requires a 16 percent rate of return on projects such as this, calculate the net present value (*NPV*) for the new cruise boat.

    b. Should Annie invest in the new cruise boat? Why or why not?

12. Nakazawa Hotels is considering installing its own vending machines **EXCEL** throughout one of its hotels. The vending machines will cost $100,000. An additional $7,000 will be needed for delivery and installation. Another $3,000 will be needed for initial net working capital. The vending machines have an expected life of 10 years and will be depreciated over 10 years on a straight-line basis to $0. The vending machines are expected to have a salvage value of $5,000 at the end of 10 years.

    The vending machines are expected to increase annual revenue by $20,000 and to increase annual cash operating costs by $7,000. Nakazawa's effective tax rate is 40 percent, and the required rate of return is 14 percent. Compute the net present value (*NPV*). Should the project be accepted?

13. A capital budgeting project has the following expected cash flows. **EXCEL**

Year	Cash flows
0	−$400,000
1	$850,000
2	$150,000
3	$150,000
4	−800,000

    a. What is different about this capital budgeting project?

    b. Compute the net present value for this project at required rates of return of 0 percent, 3.55 percent, 15 percent, 20 percent, 25 percent, and 118.32 percent.

    c. What can you say about this project's internal rate of return?

    d. How would you make a decision to accept or reject this project?

APPENDIX 10.1—COMPUTING *NPV* AND *IRR* WITH FINANCIAL CALCULATORS

Several business calculators have a cash flow function for the computation of project net present values (*NPV*) and internal rates of return (*IRR*). We will show how to use the cash flow function on two business calculators to compute the

NPV and *IRR* for both Ramdeen's expansion project and Ramdeen's new restaurant project.

First we calculate Ramdeen's expansion project's *NPV* and *IRR*. The cash flows are as follows.

Year	Cash flow
0	−$200,000
1	$ 70,000
2	$ 70,000
3	$ 70,000
4	$ 70,000
5	$ 70,000

Using the Hewlett-Packard hp 10BII calculator step-by-step:

1. Clear the calculator: [orange], [C ALL].
   Notice [C ALL] is the secondary key for [C].
2. Enter the $200,000 net investment: [200,000], [+/−], [CFj].
   When you hold down [CFj], you will see a "0" on the left side of the screen. This indicates −$200,000 is the cash flow at time "0."
3. Enter the $70,000 annual net cash flow: [70,000], [CFj].
   When you hold down the [CFj], you will see a "1" on the left side of the screen. This indicates $70,000 is the cash flow at time "1."
4. Let $70,000 be the annual cash flow for 5 years: [5], [orange], [Nj].
   Notice [Nj] is the secondary key for [CFj]. When you hold down the [Nj], you will see a "1" on the left side of the screen. This indicates the cash flow for year "0" ($70,000) will occur for "5" years.
5. Enter the 10% required rate of return: [10], [I/YR]. You will see "10.00."
6. Compute the *NPV*: [orange], [NPV]. Notice [NPV] is the secondary key to [PRC]. You will see "65,455.07." This means the *NPV* is $65,455.07.
7. Compute the *IRR*: [orange], [IRR/YR]. Notice [IRR/YR] is the secondary key to [CST]. You will see "22.11." This means the *IRR* is 22.11%.

Using the Texas Instruments BA II PLUS calculator step-by-step:

1. Prepare the calculator to use the cash flow function: [CF]. You will see "$CF_0=0.00$" or there may be some other number there besides 0.00.
2. Clear the cash flow function: [2nd], [CLR Work]. Notice [CLR Work] is the secondary key to [CE/C]. You will see "$CF_0=0.00$."
3. Enter the $200,000 net investment: [200,000], [+/−], [ENTER]. You will see "$CF_0=-200,0000.00$." This indicates −$200,000 is the cash flow at time "0."
4. Prepare the calculator for the first net cash flow: [↓] key. You will see "C01" on the left and "0.00" on the right.
5. Enter the $70,000 annual net cash flow: [70,000], [ENTER]. You will see "C01=70,000.00." This indicates $70,000 is the cash flow at time "1."
6. Let the cash flow for time "1" be the annual cash flow for 5 years: [↓], [5], [ENTER]. You will see "F01=5.00."

7. Prepare to calculate *NPV*: [NPV]. You will see "I=0.00."

8. Enter the 10% required rate of return: [10], [ENTER]. You will see "I=10.00."

9. Compute the *NPV*: [↓], [CPT]. You will see "NPV=65,355.07." This means the *NPV* is $65,455.07.

10. Compute the *IRR*: [IRR], [CPT]. You will see "IRR=22.11." This means the *IRR* is 22.11%.

Next we will calculate the *NPV* and *IRR* for Ramdeen's new restaurant project. The cash flows are as follows.

Year	Cash flow
0	−$300,000
1	$ 50,000
2	$ 70,000
3	$100,000
4	$120,000
5	$150,000

Using the Hewlett-Packard hp 10BII calculator step-by-step:

1. Clear the calculator: [orange], [C ALL]. Notice [C ALL] is the secondary key to [C].

2. Enter the $300,000 net investment: [300,000], [+/−], [CFj]. When you hold down [CFj], you will see a "0" on the left side of the screen. This indicates −$300,000 is the cash flow at time "0."

3. Enter the $50,000 net cash flow for year 1: [50,000], [CFj]. When you hold down [CFj], you will see a "1" on the left side of the screen. This indicates $50,000 is the cash flow at time "1."

4. Enter the $70,000 net cash flow for year 2: [70,000], [CFj]. When you hold down [CFj], you will see a "2" on the left side of the screen. This indicates $70,000 is the cash flow at time "2."

5. Enter the $100,000 net cash flow for year 3: [100,000], [CFj]. When you hold down [CFj], you will see a "3" on the left side of the screen. This indicates $100,000 is the cash flow at time "3."

6. Enter the $120,000 net cash flow for year 4: [120,000], [CFj]. When you hold down [CFj], you will see a "4" on the left side of the screen. This indicates $120,000 is the cash flow at time "4."

7. Enter the $150,000 net cash flow for year 5: [150,000], [CFj]. When you hold down [CFj], you will see a "5" on the left side of the screen. This indicates $150,000 is the cash flow at time "5."

8. Enter the 10% required rate of return: [10], [I/YR]. You will see "10.00."

9. Compute the *NPV*: [orange], [NPV]. Notice [NPV] is the secondary key to [PRC]. You will see "53,537.08." This means the NPV is $53,537.08.

10. Compute the *IRR:* [orange], [IRR/YR]. Notice the [IRR/YR] is the secondary key to [CST]. You will see "15.63." This means the IRR is 15.63%.

Using the Texas Instruments BA II PLUS calculator step-by-step:

1. Prepare the calculator to use the cash flow function: [CF]. You will see "CF_0=0.00," or there may be some other number there besides 0.00.
2. Clear the cash flow function: [2nd], [CLR Work]. Notice [CLR Work] is the secondary key to [CE/C]. You will see "CF_0=0.00."
3. Enter the $300,000 net investment: [300,000], [+/−], [ENTER]. You will see "CF_0=−300,0000.00." This indicates −$300,000 is the cash flow at time "0."
4. Prepare the calculator for the first net cash flow: [↓]. You will see "C01=0.00."
5. Enter the $50,000 net cash flow for year 1: [50,000], [ENTER]. You will see "C01=50,000.00." This indicates $50,000 is the cash flow at time "1."
6. Enter the $70,000 net cash flow for year 2: [↓], [↓], [70,000], [ENTER]. You will see "C02=70,000.00." This indicates $70,000 is the cash flow at time "2."

Notice we skipped by the "F01=0.00." This is the frequency for how many times the first cash flow will occur. If a cash flow only occurs once, you may skip "F01" because it will default to "1" automatically. Because all our cash flows occur once in this example, we will skip the cash flow frequency key for all cash flows.

7. Enter the $100,000 net cash flow for year 3: [↓], [↓], [100,000], [ENTER]. You will see "C03 = 100,000.00." This indicates $100,000 is the cash flow at time "3."
8. Enter the $120,000 net cash flow for year 4: [↓], [↓], [120,000], [ENTER]. You will see "C04 = 120,000.00." This indicates $120,000 is the cash flow at time "4."
9. Enter the $150,000 net cash flow for year 5: [↓], [↓], [150,000], [ENTER]. You will see "C05 = 150,000.00." This indicates $150,000 is the cash flow at time "5."
10. Prepare to calculate *NPV*: [NPV]. You will see "I = 0.00."
11. Enter the 10% required rate of return: [10], [ENTER]. You will see "I = 10.00."
12. Compute the *NPV*: [↓], [CPT]. You will see "NPV = 53,537.08." This means the NPV is $53,537.08.
13. Compute the *IRR*: [IRR], [CPT]. You will see "IRR = 15.63." This means the IRR is 15.63%.

APPENDIX 10.2—HOSPITALITY CAPITAL BUDGETING EXAMPLE

Assume you are working for Brennan Corporation and the company is trying to decide whether or not to build a new hotel. You are to consider the total net investment in the hotel and five years of cash flows. At the end of five years, you will sell the property.

Operating Information—Proposed Brennan Hotel	
Hotel size (rooms)	100
Occupancy/ADR year 1	68%/$80
Occupancy/ADR year 2	72%/$83
Occupancy/ADR year 3	74%/$86

Occupancy/ADR year 4	74%/$89
Occupancy/ADR year 5	74%/$92
Cash expenses year 1	$1,100,000
Cash expenses year 2	$1,300,000
Cash expenses year 3	$1,400,000
Cash expenses year 4	$1,500,000
Cash expenses year 5	$1,500,000

The following provides some additional information about the property's fixed assets.

Fixed asset information—Proposed Brennan Hotel	
Land cost	$1,000,000
Building cost	$5,000,000
Equipment cost	$2,000,000
Building life	39 years—no salvage
Equipment life	7 years—no salvage

The following provides information about the financing of the hotel.

Financing information—Proposed Brennan Hotel	
Amount of loan	$4,800,000
Amount of equity	$3,200,000
Cost of debt (before tax)	9%
Cost of equity	14%
Average tax rate	30%
Working capital needed year 1	$ 200,000
Working capital needed year 2	$ 100,000

The hotel will be sold based on a projection of year 6 cash flow. This is estimated to be 4 percent higher than year 5's cash flow. Additionally, the purchaser will capitalize year 6 cash flow at the weighted average cost of capital.

Step 1. Calculate the revenue stream generated by the hotel using the number of rooms, occupancy, and average rate. The cash expenses are then subtracted from revenue. Note that although interest expense is a cash expense, it is excluded from our analysis because we are using the weighted average cost of capital that accounts for the interest expense as well as the tax benefits from the interest expense. The depreciation calculations should be based on the straight-line method described in the chapter and assume no salvage value.

Asset	Cost	Life	Salvage	Annual amount
Building	$5,000,000	39	$0	$128,205
Equipment	$2,000,000	7	$0	$285,714
Total	$7,000,000	—	—	$413,919

Year	Revenue	Less: Cash expenses	Less: Depreciation	Equals: Taxable income	Less: Income taxes	Equals: Net income	Plus: Depreciation Equals: Operating cash flow
1	$1,985,600	$1,100,000	$413,919	$471,681	$141,043	$330,638	$744,557
2	$2,181,240	$1,300,000	$413,919	$467,321	$140,196	$327,125	$741,044
3	$2,322,860	$1,400,000	$413,919	$508,941	$152,682	$356,259	$770,178
4	$2,403,890	$1,500,000	$413,919	$489,971	$146,991	$342,980	$756,899
5	$2,484,920	$1,500,000	$413,919	$571,001	$171,300	$399,701	$813,620

Exhibit A10-1 Operating cash flows.

The total amount of depreciation, $413,919, is shown on the income statement to reduce our taxable income. After taxes are calculated, it is added back to net income because of its status as a noncash expense. This is shown in Exhibit A10-1.

Step 2. The next step is to calculate the net investment and the net incremental cash flows from the operation of the property. Exhibit A10-1 showed the operating cash inflows. We now must consider the cash outflows for the property. These would include the cost of the asset (including delivery and setup cost of equipment) as well as the working capital expenditures during the first two years of operation.

If the cash outflows and inflows occur during the same period, we can add them together to find the net cash flows. This is shown in Exhibit A10-2.

Step 3. The benefits of ownership of an asset can generally be categorized into two broad categories: dividends (operating cash flows) and capital gains (proceeds from sale). Because we already have calculated the net operating cash flows, we must determine the gross sales price of the property before taxes and commissions.

As discussed in the introduction of the example, the gross sales price is based on a projection of year 5's operating cash flow. This amount is expected to be 4 percent higher than that of year 5. Therefore, year 6's net operating cash flow must be

$$\$813,620 + 4\% = \$846,165$$

Investors often base sales prices on projected future benefits. Assuming this level of benefits will continue forever (like a perpetuity), the gross sales price is based on dividing the cash flow by a discount rate.

Year	Initial investment	Working capital	Operating cash flow	Net cash flow
0	($8,000,000)	—	—	($8,000,000)
1	—	($200,000)	$744,557	$ 544,557
2	—	($100,000)	$741,044	$ 641,044
3	—	—	$770,178	$ 770,178
4	—	—	$756,899	$ 756,899
5	—	—	$813,620	$ 813,620

Exhibit A10-2 Calculation of net operating cash flows.

Step 4. Calculating the weighted average cost of capital is important because it is going to be used to determine the gross sales price as well as the net present value of the project overall. The calculation is as follows.

$$60\% \times [.09(1 - 30\%)] + [40\% \times .14] = 9.38$$

Therefore, the gross sales price is the year 6 operating cash flow divided by this discount rate.

$$\$846,165/.0938 = \$9,020,949$$

Step 5. We now have to calculate the net sales price, which is the gross sales price less any taxes and commissions. Assuming the property was appraised at the sale, let us assume the following values at the date of sale.

Asset	Acquisition cost	Book value	Value at sale
Land	$1,000,000	$1,000,000	$1,600,000
Building	$5,000,000	$4,358,975[a]	$5,700,000
Equipment	$2,000,000	$571,430[b]	$1,720,949

[a]$5,000,000 − (5 × $128,205) = $4,358,975
[b]$2,000,000 − (5 × $285,714) = $571,430

The following chart details the calculation of capital gains and recaptured depreciation taxes. We will assume a flat income tax rate of 30 percent for both types of taxes.

Asset	Recaptured depreciation (cost less book value)	Recaptured depreciation tax	Capital gain (sales price less cost)	Capital gains tax
Land	N/A	N/A	$600,000	$180,000
Building	$ 641,025	$192,308	$700,000	$210,000
Equipment	$1,428,570	$428,571	($279,051)	($ 83,715)
Totals		$620,879		$306,285

Therefore, the total taxes at sale equal $620,879 + $306,285 or $927,164. Additionally, assume we used the services of a hotel broker who charges us a commission equal to 2 percent of the hotel sales price. Two percent of $9,020,949 equals $180,419. In summary, the net sales price is shown as follows.

Gross sales price	**$9,020,949**
Less: Recaptured depreciation tax	$ 620,879
Less: Capital gains tax	$ 306,285
Less: Sales commission	$ 180,419
Equals: Net sales price	$7,913,366

Therefore, the net cash flow from sale is $7,913,266.

Step 6. In addition to the sale of the property, we assume we will collect all of our receivables and sell our inventory. Thus, the working capital expenditures we made at the beginning of the project (a cash outflow) will become a cash inflow upon sale of the hotel. A total of $300,000 in working capital will become an inflow at the end of year 5 and be added to the positive net cash flow from the sale of the property.

Step 7. We can now organize the net cash flows on a timeline or in a table as follows.

Year	Initial investment	Working capital	Operating cash flow	Termination cash flow	Net cash flow
0	($8,000,000)	—	—	—	($8,000,000)
1	—	($200,000)	$744,557	—	$ 544,757
2	—	($100,000)	$741,044	—	$ 641,044
3	—	—	$770,178	—	$ 770,178
4	—	—	$756,899	—	$ 756,899
5	—	$300,000	$813,620	$7,913,366	$9,026,986

Step 8. We now have one net cash flow per year organized in such a fashion where we can calculate net present value, payback, or internal rate of return. As discussed in the chapter, net present value is the best criterion for a capital budgeting project. Therefore, we will calculate *NPV* using the weighted average cost of capital previously calculated (9.38 percent). This is shown in Exhibit A10-3.

According to the net present value, the project should be rejected. The project costs $83,322 more than the benefits it generates (in present value terms).

Step 9. It would now be a good time to reexamine our analysis. After going through this process, it may seem disappointing to arrive at a rejection decision. Some may argue that the project should go ahead because "we've already spent all this time and money on it." This is not the appropriate way to look at those costs. First, those costs are now sunk costs and are irrelevant in the analysis. Second, it is well worth the price (probably a few thousand dollars) to reject a project that could destroy $83,322 of shareholder wealth.

At this point, a "tweaking" process may begin in which analysts will change assumptions to increase cash flows. This may involve increasing occupancies,

Year	Net cash flow	PV Factor at 9.38%	PV of cash flow
0	($8,000,000)	1.00	($8,000,000)
1	$ 544,757	.9142	$ 498,017
2	$ 641,044	.8358	$ 535,785
3	$ 770,178	.7642	$ 588,570
4	$ 756,899	.6986	$ 528,770
5	$9,026,986	.6387	$5,765,536
Total			($ 83,322)

Exhibit A10-3

reducing expenses, or even altering discount rates, which is appropriate if there are serious errors in the preliminary analysis. However, a trained hotel analyst knows that reducing critical expenses such as training and advertising could have a serious negative impact on future cash flows, causing a drop in revenue that outweighs the expense savings.

An Introduction to Hotel Valuation

11

Chapter Objectives

- To be introduced to the process of hotel valuation
- To understand the different types of users and preparers of market studies and appraisals
- To be aware of the agency relationships inherent in the hotel appraisal process
- To understand the different components of hotel market analysis
- To be introduced to the cost approach
- To be introduced to the sales comparison approach
- To be introduced to the income capitalization approach

HVS INTERNATIONAL HOTEL APPRAISAL SPECIALISTS

HVS International (formerly known as Hospitality Valuation Services) is one of the largest hotel appraisal organizations in the world. Starting with one office in Mineola, New York, the company now has offices in Canada, Europe, Australia, Singapore, Hong Kong, and South America. They specialize in hotel market studies, appraising, and general hotel consulting. Since 1980 they have conducted consulting engagements with more than 10,000 hotels worldwide.

In addition to consulting engagements, the company publishes a wide variety of surveys about the industry. Some of these include an overview of the lodging industry, hotel wage surveys, and franchise fee analyses. Additionally, they track hotel sales transactions with date, sales price, and capitalization rate information. Finally, they also produce software that can quantify rooms demand as well as forecast income and expenses. The company also sends via e-mail a daily lodging report that discusses important events affecting the hotel industry.

11.1 INTRODUCTION

A hotel appraisal is an opinion of value at a certain point in time. Hotel valuation, or hotel appraisal, is an important aspect of hospitality financial management and is generally considered a specialization within the appraisal profession. Although hotel appraising follows all the standard appraisal procedures, hotels are operated differently from other types of commercial real estate endeavors such as shopping malls, apartment buildings, or office complexes. A hotel is both a business and a real estate asset.

This chapter is only intended to be an introduction to the topic of hotel valuation. We have included a section in this textbook because students may someday be asked to appraise a hotel. On the other hand, a hotel manager could also be expected to commission an appraisal and needs to understand how the value was determined. The overall objective of this chapter is to provide a general introduction to hotel appraising for the hospitality student.

11.2 REASONS FOR A HOTEL APPRAISAL

Hotels are appraised for a variety of reasons. One general reason is because owners of the hotel are interested in the current market value of an asset they own. The **market value** is considered the most likely price that a buyer and seller would agree to under normal circumstances. It is also important to recognize that each appraisal has an effective date. After that date, market conditions could change, altering the cash flows and, thus, the value of the property.

Lenders are also interested in the hotel's value to help assess the risk of their investment. Furthermore, because many loans to hotels are made by commercial banks, federal law requires most commercial loans to be backed by an appraisal. This is because the hotel property represents **collateral** for the loan from the lender. Lenders will write a loan representing a certain proportion of the market value (say 60 percent) of the hotel property. As long as the market value of the hotel remains above the amount of the loan, the lender's loan is not at risk. If the hotel is involved in a bankruptcy proceeding, the hotel can be sold, and the loan will be repaid. However, if the market value is below the amount of the loan, the lender is "exposed" and is at much greater risk. This is one of the reasons why the market value of the property is important.

Other appraisals involve those completed for tax assessment purposes. An assessed value is often different than market value; assessments are made by government authorities in order to charge real estate taxes to make improvements to local communities such as roads and schools. Many hotels appeal their assessments to lower the amount of real estate taxes they are forced to pay. Another type of value is liquidation value—the price the property would obtain in a very quick sale. This is not the same as market value because the seller is being forced to sell the property under duress. Although there are many different types of value, the focus of this chapter will be on market value.

11.2.1 Parties Involved in the Process

As previously discussed, appraisals are usually completed so that lenders can have some level of confidence about the value of the property that is backing up the loan. Appraisals are now required for commercial properties such as hotels if the loan is being made by a bank whose deposits are federally insured. In earlier chapters, we discussed agency relationships between owners and managers and owners and lenders. In fact, the appraisal process also involves agency relationships.

In the 1980s, hotel developers (who were also borrowers) would commission appraisals directly from appraisal firms. As the principal in this agency relationship, the developer would want to secure the necessary loan for the hotel project. The appraiser, who was required to obtain a large amount of information about the project, could rely significantly on the information from the developer. This information could be incomplete or biased in such a way that affected the appraised value. The failure of numerous banks and savings and loans in the 1980s exposed some of the problems in the appraisal process regarding agency problems and motivations. Some research indicates that hotel appraised values may be subject to the agency relationships and economic circumstances surrounding the appraisal.[1] In late 1985, Congress held hearings examining the appraisal process and concluded that the direct hiring of appraisers by developers helped cause inaccurate appraisals. In 1989 Congress passed the Federal Institutions Reform Recovery and Enforcement Act of 1989. This law required appraisals to be commissioned by lenders directly and helped lead to the state licensing and regulation of commercial real estate appraisers. Although it is still not clear whether or not this legislation has helped remove bias from appraised values, it recognized the importance of agency relationships in the process and had a major impact on how appraisals were to be completed.

Although anyone can conduct an appraisal, those completed for loan underwriting purposes must be completed by real estate appraisers who are licensed by the states. Different states have different requirements, but all require a certain number of hours of practical experience along with real estate courses to help improve the quality of the appraisal. Many commercial appraisers also have earned special private designations. One of the most common is the MAI designation, which stands for "Member, Appraisal Institute." The Appraisal Institute is an institution that is responsible for imposing strict educational and practical experience requirements on potential candidates. Moreover, members must take courses in appraisal practice, standards, and ethics and must continue to take courses throughout their appraisal careers. Many accounting firms have appraisers with MAI designations; a variety of other firms also conduct hotel appraisals, including HVS International and PKF Consulting. More detailed information about the Appraisal Institute is available from their Web site at http://www.appraisalinstitute.org.

11.3 THE HOTEL APPRAISAL PROCESS

Throughout this textbook we have shown that the value of an asset is the present value of its economic benefits. Accordingly, the hotel appraisal attempts to assess the future economic benefits of a hotel. Therefore, it is the job of the appraiser to attempt to quantify those future benefits. More specifically, an appraiser is expected

---

[1]For further reading, see. M. Dalbor and W. Andrew, "Agency Problems in the Hotel Appraisal Process: An Exploratory Study," *International Journal of Hospitality Management* 19 (2000), 353–60.

to carefully examine any factors that will affect the size, timing, and risk associated with those benefits. The process follows a specific order and is described in the following sections.

11.3.1 Purpose of the Appraisal

The first step in the appraisal process is determining the nature of the appraisal problem. A major concern is which type of value is being appraised and for whom. As previously discussed, most appraisals are completed to determine market value. Another important question to be answered is the specific property to be appraised. It is not uncommon for a hotel to be appraised along with a parcel of "excess" land next to it or a freestanding restaurant that is adjacent to the property. In terms of the hotel itself, both existing and proposed hotels can be appraised.

Because a hotel appraisal is an appraisal of real estate, it is important to understand the definition of real estate. **Real estate** represents the land and everything permanently attached to it. Land is not only considered to be the ground surface but also that which extends through the earth and also into the sky. This use is somewhat restricted by rights granted to utilities, called easements. On the other hand, fixtures, furniture, and equipment (commonly abbreviated FF&E) is often included in the market value of the hotel (because you cannot operate the hotel without it) but is considered personal property, and its value is segregated from the rest of the hotel.

Real property includes real estate along with the benefits of ownership. Different parties may have different ownership interests in real estate. The ownership interest with the most rights is a **fee simple interest,** implying all privileges available for use and enjoyment of the real estate. This is the most interest valued in a hotel appraisal assignment. On the other hand, a landlord in an apartment building has what is known as a leased fee interest. A landlord must allow a tenant to use a certain space in the building that is known as a leasehold interest. Examples of special interests, called partial interests, include the right to minerals under the ground (mineral rights) or the air space above the property (air rights). Each of these types of interest can be valued, and it is imperative that the appraiser understands the interest to be valued before beginning the assignment.

11.3.2 Data Collection

This portion of the appraisal process is one of the most critical and most difficult. However, in recent years the availability of secondary data on the Internet has made this task easier. Nevertheless, the appraiser must always consider carefully the accuracy of the data obtained and attempt to verify the information whenever possible. This is particularly true for information that is not publicly available (such as information about a hotel in the competitive market). Information that is later discovered to be inaccurate can have a serious impact on the valuation conclusion.

We have stated previously that the value of an asset is the present value of its current and future economic benefits. Accordingly, any and all information that can affect the size, timing, and risk of these benefits needs to be examined. In general, the process begins with very general information about the market area and becomes progressively more specific. For our purposes, we will discuss the process for the appraisal of an existing hotel.

11.3.2.1 Market Area Information   Location is a key success factor for all types of real estate, and hotels are no exception. Moreover, a hotel's location relative to its surrounding geographic area is also important. The first unit of analysis that is taken into consideration is usually a county, city, or both. The factors to be examined are those that will impact future hotel room night demand. Although a historical analysis is important and often presented in appraisal reports, the focus should remain on the future growth prospects for an area. We need to remember that the value of an asset is based on the present value of its *future* economic benefits. It is rarely the case that the future represents simple repetition of the past.

Some of the key information that can help indicate future room night demand includes the following.

- Employment information including labor force, unemployment rates, breakdown of employment by sector, names of major employers, and employers entering or leaving the area. Many municipalities will discuss new employment entering an area; however, are any employers leaving the market? In other words, is there a *net gain* in employment? The nature of employment in the area also has a significant impact on the market orientation of room night demand in the area.
- Information about office and industrial space such as total square footage, vacancy rates, historical absorption patterns, and future construction/expansion projects should be gathered and considered carefully by the appraiser.
- Convention activity in terms of facilities available to attract groups, number of room nights generated by previous convention groups, and a forecast of future group bookings.
- Demographic statistics, including population and household income information.
- The availability of higher education facilities. Colleges and universities usually create demand through medical and research facilities as well as special events such as graduation, parents' weekends, and sporting events.
- Tourism plays a key role in hotel room night generation. Natural features such as beaches as well as festivals, concerts, and exhibits are all factors that can generate significant demand.

The sources for the foregoing information vary from area to area, but the local office of economic development and the local chamber of commerce are good places to start. The previously listed factors represent a partial list of those that are typically considered in the area analysis section of a report. However, the appraiser needs to have a solid understanding of the key elements in the specific market in which the hotel is located. For example, an appraiser in New Orleans must understand the impact of Mardi Gras and Jazzfest on the local hotel market. A careful analysis of these factors will enable the appraiser to understand the segmentation of the existing market demand as well as make estimates of future growth.

11.3.2.2 Submarket Analysis   One of the most important features of a quality hotel appraisal is a thorough assessment of the competitive market in which the hotel operates. If an appraiser merely assumes the current occupancy of the hotel will continue indefinitely, the appraiser has ignored the highly competitive nature of the hotel business. A hotel is not merely an apartment building with short-term leases; it is a business within a property that competes for business largely based on its specific location and reputation.

Accordingly, the establishment of the competitive market, or the competitive supply in which the subject property operates, is of critical importance. The names of the hotels with which the subject hotel competes are generally obtained from interviews with the general manager and/or sales managers of the subject hotel. This information can be verified later when interviewing other properties.

Hotels are considered to compete with the subject property based on the following factors.

- Location or proximity to the subject
- Comparable price
- Comparable quality
- Comparable amenities and facilities
- Accommodate same type of demand

Once the hotels in the area are chosen, a significant amount of information needs to be gathered. Even though it is fairly common for appraisers to take photographs of competitive hotels, the goal of the appraiser should be to provide a verbal description that is adequate for an outside reviewer who is unfamiliar with the market to understand the property. The following is a suggested list of information to be obtained from competitive hotels.

- Name and address
- Location relative to subject hotel
- Number of available rooms
- Potential expansion/renovation plans
- Rack room rates
- Historical average occupancy and average rates
- Allocation of accommodated demand by market segment
- Description of food and beverage facilities
- Description of meeting and banquet space
- Seasonality, number of fill nights, and estimate of turnaway demand
- Age
- List of hotels they consider to be competitive

Some of the information on this list is sensitive or proprietary. Many hotel managers are reluctant to provide sensitive information, particularly about average rates and occupancy. One source of this information may be the local tax assessor, who calculates occupancy taxes. Another potential source may be other hotels; many hotels share this information with each other on an informal basis. Sometimes the respondent will answer about occupancy if the question is expressed in terms of a five-point range. Nevertheless, the appraiser must be careful about sensitive information obtained from personal interviews because it could be biased.

Of particular importance regarding the information gathered from competitive properties is an accurate breakdown of the segmentation of demand. It is also important to understand that although there are some "standard" segments of demand—such as commercial transient, convention group, and leisure—not all hotels in all markets categorize their demand in the same fashion. For example, where does the market include bus groups of tourists? In group business or leisure business? Additionally, there may be segments of demand that are specific to a particular market, such as military, airline crews, and long-term stay/relocation demand. The appraiser is expected to classify demand in a manner emulating the competitive market. Market segmentation also will have a significant effect on analyzing the average rate of the market.

Eventually, the appraiser should compile a spreadsheet detailing the composition of the competitive market in terms of historical supply and demand. A historical range of three to five years is fairly common but is not always obtainable. An example of historical supply and demand is shown in Exhibit 11-1.

Exhibit 11-1 details the historical performance of our hypothetical hotel market for one year (as previously mentioned, it is advantageous to have three to five years of historical data). The historical data is important for a number of reasons. First, it gives the appraiser important information about the current condition of the competitive hotel market. Second, it quantifies the demand by segment, and a historical analysis shows which segments have been increasing or decreasing in the number of occupied rooms. Finally, it relates information about how the subject hotel is competing in the marketplace in overall terms and by segment.

An examination of Exhibit 11-2 reveals the estimated change in accommodated demand for the three-year period. Our simulated market reveals strong historical growth in commercial demand, a decrease in group business, and a modest increase in tourist demand. The appraiser must then attempt to relate the performance of the competitive market to the information about patterns for the overall area. It is important to remember that what is happening in the overall metropolitan area may not be analogous to patterns at competitive hotels. For example, it may be such that the overall market area has accommodated an

Hotel	Rooms	Available rooms	Average rate	Occupancy %	Occupied rooms	Rooms revenue
Holiday Inn	200	73,000	$62.00	70	51,100	$3,168,200
Ramada Inn	165	60,225	59.00	64	38,544	2,274,096
Subject Hotel	175	63,875	63.00	68	43,435	2,736,405
Overall Market	540	197,100	$61.45	67.52	133,079	$8,178,701

Segmentation of Market Demand for Calendar Year 2002

Hotel	Commercial %	Group %	Tourist %	Commercial demand	Group demand	Tourist demand
Holiday Inn	45	25	30	22,995	12,775	15,330
Ramada Inn	20	15	65	7,709	5,782	25,053
Subject Hotel	55	30	15	23,889	13,031	6,515
Overall Market	41.1	23.7	35.2	54,593	31,588	46,898

Exhibit 11-1 Historical supply and demand analysis occupancy and average rate performance for calendar year 2002.

Year	Available rooms	Occupied rooms	Average rate	Occupancy %	RevPar
2000	197,100	126,538	$58.60	64.20	$37.62
2001	197,100	128,903	$60.75	65.40	$39.73
2002	197,100	133,079	$61.45	67.52	$41.49
Growth[a]	0.00%	2.55%	2.40%	2.55	5.02%

Year	Commercial %	Group %	Tourist %	Commercial demand	Group demand	Tourist demand
2000	39.5	25.2	35.3%	49,983	31,886	44,669
2001	38.7	26.2	35.1%	49,885	33,773	45,254
2002	41.1	23.7	35.2%	54,593	31,588	46,898
Growth[a]	—	—	—	4.51%	−.47%	2.46%

[a]Growth is expressed in compound annual terms.

Exhibit 11-2   Historical supply and demand growth.

increasing number of groups in the metropolitan area. However, they may not be staying at hotels in the competitive market or else they may be staying for a shorter period of time. Other factors could come into play such as a renovation or removal of meeting space at one of the competitive properties during the period of analysis. Overall, it is not enough for the appraiser to report what has happened in the competitive market in recent years; they must know *why* the demand changed.

The most common way to evaluate the occupancy and average daily rate (ADR) performance of the subject hotel is by relative comparisons. Although this can also be done with ADR, it is most commonly done with average annual occupancy. The performance of the subject hotel is judged based on the amount of demand it actually captured versus what it "should" have captured. For example, our hypothetical competitive market contains 540 total daily hotel rooms (197,100 annual). The subject hotel contains 175 rooms and represents approximately 32.41 percent of the total market. Therefore, all else being equal, the subject hotel should accommodate 32.41 percent of the demand in the market. This is called its **fair share.** This is also true for each of the three market segments. This is called a market penetration analysis and is shown for 2002 in Exhibit 11-3.

A market penetration analysis by segment can be completed for each year when historical data are available. In our example, we can see that the subject hotel has received more than its fair share of demand in two segments—commercial and group demand. The appraiser also needs to consider why this is the case. It is usually a function of the marketing strategy of the property along with location, facilities, and rack rate positioning. On the other hand, we can see the subject hotel has received far less of its fair share in the tourist segment. It might be the case that the subject hotel is not located near tourist attractions or simply does not discount its rates enough to the very rate-sensitive tourist demand segment. This is a common situation for many commercially oriented hotels that accommodate a significant amount of demand during the weeknights but have much lower occupancies on weekends. This has important implications for future occupancy projections for the subject hotel.

Subject hotel rooms (annual)	63,875
Total rooms in competitive market	197,100
Subject fair share percentage	32.41%
Commercial demand in market	54,593
Subject hotel fair share	17,692
Demand accommodated	23,889
Market penetration rate	135.03%
Group demand in market	31,588
Subject hotel fair share	10,237
Demand accommodated	13,031
Market penetration rate	127.29%
Tourist demand in market	46,898
Subject hotel fair share	15,198
Demand accommodated	6,515
Market penetration rate	42.87%

Exhibit 11-3 Historical market penetration analysis for the subject hotel calendar year 2002.

In terms of ADR, the subject hotel is currently the rate leader in this market. This is probably because the hotel accommodates a significant amount of commercial demand, which is much less rate sensitive than the other segments. It may also reflect a lack of discounting practiced by the subject hotel in all market segments, something the appraiser should consider when making future projections regarding ADR for the subject hotel. Projections for the overall competitive market as well as the subject hotel are usually included in the income capitalization approach to value section of the appraisal report.

11.3.2.3 Neighborhood Analysis As the appraiser moves from a general form of analysis to a specific one, the next step in the appraisal process is an examination of the neighborhood in which the subject hotel is located. The major feature of a neighborhood is complementary land uses. Most jurisdictions have similar land uses in an area because of zoning regulations. However, commercial properties can be considered to be part of a neighborhood because they serve the residents. Neighborhoods are often bounded by geographic features and/or roads, but this is not always the case. The neighborhood ends where there are no direct factors influencing the subject hotel.

Neighborhoods, much like products, have life cycles. Appraisals usually define the life cycle by four distinct periods: growth, stability, decline, and revitalization. This can generally be assessed by examination of the effective age of the real estate in the neighborhood, although there is no number definitively indicating when a neighborhood has moved into the next stage of the cycle. Decline is often caused by a change in an exterior factor such as the closing of a major employer or a change in the transportation network. The appraiser can obtain historical sales prices for both commercial and residential sales to assess the pattern of increasing, decreasing, or stable values.

Another important aspect of the neighborhood is the development activity around the subject hotel. This reveals the interest in the neighborhood by developers and can help determine its stage in the life cycle. This development could also help supply demand for local hotels. This is particularly true for new office and/or industrial development that could house employers needing hotel rooms. Moreover, the appraiser should consider the investment demand for similar hotels in the neighborhood. If there are a number of closed hotels or hotels that have been converted to other uses, this is another indication of the desirability of the neighborhood in terms of hotel investment.

The final consideration in regard to the neighborhood is the availability of nearby amenities. The proximity of the subject hotel to demand generators is always critical to the success of a hotel, but many hotels only offer limited amenities. Accordingly, although many hotels do not supply these amenities themselves, they choose to be located near amenities valued by their guests. A classic example is a limited-service hotel that is located next to a restaurant. However, there are many other potential examples. A location near a health club may be important to hotel guests; additionally, the proximity of a grocery store and a dry cleaner could be very helpful to a hotel that accommodates long-term stay demand.

11.3.2.4 Analysis of Site and Improvements   The desirability of the site is a critical element of the analysis. Because many hotels rely significantly on "drive-by" traffic, aspects that can affect a hotel's ability to attract this type of hotel demand need to be carefully considered. The first step in site description is the identification of the appropriate property. A mailing address is not a legal address; a legal address is usually found in the original deed of the property in governmental records. Properties also are identified by the tax assessor of the region with a tax identification number. The zoning regulations regarding the site should be verified to ensure the subject hotel is a conforming use. Any prospective changes in the zoning laws affecting the subject hotel should also be noted.

An inspection of the property is made to examine the physical characteristics of the site, including size, shape, and topography. Information regarding the flood plain (found by examining FEMA flood plain maps) and availability of the necessary utilities should be verified. Although appraisers are usually not experts about environmental hazards, an appraiser may become aware of this type of problem. If this is the case, the appraiser should notify the client and defer this analysis to an appropriate expert.

The rest of the site analysis relates primarily to a prospective guest's desire to stay at the property. Is the hotel accessible? From how far away is the property visible? Is the property visible but difficult to get to? How far away from the interstate is it? Is there enough parking on-site? Does the hotel have a corner location or exposure to a major thoroughfare? Even such small factors as the availability of a left-hand turn signal into the property can affect its desirability. Sometimes a relatively poor site can hamper the performance of a well-constructed hotel property.

The description of the improvements is often obtained from a combination of sources: the client or an engineer, a physical building inspection, or an examination of the building plans. The purpose of the improvements description is completed in large part to help complete the cost approach to value, if one is conducted. The other reasons are to help assess the effective age of the property (as opposed to merely the chronological age) and to assess the need for any cash expenditures to be made for repairs and deferred maintenance.

The description of the improvements includes structural items, the nature of the systems (electrical, heating and cooling, plumbing, air-conditioning, and fire safety). Interior finishes of the public areas and guest rooms should also be described. Included in this section should be a description of any other areas affiliated with the hotel such as a health club, pro shop, retail space, banquet space, and the like. Any deferred maintenance items noted will have to be estimated and subtracted from the various conclusions to value estimated by the appraiser. This amount must be considered to enable the hotel to function in a competitive market. This is just one example of one of the major tasks of the appraiser: to consider the property from a market participant's perspective.

11.3.3 Highest and Best Use Analysis

Highest and best use is defined as "the reasonably probable and legal use of vacant land or an improved property, which is physically possible, appropriately supported, financially feasible, and that results in the highest value."[2] The market analysis that has been completed up to this point is instrumental in determining the highest and best use for the property, both as if vacant and as if improved.

The overall idea of the highest and best use analysis is to find the property use that will produce the greatest return to the land. Armed with knowledge about the market, what should occupy this parcel of land if it were vacant? It is possible for hotel market conditions to deteriorate to the point where other types of commercial development may be more productive. This, however, is rarely the case. If it were, the client would be notified, and the appraiser would expect to support his or her conclusions in this regard.

The criteria for highest and best use as vacant and as improved are the same. The highest and best use must be legally permissible (relative to zoning), physically possible (size limitations), financially feasible, and maximally productive. The first two tests are relatively easy to assess. Information from the area and market analysis should help assess the latter two tests. These involve projecting income and expenses from each potential use. The economic benefits are subsequently discounted to determine feasibility and maximum return.

In nearly all cases, however, the existing use as a hotel is the highest and best use as both vacant and improved. This does not mean, however, that there are no deferred maintenance items that could be subtracted from the final conclusion of value. Nevertheless, all hotel appraisals must contain statements regarding highest and best use as vacant and as improved.

11.4 APPROACHES TO VALUE

Appraisers have three major valuation methods at their disposal to value an existing hotel: the cost approach, the sales comparison approach, and the income capitalization approach. The reason for using three different approaches is to provide a check for reasonableness of one value conclusion as compared to the others. Although many appraisers use all three approaches to value, this is not required. The appraiser is expected to value the property in a manner similar to that used by active hotel buyers and sellers in the marketplace. We will discuss each of the three approaches next.

[2]Appraisal Institute, *The Appraisal of Real Estate* (10th ed.), p. 275.

11.4.1 The Cost Approach to Value

The cost approach is based on the principle whereby no one would pay more for a hotel property than the cost of construction. The market value determined using the cost approach is based on replacement cost, not reproduction cost. Reproduction cost would be the cost to reproduce the existing property exactly as constructed. On the other hand, the more common type of cost in this approach is replacement cost. This involves constructing another hotel property with similar utility for the buyer, not the construction of an exact replica.

The cost approach is completed in a series of steps.

- Land valuation
- Cost of improvements, as if newly constructed
- Estimated value of furniture, fixtures, and equipment (FF&E)
- Subtract depreciation from three sources:
  1. Physical deterioration
  2. Functional obsolescence
  3. Economic obsolescence

Even if a hotel appraisal does not contain a complete cost approach to value, an estimate of the land value is often calculated. The most common way to value land is through the use of comparable sales. Appraisers obtain land sales with similar characteristics including size, zoning, and overall utility to the subject. Common sources for vacant land sales include brokers, tax assessors, and public records. Sales prices must subsequently be adjusted to make them more comparable to the subject. Sales with superior attributes to the subject are adjusted downward; sales with inferior attributes are adjusted upward. Land value is often reported on a price per square foot or price per acre basis.

Information regarding improvements and FF&E can be obtained from a variety of sources. Developers and construction companies are excellent sources for this information. Other companies offer subscription services detailing cost of construction on a per-square-foot basis or a per-item basis. If the subject hotel was recently constructed, the construction information should be available from management or the owner. The costs of FF&E are updated every year in surveys published by HVS International, who estimate the costs per room, depending on the market orientation of the hotel. Obviously, luxury hotels have more expensive furnishings than budget properties.

The estimate of depreciation from three sources is one of the most difficult tasks for an appraiser. The physical deterioration is probably the easiest component to assess and understand. These items are noted in the on-site inspection of the hotel. Functional obsolescence is the loss in value extracted by the market because of outmoded design of the hotel. Examples may include a hotel with guest rooms that are much smaller than the rest of the market or use of an old-fashioned "two-pipe" heating and cooling system. Economic obsolescence is the loss in value due to factors outside the structure. A classic example for hotels is an older property located on a highway that is currently bypassed by an interstate or new highway. The loss is calculated by capitalizing the estimated loss in income. All depreciation is subsequently subtracted from the land value and the cost of new improvements.

Overall, the cost approach is rarely used to appraise existing hotels. Although it is sometimes used for new hotels, it is really best for special-use properties such as public buildings (libraries, museums, etc). The cost approach is heavily dependent on recent, reliable land sales, which may not always be available. Second, the difficulty in accurately assessing all three types of depreciation can be formidable. The task becomes increasingly difficult as a hotel ages over time.

Finally, and most importantly, the task of the appraiser is to value the property in a manner that emulates the market. Because a hotel is an income-producing property, it is rare for a hotel investor to be concerned with the cost to build it. Accordingly, the appraiser may not utilize the cost approach to value in an appraisal of an existing hotel. Nevertheless, the appraiser must state why the cost approach was not used in the appraisal report.

11.4.2 The Sales Comparison Approach

The sales comparison approach to value is based on the idea that hotels offering the same amount of utility should sell for the same price. Hotel sales can be obtained in a variety of places. Sources such as hotel brokers and public information sources such as county or city records can be examined. Another good source of information about hotel sales is from interviews with competitive hotels. Generally, hotels that compete with the subject or else are located in the neighborhood should be analyzed if not at least mentioned in the appraisal report. As the use of the World Wide Web has increased in recent years, a variety of online sources for hotel information can be found. These sources can save time but usually charge for each comparable sale requested.

The methodology employed in land valuation is similar to that used in this approach. Once comparable sales are obtained, adjustments must be made to these sales. Appraisers must be careful to consider all of the specific circumstances surrounding the sale of other hotels. Interests conveyed, use of special financing, deferred maintenance items, and other considerations need to be verified before the sale can be used in an approach to value. Other important information to be gathered from each sale (if possible) includes rooms revenue and income information. Each sale should be verified with a knowledgeable party related to the transaction.

A major problem when using this approach is the availability of recent sales. As the student may be aware, the hotel business is subject to general business cycles. Accordingly, there may be times when certain hotels or even particular hotel markets are not generating interest for hotel buyers and sellers. This requires appraisers to use older sales or sales in other competitive markets. Another important consideration is to understand the unique nature of hotels. It is very difficult to find two hotels exactly alike, which makes the adjustment process much more difficult.

Accordingly, techniques have been developed to help deal with the adjustment process. One can argue that if one hotel is superior to another, the superior hotel should earn higher income. In order to standardize the comparison, the income per room is utilized. The amount of **net operating income (NOI)** is obtained from each comparable sale and compared to the subject property. We will discuss NOI in greater detail later in this chapter, but it is similar to earnings before interest, taxes, depreciation, and amortization. Let us look at an example.

Sale #	Subject NOI/room	Comparable NOI/room	Factor	Comparable price/room	Adjusted price/room
1	$5,000	$5,500	1.10	$65,000	$59,091
2	$5,000	$4,700	.94	$61,000	$64,893
3	$5,000	$5,400	1.08	$62,000	$57,407

Exhibit 11-4   NOI per room grid.

As shown in Exhibit 11-4, the appraiser assumes the adjustments are built into the differences in the NOI/room achieved by the two hotels. Hopefully, a relatively small range is produced, and the appraiser merely multiplies the adjusted price per room times the number of hotel rooms in the subject to find the value via the sales comparison approach.

The drawbacks to this method include the availability of NOI information from each of the comparable sales. Moreover, a significant portion of the income capitalization approach must be completed before the sales comparison approach can be finished. Additionally, the appraiser assumes the important differences to active market participants are reflected in the NOI. By using this approach, the appraiser cannot really pass judgment on the key individual factors of each comparable sale that may be either superior or inferior to the subject property.

After completing the table shown in Exhibit 11-4, the appraiser must still examine the sales and decide on a price per room. The appraiser may weigh one sale or another more in the final value conclusion from this approach. However, much like the cost approach, it is not always the case that hotel investors consider the prices of other hotels when setting prices. Nevertheless, the sales comparison approach can be used to check the validity of value via the other approaches, particularly the income capitalization approach.

11.4.3 The Income Capitalization Approach

The income capitalization approach is generally the most heavily relied on when an appraiser considers a final opinion of value. This is consideration of the fact that a hotel is an income-producing property and is valued by active market participants based on the present value of its economic benefits. The purpose of this section is to provide further insight into the process of how those benefits are determined.

The first step is to utilize the historical market information gathered by the appraiser during the fieldwork portion of the appraisal assignment. Exhibit 11-1 indicates the market achieved an occupancy of 67.52 percent for calendar year 2002 with an ADR of $61.45. The total amount of accommodated demand was 133,079. An examination of Exhibit 11-2 indicates no new supply in the past three years with overall occupied rooms increasing at a compound annual rate of 2.55 percent. It is important to notice how each of the segments has increased (or decreased) at different rates. The next step in the process is to project demand growth by market segment using the information gathered from interviews in the market and trends in the secondary data gathered.

The amount of demand for 2002 shown in Exhibits 11-1 and 11-2 represents the amount of demand *accommodated*, which is not necessarily all the demand that could be captured by the competitive hotels. There may be demand in the market that is currently being turned away during peak periods that could be captured by new hotels. This amount of demand is estimated based on turnaway information from the hotel interviews. This demand cannot be accommodated until new rooms are added to the market. Additionally, there is usually a positive correlation between market occupancy and turnaway demand. The lower the market occupancy, in general, the smaller the amount of unaccommodated demand in the market.

Another type of demand is known as latent demand. This demand usually represents customers who are particularly loyal to one hotel franchise or another and will not stay in the market until this type of property becomes available in the market. Hotel loyalty will vary by franchise, but it is not uncommon for hotels to receive 15 to 20 percent of their occupied room nights from their reservation system. An estimate is made for the total latent demand for the new property and then allocated between the appropriate demand segments.

The projection of new supply is relatively easy because information on building permits is publicly available. Additionally, a physical inspection of the proposed hotel site may indicate construction activity. It can be difficult with proposed projects in terms of their timing. Building plans for new hotels must be submitted and approved, and financing must be obtained before construction begins. The appraiser must carefully investigate information about new hotels to determine size, timing, and market orientation of the new property. For the purposes of our hypothetical hotel market, we will assume a 146-room Courtyard by Marriott is going to open at the beginning of 2005.

The base level of demand must be projected by segment. This is one of the most important yet difficult tasks in the market study section of the appraisal. The appraiser must carefully consider what has happened in the past. For example, our market shows strong increases in commercial demand, a modest increase in tourist demand, and a decrease in group demand. The increase in the first two segments may be attributable to more businesses and opening of new tourist attractions. The decline in group demand may be attributable to factors such as renovation of hotel convention space in 2002 or a conscious effort by one of the competitive hotels to block out lower-priced group rooms in favor of commercial transient customers. Other factors from the market such as new employers must also be considered. A five-year projection period is often used because of the increasing uncertainty as the projection period increases. Our projections of market demand by segment are shown in Exhibit 11-5, and the projections of total demand and supply are shown in Exhibit 11-6.

11.4.3.1 Occupancy Projection/Market Penetration Analysis The appraiser begins this section of the analysis with an examination of the historical penetration performance of the subject hotel. Once again, the analysis is conducted for the overall property as well as within the specific market segments. A penetration rate of 100 percent indicates the hotel is receiving its "fair share" of demand; penetration rates exceeding this amount indicate a competitive advantage of the hotel. On the other hand, penetration rates below 100 percent represent a competitive disadvantage. For example, the subject hotel is at a competitive disadvantage within the tourist demand segment.

A number of considerations need to be made when projecting occupancies for the subject. It should be understood that market penetration analysis is an

Commercial Demand Segment

Year	Projected growth rate (%)	Commercial segment (accommodated)	Latent demand	Total demand
2002	—	54,593	0	54,593
2003	2.0	55,685	0	55,685
2004	2.0	56,799	0	56,799
2005	1.0	57,367	10,000	67,367
2006	1.0	68,041	0	68,041
2007	1.0	68,721	0	68,721

Group Demand Segment

Year	Projected growth rate (%)	Group segment (accommodated)	Latent demand	Total demand
2002	—	31,588	0	31,588
2003	3.0	32,536	0	32,536
2004	2.0	33,186	0	33,186
2005	1.0	33,518	0	33,518
2006	1.0	33,853	0	33,853
2007	1.0	34,192	0	34,192

Tourist Demand Segment

Year	Projected growth rate (%)	Tourist segment (accommodated)	Latent demand	Total demand
2002	—	46,898	0	46,898
2003	2.0	47,836	0	47,836
2004	3.0	49,271	0	49,271
2005	2.0	50,246	10,000	60,246
2006	1.0	60,848	0	60,848
2007	1.0	61,457	0	61,457

Exhibit 11-5   Market demand projection.

Year	Total demand	Total supply	Market occupancy %
2002	133,079	197,100	67.5
2003	136,057	197,100	69.0
2004	139,256	197,100	70.7
2005	161,131	250,390	64.4
2006	162,742	250,390	65.0
2007	164,370	250,390	65.7

Exhibit 11-6   Market supply and demand projection.

extremely subjective method of projecting occupancies. Nevertheless, there are important factors to be considered that can help improve the quality of the analysis. The first consideration is the balance of supply and demand within the market. The projected market occupancies indicate an impact on the overall market from the addition of new hotel rooms (the Courtyard by Marriott). The appraiser needs to consider the impact of the opening of this new supply on the occupancy of the subject.

Additionally, the market orientation of the property should be considered. Based on the fieldwork interviews, the mix of demand at the subject hotel is 55 percent commercial individual and 30 percent group. Although a portion of the accommodated group demand may indeed stay on weekends, it is likely that this demand segment is accommodated during the week along with the commercial transient demand. This means the subject hotel may be achieving very high occupancies during the Sunday–Thursday night period. Therefore, any additional room nights accommodated by the subject hotel will have to occur on weekends. This simply may not be possible, and therefore, the hotel may not be able to increase occupancy above its current level.

The appraiser must also carefully consider a win–lose scenario based on the market occupancies projected. It is sometimes the case that an appraiser can make overly aggressive projections for the hotel being appraised. However, the appraiser should remember that the accommodation of demand in the future is essentially a zero-sum game—any demand accommodated by the subject property is demand that cannot be accommodated by any other property. Therefore, a thoughtful exercise is for the appraiser to divide up the accommodated demand among all the hotels in the market—both existing and projected—in order to project occupancies for each of the properties. Which hotels are going to have a competitive advantage, and which will be at a disadvantage? This type of analysis helps keep the appraiser in perspective in terms of the overall market.

The objective of the market penetration analysis is to project occupancy for the subject hotel over the projection period. For new hotels, appraisers usually show a buildup of occupancy of three or four years to a stabilized occupancy. Some appraisals assume this occupancy level will continue throughout the projection period. Although this may or may not occur, the appraiser must choose a stabilized year of operation to use a particular year for a value using a direct capitalization technique. In other cases, the stabilized occupancy represents an average with actual occupancies potentially falling above or below the number. The projected occupancies are shown in Exhibit 11-7.

As shown in Exhibit 11-7, the hotel is projected to maintain approximately the same mix of accommodated demand over the projection period. The occupancy declines somewhat after the opening of the Courtyard by Marriott. Given the expected market orientation of the new hotel, the impact on the subject property is primarily in the commercial transient and group segments. By the fourth year of the projection period, the subject hotel is expected to achieve a stabilized occupancy level of approximately 68 percent. Many hotel appraisals round the occupancy to the nearest whole number. However, this rounding can have an increasing impact on the financial projections of the hotel, particularly for larger hotels. This effect is not necessarily intentional but reflects an estimated number consistent with the other estimates used in the market penetration analysis.

	2003	2004	2005	2006	2007
Commercial demand	55,685	56,799	67,367	68,041	68,721
Fair share %	32.41%	32.41%	25.51%	25.51%	25.51%
Fair share demand	18,048	18,409	17,185	17,357	17,531
Penetration rate	135%	135%	135%	135%	134%
Accommodated demand	24,364	24,852	23,200	23,432	23,492
% of total accommodated	55.7%	55.6%	53.9%	53.9%	53.8%
Group demand	32,536	33,186	33,518	33,853	34,192
Fair share %	32.41%	32.41%	25.51%	25.51%	25.51%
Fair share demand	10,545	10,756	8,550	8,631	8,722
Penetration rate	125%	125%	160%	160%	159%
Accommodated demand	13,181	13,445	13,680	13,810	13,868
% of total accommodated	30.1%	30.1%	31.8%	31.8%	31.8%
Tourist demand	47,836	49,271	60,246	60,848	61,457
Fair share %	32.41%	32.41%	25.51%	25.51%	25.51%
Fair share demand	15,504	15,969	15,369	15,522	15,678
Penetration rate	40%	40%	40%	40%	40%
Accommodated demand	6,202	6,386	6,148	6,209	6,271
% of total accommodated	14.2%	14.3%	14.3%	14.3%	14.4%
Total accommodated demand	43,747	44,683	43,028	43,451	43,631
Total available rooms	63,875	63,875	63,875	63,875	63,875
Subject hotel occupancy	68.5%	70.0%	67.4%	68.0%	68.3%

Exhibit 11-7 Market penetration analysis.

11.4.3.2 Average Daily Rate Projection The projection of ADR for the subject hotel is almost as important as the occupancy projection. However, the forecast of ADR is generally less problematic. An existing hotel should have historical records available regarding the ADR ratio for the property. The historical growth in average rate is a consideration in future expected rate growth. Other important information to gather is rack rates from competitive hotels. By comparing the rack rates of competitive hotels with actual achieved rates for those hotels, the appraiser can gather information about discounting policies. Additionally, the appraiser can evaluate discounting policies within market segments.

The overall ADR is going to be affected by demand in each market segment, rack rates per segment, discounting within each segment, and the mix of single and double rooms. Most of this information should be available from the sales and marketing department of the subject hotel. Once each of these elements is known, then a relatively sophisticated ADR projection can be made.

On the other hand, there are other simple ways to project ADR for an existing hotel. If the projected mix of accommodated demand is not going to change, then the appraiser may estimate future ADR by simply using the existing ADR and compounding it into the future with a growth rate. Another method is a market positioning approach that compares the rack rates and achieved average rates of those properties with the subject. Given the location, facilities, and amenities of the subject hotel, this should have an effect on how the subject hotel positions itself relative to the competition. This estimated rate is then projected into the future based on future growth rates.

Segment	% of demand	% of single occupancy	Single rate	% at rate	Contribution
Commercial					
Full rate	54	90	$70	25	$ 8.51
Corporate rate	54	90	$63	75	$22.96
Group					
Full rate	32	50	$70	10	$ 1.12
Group rate	32	50	$60	90	$ 8.64
Tourist					
Full rate	14	10	$70	10	$ 0.10
Discounted rate	14	10	$59	90	$ 0.74

Segment	% of demand	% of double occupancy	Double rate	% at rate	Contribution
Commercial					
Full rate	54	10	$80	25	$ 1.08
Corporate rate	54	10	$73	75	$ 2.96
Group					
Full rate	32	50	$80	10	$ 1.28
Group rate	32	50	$70	90	$10.08
Tourist					
Full rate	14	90	$80	10	$ 1.01
Discounted rate	14	90	$69	90	$ 7.82
Estimated average daily rate					$66.30
Rounded					$66.50

Exhibit 11-8 Estimated average daily rate in a stabilized year.

The most sophisticated methodology makes use of the market penetration analysis previously conducted. The mix of demand from the stabilized year is utilized along with rack racks, discounted rates, and estimates of single versus double occupancy. An example of this is shown in Exhibit 11-8.

As shown in Exhibit 11-8, the weighted average rate equals $66.30, which rounds to approximately $66.50. Average rates were once rounded to the nearest $1, but because of the potential impact on the financial results, they are often rounded to the nearest $.50 or $.25. The ADR is inflated based on expected rates of inflation, obtainable from a variety of econometric forecasting sources. Given the estimated occupancies and assuming an inflation rate of 3 percent for each year of the projection period, Exhibit 11-9 shows the projected rooms revenue for the years 2003–2007.

The importance of rooms revenue cannot be overemphasized, as it is generally the largest revenue category for a hotel, even a casino property. Additionally, the rooms division is often the most or second most profitable division within the hotel. Finally, the occupied room nights are the impetus for revenue generation in other areas of the hotel.

11.4.3.3 Preparation of Financial Estimates As previously discussed, most hotel appraisals require an estimate of market value. This has important implications regarding how the appraisal is to be completed. For one, the appraiser is expected to emulate the marketplace in terms of the valuation methodology

Year	Occupied rooms (rounded)	ADR	Rooms revenue
Stabilized	43,500	$66.50	$2,892,750
2003	43,700	$68.50	$2,993,450
2004	44,700	$70.50	$3,151,350
2005	43,000	$72.50	$3,117,500
2006	43,500	$75.00	$3,262,500
2007	43,600	$77.00	$3,357,200

Exhibit 11-9 Projected rooms revenue for the subject hotel.

employed. Additionally, the revenue and expense projections are expected to be market oriented. This means that as of the date of appraisal, the hotel property is assumed to be under the guise of competent and efficient management. This has implications for all expense categories, including marketing and maintenance. Accordingly, this implicitly affects occupancy and average rate estimates as well.

A logical starting point for the compilation of financial estimates is an in-depth analysis of the historical financial statements of the subject property. In fact, appraisal practice currently requires presentation of three years of historical income statements in the final appraisal report (assuming the property is at least three years old). An appraiser may present more than three years of data if it is available. The appraiser can analyze the historical revenues and expenses in a number of ways, including

- Total dollars
- Percentage of total or departmental revenue
- Dollars per occupied room
- Dollars per available room

Most appraisers utilize the last three methods of comparison to analyze income statement line items. Additionally, most appraisers use more than one method of comparison to provide a check for the reasonableness of the estimates.

However, because the appraiser is projecting market-oriented revenues and expenses, one cannot merely rely on the historical income statements of the subject hotel. The appraiser must also analyze the income statements of comparable properties that are similar in size, facilities, and average rate to the subject. Many appraisal firms have a database of comparable hotel income statements to draw on for analysis. If these are not available, accounting and consulting firms, such as PKF Consulting, survey hotels in the United States annually and publish these figures. *Trends in the Hotel Industry* is a commonly used publication, although it is not the only one available. Consulting firms charge fees for a subscription, but these publications may be available in your local or campus library.

The hotel data found in the aforementioned publications should be analyzed in a similar fashion to that of the subject hotel. Approximately three to five other hotels are used for comparison purposes, and a range is obtained for each income statement line item. The appraiser will usually choose an amount within the indicated range unless there is specific evidence regarding a certain item to justify a selection outside the range of the comparables.

Departmental revenues
Less: Departmental expenses
Equals: Operated department income
Less: Undistributed operating expenses
Equals: Income before fixed charges
Less: Property taxes
Less: Building and contents insurance
Less: Management fees
Equals: Income before reserve for replacement
Less: Reserve for replacement
Income before other fixed charges (NOI)

Exhibit 11-10 Income statement—appraisal format.

An income statement is first produced for a representative year in current value dollars. This statement should follow the Uniform System of Accounts format discussed earlier in the text. The format is slightly different than what may be produced for internal hotel use. The general format is shown in Exhibit 11-10.

This format is very similar to the one presented earlier in the text with a few important exceptions. First of all, fixed expenses such as interest, depreciation, amortization, and income taxes are ignored for the purposes of the income projection. Interest expense is ignored because most hotel appraisals are completed assuming all equity financing. Income taxes are excluded because of the uncertainty regarding the marginal tax rate of the owner(s). Accordingly, because income taxes are deleted from the analysis, the tax shield from depreciation and amortization cannot be calculated.

An important item often excluded from statement of operations is the reserve for replacement. This reserve is an allocation to the replacement of FF&E, which wears out over time. Although the expense of capital expenditures does not appear in the operating statements of a hotel, these items are important to the cash flows of the property and are represented by this expense, which is typically shown as a percentage of revenues. Historically, a range of 3 to 5 percent of gross revenues has been most often used by appraisers and consultants for this line item. However, studies of these expenditures reveal this range to be too low. A more appropriate allocation should be 5 to 7 percent of gross revenues.

Once an income statement for a typical year is compiled, the projected financial statements are completed using the previously determined ADR and occupancy. However, some important adjustments need to be made from the base year estimate. First, inflation rates need to be considered to reflect dollar values in future years. Although it is common for all revenues and expenses to be inflated at the same rate, this is usually not appropriate. Wage rates will most likely increase at a different rate than property insurance or utilities. Accordingly, the rate of future increases utilized in the report should be discussed.

Another important feature of the projection is the breakdown between fixed and variable components of revenue and expense items. In general, items before undistributed operating expenses tend to have a more significant variable component than fixed. On the other hand, expenses such as administrative and general, maintenance, and energy are primarily fixed. The appraiser must calculate the variable component (usually on a per-occupied-room basis) as well as the

Year	NOI
Stabilized	$ 832,000
2003	$ 748,000
2004	$ 827,000
2005	$ 857,000
2006	$ 938,000
2007	$1,007,000

Exhibit 11-11   NOI stream for the subject hotel.

fixed component for each item on the income statement. Both elements are inflated and totaled to compile the NOI for the number of years in the future required by the appraisal assignment.

11.4.4 Direct Capitalization

The direct capitalization technique involves the use of a stabilized year's NOI in a present value of perpetuity formula. The formula to determine the value is as follows.

$$\text{Market value} = \frac{\text{Stabilized NOI}}{\text{Overall capitalization rate}}$$

Assuming we have compiled the financial statements in a manner consistent with the preceding text, we have derived the NOI stream for the subject hotel as shown in Exhibit 11-11.

Exhibit 11-11 indicates an NOI of $832,000 in a stabilized year in current value dollars. The denominator of the formula can be obtained in two ways. The first is a derivation from comparable sales. If the appraiser uses rates obtained from comparable sales, the details of the transaction must be verified. Was the property stabilized at the time of sale? Were there any deferred maintenance items at the property? Did the NOI estimates of the comparable sales include a reserve for replacement? Overall, the income projection for the comparable sales must be completed in a similar manner to the subject property to be useful. If reliable income information has been obtained from the comparable sales, the overall capitalization rate is found as follows.

$$\text{Overall rate} = \frac{\text{Stabilized NOI}}{\text{Sales price}}$$

We then examine the range of overall capitalization rates for our sales. Hopefully, the sales will help form a relatively small range for the appraiser to derive an overall capitalization rate from this method. If the appraiser has found five other sales with overall capitalization rates ranging from 11.5 percent to 14 percent, the appraiser may select a 13 percent rate to use for the direct capitalization method.

Another method of finding an overall capitalization rate is the band of investment method. It involves using a weighted average of a capitalization rate for debt and a required rate of return on equity. The overall capitalization rate is derived in the following manner.

$$\text{Overall capitalization rate} = (\text{Loan to value \%} \times \text{Mortgage constant}) + (\text{Equity \%} \times \text{Return on equity})$$

As previously mentioned, the mortgage constant is the rate of capitalization for debt. It is the ratio of annual debt service to the amount of the original loan. For example, assume a hotel is constructed with a $5,000,000 loan at an interest rate of 10 percent for 20 years. The mortgage constant is as follows.

$$\text{Annual payment} = \frac{\$5,000,000}{8.5136} = \$587,296$$

$$\text{Mortage constant} = \frac{\$587,296}{\$5,000,000} = .1175$$

After consulting the market participants, the appraiser finds 70 percent loan-to-value ratios to be typical for hotels, and equity investors are requiring returns of 18 percent. The overall capitalization rate is as follows.

$$\text{Overall capitalization rate} = (.70 \times .1175) + (.30 \times .18) = 13.62 \text{ percent}$$

The two rates should be reasonably similar, although differences may occur because of changes in investment terms since the comparable hotels were sold. Assuming the appraiser uses a 13 percent overall capitalization rate, the value conclusion would be as follows.

$$\text{Value via direct capitalization} = \frac{\$832,000}{.13} = \$6,400,000$$

Accordingly, the value using this approach is $6,400,000 (rounded). However, given the competitive nature of hotel markets and the changes in NOI from year to year, the use of an average NOI is usually not appropriate. Although this approach may be used by apartment building or office building investors from time to time, it is rarely used for hotel properties. Therefore, we will attempt to value the property utilizing the projected NOI stream.

11.4.5 Yield Capitalization

Generally, the discounting of the projected NOI stream is more widely used by active market participants because of the variability in the NOI stream for most hotel properties until the property becomes stabilized. Projection periods can vary from three to ten years or more, although a five- to ten-year projection period is fairly common.

The value of the subject hotel is arrived at in a manner similar to a share of stock—it is the present value of current and future economic benefits. The NOI is discounted using an **equity yield rate.** Equity yield rates are best obtained through surveys of hotel buyers in the marketplace. Appraisers may also subscribe to newsletters containing investor opinions about yield rates of return on different types of commercial real estate. The equity yield rate is the long-term holding period return for an equity investor.

Most appraisers also assume the hotel will be sold after a certain period of time. Accordingly, the sales price should be based on the present value of economic benefits. In our case, year 5's NOI is inflated to represent an estimate of NOI for year 6. The present value of this NOI is based on a simple perpetuity formula. The NOI is divided by a **terminal capitalization rate,** or a "going-out" rate. This rate is similar to the overall capitalization rate discussed in the previous section except for the notion that the investor is bearing more risk at the time of sale because of general uncertainty further into the future as well as the increasing age

Year 5's NOI inflated by 3 percent	$1,037,000
Terminal capitalization rate	.14
Gross sales price (rounded)	$7,407,000
Broker's fee (2 percent; rounded)	$ 148,000
Net sales price	$7,259,000

Exhibit 11-12 Net sales price calculation.

Year	NOI	PV factor at 14%	Present value
1	$ 748,000	.8772	$ 656,146
2	$ 827,000	.7695	$ 636,350
3	$ 857,000	.6750	$ 578,451
4	$ 938,000	.5921	$ 555,371
5	$1,007,000	.5194	$ 523,004
Reversion[a]	$7,259,000	.5194	$3,770,325
Total Present Value			$6,719,647
Rounded			$6,720,000

[a]The sale of the property is assumed to occur at the end of year 5.

Exhibit 11-13 Estimate of market value for the subject hotel utilizing yield capitalization.

of the property. Finally, a broker's fee of 2 to 3 percent should be deducted from the gross sales price to obtain the net price. This net sales price is subsequently discounted at the equity yield rate with the rest of the NOI stream. The net sales price is also called the reversion value. The calculation for the net sales price for the subject hotel is shown in Exhibit 11-12.

With the NOI stream for the subject hotel from Exhibit 11-11 and the net sales price from the preceding text, we can find the market value of the property by finding the present value of these benefits. Assuming an equity yield of 14 percent, the present value calculation is shown in Exhibit 11-13.

There is a relatively small difference between the value conclusions between the direct and yield capitalization methods. This is not unusual for the two conclusions to differ slightly; the direct capitalization usually only serves as a check against the value conclusion via yield capitalization.

11.5 A RULE OF THUMB APPROACH AND REVENUE MULTIPLIERS

There are at least two other appraisal approaches utilizing income statement information that can be considered rule-of-thumb techniques. The first is based on project cost. If the ADR is $63, then the value should be approximately $63,000 per room. In the case of the subject hotel, $63,000 multiplied by 175 equals $11,025,000. This number is not very close to the value conclusions from the income capitalization approach. Sometimes this approach is remarkably accurate, but at other times it does not seem very useful. And therein lies the problem with rule-of-thumb approaches—sometimes they work, and sometimes they do not. The problem is we cannot be sure when they will work. Although there may be some useful underlying economic intuition in these approaches, they simply may not be applicable to all types of hotels in all hotel markets.

A much more commonly used technique is a gross revenue multiplier. However, because the majority of revenue generated by a hotel is in the rooms department, a gross rooms revenue multiplier is often used. The multipliers will vary by hotel type and market, but the range of gross rooms revenue multipliers is between two and five times. For the subject hotel, the gross rooms revenue multiplier is calculated as follows.

Value conclusion via direct capitalization	$6,400,000
Divided by rooms revenue (stabilized year)	$2,892,750
Equals	2.2

This approach to value is really a combination of the income capitalization and sales comparison approaches because the sales prices and rooms revenue information are obtained from comparable sales. Once again, this method can be used but rarely stands alone in a formal written appraisal report. It also requires the sales used to be very comparable to the subject.

11.6 FINAL RECONCILIATION OF VALUE

The final section of the appraisal report is a reconciliation of the different approaches to value used by the appraiser. It reports the values obtained through the approaches used (cost, sales comparison, and income capitalization). The final value is based on the previous value conclusions and the appraiser's judgment regarding the underlying reliability of each approach. If, for example, the appraiser could only find a few sales that were not very comparable, the appraiser may place very little reliance on this approach. The value conclusion should not merely be a simple average of the approaches used. It can be within the range of values indicated or it can be the actual value obtained from one of the approaches. The key is for the appraiser to justify the final value conclusion. In most hotel appraisals, the income capitalization approach usually receives the most significant consideration.

11.7 SUMMARY

This chapter described in detail the hotel appraisal process, which includes the definition of the appraisal problem, the interest to be valued, and the area and neighborhood analyses. The heart of the hotel appraisal report is the competitive market analysis, which includes an in-depth description of historical, current, and projection supply and demand. From these, projections about hotel occupancy, ADR, and estimated operating results are made. The appraiser subsequently values the property in a manner congruent with active hotel investors in the market, using the cost approach, sales comparison, and/or income capitalization as necessary. After the values are determined, a reconciliation is made to determine the final value for the property.

KEY TERMS

Collateral
Equity yield rate
Fair share
Fee simple interest
Market value
Net operating income (NOI)
Real estate
Terminal capitalization rate

DISCUSSION QUESTIONS

1. What are the reasons for appraising hotels?
2. What are the steps in the appraisal process?
3. Why is the submarket (competitive market) analysis so important for hotels?
4. What are the major features of the site analysis?
5. What are the three major approaches to value? Which one is most commonly used for hotel valuation?
6. What are some limitations associated with the cost approach to value?
7. How are occupancies for appraised hotels determined?
8. In terms of the income capitalization approach, how are most hotel properties valued? Why?
9. Where do hotel revenue and expense projections come from?
10. How does the appraiser reconcile the different approaches to value?

PROBLEMS

Problems designated with **Excel** *can be solved using* **Excel** *spreadsheets accessible at* http://www.prenhall.com/chatfield.

1. You are provided with the following information about a hotel and its competitive market.

	Number of rooms	Total demand	Commercial demand	Group demand	Tourist demand
Market	500	118,625	73,547	33,215	11,863

	Number of rooms	Total demand	Commercial demand	Group demand	Tourist demand
Subject	100	24,820	17,374	1,241	6,205

Calculate the subject hotel's total penetration rate and penetration rate by segment. Comment on these penetration rates for the subject.
2. You collect the following information from comparable sales.

	Hotel sale #1	Hotel sale #2	Hotel sale #3	Hotel sale #4
Sales price	$10,000,000	$7,500,000	$6,000,000	$9,500,000
Rooms revenue	$ 4,500,000	$3,000,000	$2,200,000	$5,000,000

If the hotel you are appraising is a 250-room property with a 65 percent occupancy and ADR of $80, what is a reasonable value for the hotel?
3. An appraiser has collected the following information about some recent sales in the competitive market area.

	Hotel sale #1	Hotel sale #2	Hotel sale #3	Hotel sale #4
Sales price	$12,000,000	$4,500,000	$5,000,000	$6,500,000
Number of rooms	250	130	140	155
NOI	$ 1,560,000	$ 520,000	$ 650,000	$ 900,000

The subject hotel has 175 rooms and a stabilized NOI of $1,250,000. Can you form an opinion of value?
4. A recent survey of hotel investors indicated expected equity yield rates of 16 percent. The hotel you are appraising could be financed today with a $7,000,000 loan at an interest rate of 9 percent for 15 years. The typical loan-to-value ratio is approximately 60 percent. Calculate the mortgage constant and the overall capitalization rate.
5. You have determined the NOI of the hotel you are appraising to be $1,350,000. The expected equity yield for hotel investments is currently 18 percent. The mortgage constant for typical hotel investments is 12 percent, and hotels are currently financed with 65 percent debt.
   Determine an estimated value for your hotel using direct capitalization.
6. You collect the following sales during your fieldwork.

	Hotel sale #1	Hotel sale #2	Hotel sale #3
NOI	$ 1,500,000	$ 800,000	$ 900,000
NOI as % of revenue	20%	18%	24%
Sales price	$12,500,000	$6,200,000	$6,500,000
Overall cap rate	12%	12.9%	13.85%

However, on further investigation, you discover that although all of the comparable hotel sales are stabilized, a reserve for replacement has not been deducted. Provide the revised range of overall capitalization rates after adjusting for a 5 percent reserve for replacement.

7. You have made the following five-year projection for a hotel you are appraising.

Year	NOI
1	$250,000
2	$306,000
3	$315,000
4	$328,000
5	$341,000

Cash flows are expected to increase by approximately 4 percent per year after the projection period. Overall capitalization rates are currently 12 percent; these can be expected to increase by 150 basis points at the termination of the investment. Furthermore, sales brokerage fees are three percent of the sales price.

Determine the terminal value of this property.

EXCEL 8. According to your interviews with hotel investors, equity yield rates are 14 percent. Year 6 NOI is expected to be 3 percent higher than year 5. Terminal capitalization rates are expected to be 13 percent at the time of sale. Brokers charge 3 percent of the gross sales price to market the property. You have also estimated the following NOI stream for the first five years of the property.

Year	NOI
1	$875,000
2	$901,000
3	$928,000
4	$956,000
5	$985,000

Calculate the market value of the property using the income capitalization approach.

Capital Structure | 12

Chapter Objectives

- To understand the meaning of a firm's capital structure
- To understand the meaning of optimal capital structure
- To understand financial risk, business risk, and the trade-off between these two risks
- To understand the trade-off between the benefits of debt financing and the costs of debt financing that causes most firms to use a significant amount of both debt and equity financing in their capital structure
- To understand the various factors affecting a firm's capital structure such as taxes, bond rating factors, industry standards, and so forth

12.1 INTRODUCTION

Capital structure is a firm's mix of debt and equity financing. More precisely, it is a firm's proportion of long-term financing provided by debt, preferred stock, and common equity. A firm's capital structure is a relevant input into the weighted average cost of capital estimation. Recall from Chapter 8 the weighted average cost of capital equation

$$k_a = w_d \times k_d + w_p \times k_p + w_e \times k_e$$

where the w's represent the firm's target capital structure and are measured as proportions. All the w's must add up to 100%.

$$w_d + w_p + w_e = 100\%$$

The terms of the equation are defined as

w_d = the proportion of debt in the capital structure
w_p = the proportion of preferred stock in the capital structure
w_e = the proportion of equity in the capital structure
k_d = the after-tax cost of debt
k_p = the cost of funds raised from preferred stock
k_e = the cost of funds raised from common equity

The weighted average cost of capital is an average cost of a firm's various components of capital. The weights in the average cost of capital are a measurement of a firm's target capital structure. The focus of this chapter is how a firm's capital structure affects its cost of capital and its stock price. An **optimal capital structure** should minimize a firm's cost of capital and maximize its stock price. A firm's capital structure is affected by many different factors, including the following.

- Financial risk and business risk
- Taxes
- Costs of financial distress
- Agency costs
- Creditor requirements and bond rating factors
- Industry standards
- Desire by owners to retain firm control
- Risk aversion by management
- Borrowing capacity
- Profitability

Even though it is not possible to determine a firm's optimal capital structure precisely, we will cover the basic issues involved to assist managers in better understanding capital structure decisions they may face.

12.2 FINANCIAL RISK

Financial risk is the risk arising from a firm's use of fixed cost sources of financing. Fixed cost sources of financing include both debt and preferred stock. Debt and preferred stock create risk because they have fixed financial costs such as interest expense and preferred dividend payments. If the firm cannot afford to pay these fixed financial costs, financial distress occurs. Increasing use of debt and preferred stock increases the fixed costs a firm must pay regardless of its level of sales and profitability.

A firm's use of debt and preferred stock financing is called *financial leverage*. Thus, a firm using debt or preferred stock as part of its capital structure is said to be using financial leverage. Financial leverage increases the risk on the owners of a firm by increasing the volatility of a firm's return on equity or its earnings per share. When times are good, financial leverage causes owners' returns to increase more than otherwise. But when times are bad, financial leverage will causes owners' returns to decrease more than otherwise. Let us consider the example in Exhibit 12-1 to illustrate this concept.

In Exhibit 12-1, Fried's Gourmet Catering Company has $400,000 in total assets. In the first column, we let Fried's be all equity financed with no debt. The next column shows 25 percent of assets financed with debt, and the last column has 50 percent of assets financed with debt. Starting with earnings before interest and taxes (EBIT) of $50,000, we subtract interest expense to obtain earnings before taxes (EBT) and then subtract taxes to obtain net income. Return on equity is then computed by dividing net income by the amount of equity. Notice that with more debt, there is more interest expense to pay, and Fried's net income declines (as

EBIT = $50,000

Financial leverage	0%	25%	50%
Total assets	$400,000	$400,000	$400,000
Debt	0	100,000	200,000
Equity	400,000	300,000	200,000
EBIT	$ 50,000	$ 50,000	$ 50,000
−Interest (10%)	0	10,000	20,000
EBT	50,000	40,000	30,000
−Tax (40%)	20,000	16,000	12,000
Net income	30,000	24,000	18,000
ROE (Net income/equity)	7.5%	8%	9%

If EBIT increases to $100,000

EBIT	$100,000	$100,000	$100,000
−Interest (10%)	0	10,000	20,000
EBT	100,000	90,000	80,000
−Tax (40%)	40,000	36,000	32,000
Net income	60,000	54,000	48,000
ROE (Net income/equity)	15%	18%	24%

If EBIT Decreases to $15,000

EBIT	$ 15,000	$ 15,000	$ 15,000
−Interest (10%)	0	10,000	20,000
EBT	15,000	5,000	−5,000
−Tax (40%)	6,000	2,000	−2,000
Net income	9,000	3,000	−3,000
ROE (Net income/equity)	2.25%	1%	−1%

Exhibit 12-1 Fried's Gourmet Catering Company financial leverage and return on equity.

interest expense goes from 0 to $10,000 to $20,000, net income goes from $30,000 to $24,000 to $18,000, respectively). But debt financing not only increases interest expense, it also replaces equity financing. So despite the lower net income, our example shows return on equity increasing with more financial leverage (return on equity increases from 7.5 percent to 8 percent to 9 percent). This is due to the smaller amounts of equity used with more debt financing.

The second part of Exhibit 12-1 shows the benefits of financial leverage when times are good. If earnings before interest and taxes are $100,000 instead of $50,000, of course return on equity will improve for Fried's Gourmet Catering Company. In the case of no financial leverage, return on equity doubles from 7.5 percent to 15 percent, whereas in the case of 50 percent debt financing, return on equity more than doubles from 9 percent to 24 percent!

The third and last part of Exhibit 12-1 shows the downside of financial leverage when times are bad. If earnings before interest and taxes are $15,000 instead of $50,000, of course return on equity will decline for Fried's Gourmet Catering Company. In the case of no financial leverage, return on equity drops significantly from 7.5 percent to 2.25 percent. In the case of 50 percent debt financing, return on equity drops drastically from 9 percent to −1 percent.

Exhibit 12-1 illustrates the positive impact of financial leverage on returns to owners. But it also shows the higher risk incurred by taking on financial leverage. Financial leverage increases the volatility of owners' returns. Exhibit 12-1 shows owners' returns varying from 2.25 percent to 15 percent with no financial leverage and from −1 percent to 24 percent with 50 percent financial leverage.

$$(\text{Debt}/\text{equity} = \frac{\$200,000}{\$400,000} = 50\%)$$

Keep in mind that Exhibit 12-1 shows only three possible scenarios for the earnings before interest and taxes level. Many other scenarios are possible. Essentially, the greater the financial leverage, the greater the possible variance in owners' returns. But as long as earnings before interest and taxes is greater than zero, Fried's return on equity will be positive if no financial leverage is used. Financial leverage can increase the return to owners, but it also increases the risk of those returns and increases the risk that those returns will be negative.

12.3 BUSINESS RISK

All firms have a risk involved with the basic operations of the business. Even in the absence of debt, there is a risk that sales may be low, cost of goods sold may be high, or operating expenses may be high. Any of these factors could cause a firm's earnings before interest and taxes to be low or even negative and in turn cause the firm's returns to owners to be low or negative. This basic risk inherent in the operations of a firm is called business risk. Business risk can be viewed as the volatility of a firm's earnings before interest and taxes (EBIT).

Many factors influence business risk, and they can be categorized two ways. First are those factors affecting a firm's sales revenues, and second are those factors affecting costs. Many factors can affect a firm's sales, including

- *Volatility of demand for a firm's product and services.* This includes sensitivity to the business cycle. Sales of hospitality firms tend to fluctuate a great deal along with the business cycle, so hospitality firms generally have a high degree of business risk.
- *Volatility of price for a firm's product and services.* More stable selling prices lead to more stable sales revenue and lower business risk. Whether a firm has significant market power or operates in a very competitive market can play a large role. A firm with significant market power can control, to some extent, the selling price and will generally have less business risk than firms operating in competitive markets.
- *Diversification will reduce a firm's business risk.* It can take place in several different ways. A geographically diversified firm will not suffer the same decrease in sales from a regional recession as a firm operating only in that one particular region. A firm diversified across the low, middle, and high ends of a market will survive a decline in one segment of the market better than a firm operating only in one sector.

Because a firm's cost of goods sold and operating costs are deducted from sales revenue to arrive at EBIT, the volatility of a firm's costs is a determinant of business risk. Many factors can affect a firm's costs, including

- *The inherent volatility of a firm's input costs.* For example, any company extensively using energy sources such as oil, gas, or electricity will have more business risk than otherwise because the cost of energy is highly volatile.
- *The degree to which a firm's operating costs are fixed rather than variable.* Fixed costs do not decline when a firm's sales decline. Fixed operating costs may include the wages and salaries of personnel that cannot be laid off, insurance premiums, and property taxes. As such, when a firm's sales decline, higher fixed costs will cause a greater decline in EBIT than otherwise. Higher fixed costs are associated with higher business risk.

A firm's level of business risk is determined to some extent by the market it operates in as well as the management of the firm. For example, restaurants are generally hurt by recessions because people will generally not eat out as much during bad economic times. But management can minimize this to an extent by advertising or by other methods used to induce customers to patronize restaurants.

Generally, the higher a firm's business risk, the less will be the firm's use of financial leverage in its optimal capital structure. Remember, the use of financial leverage means a firm is using fixed cost sources of financing to include debt or preferred stock financing. Increasing the use of financial leverage means increasing the level of EBIT a firm needs to generate in order to meet its obligations to pay for these fixed cost sources of financing. If we look back at Exhibit 12-1, we see the more financial leverage used by Fried's Gourmet Catering Company (debt ratio increasing from 0% to 25% to 50%), the more EBIT needed to just cover the interest expense ($0, $10,000, and $20,000, respectively). In fact if we look at the case of "If EBIT Decreases to $15,000" in Exhibit 12-1, we see that owners' returns were negative when financial leverage is the highest (debt ratio = 50%), and owners' returns are the highest when there is no financial leverage (debt ratio = 0%).

More financial leverage means a firm requires a greater level of EBIT just to cover fixed financial expenses. More business risk means a firm's EBIT is more volatile. Of course, having a high level of financial leverage and a high level of business risk is a very risky combination. High financial leverage will require a high level of EBIT for firm survival, and a high level of business risk means the firm is not very certain of generating a high level of EBIT. Generally, firms with relatively more business risk should take on relatively less financial leverage to obtain the optimal capital structure.

12.4 CAPITAL STRUCTURE THEORY

There are many different theories of capital structure. Here we will present a basic capital structure theory based on the trade-offs between the tax effects of using debt financing and the additional distress costs and agency costs arising from the use of debt financing. It is a basic theory that will help to illustrate the issues involved in the determination of a firm's optimal capital structure. In the following discussion, we will assume a firm's capital structure consists of only long-term debt and common equity. By assuming a firm does not use other sources of capital (short-term debt and preferred stock), we will make the discussion easier to understand, but not affect the relevance of our results.

A firm's weighted average cost of capital is estimated as follows.

$$k_a = w_d \times k_d + w_p \times k_p + w_e \times k_e$$

But if a firm has no preferred stock financing, then we eliminate the preferred stock component from the equation.

$$k_a = w_d \times k_d + w_e \times k_e$$

12.4.1 The Cost of Debt Versus the Cost of Equity

A firm's cost of debt is always less than the cost of equity (k_e) because debt has less seniority risk and has a fixed return. In other words, in the case of financial difficulty, a firm will make payments to debt holders before making payments to owners (equity). The return on debt is also fixed and not dependent on the profitability of the firm, whereas the return on equity generally varies up and down with the profitability of the firm. Furthermore, the interest cost of debt (k_d) is a tax-deductible cost, and the cost of equity (k_e) is not tax deductible. Between the lower seniority risk, the more certain return, and the tax-deductibility of interest expense, the cost of a firm's debt is generally much lower than the cost of a firm's equity. It may appear a firm should use as much debt and as little equity as possible so as to minimize the weighted average cost of capital. But this logic ignores the higher risk and the resulting financial distress costs and higher agency costs brought on by more debt financing.

12.4.2 The Cost of Financial Distress

The costs of financial distress are brought on by the use of debt financing. The more debt financing used, the greater will be a firm's cost of financial distress. Among other costs, bankruptcy costs are one type of financial distress. In the case of bankruptcy, a firm's assets often decline in value as the various parties to the bankruptcy argue over the firm's reorganization or its liquidation. The bankruptcy proceedings often take years, and in the meantime, assets are declining in value and investors' funds are tied up, receiving little or no return. There are also lawyers' fees, other legal fees, and accounting costs to be paid in a bankruptcy proceeding.

Even in the absence of bankruptcy, there may be significant financial distress costs. If a firm has a very high debt load and is viewed as risky and possibly near bankruptcy, it will usually change customer and supplier actions. Do you really want to stay at a hotel that might close down during the middle of your stay? Do you want to sign up and pay for a cruise if there is a good chance the cruise ship company will stop operations and declare bankruptcy before you can take your cruise? A company in financial distress may lose customers.

Financial distress may not only drive away customers, but also suppliers will be reluctant to sell unless they receive cash on delivery. Do you really want to sell a shipment of steaks to a restaurant on credit if you know the restaurant is struggling to make enough income to pay the interest expense on its debt?

Financial distress also may cause management to take actions harmful to the value and long-term health of the company but ensure the survival of the company in the short-term. For example, valuable assets may be liquidated at bargain basement prices, key employees may be let go, and crucial maintenance may be delayed. While trying to preserve their jobs, management may actually reduce firm value.

We can see that financial distress not only includes bankruptcy costs but also costs arising from the impact of financial distress on customers, suppliers, and management. Financial distress is generally caused by the use of debt financing. The presence of fixed interest expense puts pressure on a firm to earn an EBIT level at least sufficient to pay the fixed interest expense. Thus the more debt financing used, the greater the possibility of financial distress.

12.4.3 The Agency Cost of Debt Financing

The concept of agency problems and agency costs was introduced in earlier chapters. One potential agency problem is the relationship between the owners of a firm (stockholders) and the creditors of a firm (bondholders). Remember, the owners of a firm receive both the upside benefits and the downside costs of risk. If the firm performs superbly and firm value increases (upside benefits), the owners receive the benefits because they hold the residual value of the firm. If the firm performs poorly, the owners lose out (downside costs). But creditors are very limited on receiving any benefits from risk. If the firm performs superbly, the creditors typically receive the fixed interest rate promised and no more. If the firm performs poorly, the creditors could lose everything. Therefore, the owners may have an incentive to increase risk and thus increase the possibility of upside benefits. Creditors do not have this same incentive because they will not gain anything more than the interest promised. Selling off low risk assets and acquiring high-risk assets or issuing additional debt and investing in high-risk projects could accomplish this. The firms' expected profitability may be expected to increase, but since creditors' return is fixed, there is no benefit to the creditors, only a greater risk of not being paid.

Because managers may take actions to benefit owners (stockholders) to the detriment of creditors (bondholders), bonds are protected by restrictive contractual stipulations. These stipulations restrict actions a firm might take possibly to include management decisions that are quite reasonable. For example, a firm might be precluded from issuing additional debt or investing in particular segments of the economy. As a result, the restrictions can reduce the efficiency of a firm's operations.

In addition to the loss of efficiency caused by restrictive contractual stipulations, there will be monitoring costs to ensure the firm follows the restrictions. So agency problems increase the cost of debt beyond the interest expense and the financial distress costs. At low levels of debt financing, creditors are not likely to demand extensive contractual protection because the risk from possible agency problems is low. At higher levels of debt financing, owners have more to gain if management takes actions unfavorable to creditors. Thus at higher debt levels, creditors are likely to require more extensive contractual protection and require more monitoring of the firm's actions. As a result, these agency costs are expected to increase along with interest rates as a firm uses greater amounts of debt financing in its capital structure.

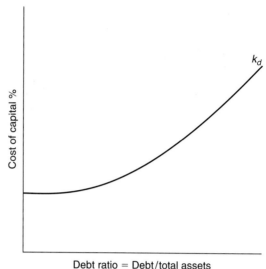

Exhibit 12-2 Financial leverage and the cost of debt.

12.4.4 Financial Leverage and the Cost of Debt

In summary, as a firm uses more debt financing in its capital structure, the interest costs of debt, the financial distress costs of debt, and the agency costs of debt will increase. Even though a firm's cost of debt is less than its cost of equity, there is a trade-off cost to using more debt The higher risk in general, the greater financial distress costs and the agency costs of using more debt will typically restrict a firm to using much less than 100 percent debt in its capital structure.

Let us see if we can better understand the relationship between the costs, of financial distress, agency costs, and optimal capital by considering Exhibits 12-2, 12-3, and 12-4. In Exhibit 12-2, the horizontal axis measures a firm's debt ratio (debt/assets), and the vertical axis measures the cost of capital as a percentage. As we move from the origin toward the right, a firm is moving from no-debt financing (at the origin) to progressively more and more debt financing. We see the cost of debt financing growing at an increasing rate as the firm becomes increasingly risky, with greater proportions of debt in its capital structure. With more debt financing comes higher costs of financial distress and greater agency costs, as explained previously.

12.4.5 Financial Leverage and the Cost of Equity

Exhibit 12-3 illustrates the relationship between the cost of equity and financial leverage. It is similar to Exhibit 12-2, except that we replace the cost of debt with the cost of equity. Remember, Exhibit 12-1 shows that financial leverage increases the risk of owners' return. More financial leverage causes greater risk. We cannot specify this relationship precisely, but without a doubt, more debt financing creates more risk to owners and thus increases the cost of equity. Also the cost of equity will increase at an increasing rate with more debt financing. This is illustrated in Exhibit 12-3.

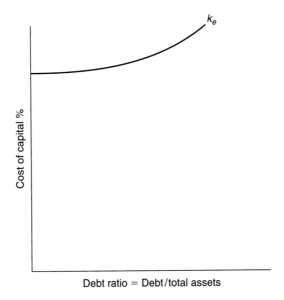

Exhibit 12-3 Financial leverage and the cost of equity.

12.4.6 The Weighted Average Cost of Capital and Optimal Capital Structure

Now, let us once again consider the weighted average cost of capital when a firm uses only debt and equity financing. In Exhibit 12-4 we show both the cost of debt and the cost of equity and the impact of financial leverage. Additionally, we show the resulting weighted average cost of capital. Remember, the weighted average cost of capital is computed with the following equation.

$$k_a = w_d \times k_d + w_e \times k_e$$

Therefore, if a firm is all equity financed ($w_e = 100\%$) with no debt ($w_d = 0\%$), the weighted average cost of capital is equal to the cost of equity. This can be seen in Exhibit 12-4 along the vertical axis where the debt ratio is 0 and the k_e curve and the k_a curve intersect.

As a firm uses some debt financing ($w_d > 0\%$ and $w_e < 100\%$), the weighted average cost of capital (k_a) should initially decrease as it moves away from the cost of equity (k_e) and approaches the cost of debt (k_d). But as a firm's use of debt financing in the capital structure increases, the cost of equity and the cost of debt both increase at an increasing rate due to higher risk, greater financial distress costs, and greater agency costs. At some point, as more financial leverage is used and the weighted average cost of capital (k_a) approaches the cost of debt (k_d), the weighted average cost of capital will begin to increase with more financial leverage. This means the weighted average cost of capital (k_a) is at a minimum when debt is used in the capital structure, but debt is less than 100 percent of capital. The proportion of debt and equity financing at this minimum point (where cost of capital is minimized) is called the *optimal capital structure*.

It is extremely difficult to calculate a firm's optimal capital structure precisely. Even if we could precisely compute it, a firm's optimal capital structure

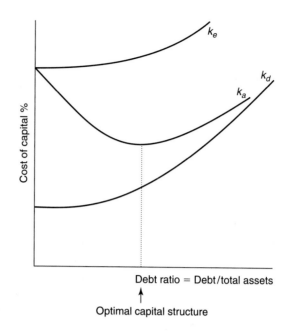

Exhibit 12-4   Financial leverage and the optimal capital structure.

changes over time. However, it is generally felt that a firm's weighted average cost of capital (k_a) curve is fairly flat over a large range of capital structures. This means that if a firm's actual capital structure is 30 percent debt financing and its optimal capital structure is 35 percent debt financing, its cost of capital will not be appreciably higher than its minimum possible cost of capital.

By combining the trade-off between the benefits of debt financing and the costs of debt financing, we can see why most firms use a significant amount of both debt and equity financing. The tax deductibility of interest provides an incentive to use debt in a firm's capital structure. But financial distress costs and agency costs become greater than the tax advantage if financial leverage is too high. The amount of financial leverage where this trade-off is optimized is called the optimal capital structure. It is at this point that the firm's weighted average cost of capital is minimized.

12.5 OTHER SIGNIFICANT FACTORS IN THE DETERMINATION OF A FIRM'S CAPITAL STRUCTURE

We have already discussed the relevance of financial risk, business risk, the tax-deductibility of the cost of debt, financial distress, and agency costs to a firm's capital structure decisions. There are many other practical factors having a significant impact on a firm's capital structure decision. In this section, we will discuss other factors likely to be relevant to a firm's capital structure.

12.5.1 Industry Standards

Generally when investors and other interested parties evaluate a firm's capital structure, it is compared to what is typical for other firms in the same industry. So a large casino/hotel's capital structure will be compared to the typical large casino/hotel's capital structure. The capital structure of a chain of family restaurants will be compared to the capital structure of a typical chain of family restaurants. There will always be some variation in the capital structures of different firms in the same industry. But there is substantial evidence indicating that firms' capital structures tend toward an industry average with the averages varying from industry to industry. This is not surprising because, as we previously discussed, business risk is a significant factor impacting a firm's capital structure, and business risk is heavily influenced by industry. So if a firm's industry significantly influences business risk, and a firm's business risk significantly influences capital structure, then a firm's industry must also significantly influence capital structure as well.

12.5.2 Creditor and Rating Agency Requirements

Firms need to follow previous debt agreements entered into. For example, a firm may have previously borrowed money and agreed to keep its debt ratio (total debt/total assets) to less than 50 percent. The firm's capital structure is restricted to debt financing no more than 50 percent of assets until this loan is repaid. Firms must also be concerned with the ability to borrow in the future and also the cost of borrowing in the future. This is determined by investors' perceptions and also by ratings on a firm's debt provided by rating agencies such as Moody's Investors Service or Standard & Poor's corporation. We previously discussed bond ratings by these companies in Chapter 6. A high bond rating (such as Aaa by Moody's or AAA by Standard & Poor's) will lower a firm's cost of debt, whereas a low bond rating (such as Ca by Moody's or Cc by Standard & Poor's) will raise a firm's cost of debt. Strong financial leverage ratios such as a low "debt ratio" and a high "times interest earned ratio" help to convince creditors and rating agencies of a firm's financial strength. This in turn helps to maintain high bond ratings and the ability to more easily borrow funds when needed in the future and also the ability to borrow at lower interest rates.

In summary, if a firm uses a small amount of debt in its capital structure, the firm is more likely to appear financially strong and less risky. This will help to maintain high bond ratings and build a strong reputation among potential creditors. This in turn will help the firm to more easily borrow in the future as needed as well as keep interest rates lower than otherwise.

12.5.3 The Need for Excess Borrowing Capacity

Firms are said to have a certain borrowing capacity. A firm would not be able to borrow beyond its capacity without paying excessively high interest rates. Successful, ongoing firms not currently in financial distress generally maintain an excess borrowing capacity. This allows a firm the flexibility to handle future developments. For example, what if an excellent project is identified but a company's investors do not know about the project despite management's confidence? If management believes the stock price is currently undervalued because it does not reflect the future earnings from this project, management may be discouraged from issuing stock to raise investment funds. But if a firm has a sufficient reserve of borrowing capacity, the project can be funded with the proceeds of new debt. In summary, successful firms usually maintain excess borrowing capacity so they have the financing flexibility to properly react to investment opportunities as they become available. The desire to maintain excess borrowing capacity will tend to reduce the use of debt in a firm's capital structure.

12.5.4 Profitability and the Need for Funds

Highly profitably firms may have little need for debt because they generate much of the firm's funding internally. Remember, profits can be paid out as dividends to stockholders or reinvested in the firm. Reinvested profits are added to retained earnings on the right-hand side of the balance sheet. If a firm generates high profits and reinvests much of the high profits in the firm, then the firm has a large continuous internal source of funds. This will reduce the need to borrow and reduce the use of a debt in a firm's capital structure.

12.5.5 Managerial Risk Aversion

A firm's management may not desire a capital structure that is optimal for the stockholders. Management incentive is most likely to have less debt than is optimal for the owners. Management income and wealth are usually very dependent on the success of the one company they work for, and thus management may be unwilling to take on a lot of debt financing and the resultant financial risk. On the other hand, a firm's stockholders can easily diversify their investment portfolio through the purchase of common stock in several different firms. Thus a well-diversified stockholder is likely to be very tolerant to a firm's financial risk and willing to see a firm rely quite heavily on debt in the capital structure. For these reasons, management is likely to prefer the use of less debt in the capital structure than is optimal for well-diversified stockholders.

12.5.6 Corporate Control

The impact of new securities on control of a firm may influence a firm's capital structure. Debt financing may be used to preserve control of a firm. If a few individuals currently control a firm, the controlling owners may not be willing to issue additional common stock unless they can afford to purchase the stock themselves. If the firm sells the new common stock to others, the control of the existing stockholders will be weakened or possibly eliminated through dilution. Debt could be used to raise new funds instead of a common stock issuance.

Avoiding a corporate takeover is another incentive for a firm to increase the use of debt in its capital structure. A firm with too little debt in its capital structure may be an excellent takeover target. Management generally desires to avoid a takeover because they run a significant risk of job loss in a takeover. The desire to avoid a takeover may motivate management to use more debt in its capital structure. Of course, takeovers are a control issue because a takeover is just a change in control of a firm.

On the other hand, another control issue could cause a firm to use more equity and less debt financing in its capital structure than otherwise. If a firm is facing financial distress, raising funds with more debt might seriously weaken the firm. This could force a turnover of control to creditors (based on previous credit agreements). Management facing such a situation may be motivated to issue common stock in place of additional debt in order to reduce the risk of losing control to creditors and possibly losing their jobs.

Corporate control can certainly be one of many variables significantly influencing a firm's capital structure. But whether corporate control concerns suggest the use of more debt or more equity depends on the specific situation.

12.6 SUMMARY

A firm's capital structure is basically the proportion of long-term funding provided by long-term debt, preferred stock, and common equity. A firm's capital structure influences its cost of capital through the tax advantage to debt financing and the effect of capital structure on firm risk. Due to the trade-off between the tax advantage of debt financing and risk, each firm has an optimal capital structure that minimizes the weighted average cost of capital. We have explained how a variety of factors influence a firm's capital structure decisions, including

- A firm's business risk affects the amount of financial risk a firm is willing to assume. Greater (lower) business risk will generally lead to lower (greater) debt use in a firm's capital structure.
- Industry standards provide guidelines for acceptable capital structures.
- Creditor and rating agency perceptions influence capital structure decisions. A desire to create a favorable impression on creditors and ratings agencies such as Moody's and Standard & Poor's will generally lead to less debt in a firm's capital structure.
- The need to maintain excess borrowing capacity will motivate a firm to use less debt in its capital structure.
- A firm's level of profitability helps to determine its needs for external funds. Very profitable (less profitable) firms generate larger (lesser) amounts of internal funding through growth in retained earnings and thus are likely to need less (more) debt in its capital structure.
- A firm's management may desire less debt in the firm's capital structure than stockholders. This is due to management's heavy dependence on the firm's performance for his or her financial well-being. Firm stockholders are likely to be well diversified and less concerned about each firm's financial risk. Thus management may desire less debt financing than stockholders.
- Corporate control is usually an important influence on a firm's choice of debt versus equity financing. But the influence depends on what the control issue is. Preserving control among the dominant owners or eliminating motivations for a corporate takeover create incentives to use more debt financing. On the other hand, minimizing the possibility of creditors taking control of a firm creates incentives to use less debt financing.

KEY TERMS

Capital structure
Optimal capital structure

DISCUSSION QUESTIONS

1. Under what circumstances can short-term debt be considered part of a firm's capital structure?
2. An optimal capital structure is optimal in what sense?
3. Explain the difference between financial risk and business risk.
4. What are the benefits of debt financing?
5. What are the costs of debt financing?
6. What factors affect a firm's level of business risk?
7. Why does a firm's financial leverage affect its cost of equity?
8. How can a firm's level of profitability affect its capital structure?
9. Explain how concerns by both owners and management about corporate control can affect a firm's capital structure.
10. Financial leverage is a double-edged sword in that it can either benefit or hurt the owners of a firm. Explain what this statement means.

PROBLEMS

1. An investment-banking firm has estimated the following after-tax cost of debt and cost of equity for Mann's Fine Dining Establishments Incorporated.

Proportion of debt	After-tax cost of debt	Cost of equity
0%		13.5%
10%	5.5%	13.6%
20%	5.6%	13.8%
30%	5.8%	14.1%
40%	6.2%	14.6%
50%	6.8%	15.4%
60%	7.7%	16.4%
70%	8.9%	17.7%

What is Mann's Fine Dining Establishments Incorporated's optimal capital structure?

2. Ramdeen's Restaurant has estimated the following cost of debt (before-tax) and cost of equity.

Proportion of debt	Before-tax cost of debt	Cost of equity
0%		11.2%
10%	7.0%	11.1%
20%	7.1%	11.3%
30%	7.3%	11.9%
40%	7.7%	12.7%
50%	8.4%	13.7%
60%	9.5%	14.9%
70%	10.9%	17.7%

What is Ramdeen's Restaurant's optimal capital structure assuming a 40 percent effective tax rate?

3. An investment-banking firm has estimated the following after-tax cost of debt and the cost of equity for Christianson's Extravagant Tours Incorporated.

Proportion of debt	After-tax cost of debt	Cost of equity
0%		10.4%
10%	3.5%	10.5%
20%	3.6%	10.8%
30%	3.8%	11.3%
40%	4.3%	12.0%
50%	5.0%	12.9%
60%	6.0%	14.1%
70%	7.2%	15.5%

What is Christianson's Extravagant Tours Incorporated's optimal capital structure?

4. Park Plaza Hotels has estimated the following cost of debt (before-tax) and cost of equity.

Proportion of debt	Before-tax cost of debt	Cost of equity
0%		14.3%
10%	9.5%	14.4%
20%	9.6%	14.7%
30%	9.7%	15.2%
40%	10.1%	16.0%
50%	10.8%	17.0%
60%	11.8%	18.5%
70%	13.0%	20.5%

What is Park Plaza Hotels' optimal capital structure assuming a 40 percent effective tax rate?

Glossary

Agency problem — A problem that arises in an agency relationship due to inefficient or ineffective contracting.

Agency relationship — A contractual relationship in which one party (the principal) hires another (the agent) to perform a task.

Amortization table or schedule — A table showing how much of each loan payment is allocated to interest and how much is allocated to repayment of the original principal.

Annuity — Two or more equal, periodic cash flows.

Balance sheet — Statement of financial position of the firm for a point in time.

Beta — The measure of an asset's risk relative to the market portfolio; a measure of systematic risk.

Bond — A long-term debt security. An investor buying a bond in the primary market is essentially lending money to a corporation. Bonds generally make interest payments every six months and pay the par value to the investor at maturity.

Bond rating — A measure of a bond's default risk provided by a rating agency such as Moody's Investors Service or Standard & Poor's Corporation.

Call feature — A bond or preferred stock feature that allows the corporate issuer to buy back the bond prior to maturity or allows the corporate issuer to buy back preferred stock.

Capital asset pricing model (CAPM) — The equation for the security market line showing that the expected return on an asset is related to its systematic risk.

Capital budgeting — The decision-making process used in the acquisition of long-term physical assets.

Capital gain — The gain on the sale of a long-term asset over and above the original cost.

Capital market line — A line connecting the risk-free rate of return and the market portfolio. The slope measures the increase in return for an increase in risk.

Capital structure — A firm's proportion of long-term financing provided by debt, preferred stock, and common equity.

Coefficient of variation — The ratio of standard deviation of returns to expected return.

Collateral — An asset representing security for a loan; if the loan fails, the asset can be sold to help repay the loan.

Common stock — Represents ownership in a corporation.

Compounding — The process of a present value earning interest and growing to a future value where the interest is earned on previously paid interest.

Compound interest — Interest paid on interest previously earned as well as being paid on principal.

Correlation coefficient — A numerical measure of the extent to which the returns of two assets move together over time. The range is from −1.0 to +1.0.

Cost of capital — The minimum rate of return a firm needs to earn on investments to succeed. It is the rate of return required to keep the firm's investors satisfied.

Coupon rate — The interest rate offered by a bond. The coupon rate is an annual rate multiplied times the par value to obtain the annual coupon payment. Corporate bonds usually pay half the annual coupon payment every six months.

Cumulative dividends — The type of dividends paid by most preferred stocks. If a corporation misses a cumulative dividend on preferred stock, then the missed dividend accumulates. The corporation can never again pay a common stock dividend until all missed accumulated preferred dividends have been paid.

Debenture — A bond that is not secured by collateral. It is backed by a corporation's cash flow.

Default — The inability of a borrower to make interest or principal payments to bondholders.

Depreciation — The apportionment of the cost of a long-term asset over some specified period of time for the purpose of financial reporting or taxes.

Discounted payback period — How many years it takes for a capital budgeting project's net cash flows, measured as a present value, to recover the project cost. The present values of the project's net cash flows are usually computed using the firm's appropriate required rate of return.

Discounting — The process of finding the present value of a future single payment or stream of payments. The interest rate used in the process is called the discount rate.

Discount rate — The interest rate used in the process of discounting.

Diversification — Holding two or more assets to maximize return and minimize risk.

Dividend decision — A decision made by the firm regarding how much dividends will be paid and when.

Dividend yield — A percentage return computed by dividing a company's annual dividend by the price of the stock.

Effective annual rate — The actual interest rate paid or received on an annual basis is referred to as the effective annual rate. For example, a 6 percent nominal annual rate compounded monthly is equivalent to a 6.17 percent effective annual rate because $100 invested at this rate for one year will earn $6.17 in interest per year.

Efficient portfolio — The portfolio providing the highest return for a given level of risk.

Equity yield rate — The rate of return an investor earns on a prospect during the holding period.

Expected value — The weighted average of potential outcomes.

Fair share — The number of hotel rooms available at the subject hotel divided by the total number of available rooms in the competitive market.

Fee simple interest — The highest ownership interest in real estate, including all rights to its use and enjoyment.

Financing decision — A decision made by the firm regarding how assets will be paid for. Represents one of the three major financial decisions of the firm.

Flotation costs — Any costs a firm incurs to issue or float a new security. Includes investment banking and legal fees as well as any other relevant costs. Same as issuance costs.

Forward contract — An agreement regarding the sale of an asset at a future date for a negotiated price.

Futures contract — Similar to a forward contract with some key exceptions, including standardized amounts, dates of delivery, and no cash payment requirement at time of contract.

Future value — The value at some future point in time of a single cash amount or several cash amounts that occur at an earlier point in time.

Holding period of return — Rate of return on an investment over a given period.

Income statement — Statement of firm performance in terms of revenues and expenses for a period of time, typically a month or a year.

Indenture — The contract setting out the agreement between investors and the issuing corporation for a bond. It details the covenants restricting future actions of the issuing corporation and also explains the various features of the bond.

Independent project — A capital budgeting project generally considered separate from other capital budgeting projects. It is not necessarily compared to another project or projects to determine which is best. The acceptance of an independent project does not necessarily cause another project or projects to be rejected.

Interest rate — The return earned on an investment expressed as a percentage rate. Also the cost paid on a loan expressed as a percentage rate.

Internal rate of return — The interest rate at which a project's net present value equals zero. It is also the interest rate at which the sum of the present values of the net cash flows equals the net investment. It is essentially the annual percentage rate of return on a capital budgeting project.

Investment decision — A decision made by the firm regarding particular assets to invest in. Represents one of the three major financial decisions of the firm.

Issuance costs — Any costs a firm incurs to issue or float a new security. Includes investment banking and legal fees as well as any other relevant costs. Same as flotation costs.

Liquidity ratios — A class of ratios that measures the ability of a firm to cover its current obligations (liabilities).

Marginal cost of capital — This is the cost of raising new funds as opposed to the historical cost of funds. It is the cost of new funds that is relevant to new investments.

Market maker — An individual who helps make markets more efficient by being ready to buy or sell securities.

Market portfolio — A theoretical portfolio of all traded assets that is also the most efficient in terms of offering the most return for a given level of risk.

Market value — The most likely sales price negotiated between a buyer and seller under normal conditions.

Modified accelerated cost recovery system (MACRS) depreciation — The method prescribed for depreciation for tax purposes in the United States since 1986.

Modified internal rate of return — The interest rate at which the project's present value of investment costs equal the project's terminal value of net cash flows. An acceptable capital budgeting project has a modified internal rate of return greater than the required rate of return.

Mortgage-backed securities — Securities that offer income from the payment of principal and interest on mortgages or other loans.

Mortgage bond — A collateralized bond. A bond backed by specific assets.

Mutually exclusive project — A capital budgeting project that is considered relative to other alternative capital budgeting projects to determine which one is best and which one should be accepted, if any. The acceptance of a mutually exclusive project does directly cause another alternative project or alternative projects to be rejected.

Net cash flow — The cash flow created by a capital budgeting project during one year of the project's life. It is computed as the change in operating earnings after taxes plus the change in depreciation minus the change in net working capital during the year.

Net investment — The cost of starting a project or the net cash outflows required to ready a project for its basic function or operation; sometimes called the initial investment or initial outlay.

Net operating income (NOI) — The income available to the owners after fixed charges and a reserve for replacement, but before interest, income taxes, depreciation, and amortization.

Net present value — The sum of the present values of the net cash flows minus the net investment. It is the expected increase in the value of the firm due to an investment in a capital budgeting project.

Nominal annual interest rate — The interest rate as stated in a contract. The nominal interest rate does not take into account compounding. For example, $100 invested at a 6 percent nominal annual rate compounded monthly for one year does not earn $6.00 but will earn $6.17.

Normal capital budgeting project — A project with all positive net cash flows after the net investment. A normal project has one sign change with its cash flows; negative to positive as the negative cash flows from the net investment turn into positive cash flows from the net cash flows. A project that is not normal will have two or more sign changes in its cash flows.

Opportunity costs — The actual value a firm loses when it makes a decision. This may or may not be the same as the accounting cost. For example, if you give a diamond ring to your daughter that you purchased 15 years ago, your opportunity costs is not what you paid for the ring 15 years ago, and it is not the retail appraised value from your local jeweler. The opportunity cost is what you could have sold the ring for if you had not given it away, or the actual dollar value you are losing by making the decision to give it away.

Optimal capital structure — The capital structure that minimizes a firm's weighted average cost of capital and maximizes the value of the firm.

Par value on a bond — The principal amount of the bond that is paid at maturity in addition to any remaining coupon payments. Sometimes called the face value. Corporate bond par values are usually $1,000.

Par value on preferred stock — An arbitrary amount assigned to preferred stock by the issuing corporation. Preferred stock par value is usually $25, $50, or $100.

Payback period — The number of years it takes for a project's net cash flows to recover the net investment.

Perpetuity — An infinite series of uniform, future payments. In other words, it is an infinite annuity.

Preferred stock — A stock with a seniority claim superior to common stock but inferior to debt. Preferred stock dividends are usually a fixed quarterly payment.

Present value — Literally the value today of a future value. More generally as used in financial mathematics, it is the value at an earlier point in time of a single future cash amount or of several future cash amounts.

Primary market — The initial sale of common stock to an investment banker or group of bankers who will later issue the stock to the general public.

Principal — The original amount of money invested or borrowed. The interest rate return on an investment or the interest rate cost on a loan is computed as a percentage of the principal.

Probability distribution — A series of outcomes and associated probabilities with each outcome.

Profitability index — The sum of the present values of the net cash flows divided by the net investment. A profitability index greater than one indicates an acceptable capital budgeting project.

Put feature — A bond feature that allows the investor to demand that the corporation repay the bond prior to maturity.

Real estate — Land and all that is permanently affixed to the land.

Required rate of return — The minimum rate of return that will satisfy an investor.

Risk — Uncertainty about whether future outcomes will differ from our expectations.

Risk aversion — The concept whereby investors must be compensated for bearing risk.

Risk-free rate of return — The return received on a government instrument (i.e., bill, bond, or note) with an appropriate maturity for the asset involved.

Secondary market — The market that represents the bulk of stock and bond trading. This market represents trading between individuals.

Securities and Exchange Commission (SEC) — An agency of the federal government established in 1933 and responsible for the regulation of securities trading in the United States.

Seniority — Seniority refers to the order in which a corporation would pay off its obligations in case of financial difficulty. A senior obligation is paid before an obligation lacking seniority.

Sinking fund on bonds — A bond feature requiring the issuing corporation to retire a portion of the bonds prior to maturity.

Sinking fund on preferred stock — A preferred stock feature requiring the issuing corporation to redeem a certain percentage of the total preferred stock each year.

Solvency ratios — A class of ratios that measure the extent of the use of debt financing by a firm.

Standard deviation — A measure of dispersion around an expected value of mean; the square root of the variance.

Statement of cash flows — Statement showing the sources and uses of cash over a period of time. The statement is divided into three major sections: operating activities, investing activities, and financing activities.

Statement of retained earnings — Statement showing changes in the retained earnings portion of the balance sheet over a period of time. Now, it is combined into a larger statement known as the Statement of Changes in Owner's Position.

Subordinated — Used to indicate seniority on a bond. A subordinated debenture will be paid after an unsubordinated debenture.

Sunk costs — Costs that have been paid in the past and are thus irrelevant because the cost has been paid whether a project is accepted or rejected.

Systematic risk — The component of total risk that is market related and cannot be eliminated in a diversified portfolio.

Target capital structure — The proportions of various capital components a firm plans to use to fund investments. Capital components may include permanent short-term debt, long-term debt, preferred stock, and common equity.

Tax carryback — The ability of a firm to use current losses as a way to offset earnings in prior years. The current limit is two years.

Tax carryforward — The ability of a firm to use current losses as a way to offset earnings in future years.

Terminal capitalization rate — A rate of return used to determine a gross sales price at the end of a holding period.

Uniform System of Accounts — Standardized income statement that allows for easier comparability between properties. Used for hotels, restaurants, and clubs.

Unsystematic risk — The component of total risk that is related to a specific business or industry that can be eliminated in a diversified portfolio.

Value creation — The outcome of an asset's prospective benefits exceeding its costs.

Variance — A measure of dispersion around an expected value, or mean.

Weighted average cost of capital — The weighted average of the costs of a firm's funds raised from debt, preferred stock, and common equity. The weights are generally equal to a firm's target capital structure.

Yield to maturity — The investor's rate of return on a security investment. The investor's rate of return on a bond held to maturity. The investor's rate of return on preferred stock if the preferred stock is not sold by the investor.

Zero coupon securities — Bonds that are bought at discount and gain value as they near maturity; no interest payments are made.

Index